The 21st Century Webster's
Family Encyclopedia

The 21st Century
Webster's
Family Encyclopedia

Volume 8
Polo - Sea

1999 Edition

IMPORTED BY/IMPORTE PAR
DS-MAX CANADA
RICHMOND HILL, ONTARIO
L4B 1H7

MALAYSIA
PRO ENTERPRISE SDN BHD
LOT 605, SS13/1K, OFF JLN.
KEWAJIPAN, 47500 SUBANG JAYA
SELANGOR D.E., MALAYSIA

ENGLAND
WENTWALK LTD.
278A ABBEYDALE ROAD, WEMBLEY
MIDDLESEX, HA0 1NT

DS-MAX
IRVINE, CA 92618
IMPORTER: #16-1241510
949-587-9207

TRIDENT PRESS INTERNATIONAL

Copyright © 1999, Uitgeverij Het Spectrum BV, Utrecht

ISBN 1-55280-463-1

The 21st Century Webster's Family Encyclopedia
is based on the Spectrum Database

editors:
Bart Drubbel
Tjeerd van der Velde
Saskia van Iperen

Polo, game played on horseback (polo ponies), with a ball and mallets. It is played between two teams of four on a field 300 yd (271 m) long and 200 yd (183 m) wide, with a goal at each end. The object is to score points by striking the 3-3.5 in (7.6-8.9 cm) diameter ball into the goal with the mallet, which is 48-54 in (122-137 cm) long. The game originated in Persia and spread through Turkey, Tibet, India, China, and Japan. It was revived in 19th-century India and learned by British army officers, who introduced it into England in 1869 and into the United States in 1876.

Polo, Marco (1254?-1324?), Venetian explorer famous for his overland journey to China (1271-95). Reaching China in 1275, he served as an envoy of the ruler, Kublai Khan. He was appointed governor of Yangchow for 3 years and assisted in the capture of the city of Sainfu. He returned home to Venice (1295) laden with a treasure in precious stones. Commanding a galley against the Genoese at the battle of Curzola (1298), he was captured. In prison he wrote an account of his travels that later inspired explorers like Christopher Columbus to search for a sea passage to the East.

Polonium, chemical element, symbol Po; for physical constants see Periodic Table. Discovered by Marie Curie in 1898. Polonium was the first element to be discovered by virtue of its radioactivity. It occurs in pitchblende and other uranium minerals in minute amounts. The element is a decay product of radium and is also called Radium F. It is produced artificially by irradiating bismuth-210 with neutrons in a high-flux nuclear reactor. Polonium is a low-melting metalloid. It resembles tellurium and bismuth. Several compounds have been synthesized, including a polonide. Polonium-210 is a powerful α-emitter and is dangerous to handle even in small amounts. It is alloyed with beryllium as a neutron source. Polonium is used in devices for removing dust particles and static electricity. It is one of the most toxic substances known.

Polyandry *See:* Polygamy.

Polychlorinated biphenyl (PCB), any of several compounds formed by substituting hydrogen (H) atoms in biphenyl ($C_6H_5C_6H_5$) with chlorine (Cl) atoms. PCBs were once widely used in the manufacture of many products, including lubricants, paints, and adhesives. However, scientific studies have concluded that PCBs are a poisonous threat to the environment, killing wildlife and creating health problems for people. Their use has been banned in the United States.

Polyclitus, name of 2 Greek sculptors. **Polyclitus the Elder** (5th century B.C.) was renowned for bronze statues of athletes, of which numerous marble copies survive. His most famous works, a colossal statue of Hera, now lost, and the *Doryphorus* (Spear Bearer), became the models for ideal proportion. **Polyclitus the Younger** (4th century B.C.) was known primarily as an architect but also produced figures of athletes.

Polyester, any of several strong, light synthetic products made from chemical substances derived from petroleum. Polyesters are manufactured in 3 forms: textiles, plastics, and films. Products made from polyester have great strength and durability. Polyester textiles are colorfast and wrinkle-resistant and are widely used in the creation of clothing and home furnishings. Polyester plastics are used to manufacture such products as bottles, household fixtures and appliances, boats, and automobile parts. Polyester films are used to create Mylar, insulation wires, sealing tapes, computer tapes, and other items.

Polyethylene *See:* Plastic.

Polygamy, marriage in which a man has more than one wife at one time (polygyny), or a woman has more than one husband (polyandry). It is still practiced in parts of Asia and Africa; both the Muslim and Hindu religions permit polygyny. It was once also a custom of U.S. Mormons but is now forbidden by them.

Polygon, closed plane figure bounded by three or more straight lines, such as triangles (3 sides), pentagons (5 sides), and dodecagons (12 sides). Convex polygons have interior angles that are all either acute or obtuse; in concave polygons one or more of these angles is reflex. A polygon with equal angles and sides equal in length is called a regular polygon. A *spherical polygon* is a closed figure on the surface of a sphere bounded by arcs of great circles.

Polyhedron, three-dimensional figure bounded by 4 or more polygon sides. There are only 5 types of convex polyhedron that can be regular (i.e., have faces that are equal regular polygons, each face being at equal angles to those adjacent to it); the tetrahedron, the octahedron, and the isocahedron, with 4, 8, and 20 faces, respectively, each face being an equilateral triangle; the hexahedron, with 6 square faces; and the dodecahedron, with 12 pentagonal faces. Regular polyhedrons may be circumscribed about or inscribed in a sphere.

Polymer, substance composed of very large molecules (macromolecules) built up by repeated linking of small molecules (monomers). Natural polymers include proteins, nucleic acids, polysaccharides, resins, rubber, and many minerals. The ability to make synthetic polymers (e.g., plastics and synthetic fibers) lies at the heart of modern technology. Polymerization, which requires that each monomer have two or more functional groups capable of linkage, takes place by condensation, with elimination of small molecules, or by simple addition. Catalysis is usually required, or the use of an initiator to start a chain reaction of free radicals. If more than one kind of monomer is used, the result is a copolymer with the units arranged at random in the chain.

Polymerization, chemical process in which many small molecules, called monomers, are joined together to produce a large molecule, called a polymer. The monomers combined can be all of one kind or of many different kinds. The characteristic of the polymer is determined by what monomers are combined. Some polymers, such as starch and rubber, are found in nature; others, like plastic and paint, are synthetically produced.

Polymorphism, in zoology, the existence of more than two forms or types of individual within the same species of animal. An example is seen in some social insects, such as ants and bees, in which many different types of worker are structurally adapted for different tasks within the colony. *See also:* Zoology.

Polynesia *See:* Pacific Islands.

Polyphony (Greek, "many sounds"), music made up of several independent melodic lines linked harmonically through counterpoint.

Polytheism, belief in many gods, as opposed to monotheism or dualism; characteristic of most religions, notably Hinduism and Greek and Roman religion. It may arise from the personification of forces worshiped at a more primitive level in animism. One god may dominate the others (e.g., Zeus); sometimes a supreme being is recognized, transcending the gods. *See also:* Gods; Religion.

Pomegranate, family of tropical shrubs and small trees native to Asia and India and cultivated in the United States. Pomegranates in the wild are shrublike; when cultivated, they grow as trees and can reach a height of 15 to 20 ft (4.6 to 6 m). A pomegranate is valued for its golden red fruit. The fruit is the size of a large apple and has a tough rind. Inside are many small seeds, each of which is enclosed by fleshy pulp. The pulp has a pleasant flavor and is eaten fresh or used to create syrup for drinks.

Pomerania, region in north-central Europe, south of the Baltic Sea. The greater part of Pomerania lies in Poland; the rest lies in Germany. Pomerania is mostly made up of fertile lowlands. Agriculture is the main occupation. Industries in the area include the manufacture of metals, ships, and paper. Pomerania was first settled as early as A.D. 100 by Germanic tribes. It has been occupied and governed by Slavs, Germans, Prussians, and Swedes. After World War II, it was divided between Germany and Poland.

Pomeranian, small dog, weighing from 3 to 7 lbs (1.4 to 3.2 kg) and standing approximately 6 in (15.3 cm) tall at the shoulder. The Pomeranian has long, fluffy hair on its body and a furry collar around its neck. Its face has sharp, foxlike features. Related to large dogs of the Arctic, the pomeranian became a popular "toy dog" pet in the late 1800s.

Pomo, Hozan-speaking tribe living in North California, noted for their intricate basket making. A wealthy tribe with many natural resources, they used shells as currency.

Pompadour, Marquise de (1721-64), mistress of King Louis XV of France from 1745. She was a patroness of the arts and had much influence on the political and artistic life of France.

Pompano, any of several saltwater fishes belonging to the jack family. Found in warm waters throughout the world, the pompano is valuable as a delicious food fish. Pompanos vary in size, shape, and color, depending on the species. The size range is 1 ft to 3 ft (46 cm to 114 cm); the weight range is from 3 lbs to 50 lbs (1.4 kg to 23 kg). Some of the species found along the Atlantic coast include the common pompano, the great pompano, and the palometa.

Pompeii, ancient Roman city in southern Italy, buried by an eruption of Mt. Vesuvius (A.D. 79). It was rediscovered in 1748. Excavations have revealed

a town preserved much as it was on the day of its destruction, even to several bodies. The site has yielded invaluable information on Roman urban life and beautiful examples of Roman art.
See also: Rome, Ancient.

Pompey the Great (106-48 B.C.), Roman general and political leader. He started his career in 83 B.C. when he helped Lucius Sulla win a war against Gaius Marius. A few years later, he was sent to Spain to end a rebellion by Marius' supporters. In 72 B.C. he suppressed the slave revolt led by Spartacus. He was elected a Roman consul in 70 B.C. In 67 B.C. he was given the task of ridding the Mediterranean Sea of pirates. The next year he fought and defeated Mithridates VI of Pontus, conquering Palestine, Syria, and parts of Asia Minor. When the senate disapproved of some of his actions, Pompey united with Julius Caesar, a senate opponent. In 60 B.C., Pompey, Caesar, and Marcus Crassus formed the First Triumvirate (a triumvirate is a trio who head a government together), which ruled for several years. However, Pompey became competitive for Caesar's power and consequently broke with him. Pompey went over to senate's side and became a consul again in 52 B.C. In 49 B.C., Caesar defied the senate and initiated military action that resulted in civil war. Pompey was defeated at Pharsala. He fled to Egypt and was captured and executed there by the Roman-controlled Egyptian government.
See also: Caesar, (Gaius) Julius.

Pompidou, Georges Jean Raymond (1911-74), president of France from 1969 to 1974. He was a literature professor before he began his political career in 1944 as an aide to Charles De Gaulle. De Gaulle was at that time a general and head of a temporary government. Pompidou's subsequent political career consisted of various posts in connection with De Gaulle. De Gaulle was elected president in 1958. When he resigned his presidency, Pompidou was elected to take his place. As president, Pompidou strove to better France's economy.
See also: France.

Ponape *See:* Pohnpei.

Ponce (pop. 161,700), city in Puerto Rico. Located in the south, near the coast, it is an important port through which a major portion of the island's imports and exports pass. Its other industries include liquor distilling, sugar refining, and tourism.
See also: Puerto Rico.

Ponce de León, Juan (c.1460-1521), Spanish discoverer of Florida. He sailed with Christopher Columbus in 1493, and in 1508 he conquered Puerto Rico and became its governor. Leading an expedition, possibly to find the mythical Fountain of Youth, he discovered and named Florida in 1513, but when he attempted to colonize it in 1521, he was driven off and mortally wounded by Indians.
See also: Florida.

Ponchielli, Amilcare (1834-86), Italian opera composer. His best-known works are *I Promessi Sposi* (1856) and *La Gioconda* (1876), with its famous ballet, *Dance of the Hours*.
See also: Opera.

Pond, still body of water smaller than a lake. Ponds can be natural or artificial. Ponds are located in many different kinds of terrain, form arctic to tropical regions. Their location, depth, soil, and water level and quality determine the kind of plant and animal life found in them.
See also: Marsh; Swamp.

Pond lily *See:* Water lily.

Pondweed, name for freshwater plants (genus *Potamogeton*) that sometimes clog streams and ponds. Their leaves may lie flat on the surface of the water or be completely submerged. The sago pondweed has branching stems and hairlike leaves. Like all pondweeds, its flowers open above the water. Its fruits are an important food for migrating ducks.

Ponomarev, Boris Nikolaevich (1905-   ), prominent official in Soviet Communist Party. He first became prominent in 1956 when he was voted into the party's Central Committee. In 1961, he became a secretary of the Central Committee. Ponomarev has also been a member of the Soviet Union's parliament since 1958.
See also: Union of Soviet Socialist Republics.

Ponselle, Rosa Melba (1897-1981), U.S. soprano, born Rosa Ponzillo. She sang in vaudeville before her sensational Metropolitan Opera debut in 1918 opposite Enrico Caruso in Verdi's *La Forza del Destino*. Until retiring in 1936, she was one of the company's leading dramatic sopranos.

Ponta Delgada (pop. 21,800), city on Saö Miguel Island, the largest of the Portuguese Azores islands. Its harbor is the main port of the Azores, exporting tropical fruits, vegetables, tea, and other products from the area. Other important industries in Ponta Delgada include sugar refining and liquor distilling. Its beautiful setting and favorable climate also makes it an active tourist resort.

Pontiac (1720-69), chief of the Ottawa Indians. He opposed the English during the French and Indian Wars, and was one of the leaders of an unsuccessful war against them, called Pontiac's Rebellion (1763-65), in which Pennsylvania, Virginia, and Maryland were seriously threatened. He signed a peace treaty in 1766.

Pontiac (pop. 76,715), city in southeastern Michigan. It lies on the Clinton River. Pontiac was founded in 1818 and became a city in 1861. In its early days, Pontiac was a leading manufacturing center of wagons and carriages. That developed into automobile manufacturing, which is still its major industry. Its plants produce many cars, trucks, and buses annually. Pontiac is situated on wooded hills and has many lakes and parks nearby. It was named for Pontiac, a Native American chief believed to be buried in the area.
See also: Michigan.

Pontifex, high priest of ancient Rome, one of the 16 members of the Pontifical College presiding over the state religion. The highest religious authority was the *pontifex maximus* (supreme pontiff); this title was adopted by the emperors and later by the popes.
See also: Rome, Ancient.

Pontiff *See:* Pope.

Pontine Marshes, swamp region in Italy. Located in central Italy, it covers an area of about 175,000 acres (70,820 hectares). The hills and mountains around this area prevent its water from being drained into the sea, creating an unhealthy environment. For centuries, it was the cause of malaria epidemics. Attempts to drain the area by digging waterways date back to as early as 312 B.C. In 1926, Benito Mussolini initiated a project that successfully drained the marshes. The reclaimed land has become a fertile agricultural area with several cities.

Pontoon bridge, bridge held up by pontoons (flat-bottomed boats), sealed metal tubes, or other floating objects. Because it can be built relatively quickly and is made up of materials that are transportable, it is especially convenient for military purposes. An army can set it up when invading or defending a territory to transport troops and equipment across a river when no bridge exists, or when the enemy has destroyed a once-existing bridge. A pontoon bridge was used as early as 480 B.C. by the Persian army. More recently, pontoon bridges were important to U.S. troops in Europe during World War II, where many bridges had been annihilated. Because a pontoon bridge blocks navigation, it is not a viable permanent structure. However, several long-span permanent concrete pontoon bridges exist. Washington has three, and Tasmania and Istanbul have one each.

Pontus, ancient kingdom in northeastern Asia Minor by the Black Sea. Dating from the 4th century B.C., it reached its height under Mithridates VI, who was, however, defeated by the Roman general Pompey in 65 B.C. Pontus was annexed by the Roman Empire in 9 B.C. after it had challenged Roman power.
See also: Mithridates VI.

Pony *See:* Horse.

Pony express, famous relay mail service between St. Joseph, Mo., and Sacramento, Calif. (Apr. 1860 to Oct. 1861). It used horses, not ponies, with riders chosen for their small size. The route covered 1,966 mi (3,164 km), with stations at 10-15 mi- (16-24 km-) intervals. The goal of 10-day delivery was often met. The pony express was superseded by the transcontinental telegraph.

Poodle, breed of intelligent dogs. Poodles have curly hair that can be trimmed in various styles. Their coats are of one solid color, and can be white, black, gray, brown, orange, or blue. There are three varieties of poodles. The *toy poodle* has a shoulder height of up to 10 in (25.4 cm) and weighs up to 6 lbs (2.7 kg). The *miniature poodle* has a shoulder height of 10 to 15 in (25 to 38.1 cm) and weighs 14 to 16 lbs (6.4 to 7.3 kg). The *standard poodle* has a shoulder height of over 15 in (38.1 cm) and weighs 40 to 60 lbs (18.1 to 27 kg). Poodles originated in Germany and were once used to retrieve game. However, they are no longer hunting dogs.

Pool *See:* Billiards.

Poor Richard's Almanac, almanac, written and published by Benjamin Franklin. The almanac was published annually from 1732 to 1757. It included weather predictions, poetry, astrological signs, as well as proverbs and advice. Franklin wrote the almanac under the pen name Richard Saunders. In the early almanacs, Richard had a foolish, dull personality, but in subsequent almanacs he developed into a witty, clever character who promoted thrift, simplicity, and hard work as the keys to success. Some of his now famous proverbs were: "God helps those who help themselves" and "a penny saved is a penny earned." The almanac was popular in its time, and the philosophies it expressed continue to be relevant.
See also: Franklin, Benjamin.

Poorwill *See:* Whippoorwill.

Pop art, modern art movement dating from the mid-1950s, based on images of advertising, commercial illustration, and mass-produced objects. Developed in England and the United States, it included the artists Richard Hamilton, David Hockney, Andy Warhol, and Robert Rauschenberg, among others.

Popcorn (*Zea mays everta*), type of corn that opens and puffs open when it is heated. It belongs to the family Gramineae. A popular snack, it is a good source of fiber and does not contain many calories. A popcorn kernel contains moist starch. When the kernel is heated, the moisture turns into steam that creates pressure and causes the kernel to burst and the starch to puff out. Native to America, popcorn was cultivated by Native Americans for thousands of years before they introduced it to settlers.

Pope, head of the Roman Catholic church and head of state of Vatican City. The pope is the bishop of Rome, successor in a long line that Roman Catholics believe began with St. Peter, the first bishop of Rome. Basing their authority upon Peter and, ultimately, upon the words of Jesus of Nazareth, the popes, as early as Clement I (c. 92-101), claimed paramount authority over all Christians and primacy over all other bishops. In succeeding centuries, the popes would maintain and extend their claim to absolute spiritual authority and eventually, to political authority as well. But over the centuries, the content and extent of papal authority, power, and prestige, spiritual and political, has varied considerably and was contested almost from the outset. The early church had been governed loosely and informally as a community of believers and bishops who were the equals of each other. The memory of that tradition persisted in Eastern Orthodoxy and when the capital of the Roman empire was moved east to Constantinople in the fourth century, the ground was laid for a contest between east and west for supreme authority over Christendom. That contest, begun in the fourth century, culminated in 1054 during the papacy of Leo IX in a complete schism, or break, between the Roman Catholic and Eastern Orthodox churches. The pope eventually faced two greater challenges to his claims in the Protestant Reformation of the 16th century and the rise of nationalism beginning in the Renaissance. The one effectively put an end to the pope's hitherto unchallenged spiritual authority among Western Christians and the other put an end to his once considerable political power. At the height of political power under Pope Innocent III (1198-1216) the popes claimed to have the power to elevate and depose monarchs as well as bishops and cardinals and the Holy See included considerable territories and drew upon revenues from throughout Europe. The rise of nationalism and the loss of church property and income eventually reduced the pope's domain. The Papal States, founded in 756 and at one time quite extensive, were all part of Italy by 1870, and what was left to the pope, Vatican City, was eventually created an independent state by the Lateran Treaty of 1929. While the modern papacy is vastly reduced politically, the popes continue to enjoy and exercise considerable political influence and prestige. As a head of state, the pope sends ambassadors, or *nuncios*, throughout the world to represent the position and policies of the papacy on a wide range of issues affecting Roman Catholics.

The history of the papacy is a story of popes who were great administrators, visionaries, saints, jurists, and politicians. Among them, too, were diplomats and scholars, discerning patrons of arts and letters, sensualists, weaklings, and scoundrels. The fall of Rome and the subsequent power vacuum ushered in a centuries' long period of lawlessness in the West known as the Dark Ages. For most of that period, the popes took a leading role in the struggle to restore order and civilized life to the West. Pope Gregory I, the Great (590-604) defended Italy from barbarian attack and imposed a measure of enduring order upon the chaos. In the 9th and 10th centuries, the pope's influence declined but was restored by a powerful reform movement. Pope Gregory VII (1073-85) established the pope's authority over clerics and kings and ushered in the greatest years of papal power and prestige. Decline set in with the capture of Pope Boniface VIII by troops of the French King Philip IV in 1303. The pope had become just one more of the many players in the ruthless game of politics. From 1309 to 1377 the popes resided in Avignon, France, and the result was the Great Schism in the western church that lasted from 1378 to 1417, a period in which rival popes claimed to be Peter's true heir and successor. The period raised fundamental questions about the papacy and church governance. In the centuries that followed the popes rapidly lost ground to the Reformation and nationalism.

Wealth and power had corrupted the ecclesiastical bureaucracy and hierarchy and many popes, among them Borgias and Medicis, led lives that scandalized pious Christians, particularly those who lived outside of Italy. But among these Renaissance popes were outstanding men, like Pope Sixtus IV (1471-84), a patron of arts and letters, and Pope Julius II (1503-13), patron of Raphael and Michelangelo. But the popes were not to recover lost ground. Despite the internal reforms and the work of the Counter-Reformation, through the 1700s and 1800s the popes were clearly taking a rear guard action, supporting politically conservative forces, and widely perceived as reactionary. Ideologically, the popes retrenched. They claimed infallibility in matters of faith and morals and there have since, for the most part, appeared departures from orthodoxy and the influences of modern thought.

The pope is elected for life. Upon his death, a conclave, or gathering, of cardinals is called to convene within 20 days. Voting is usually by ballot and for a man to be declared pope he must win a 2/3 majority plus one vote. A woman may not be pope. After a man is elected and accepts, a coronation ceremony is held. The current pope, John Paul II, was elected in 1978. He is the first non-Italian pope since Adrian VI (1522-23). John Paul II is Polish; Pope Adrian II was Dutch. The pope receives an annual salary and, in the course of discharging his many duties and responsibilities, leads a busy, demanding, and relatively spartan life absorbed in administrative, theologi-

cal, ceremonial, and political matters bearing on the lives of Roman Catholics throughout the world.
See also: Roman Catholic Church.

Popé (d. c.1692), medicine man of the Pueblo Indians who organized the so-called Pueblo Revolt in 1680 against the Spanish in New Mexico. He succeeded in driving them out of Santa Fe and temporarily destroyed Spanish practices, restoring the Pueblos' ancient traditions.

Pope, Alexander (1688-1744), the greatest English poet and satirist of the Augustan Age. He was 4 ft 6 in (1.4 m) tall and partly crippled by tuberculosis. He first set out his literary ideals in his *Essay on Criticism* (1711), written in rhymed (heroic) couplets. His best-known works are the mock epic *The Rape of the Lock* (1712), his translations of the *Iliad* (1720) and the *Odyssey* (1726), *The Dunciad* (1728, 1743), a satirical attack on literary critics, and his essays on moral philosophy, *An Essay on Man* (1733-34) and *Moral Essays* (1731-35).

Poplar, name of group of trees belonging to the willow family. Poplars are found in Europe, Asia, and North America. They grow quickly and produce a soft, light wood used in the manufacture of crates and boxes. Depending on the species, they may be heart-shaped, triangular, or diamond-shaped. The name of some poplars are: balsam poplar, white poplar, white or silver poplar, and Carolina poplar.

Popocatépetl, volcanic mountain in Mexico. Its name is the Aztec word for "smoking mountain." With an altitude of 17,887 ft (5,452 m), it is one of the highest mountains in North America, and the second-highest mountain in Mexico. Its peak is always snow-covered. "Popo," as it is sometimes called, has not had a major eruption since 1702. It does occasionally emit smoke clouds and sulfur gas, and, less frequently, ashes and stones.

Popper, Sir Karl Raimund (1902-94), Austrian-born English philosopher, best known for his theory of falsification in the philosophy of science. Popper contends that scientific theories are never more than provisionally adopted and remain acceptable only as long as scientists are devising new experiments to test (falsify) them. He attacks the doctrine of historicism (presuming to understand phenomena entirely through their development) in *The Open Society and Its Enemies* (1945) and *The Poverty of Historicism* (1957).
See also: Philosophy.

Poppy, name for annual or herbaceous perennial plants of the genus *Papaver* and related genera. There are about 100 species, which are mostly native to temperate and subtropical areas in Eurasia and northern Africa. The flower bud is enclosed by two thick, green sepals that drop off to allow the thin petals to unfold. The seeds are enclosed in a capsule. The sap of the unripe capsules of the opium poppy (*P. somniferum*) yield opium; its seeds (poppyseed) are not narcotic.

Popular music, term used to describe several kinds of music that are not classical. Classical music includes symphonies, operas, and ballet works performed by an orchestra. Popular music includes rock and roll, country and folk music, jazz, and other styles and blendings of styles. It is called "popular" because it is usually appreciated by a large number of the general public.

Population, number of or term for all the inhabitants of a designated territory. For the world as a whole, population doubled between 1930 and 1975, from 2 to 4 billion, and increased to 4.7 billion by mid-1983, with a possible 6 billion forecast for the year 2000. The sharpest increases have been in developing nations, which are least able to provide food, education, and jobs for all. Averting world famine depends on the few countries able to export food. Many nations now have population-control programs, but the control of infectious diseases and increases in the food supply because of modern growing techniques have combined to encourage population growth. In some societies, however, fertility rates have declined somewhat, and an increase in abortions, approaching the number of live births in a few countries, has helped defuse the population bomb, though not without great controversy. In the United States, a "baby boom" occurred after World War II, but after 1957 the birth rate declined and by the 1980s gave indications of approaching zero population growth.

Populism, "grass roots" agrarian political movement incorporating a farmer-labor coalition. Specifically, it refers to the doctrines of the U.S. People's Party. The post-Civil War farm depression had created agrarian reform movements like the Grange and the Farmers' Alliance. In 1891-92 delegates from the Farmers' Alliance and labor organization set up the People's Party, which espoused an eight-hour day, government ownership of railroads, graduated income tax, government postal savings banks, direct election of senators, increase of the money supply, and free silver. At first the party gained support rapidly. However, the People's Party declined following the 1896 presidential election, when the Democratic candidate, W.J. Bryan, captured most of the populist vote. The term *populism* is also applied to any policies appealing to the common citizen, such as those advocated by Huey Long and George Wallace.

Poquelin, Jean Baptiste *See:* Molière.

Porcelain, a kind of white earthenware. It is hard, fine, and translucent. Porcelain is made from a mixture of kaolin (a pure white clay) and petuntse (a hard mineral). After the mixture is shaped, it is fired at an extremely high temperature that causes the petuntse to melt into glass that is fused to the kaolin which retains the shape. Porcelain is used to create such items as tableware, vases, and figurines. It is most often decorated with painted designs. Because it was first developed by the Chinese (7th century), it is sometimes referred to as china. Europe, Japan, and the United States produce most of the world's porcelain.

Porcupine, name for large, spiny vegetarian rodents of two distinct families: Erithizontidae, confined to the Americas, and Hystricidae, to the tropics of the Old World. Old World forms, including about a dozen species in Africa and South Asia, are among the largest rodents, and the entire body is covered with spines. The American porcupines have an equal armory of spines, but when relaxed, these are concealed in a thick underfur.

Porcupinefish, slow-moving tropical fish that can blow up its body when alarmed. It takes in water through the mouth to swell its body into a sphere; at the same time, sharp spines are raised, making it very difficult to handle. Porcupinefish feed on shellfish and coral. Pacific Islanders used to make the skins into helmets.

Pore, minute opening of a gland in skin. Skin has many small glands that produce perspiration and oil. Pores serve as an outlet for the perspiration and oil. When pores are blocked up, skin becomes inflamed, resulting in a skin rash or acne.

Porgy, deep-bodied fish (family Sparidae) with powerful teeth. Porgies are found in shallow tropical and temperate seas. The largest is the 100-lb (45-kg) South African mussel-cracker. On the Atlantic coast of America there are the northern porgy, the sheepshead, and the pinfish.

Porifera *See:* Sponge.

Po River, longest river in Italy. Beginning in the Cottian Alps, it flows east for 405 mi (652 km) and drains into a huge delta in the Adriatic Sea. Most rivers in northern Italy empty into it, as do the Garda, Como, Maggiore, Lecco, and Iseo lakes. The Po carries a tremendous amount of water and has created many devastating floods. Efforts were made as early as 300 B.C. to control the river by building embankments. Several large Italian cities are situated on the Po, such as Cremona and Turin. From the mouth of the Po to Turin, the river is deep and wide enough for the navigation of freight ships transporting cargo. On the upper section of the river are several electric power plants.

Pork, pig flesh used for food. Pork may be eaten cooked. It may also be cured with salt and then smoked or dried. Smoking and drying cured pork prevents the meat from spoiling, and gives it an added flavor. Ham and bacon are cured pork. Pork may contain small worms that, when consumed, create a disease called trichinosis. Fresh pork should always be thoroughly cooked until the meat becomes gray—this kills any worms that may be in it.

Pork barrel, pejorative U.S. term for government spending on local, presumably unnecessary, projects. The term, which originated in the 19th century and derives from the practice of salting pork to store in barrels, is used to indicate the wastefulness and selfishness of legislators who vote on such expenditures to reward political allies and direct funds into their districts.

Pornography, term applied to materials, including books, pictures, magazines, and films, with obscene or offensive content designed to cause sexual excitement. The term is derived from the Greek *pornographos* ("writing of harlots") and most often refers to sexual material, though it is now sometimes applied to other forms of offensive material, such as that which portrays gratuitous violence. In the United States each state has laws concerning the publication and distribution of obscene material; these are backed up by extensive international agreements designed to inhibit the import and export of pornography.

Porphyry (A.D. 233-304), ancient Greek philosopher, author of *Introduction to the Categories*, a book which discussed how the qualities of things could be put into categories and groups. He studied in Athens before moving to Rome, where he became a member of the Neoplatonic group led by Plotinus. *See also:* Neoplatonism.

Porpoise, small toothed whale (family Phocaenidae), distinguished from dolphins in being smaller and having a rounded head with no projecting beaklike mouth. They feed mainly on shoaling fishes. The name is sometimes loosely applied in the United States to the various species of dolphin.

Porsche, Ferdinand *See:* Volkswagen.

Port, sweet wine, usually red, fortified with brandy. It comes from grapes grown in the Douro Valley, Portugal, and is shipped from Oporto, whence its name.

Portage la Prairie (pop. 13,198), city of southern Manitoba. Situated between the Assiniboine River and Lake Manitoba, it was founded in 1738 by the French who built Fort LaReine there. French fur traders carried their canoes across the prairie between the river and the lake, thus giving the city its name. Today it is a key agricultural market city and food processing center for the Portage Plains region.

Port-au-Prince (pop. 738,000), capital, largest city, and leading port of Haiti. It stands on a sheltered bay facing the Caribbean Sea. In spite of local industries, including textile, flour, and sugar milling, some imposing buildings, and a modern airport, the city is one of the Western Hemisphere's poorest capitals. French colonists founded Port-au-Prince in 1749.

Port Authority of New York and New Jersey, governing agency for port-owned facilities in New York City and adjacent New Jersey. Incorporated in 1921 to develop and improve commerce in and around New York Harbor, the Port Authority operates bridges, tunnels, marine terminals, airports, and buildings such as the "twin towers" of the 1,350 ft (411 m) World Trade Center. It is governed by 12 commissioners, 6 from each of the 2 states, and maintains trade development offices in major United States and foreign cities.

Portcullis *See:* Castle.

Port Elizabeth (pop. 652,000), city in South Africa. Situated on a bay of the Indian Ocean, it was founded in 1799. The modern city was laid out in 1820 by Sir Rufane Donkin, who named it for his wife, Lady Elizabeth. Port Elizabeth is a major seaport and manufacturing center with important rubber and automobile industries.

Porter, U.S. naval officers, father and son. **David Porter** (1780-1843) took part in the war against Tripoli (1801-5) and during the War of 1812 he became the first United States naval officer to operate a warship in the Pacific Ocean. He was also the foster father of David G. Farragut, one of the greatest Union naval commanders of the Civil War. **David Dixon Porter** (1813-91) served under Farragut in the Civil War and played key roles in the captures of New Orleans, Vicksburg, and other major Southern ports.

Porter, Cole (1893-1964), U.S. popular song composer. After World War I he achieved great success as a writer of sophisticated songs and musical comedies, providing both the words and music. His prolific output includes *Anything Goes* (1934), *Kiss Me Kate* (1948), *Can-Can* (1953), the film score for *High Society* (1956), and many classic songs.

Porter, Fitz-John (1822-1901), U.S. Army officer. During the Civil War, he served as a corps commander in the Army of the Potomac and fought in the Shenandoah Valley and Peninsular campaigns. During the second Battle of Manassas (Bull Run) in 1862, the Union commander, Gen. John Pope, accused him of failing to carry out orders. Porter was court-martialed, found guilty, and discharged from the army in 1863. In 1879 his case was reviewed and he was exonerated. He was restored to his rank 7 years later.

Porter, Katherine Anne (1890-1980), U.S. short-story writer and novelist who won the 1966 Pulitzer Prize for her *Collected Short Stories* (1965). Her collections of short stories include *Flowering Judas* (1930) and *Pale Horse, Pale Rider* (1939). *Ship of Fools* (1962) is her only novel.

Porter, William Sydney *See:* Henry, O.

Portland (pop. 215,281), largest city in Maine. Located on Casco Bay, Portland was founded in 1632 and has one of the finest harbors along the Atlantic Coast. It is a major shipping center for pulpwood and other agricultural products and oil bound for the Portland-Montreal pipeline is unloaded there. Portland is also an important seafood processing hub and its downtown business district features many good examples of Victorian architecture.
See also: Maine.

Portland (pop. 445,400), largest city in Oregon, a leading West Coast port. It stands in northwestern Oregon on the Willamette River near its junction with the Columbia River, c.60 mi (97 km) due east of the Pacific Ocean. Ocean-going ships reach Portland by river, enabling it to handle more dry cargo than any other Pacific port. Lumber, fruit, and wheat are the main exports. Important educational institutions include the University of Oregon's schools of medicine and dentistry, Portland State College, and the Roman Catholic University of Portland. The city's rose gardens are nationally famous.
See also: Oregon.

Portland cement *See:* Cement.

Port Louis (pop. 142,800), capital and largest city of the island nation of Mauritius. Located on a sheltered harbor of the Indian Ocean on the northwestern shore of the country's main island, Port Louis is a key agricultural and industrial export center. It was founded by the French in 1735 and named for King Louis XV.

Port Moresby (pop. 145,300), capital and largest city of Papua New Guinea. It lies on a harbor of the Coral Sea in the southeastern part of the country and was founded in 1873 by the British explorer Capt. John Moresby. During World War II (1939-45) Port Moresby served as an Allied military operations center for the South Pacific.

Porto, or Oporto (pop. 327,400), second largest city in Portugal. Situated on the Douro River near its mouth at the Atlantic Ocean, Porto was founded during the Roman Empire and several of its medieval landmarks, including a cathedral, survive today. Porto is the major commercial and industrial hub of northern Portugal and is famous for its port wines. Fishing and food processing also contribute greatly to the city's economic base.

Pôrto Alegre (pop. 1,262,600), city in southeastern Brazil. It is located on the Guaíba River near the Atlantic Ocean and is the capital of the state of Rio Grande do Sul. Pôrto Alegre is a key shipping and commercial port, as well as an important cultural and educational center.

Portobelo (pop. 550), village in Panama. Named by Columbus in 1502 and founded as a Caribbean shipping port, Portobelo was often the starting point for Spanish treasure ships bound for Spain from its New World colonies. Repeated attacks by English pirates in the 17th and 18th centuries destroyed much of the town and its importance declined after the opening of the Panama Railroad in the 1850s.

Port-of-Spain (pop. 51,100), capital and largest city of Trinidad and Tobago. Situated on the northwest coast of the island of Trinidad, Port-of-Spain was founded by the Spanish around 1560 and was briefly the capital of the Federation of the West Indies (1958-62), a group of British-owned Caribbean islands. It is a major agricultural export center for the nation and the southern Caribbean region.

Portolá, Gaspar de (1723?-?84), Spanish colonizer of California. In 1769, as governor of the Californias, he mounted an expedition from Mexico that founded San Diego and Monterey. He was governor of Puebla, Mexico, from 1776.
See also: California.

Porto-Novo (pop. 144,000), capital and second largest city of Benin. Lying on the Gulf of Guinea, it was founded and named by the Portuguese in the 17th century and became a hub for the West African slave trade. Captured by the French in 1883, Porto-Novo was made the capital of the colony of Dahomey and remained the capital when independence was granted in 1960. It is a major port and rail terminal for the rest of the nation.

Port Said (pop. 399,800), port city in Egypt. Located on the Mediterranean Sea at the northern terminus of the Suez Canal, Port Said was founded in 1859 as a camp for workers building the canal. Because of its key location, it is a major commercial center for ships using the canal and the site of a free trade zone established by the Egyptian government to encourage commerce.
See also: Egypt.

Portsmouth (pop. 187,900), major port and naval center in southern England. Situated on the English Channel, Portsmouth was founded in the 1100s and became a key shipbuilding city in the 16th century. Shipbuilding and naval activity provide the city with much of its economic base and its busy harbor handles much of the country's import and export trade. Historic sites there include the 12th century cathedral, the birthplace of Charles Dickens, and Lord Nelson's flagship, *Victory.*
See also: England.

Portsmouth (pop. 26,254), New Hampshire, major seaport on the state's Atlantic coast. Founded in the early 1600s at the mouth of the Piscataqua River, Portsmouth is the site of an important naval shipyard and Air Force base. It is the oldest settlement in New Hampshire and the site of its first capital. The Treaty of Portsmouth, ending the Russo-Japanese War, was signed at the naval base in 1905.
See also: New Hampshire.

Port Sudan (pop. 206,700), chief port city of Sudan. It is on the Red Sea and was built between 1905 and 1909 to replace an earlier Arab port that became choked off by coral reefs. With modern harbor facilities, Port Sudan handles most of the nation's overseas trade and is the fourth largest city in Sudan.
See also: Sudan.

Portugal, republic on the Iberian peninsula in the extreme southwest of continental Europe.
Land and climate. Excluding the Azores and Madeira, Portugal covers an area of 34,340 sq mi/88,941 sq km and is bordered by Spain to the east and north and by the Atlantic Ocean to the west and south. Portugal lies at the point where the western ridge of the high Spanish plateau slopes downward towards the Atlantic Ocean. Most of the highest land lies in the northeast gradually giving way to undulating hills and low fertile plains. Three large rivers, all rising in Spain, cross the country: the Douro, the Tagus, and the Guadiana. Coastal Portugal has a mild climate; the interior has colder winters and is often subject to drought. The capital is Lisbon.
People. The Portuguese people are a mixture of the original inhabitants of the land and successive waves of invaders. The Portuguese language is closely related to Spanish and almost everyone in Portugal is Roman Catholic.
Economy. Portugal is one of Europe's poorer countries. Most of the people live in villages and small towns and agriculture is an important occupation. Most farms are small and poor. Portuguese raise livestock, olives, grapes, citrus fruits, and almonds and produce wine and olive oil. Portugal is a major producer of cork. Fishing is important, the chief catches being sardines and tuna. Industries include food processing, textiles, metals, mining, and hydroelectricity.
History. Over the centuries, the area that is now Portugal was invaded by Celts, Greeks, and Romans and later by Visigoths, Berbers, and Moors. The Moors arrived in 711 and remained until 1249. Their influence upon Portuguese culture has been deep. Portugal became an independent Christian kingdom in 1143 under Alfonso I and over the next century the country was completely reconquered from the Moors. In 1385, John I founded the Aviz dynasty and by the second half of the 16th century, Portugal was at the

Portugal

Capital:	Lisbon
Area:	35,672 sq mi
	(92,389 sq km)
Population:	9,926,000
Language:	Portuguese
Government:	Republic
Independent:	1910 (republic)
Head of gov.:	Prime minister
Per capita:	U.S. $9,740
Mon. unit:	1 Escudo = 100
	centavos

pinnacle of its power with an empire that included much of South America, Africa, and South and Southeast Asia. Philip II of Spain seized Portugal in 1580 and the Spanish ruled until a successful revolt established the ruling house of Braganza in 1640. By then, Portugal had lost most of her former power and influence. During the Napoleonic Wars, Portugal was invaded by both the French and the Spanish. By 1825 Brazil had become an independent empire. A Portuguese republic was declared in 1910 and after a military coup in 1926 Antonio de Oliveira Salazar rose to power and became virtual dictator until he was succeeded by Marcello Caetano in 1968. A coup in 1974 ushered in a government that brought democratic reforms. Subsequently, Portugal shed virtually all of its overseas territories. Guinea-Bissau became independent in 1974, followed by Angola, the Cape Verde Islands, Mozambique, and São Tomé and Príncipe in 1975. In 1976 Portuguese Timor became part of Indonesia and Macao will revert to China in 1999. In the process, Portugal has also recovered a measure of political stability. In 1987 the government, headed by Premier Anibal Cavaco Silvas, was democratically elected. The 1995 elections were won by the Socialistst, led by António Guterres.

Portuguese, official language of Portugal and Brazil. It is one of the Romance Languages and developed from the Latin spoken in Roman Iberia. Brazilian Portuguese has absorbed words and phrases from the languages of the Native American and African slave populations.

Portuguese Guinea *See:* Guinea-Bissau.

Portuguese man-of-war (*Physalia physalis*), colorful jellyfish of the order Siphonophora. It consists of an assemblage of four kinds of polyps, the most obvious of which is a gas-filled bladder about 1 ft (30.5 cm) long, which carries a high crest and is colored blue or purple. Below this float are supported other polyps, including the long, stinging tentacles used for catching prey. The sting can be painful to humans.

Portuguese water dog, web-footed dog capable of swimming great distances. Portuguese fishermen trained and used the dogs to retrieve fish and nets from the water and they have also been used to carry messages between ships. Males range from 20 to 23 in (51 to 59 cm) tall and weigh between 42 and 60 lb (19-27 kg), while females are smaller.

Portulaca, flower of the purslane family. Producing colorful blossoms that open only in full sunlight, portulacas are cultivated in gardens and several species are used as potted plants. The petals are most commonly red, yellow, pink, white, or purple and the plant may grow from 1 to 1.5 ft (30-46 cm) tall.

Poseidon, in Greek mythology, god of the sea. The son of Cronus and Rhea and brother of Zeus, Poseidon was also the god of horses, earthquakes, and sea storms. He was often pictured with a long white beard driving a chariot and wielding a trident with which he stirred up the earth or sea when venting his wrath. His Roman counterpart was Neptune.

Positivism, philosophical theory of knowledge associated with the 19th-century French philosopher Auguste Comte. It holds that the observable, or "positive," data of sense experience constitute the sole basis for assertions about matters of fact; only the truths of logic and mathematics are additionally admitted. The speculative claims of theology and metaphysics, regarded as the primitive antecedents of "positive" thought, are discounted.
See also: Comte, Auguste.

Positron emission tomography (PET), technique used to study brain activity. A person undergoing a PET scan is injected with a glucose solution containing low-level radioactive particles that produce positrons, electrically charged particles that help produce gamma rays. The person places his or her head inside a ring containing sensors that measure gamma ray signals from the brain, and these signals are translated by colors onto a screen. Scientists reading the screen can interpret the colors in a way that measures brain activity.
See also: Brain.

Possum, tree-dwelling mammal of the family Phalangeridae, native to Australia and New Guinea. There are about 40 species of possums, ranging in weight from 1/2 oz (14 grams) to 11 lb (5 kg). They are nocturnal animals, foraging through forests and garbage cans for their food. As with other marsupials, the babies are born prematurely and are nurtured in the mothers' pouches. Their practice of lying absolutely still when frightened gives rise to the term "playing possum."

Post, Emily Price (1872-1960), U.S. writer, accepted authority on correct social behavior because of her book *Etiquette* (1922).

Postal Service, U.S., independent federal agency that provides mail service nationwide. The Postal Service began operation on July 1, 1971, replacing the United States Post Office Department founded in 1775. The current arrangement calls for an 11-member independent board of governors, headed by the Postmaster General, to oversee all facets of the postal system's operations. They set postage rates, appoint postmasters, and set salaries for employees. There are about 30,000 post offices in the United States and the USPS employs about 730,000 people.

Postal Union, Universal (UPU), United Nations agency governing the international flow of mail. Begun in 1874 with 22 nations attending the first International Postal Congress in Berne, Switzerland, the UPU became a UN agency in 1947. Today it includes all 170 member nations. The UPU sets policies and uniform procedures for the exchange of mail and parcels between countries and establishes reasonable postal rates. It also provides technical assistance and advice to its members and strives toward the improvement of all services under its supervision.

Post, Wiley (1899-1935), U.S. aviator. In 1933 he was the first person to fly solo around the world, a feat he accomplished in a little over a week (July 15-22). During this flight, which covered 15,596 mi (25,099 km), Post proved the effectiveness of an automatic pilot system that enabled the plane to stay aloft while he rested. On Aug. 15, 1935 he was killed in a plane crash near Point Barrow, Alaska.

Postimpressionism, term coined by critic Roger Fry to describe the work of certain painters (1880-90) whose styles, though dissimilar, flowed from, and were a reaction to, impressionism. Paul Cézanne, Paul Gauguin, Georges Seurat, and Vincent Van Gogh are considered the principal postimpressionists.

Post mortem *See:* Autopsy.

Pot *See:* Marijuana.

Potash, potassium-based salts used in fertilizers. Most potash comes from the mineral sylvite and is often found in underground salt beds or in salt lakes. Potassium chloride (KCI) is the most important type of potash but another type, potassium carbonate (K_2CO_3), can be manufactured by running water through wood ashes and boiling the solution in large iron pots.

Potassium, chemical element, symbol K; for physical constants see Periodic Table. Potassium was discovered by Sir Humphrey Davy in 1807. It was the first metal isolated by electrolysis. It is found mainly as *sylvite* (potassium chloride) but occurs in many other minerals. It is obtained commercially by electrolysis of the hydroxide. Potassium is a silvery-white, soft, reactive metal of the alkali metal group. It catches fire spontaneously in water and oxidizes rapidly in air and must be stored in a dry oxygen-free liquid such as mineral oil. It is essential to plant growth and is found in most soils. Potassium and its compounds are used in fertilizers, photography, organic synthesis, and heat transfer media.

Potassium nitrate *See:* Saltpeter.

Potato (*Solanum tuberosum*), herbaceous plant of the nightshade family, with an edible, fleshy, tuberous, underground stem. It originated in the South American Andes. The tubers became a popular European foodstuff in the 18th century, the Irish in particular becoming dependent on the high-carbo-hydrate crop.

Potato beetle (*Lema trilineata*), destructive insect of the leaf beetle family. The larvae feed on the leaves and stems of potato plants, causing extensive damage and diseases that harm proper potato tuber growth. The most common type is the Colorado potato beetle (*Leptinotarsa decemlineata*), which measures 1/2 in (13 mm) long and is yellow with black stripes on its wing covers.

Potato famine, in 19th-century Ireland, famine caused by potato blight. In 1845 and 1846 potato crops failed; in the subsequent famine nearly a million people died, and over a million emigrated, particularly to the United States. Ireland's population fell from about 8.5 million in 1845 to 6.55 million in 1851.
See also: Ireland.

Potawatomi, North American tribe of the Algonquian language family. In the 18th century they lived around the south shore of Lake Michigan. They allied with the French colonists and joined Pontiac in his rebellion (1763). They later supported the British in the Revolutionary War and in the War of 1812. Coming under pressure from settlers, they moved west, and in 1846 most of them were forced into a reservation in Kansas. The Potawatomi in Kansas have preserved much of the aboriginal culture.

Potemkin, Grigori Aleksandrovich (1729-91), Russian soldier and favorite of Catherine the Great. For the last 20 years of his life, he was the most powerful man in Russia. He enlarged the Russian army and navy, and annexed (1783) and administered the Crimea.

Potential, electric, work done against electric fields in bringing a unit charge to a given point from some arbitrary reference point (usually earthed), measured in volts (i.e., joules per coulomb). Charges tend to flow from points at one potential to those at a lower potential; potential difference, or voltage, thus plays the role of a driving force for electric current. In inductive circuits, the work done in bringing up the charge depends on the route taken, and potential ceases to be a useful concept.

Potentiometer, device used to obtain a precise measure of the electromotive force (emf), or voltage, of an electrical cell. It employs a special circuit incorporating a variable resistor (rheostat) and a galvanometer. Using a standard cell of known emf, the rheostat is adjusted until no current flows in the circuit, as indicated by the galvanometer. The cell of unknown emf is then placed in the circuit instead of the standard cell, and the rheostat is adjusted again so that no current flows. The difference in the 2 settings of the rheostat indicates the emf of the unknown cell. The potentiometer can be used to calibrate electrical instruments and as a variable resistor. The volume control in a radio is a type of potentiometer.

Potlatch, in many tribal cultures, especially among the Native Americans of the Northwest Coast, an elaborate ceremonial feast at which the host distributes or destroys his own wealth to gain status or office in his tribe. Wealthier guests are expected in turn to match or exceed this in future potlatches. Although banned for a while in Canada, the potlatch is still an important tribal institution.

Potomac River, U.S. river flowing through Washington, D.C. Formed by the confluence of the 110-mi (177-km) long northern branch and the 140-mi

(125-km) long southern branch, it flows 287 mi (462 km) into Chesapeake Bay. Navigation for large ships is prevented above Washington, D.C., by the Great Falls. The river is noted for its scenic attraction.

Potsdam (pop. 142,300), city in eastern Germany, near Berlin. In the 18th century it was chosen by Frederick II as his principal residence and became a center and symbol of Prussian militarism. Noted for its royal palaces, it is now also an industrial city. It was the site of the 1945 Potsdam Conference.

Potsdam Conference (July 17 to Aug. 2, 1945), a summit meeting at Potsdam, Germany, between Premier Joseph Stalin, President Harry S. Truman, and in succession, Prime Ministers Winston Churchill and Winston Attlee. They agreed that a four-power Allied Control Council would rule defeated Germany, disarming it and fostering democratic government; Poland would gain part of East Germany; the German economy would be decentralized; Germans in Hungary, Poland, and Czechoslovakia would be repatriated. The conference also discussed reparations payments and issued an ultimatum to Japan. Almost all the agreements were breached as the Cold War hardened.
See also: World War II.

Potter, Beatrix (1866-1943), English author and illustrator of children's books. Her works, illustrated by herself, have become classics, including *The Tale of Peter Rabbit* (1902), *The Tailor of Gloucester* (1903), *Benjamin Bunny* (1904), *Mrs. Tiggy-Winkle* (1905), *Jemima Puddle-Duck* (1908), and *Pigling Bland* (1913).

Pottery and porcelain, ceramic articles, especially vessels, made of clay (generally kaolin) and hardened by firing. In the manufacture of pottery the clay is made plastic by blending with water. The article is then shaped—traditionally by hand, by building up layers of strips (coiled pottery), by "throwing" on the potter's wheel, or by molding, industrially by high-pressure molding or by a rotating template. The clay is fired in a kiln, slowly at first, then at higher temperatures to oxidize and consolidate it. The glaze (if desired) is then applied by spraying or dipping and the article is refired.

Potto (genus *Perodicticus*), various slow-moving African primates related to the lorises. The potto has large, staring eyes, thick, woolly fur, and a short tail; spines from the neck bones protrude through the skin. It leads a solitary life, emerging at dusk to search for fruit, insects, lizards, or birds' nests.

Poulenc, Francis (1899-1963), French composer, member of the post-World War II group of composers called *Les Six*. His music is light in texture, although serious. His best-known works include *Mouvements perpetuels* for piano (1918), the ballet *Les Biches* (1924), and the opera *Dialogue des Carmélites* (1957). He was also a notable songwriter.

Poultry farming, rearing of all types of domesticated farm fowls for eggs and flesh. Chickens are the most popular bird, followed by turkeys, ducks, geese, and other types. Important chicken breeds are the leghorn and Rhode Island Red for eggs and the Plymouth Rock and Cornish for meat. Nearly all economically valuable fowls live in controlled environments, with artificial lighting and heating and small pens for individuals or groups. Chickens are hatched in incubators, reared in brooders and transferred to laying or fattening quarters. An annual output of 200-250 eggs per bird is essential for good profits. Marketing is organized through farmers' cooperatives and marketing boards.

Pound, Ezra Loomis (1885-1972), U.S. poet, critic, and translator. A gifted linguist, he went to Europe in 1908 and soon won recognition. His most important works are *Homage to Sextus Propertius* (1918), *Hugh Selwyn Mauberley* (1920), and the epic *Cantos* (1925-60). He championed the imagist and vorticist movements, and influenced T.S. Eliot, Robert Frost, and W.B. Yeats, among others. He supported Benito Mussolini, and after broadcasting pro-Fascist propaganda during World War II, he was indicted for treason by the United States; he was found unfit to plead and confined to a mental institution until 1958.

Pound, Roscoe (1870-1964), U.S. jurist and educator who championed flexibility in the law and efficiency in court administration. Professor of law at Harvard (1910-37), he advocated a "sociological jurisprudence" that would adapt the law to changing social and economic conditions.

Poussin, Nicolas (1594-1665), greatest 17th-century French Baroque painter. He worked mostly in Rome and based his style on Raphael and antiquities. He was first painter to Louis XII. His classical and religious subjects, such as *Shepherds of Arcadia* (1629), *The Rape of the Sabine Women* (1635), and *The Seven Sacraments* (1644-48) are rich in color, austere in handling, dramatic, and evocative in mood. He influenced Jacques-Louis David, Paul Cézanne, and Pablo Picasso.

Poverty, shortage of income or resources necessary for a minimum standard of living in a particular society. In the United States, where a poor minority exists in the midst of an affluent society, a major element in poverty is the feeling of psychological deprivation. In the poor countries of Asia, Africa, and Latin America, where the poor constitute a majority of the people, poverty consists more of physical deprivation, but even in the third world the economic expectations of the poor have been substantially raised by exposure to the mass media.

Powder metallurgy, process of reducing metals into powder. The process is used to make metal alloys by mixing them as powder and heating them to bind the powders together. They are then pressed into the desired shape or form. Metals can be broken down into powders by crushing them or by submittting them to intense heat. They can also be reduced through electrolysis or by atomization of the metal in molten form.

Powder River, river of western United States. From its source in the foothills of Wyoming's Bighorn Mountains, the Powder River flows northward into Montana and joins the Yellowstone River near Terry, Mont. It is 486 mi (782 km) long.

Powell, Adam Clayton, Jr. (1908-72), U.S. politician. Minister of the Abyssinian Baptist Church, he was New York's first black city council

member (1941). He founded *The People's Voice* (1942) and, as the flamboyant "Voice of Harlem," was a Democratic representative (1945-70). Excluded from Congress for alleged misuse of public funds (1967), the
expulsion was overturned by the U.S. Supreme Court and he was reelected
twice until he was defeated in 1970.

Powell, Anthony Dymoke (1905-   ), English novelist, best known for his
contemporary comedy of manners *A Dance to the Music of Time*, a 12-vol-
ume series of novels starting with *A Question of Upbringing* (1951) and
ending with *Hearing Secret Harmonies* (1976).

Powell, Colin (1938-   ), youngest person and first black officer ever to
become Chair of the Joint Chiefs of Staff (1989-93), the highest-ranking military
post in the United States. Powell, a 4-star general, co-directed (with Secretary of
Defense Dick Cheney) the allied effort during the Persian Gulf War (1991).
See also: Persian Gulf War.

Powell, John Wesley (1834-1902), U.S. geologist and ethnologist best
known for his geological and topographical surveys and for his anthropo-
logical studies of Native Americans. He helped establish and headed the U.S.
Geological Survey (1881-94).
See also: Geology.

Powell, Lewis Franklin, Jr. (1907-   ), associate justice of the U.S. Supreme Court (1971-87). A lawyer and former president of the American Bar
Association, he was appointed to the court by President Richard M. Nixon.

Power, in physics, the time rate at which work is done. The amount of power
that is put forth determines the amount of work that can be done per unit
time. Power can be calculated with the following formula:

$$P = \frac{W}{t}$$

In this formula, P stands for power, W for work, and t for time. Work is
measured by multiplying the force times the distance. The formula for power
is then written:

$$P = \frac{Fd}{t}$$

In this formula, F stands for force and d stands for distance.
The basic unit of power in the English system of measurement is *foot-pounds
per second*. When a force of 1 pound moves an object 1 foot, 1 foot-pound
of work is done. In the metric system, the customary unit of power is the
watt. A watt is the power needed to do 1 joule of work per second.

Power, in the social sciences, the ability to exercise control over others.
Power is most often exerted by individuals, groups, or nations through
superior physical strength, social position, or intellect. Greater resources or
attributes usually give a person or entity power to impose penalties on those
who fail to yield to their demands. Fear of the imposition of those penalties
is what most often keeps weaker individuals or nations from rebelling against
those holding power over them.

Power, in mathematics, the total of a number multiplied by itself a given number of times. It was developed as a shortcut to having to write the same number multiplied by itself many times, for example, 5 to the fourth power means that the number 5 is multiplied by 5 four times. It is written as a cardinal number with a superior number to the upper right of it (5^4=625). In the example, 5 is called the base and 4 is the exponent.
See also: Mathematics.

Power of attorney, in U.S. law, legal document authorizing a person to act on behalf of the signatory, usually in business and financial matters. To be officially recorded, it usually must be certified by a notary public. A general power allows the agent to act for the signatory in all circumstances, while a special power covers only specified items.

Powers, Hiram (1805-73), U.S. sculptor. He worked in Florence, Italy, from 1837. His work includes the neoclassical *Greek Slave* (1843) and busts of eminent Americans, including Andrew Jackson, Thomas Jefferson, and Benjamin Franklin.

Powhatan (c.1550-1618), personal name Wahunsonacock, chief of the Powhatans and head of the Powhatan Confederacy of tribes, which he enlarged until it covered most of the Virginia tidewater region and part of Maryland. He befriended the Jamestown settlers under their leader John Smith (1608). Later hostilities were settled when his daughter Pocahontas married John Rolfe (1614).

Powhatan, North American tribe in eastern Virginia, of Algonquian linguistic stock. They grew corn, hunted, fished, and lived in villages with palisades. Under Powhatan their confederacy dominated some 30 tribes. After his death (1618) violent clashes with encroaching settlers led to their defeat. Some 3,000 Powhatan live in Virginia today.

Poznan (pop. 1,300,000), city in Poland. Located on the Warta River in the west-central part of the country, it was founded in the 9th century A.D. It became part of Poland in 1919 when the national boundaries were realigned following World War I. In 1956 labor riots against communist government policies there led to major reforms for the Polish people. Today, Poznan is an important industrial and educational center.

PR *See:* Public relations.

Prado *See:* Madrid.

Praetor, in ancient Rome (from 366 B.C.), a magistrate elected annually to administer justice, 2nd in rank to the consul. By 197 B.C. there were six praetors; four were responsible for provincial administration.

Praetorian Guard, elite household troops of the Roman emperors, consisting of 9 (later 10) cohorts of 1,000 foot soldiers with higher rank and pay than ordinary troops. Instituted by Augustus in 2 B.C., they assumed enough power to overthrow emperors. Constantine disbanded them in 312.

Pragmatic sanction, edict by a ruler pronouncing on an important matter of state, such as the succession. The most famous was issued by the Holy Roman Emperor Charles VI in 1713 (published 1718), declaring that his eldest daughter, Maria Theresa, would inherit the Austrian throne in the absence of a male heir. This resulted in the War of the Austrian Succession (1740-48).

Pragmatism, philosophical method whose criterion of truth is relative to events and not, as in traditional philosophy, absolute and independent of human experience. A theory is pragmatically true if it "works"—if it has an intended or predicted effect. All human undertakings are viewed as attempts to solve problems in the world of action; if theories are not trial solutions capable of being tested, they are pointless. The philosophy of pragmatism was developed in reaction to late 19th-century idealism, mainly by the U.S. philosophers C.S. Peirce, W. James, and John Dewey.
See also: Dewey, John; James, William; Peirce, Charles Sanders.

Prague, or Praha (pop. 1,214,200), capital and largest city of the Czech Republic, on the Vlatava River. One of Europe's great historic cities, it became prominent under Emperor Charles IV, who founded the university in central Europe (1348). The Hapsburgs ruled Prague for nearly 300 years, beginning in 1526, until Czechoslovakia's independence after World War I. Prague was invaded by the Nazis in 1939 and by Warsaw Pact countries in 1968. The city has great cultural, commercial, and industrial importance and is the center of the country's manufacturing industries.
See also: Czech Republic.

Prairie, rolling grassland that once covered much of interior North America. There are three types of prairie: tall-grass, midgrass (or mixed-grass), and shortgrass, which is found in the driest areas. Typical prairie animals are the coyotes, badgers, prairie dogs, and jackrabbits and the now largely vanished bison and wolf.

Prairie chicken, name for two species of grouse (genus *Tympanuchus*) that were once common in the eastern half of North America. Plowing of the prairies and cutting down of the woodlands have destroyed their homes. The males have airsacs on their throats for making booming calls. The airsacs are orange in the greater prairie chicken and violet in the lesser prairie chicken. The heath hen, which was a race of the greater prairie chicken, has been extinct since 1932.

Prairie dog, ground squirrel of the genus *Cynomys*. Social animals of the open plains of North America, they live in large colonies in connected burrows. They are short-tailed, marmot-like creatures, active by day, feeding, grooming, or sunbathing near their burrows. They frequently raise themselves on their hindlegs to watch for danger. A sharp whistle, given as warning, sends the colony dashing into the burrows.

Prairie Provinces, popular name for the Canadian provinces of Manitoba, Saskatchewan, and Alberta.

Prairie wolf *See:* Coyote.

Praseodymium, chemical element, symbol Pr; for physical constants see Periodic Table. Praseodymium was discovered by C.A. von Welsbach in 1885 after he separated didymia into earths (oxides) called praseodymia and neodymia. The element occurs in the minerals monazite and bastnasite, the two principal sources of the rare-earth elements. It is prepared by reducing the anhydrous chloride with calcium. Praseodymium is a silvery, soft, reactive metal, belonging to the series of elements known as the rare-earth metals. Ion-exchange and solvent extraction techniques have led to much easier isolation of the so-called rare-earth elements. Praseodymium and its compounds are used in carbon lighting applications, special glasses and enamels, and refractory materials.

Prawn *See:* Shrimp.

Praxiteles (active c.370-330 B.C.), greatest Greek sculptor of his time. Of his major works, which introduced a new delicacy, grace, and sinuosity of line, only the marble statue *Hermes with the Infant Dionysus* survives. There are Roman copies of his *Aphrodite of Cnidus* and *Apollo Sauroctonus*.

Prayer book, collection of commonly used prayers in Judeo-Christian religious services. They contain statements of doctrine, ordinances, and explanations of the sacraments, in addition to prayers. The Church of England developed its *Book of Common Prayer* in 1549 and other Christian faiths have devised similar concepts. Prayer books are also widely used in Jewish temple (synagogue) services and ceremonies.

Preble, Edward (1761-1807), U.S. naval officer. He commanded the first U.S. warship to go beyond the Cape of Good Hope (1799) and in 1804 led the unsuccessful assault on Tripoli.

Precambrian, whole of geological time from the formation of the planet Earth to the start of the Phanerozoic (the eon characterized by the appearance of abundant fossils in rock strata), thus lasting from about 4.55 billion to 570 million years ago. It is essentially equivalent to the Cryptozoic eon.

Precipitation, in meteorology, all water particles that fall from clouds to the ground, including rain and drizzle, snow, sleet, and hail. Precipitation is important in the hydrologic cycle (the circulation of water between the surface of the earth and the atmosphere).

Pre-Columbian art, art of what is now Latin America prior to Columbus' discovery of the Americas (1492). The two main cultural areas were the central Andes (southern Colombia, Ecuador, Peru, Bolivia, northwestern Argentina and northern Chile) and Meso-America (Mexico and Central America). In both areas artistic development took place after 3000 B.C. Monochrome-decorated pottery, female figurines, and elaborately designed textiles have been discovered in Ecuador and Peru dating from 3000-2500 B.C. The great Andean classical period noted for textiles, ceramics, gold and silver work, jewelry, and stone masonry took place in 1000 B.C.-A.D. 800, prior to the Inca kingdom. The great city buildings at Cuzco, Machu Picchu, and Tiahuanaco are striking achievements. The Meso-Americans excelled in the graphic and plastic arts. From about A.D. 1000 the illuminated codex writings of the Mayas, Mixtecs, and Aztecs recorded mythological stories. Their temples, as at Chichén Itzá, are decorated with elaborately carved stone sculptures and reliefs, with wall frescoes inside. The Olmecs made small jade carvings and colossal stone heads. In Colombia the Chibcha Indians were skilled in ceramics, textiles, and jewelry.

Predestination, in theology, doctrine that through God's decree the souls of certain persons (the elect) are destined to be saved. Premised on God's omniscience and omnipotence and buttressed by the doctrines of God's providence and grace, predestination was taught especially by St. Paul and was elaborated by St. Augustine in opposition to Pelagianism (which denied Original Sin and asserted that people are free to do good or evil). Calvinism taught additionally the predestination of the nonelect to damnation, denying individual free will and regarding saving grace as irresistible and wholly gratuitous. Jansenism was a similar Roman Catholic movement. Islam likewise teaches absolute predestination.
See also: Religion; Theology.

Pre-emption, right of individuals to purchase land or goods before others and the act of such purchases. During the 1800s more than 200 million acres (81 million hectares) of government-owned land in the United States passed into private hands through pre-emption. Squatters settled lands they didn't own and usually built homes there. The federal government passed laws allowing them to purchase the land cheaply before it was offered for sale to anyone else. The practice was abolished in 1891.

Pregnancy, time between conception and birth. In the human female this takes about 39 weeks, or 9 months. The first symptom of pregnancy is usually a missed menstrual period (though this in itself is not proof) followed perhaps by "morning sickness," which can continue for some weeks. Tenderness of the breasts and darkening of the nipples usually occur, and frequent urination is common. As the fetus develops, swelling of the abdomen can first of all be felt and then seen. Inside the womb the fetus develops rapidly, and is well formed by 3 1/2 months. After the 28th week, the child is capable of surviving outside the womb, but infant mortality is higher in premature babies than in those carried to full term.
See also: Reproduction.

Prehistoric animal, animal that became extinct before human beings began to produce written records. Our knowledge of these animals is therefore derived almost completely from fossils. Although scientists believe life on earth began over 3 billion years ago, few fossils have been found that are more than 600 million years old. The earliest are all invertebrates, or animals without skeletal backbones. These include ammonites, snails, clams, worms, and animals resembling jellyfish. The most common prehistoric invertebrate seems to have been the trilobite—a kind of flat shellfish with jointed legs. The first fishes appeared about 480 million years ago. They had no jaws and were covered with heavy, bony armor. Fishes as we know them did not appear until about 130 million years later. Some of these had fleshy fins that probably evolved into legs. The first amphibians appeared about 400 million years ago.

An extensive fossil record indicates that the first land vertebrates—the reptiles—evolved about 290 million years ago. They were bigger and more powerful than the amphibians, and were able to hatch their eggs on land. Reptiles dominated the earth for about 100 million years. Dinosaurs are perhaps the best known of the prehistoric animals. Although some grew to enormous size and were very powerful, they all became extinct, although the reason why remains a subject of controversy. Among the dinosaurs was the carnivorous Tyrannosaurus rex, the 85-ton Brachiosaurus, the 87-foot-long Diplodocus, the horned Triceratops, and the armored vegetarian Stegosaurus. Flying reptiles began to appear during the Jurassic period. One of these—the Archaeopteryx—is believed to be the earliest ancestor of modern birds.

Placental mammals, or animals who carry their young within their bodies, have been on earth for about 65 million years. Later, when mammals came to dominate the land, larger variants of modern-day mammals existed. Megatherium was a 20-foot-long mammoth that resembled a large, hairy elephant. Some of these prehistoric mammoths have been found deep-frozen in the icy soil of Siberia.

Prehistoric people, general term for a variety of species of human ancestors. Humans and apes, who share common ancestors, began to diverge in their evolutionary development about 14 million years ago. The first certain ancestor of modern humans is *Australopithecus afarensis*, discovered in 1978, a species that flourished in Ethiopia and Tanzania 3.8-2.5 million years ago. Adult individuals walked upright and had a brain size of about 400 cc. They inhabited grasslands and ate a wide variety of food, including some meat. There were other species within the genus *Australopithecus*, but they are believed to have left no descendants. *Homo habilus*, the earliest true human being, dates back about 2 million years. They used primitive tools, hunted in groups, and had a brain capacity of 500 to 750 cc. *Homo erectus*, whose earliest remains date back about 1.5 million years, had a brain size of 800 cc, which increased to 1,300 cc over the next million years. *Homo erectus* lived originally in Africa and used fire and the ax. This species evolved into an early form of *Homo sapiens* some 400,000 years ago. These ancestors of ours cooked meat, wore clothes, made wooden tools, and built huts. It is unknown whether the Neanderthal, who flourished about 75,000 to 35,000 years ago, was within the human line of descent or represented a competitor exterminated by the expansion of modern humans. There is much evidence that *Homo sapiens sapiens*, modern humans, first appeared about 40,000 years ago. Cro-Magnon, an example of this modern species, used a variety of tools, domesticated animals and plants, and created cave paintings.

Prejudice, opinions and attitudes formed by individuals or groups about other individuals or groups, usually without ample sustaining evidence. Most forms of prejudice are unfavorable or even hostile, based on fears or preconceived notions against a religious, ethnic, or national group. Extreme forms have resulted in persecution or acts of violence by one group of people against another. Prejudice can be overcome or eliminated through openmindedness, understanding, education, and interaction with groups or individuals targeted for discrimination.

Premature birth, birth of a baby before the 40th week of pregnancy. A birth before the 28th week of pregnancy, when the fetus is not viable, is a miscarriage. *See also:* Birth.

Prendergast, Maurice Brazil (1859-1924), U.S. painter influenced by postimpressionism, a member of the ashcan school founded by 8 U.S. painters in 1908. His works include *Umbrellas in the Rain* (1899) and *Central Park* (1901).
See also: Ashcan School.

Presbyterian Church (U.S.A.), largest Presbyterian denomination in the United States, formed in 1983 when the Presbyterian Church in the United States and the United Presbyterian Church in the U.S.A. were united. Local congregations are organized into regional groups called presbyteries, which, in turn, are organized into larger synods.

Presbyterianism, form of Christian church government based on bodies of clergy and lay presbyters. Midway between episcopacy and congregational-ism, it was espoused at the time of the Reformation by the reformed churches, which viewed it as a rediscovery of the apostolic practice of church govern-ment. There is a hierarchy of church courts. The lowest is the kirk-session, composed of the minister and elders elected by the local congregation. This is followed by the presbytery, including representative ministers and elders from a given area, the synod, composed of members chosen from several presbyteries, and the general assembly, the supreme body, consisting of ministers and elders from all the presbyteries. (Various names are used for these courts.) Presbyterian doctrine is biblical Calvinism.

Prescott, William (1726-95), American Revolutionary colonel. He com-manded the militia in the Battle of Bunker Hill (1775) and took part in the battles of Long Island (1776) and Saratoga (1777).
See also: Bunker Hill, Battle of.

Prescott, William Hickling (1796-1859), U.S. historian. Despite the handi-cap of near blindness, he became an authority on Spain and the Spanish conquest of America. His *History of the Reign of Ferdinand and Isabella the Catholic* (1837), *History of the Conquest of Mexico* (1843), and *History of the Conquest of Peru* (1847) became classics, admired for their narrative skill as well as their historical rigor.

Presidential libraries, collections of documents, personal papers, and other memorabilia of former U.S. presidents. There are nine such libraries in the United States preserving the historical records of former presidents Ruther-ford B. Hayes, Herbert Hoover, Franklin D. Roosevelt, Harry Truman, Dwight Eisenhower, John F. Kennedy, Lyndon B. Johnson, Gerald Ford, and Jimmy Carter. Scholars and historians use these libraries and their adjoining museums to do research.

Presidential Medal of Freedom *See:* Decorations, medals, and orders.

Presidential succession, system of selecting a new U.S. president when the incumbent dies in office, resigns, is removed from office, or is unable to discharge his duties. Under Article II of the Constitution, the vice president is next in line for the presidency and the 20th and 25th Amendments further ensure that the succession will continue through a vice president or vice president-elect. The Presidential Succession Act of 1886, amended in 1947, specifies that the Speaker of the House, the president pro tempore of the Senate, and the 14 members of the president's Cabinet follow the vice president in line to succeed the president.

President of the United States, elected official, head of the executive branch of the U.S. government. The office of president derives its authority from the U.S. Constitution. In order to avoid concentration and abuse of political power, the Constitution established a system of checks and balances whereby power in the U.S. government is divided among the Congress, an independent judiciary, and the president. Defined by the Constitution in less detail than the other two branches, the presidency was given its fundamental form and character by George Washington, but its role and the range of its powers have changed with the nation and with the men who have held the office. To date, no woman has yet been elected to the presidency.

The president's basic roles and duties include being the country's chief executive in charge of enforcing federal law, commander in chief of the armed forces responsible for the country's defense, the formulator of foreign policy, lawmaker, head of a political party, a popularly elected leader, and head of state.

In most cases, presidents have been nominated by one of the major political parties and have won the presidency in contested elections. A majority of popular votes generally translates into a majority of votes in the electoral college. The electoral college consists of 538 delegates, selected by state and according to the number of representatives and senators in that state. To win the presidency, the successful candidate must have 270 electoral votes. The electoral vote is the last formal step in the process of a president's election and can almost always be determined by the outcome of the popular vote. A person can also become president by succeeding to the presidency from the vice presidency. And, in the event no candidate in an election receives a majority of electoral votes, the president is elected by a vote of the House of Representatives. To be eligible for president, one must be a natural-born citizen, at least 35 years of age, and living in the United States 14 years. In the event the office is vacant between elections, succession to the presidency is to the vice president, followed by the Speaker of the House, the president *pro tempore* of the Senate, then to the various secretaries of the president's cabinet beginning with the secretary of state. Presidents serve for a term of 4 years and, since the 22nd Amendment in 1961, no one can serve more than two terms. Presidents may also be removed from office. The process requires first that a president be impeached, that is, charged with some offense or offenses. The president is then tried by the Senate, the chief justice of the Supreme Court presides, and the outcome is determined by vote. A two-thirds majority is required for conviction.

The office of the presidency is supported by a vast bureaucracy consisting of 14 departments, more than 100 separate agencies, and more than 5 million civilian and military employees. The executive departments are headed by secretaries, who are members of the president's cabinet. They include the Secretaries of State, the Treasury and Defense, Justice (headed by the Attorney General), the Interior, Agriculture, Commerce, Labor, Health and

Human Services, Housing and Urban Development, Transportation, Energy, Education, and Veterans' Affairs. Among the more important agencies in the executive branch are the Council of Economic Advisers, the National Security Council, the Office of Management and the Budget, the Federal Reserve System, and the Federal Communications Commission. The president also has the power to appoint judges to the federal bench, including the Supreme Court, though these appointments must be approved by the Senate.

Up to the Civil War, strong personalities defined and strengthened the office of president. Thomas Jefferson, Andrew Jackson, and Abraham Lincoln greatly enhanced the power of the office. In the decades between the end of the Civil War (1865) and the Spanish American War (1898), Congress became the dominant branch of government. But the presidency of Theodore Roosevelt (1901-9) marked the beginning of the rise of America as a major military power and player on the international political scene. With this change, a greater measure of power and prestige returned to the presidency. The trend increased under Woodrow Wilson (1914-18), who led the country through its involvement in World War I and culminated in the presidency of Franklin D. Roosevelt (1933-45), the most powerful president of modern times. The end of World War II found the United States at the pinnacle of international power and prestige and the presidency, though a troubled office, has retained its place as the focus of power and decision making within the government. But there have been setbacks and there continues to be debate over the limits of presidential power. At the heart of the debates have been the legacies of Roosevelt's presidency, Truman's decision to use the atomic bomb, the debacle of the Korean War and defeat in the Vietnam War, the Watergate scandal, and the Iran-contra scandal.

Presley, Elvis (1935-77), U.S. singer, first major rock star, and present-day cult hero. From 1956 to the mid-1960s, Presley's versions of rhythm-and-blues songs ("Hound Dog") and ballads ("Love Me Tender") were instant hits, as were his 33 films. His Memphis, Tenn., home, Graceland, became a shrine for his many fans.

Pre-Socratic philosophy, general term applied to the thought of the early Greek philosophers (c.600-400 B.C.) who lived before Socrates. Their writings survive mostly in obscure fragments, but their fame and importance lie in their being the first to attempt rational explanations of the universe. Some of the major pre-Socratics were Anaximander, Anaxagoras, Heraclitus, Parmenides, and Pythagoras.
See also: Philosophy.

Press *See:* Journalism; Newspaper; Printing.

Pressburg *See:* Bratislava.

Pressure, force acting on a surface per unit of area. All liquids and gasses exert pressure on any body immersed in them and on the walls of their containers, if any. According to the kinetic theory of matter, the pressure in a closed container of gas arises from the bombardment of the container walls by gas molecules: it is proportional to the temperature and inversely proportional to the volume of the gas.
See also: Physics.

Prester John, legendary Christian priest-king. A purported letter from "Presbyter John," probably of Western authorship, reached the papal court in 1165. It described a great Christian utopia in the "three Indies," identified in later legend as Ethiopia.

Pretoria (pop. 822,900), administrative capital of South Africa. It is also the capital of the province Pretoria-Witwatersrand-Vereeniging. Founded by the Boers in 1855, the city was named for Andries Pretorius, who defeated the Zulus in 1838. It became the administrative capital of the Union of South Africa when it was formed in 1910 and is a major manufacturing and cultural center.
See also: South Africa.

Pretorius, Andries Wilhelmus Jacobus (1799-1853), commandant of the Boers and Great Trek leader. His defeat of the Zulus at Blood River (1838) led to the founding of the Republic of Natal. He led the 1848 trek into the Transvaal.

Pretzel, popular snack biscuit. Pretzels are made from twisted dough that is usually glazed, salted, and baked until hardened, but some varieties are large and soft. They are believed to have originated in southern Europe where monks gave them to children as a reward for learning their prayers, and the name comes from a Latin word meaning "small reward." Its popularity spread to the United States in the 1860s and is a favorite snack food today.

Prévert, Jacques (1900-77), French writer. His popular poems, sometimes satirical, sometimes melancholy, include *Paroles* (1946). Among his screenplays is that for Marcel Carné's *Les Enfants du Paradis* (1944).

Previn, André (1929-   ), German-born U.S. musician. Originally an adapter of stage musicals for the screen, he won Academy Awards for his arrangements in the films *Kiss Me Kate* (1953) and *Gigi* (1958). As a jazz pianist he made several successful recordings and is also a classical composer and pianist. Principally a symphony conductor since 1960, he has led seasons of the Houston Symphony, the London Symphony, and the Pittsburgh Symphony, recording widely as well.

Prévost d'Exiles, Antoine François, or Abbé Prévost (1697-1763), French writer, priest, and adventurer. *Manon Lescaut* (1731), a love story, is the masterpiece among his novels. It is the basis of operas by Jules Massenet and Giacomo Puccini.

Pribilof Islands, group of 4 small islands of volcanic origin in the Bering Sea, about 300 mi (483 km) southwest of Alaska. St. Paul and St. George are the largest. Every spring some 80% of the world's fur seals visit the islands to breed. Since 1911 the seal herds have been protected, and the United States, which acquired the islands in 1867, regulates the harvesting of seals.

Price, Leontyne (1927-   ), U.S. soprano. Her first success was as Bess in Gershwin's *Porgy and Bess* (1952-54). She made debuts in televised operas (1955), at the San Francisco Opera (1957), and at the New York Metropolitan

Opera (1961), winning international fame for her performances in works by Verdi and Puccini. She retired from opera in 1985 but continues as a recitalist. *See also:* Opera.

Prickly ash, shrub or tree (*Zanthoxylum americanum*) growing in damp soils. The bark and fruit are used for medicinal purposes in the treatment of rheumatism and such stomach problems as flatulence and poor digestion.

Prickly heat, or heat rash, uncomfortable itching sensation caused by excessive sweating in hot weather.

Prickly pear, any of a genus (*Opuntia*) of branching cactus with flat stems and yellow flowers. It is found in most of the southern United States and grows farther north (into New England) than other cacti. Prickly pears are grown in many places as hedges. Introduced to Australia, they spread so rapidly as to become a pest, but were brought under control by introducing a moth whose caterpillars burrowed into the stems.

Priest, in most religions, a cultic officer who communicates the sacred to the followers; a spiritual leader expert in ritual and generally the offerer of sacraments.

Priestley, J(ohn) B(oynton) (1894-1984), English writer and critic. Besides many plays, he wrote popular novels such as *The Good Companions* (1929) and *Angel Pavement* (1930), and criticism, of which his major work is *Literature and Western Man* (1960).

Priestley, Joseph (1733-1804), British theologian and chemist. Encouraged and supported by Benjamin Franklin, he wrote *The History and Present State of Electricity* (1767). His most important discovery was oxygen (1774; named later by Lavoisier), whose properties he investigated. He later discovered many other gases—ammonia, carbon monoxide, hydrogen sulfide—and found that green plants require sunlight and give off oxygen. His association in the 1780s with the Lunar Society brought him into contact with scientists such as James Watt and Erasmus Darwin. Priestley's theological writings and activity led some English Presbyterians into Unitarianism, and he is regarded as a principal architect of the Unitarian church. He was also an opponent of the slave trade and a supporter of the French Revolution. When his house and laboratory were destroyed by people enraged by these ideas, he emigrated to the United States (1794).
See also: Oxygen; Unitarianism.

Primary color *See:* Color.

Primary election, in the United States, an election in which supporters of a political party elect candidates to run in a subsequent general election. Primary elections are used throughout the United States to select candidates for Congress, state offices, and local government posts. In some states the candidates are proposed by petition; in others they simply file for the office. Most states operate "closed" primaries in which only registered party members may vote. Presidential primaries are a prelude to a party's national convention. Although some states choose delegates to the national convention by the caucus system, most have adopted the primary in one form or another. Voters indicate their preference either directly or by voting for delegates who are pledged to support a particular presidential candidate.

Primate, member of an order of mammals including humans, anthropoid apes, monkeys, tarsiers, pottos, galagos, and lemurs. Compared with most mammal groups, primates are anatomically less specialized; the brain, however, is larger and more developed.

Prime meridian, meridian that indicates zero degree longitude. Meridians are imaginary lines drawn on the earth's surface from the North to the South Pole. The prime meridian passes through Greenwich, England. All other longitudes are identified in degrees by their distance from the prime meridian.
See also: Longitude.

Prime minister, or premier, head of the government in a parliamentary system. The prime minister appoints and directs his or her own cabinet, which is the source of all major legislation, and also has the power to make and dismiss ministers and to call an election before the full term of a government. The office developed in 18th-century England under Robert Walpole. Most parliamentary democracies distinguish between the head of state (a monarch or president) and the prime minister, who is head of the government.

Prime minister of Canada, highest-ranking elected official of Canada and leader of the government. The prime minister is traditionally the leader of the majority party in the Canadian House of Commons and is responsible for directing the affairs of the government and the nation's foreign and domestic policies. A prime minister must have the support of a majority of the House to remain in office and if the House passes a vote of no confidence, he or she must resign or call a new election. Since independence in 1867, 18 men have held the office.

Primo de Rivera, Miguel (1870-1930), Spanish general and politician. Supported by King Alfonso XIII, he overthrew the government in 1923 and became dictator. Popular discontent, economic failure, and loss of army support forced him to resign in 1930. His son, **José Antonio Primo de Rivera**, founded the Falanga (a Fascist political party) and was executed by Loyalists (republicans) in 1936.

Primogeniture, law by which the eldest son inherits all the lands of a family. It originated in medieval Europe as a reward for the son who gave military service to his king. Never widely established in the United States, primogeniture is still customary in England.

Primrose, perennial plant (*Primula officinalis*) growing in dry meadows, lightly wooded areas, and along forest edges; the flowers, herb, and rootstock are used for medicinal purposes.

Primrose, William (1904-82), Scottish violist, U.S. resident from 1937. He cofounded the Festival Quartet in 1956. Several composers, including Béla Bartók, wrote works especially for him.

Prince Albert (pop. 33,700), city in central Saskatchewan. Situated on the North Saskatchewan River, it was founded in 1866 and named for Queen Victoria's prince consort. It is an important lumbering and manufacturing center and due to its location near the entrance to Prince Albert National Park, it is a major tourist center as well.
See also: Saskatchewan.

Prince consort, husband of a reigning queen. A prince consort is not given the title of king in European countries where the sovereign's daughter may inherit the throne and he has no place in the royal succession under ordinary circumstance. These rules apply in the monarchies of Denmark, the Netherlands, and the United Kingdom.

Prince Edward Island, one of Canada's maritime provinces, and the smallest of all Canada's provinces both in area and population.
Land and climate. Prince Edward Island is about 10 mi/16 km from the mainland, separated from it by the Northumberland Strait. The maximum length is about 145 mi/233 km and its greatest width about 55 mi/89 km. The shoreline is deeply serrated with tidal inlets. The surface of the island is gently rolling, with some small hills in the center and southeast. Because of its agricultural resources, it is sometimes called the "Garden of the Gulf" and "The Million Acre Farm." The island's climate is variable but generally milder than that of the mainland. The capital is Charlottetown.
People. Some 80% of the population are descendants of British and Scots settlers, about 15% are descendants of Acadian French settlers, and the balance are Micmac Indians living on reservations.
Economy. Prince Edward Island's economy is based upon farming, fishing, tourism, and light industry. Tobacco, strawberry, and blueberry crops are exported. Potatoes are an important crop and about half of the crop is processed, mainly into frozen French fries. Processing of lumber is important to the island as is lobster fishing. There is also manufacturing of fisheries' products.
History. Prince Edward Island was originally inhabited by nomadic Micmacs, Native Americans of the Algonquian tribe. Jacques Cartier landed in 1534, becoming the first European to explore the island for France, and named it Île Saint-Jean. Some 2,000 Acadians, French settlers expelled from Nova Scotia by the British, settled on the island between 1749 and 1755. With the Treaty of Paris in 1763, the island became British, most of the French settlers were expelled, and its name was changed to St. John's Island. Originally annexed by the British to Nova Scotia, St. John's Island became a separate colony in 1709. In 1799, the British changed the name of the island to Prince Edward Island in honor of the Duke of Kent. In 1851, the island won control of its local affairs. After some hesitation, Prince Edward Island decided to join the Dominion of Canada and on July 1, 1873, became the seventh province.
See also: Canada.

Prince George (pop. 67,600), city of central British Columbia. Located at the junction of the Fraser and Nechako rivers, the city was founded in 1807 by Simon Fraser as a fur-trading post named Fort George. It is the site of several major pulp mills and is a major manufacturing and energy center for the province.
See also: British Columbia.

Prince Rupert (pop. 15,800), port on the west coast of British Columbia. Lying on an island at the mouth of the Skeena River, Prince Rupert developed in the early 1900s as a western rail terminus for the Grand Trunk Railway. It is a major fishing, lumbering, and pulp processing center, and its ice-free harbor makes it a key Canadian west coast port.
See also: British Columbia.

Princeton (pop. 25,718), borough and township in central New Jersey, site of Princeton University, Princeton Theological Seminary, and the Institute for Advanced Study. The region was settled by Quakers in 1696. In 1777 it was the scene of a Revolutionary War battle in which George Washington defeated British forces. The Continental Congress met in Princeton for 5 months in 1783.
See also: New Jersey.

Princeton University, private university in Princeton, N.J. Chartered as the College of New Jersey in 1746, it was renamed in 1896, when it became a university. A leading U.S. educational institution, it includes world-famous graduate schools of public and international affairs, architecture, and scientific research. It has admitted women since 1969.

Príncipe Island *See:* São Tomé and Príncipe.

Printing, reproduction of words and pictures in ink on paper or other suitable media. Despite the advent of information retrieval systems, the storage and dissemination of knowledge are still based primarily on the printed word. Modern printing began with the work of Johann Gutenberg, who invented movable type and type metal in the 15th century. Individual characters could be used several times. The process was little changed for 400 years, until the invention of machines that could cast type as it was required.
Letterpress and lithography are today the two most used printing techniques. Letterpress uses raised type that is a mirror image of the printed impression. The type is inked and the paper pressed to it. Lithography depends on the mutual repulsion of water and oil or grease. In fine art a design is drawn with a grease crayon on the surface of a flat, porous stone, which is then wetted. Water is repelled by the greasy areas; but ink is repelled by the damp and adheres to the greasy areas. Modern mechanized processes use the same principle. Commonest is photo-offset, where the copy to be printed is photographed and the image transferred to a plate such that the part to be printed is oleophilic (oil-loving), the rest hydrophilic (water-loving). Gravure is another major printing technique. The plate is covered with a pattern of recessed cells in which the ink is held, greater depth of cell increasing printing intensity. Little-used for books, it is used extensively in packaging.

Prion, microscopic particle that produces a fatal disease in goats and sheep. Prions are linked to scrapie, a disorder that attacks and destroys the central nervous systems of the grazing animals, but scientists do not fully understand how the disease is caused. It is believed that prions contain an excess of protein that disrupts normal cell activity in infected animals and might possibly affect humans as well. Stanley Prusiner, who discovered prions, received the Nobel Medicine prize in 1997.

Prism, in geometry, a solid figure having 2 equal polygonal faces (the bases) lying in parallel planes and several others (the lateral faces) that are parallelograms. Prismatic pieces of transparent materials are much used in optical instruments. In spectroscopes and devices for producing monochromatic lights, prisms are used to produce dispersion effects, just as Newton first used a triangular prism to reveal that sunlight could be split up into a spectrum of colors. In binoculars and single-lens reflex cameras, inflecting prisms (employing total internal reflection) are used in preference to ordinary mirrors. The Nicol prism is used to produce polarized light.

Prison, institution for confining people convicted of breaking a law. There are three types of prisons in the United States: jails and lockups, run by city and county governments mainly for those awaiting trial; state prisons, operated by the individual states containing the majority of convicted criminals, and federal prisons, which house society's most violent offenders and those who break federal laws. By the early 20th century imprisonment had replaced corporal punishment, capital punishment, and exile as the chief method of dealing with criminals. The purpose of prisons is threefold: to punish the wrongdoer; to protect society; and to act as a deterrent. Overpopulation is a serious problem in modern prisons, leading to the 1981 Supreme Court ruling that two prisoners may be kept in a cell built for one if prison conditions on the whole are humane. At the end of 1989 U.S. federal and state prisons held about 710,000 inmates; nearly 0.3% of the U.S. population.

Prisoners of war, combatant who has been captured by or has surrendered to an enemy state. The Hague Convention of 1907 and the Geneva Conventions of 1919 and 1949 established rules in international law for the protection of such prisoners, notably that they should not be maltreated nor required to give any information other than their name, rank, and serial number, and that they should be repatriated upon the cessation of hostilities.
See also: Geneva Conventions.

Pritchett, V(ictor) S(awdon) (1900-97), English novelist, short-story writer, and literary critic. Many of his works are based on his travels in Spain. They include *Marching Spain* (nonfiction, 1928), *The Spanish Temper* (nonfiction, 1954), and *Clare Drummer* (novel, 1929). *A Cab at the Door* (1968), and *Midnight Oil* (1971) are autobiographical.

Privacy, Right of, customary right of a citizen to have a private life free of "undue" interference or publicity. The concept represents a balance of interests between the individual and the state. In general, privacy may be interfered with only in limited, prescribed ways.

Privateer, armed vessel that was privately owned but commissioned by a government to prey upon enemy ships in wartime. Privateers thus often supplemented a nation's navy. The practice of privateering was outlawed (1856) by the Declaration of Paris, but the United States refused to sign it, and privateers operated during the U.S. Civil War. The practice has been abandoned by all nations.

Privet, shrub whose dense growth makes it popular for hedges. California privet comes from Japan and is suitable for use in colder climates, as it retains its leaves in freezing conditions.

Privy Council, honorary group of appointed advisers to the reigning sovereign of Great Britain. Instituted by William the Conqueror (William I) in the late 11th century, the privy council once had the important function of advising the king on matters of national importance. As parliament and the prime minister replaced the monarchy in the nation's governing structure, the privy council declined in importance. Today it serves a largely ceremonial function, overseeing matters of commerce, scientific research, and the arts.

Probability, branch of mathematics that deals with the likelihood that an event will occur. Most commonly, the number of possible outcomes is counted, and the probability of any particular outcome is expressed as a fraction between 0 and 1. For instance, in rolling 2 dice there are 36 possible outcomes. Only one of these is that a 12 will turn up (a 6 on each die). The chance of rolling a 12 is therefore 1/36. On the other hand, there are 6 possible ways of rolling a 7: 1-6, 6-1, 5-2, 2-5, 3-4, 4-3. The chance of rolling a 7 is therefore 1/6. As more complicated theories and problems arise, more sophisticated techniques arise, such as permutations and combinations. Probability theory has contributed vital understanding in many fields of physics, including statistical mechanics. Its importance in science has risen dramatically in recent decades. Statistics, a related field, is the application of probability theory to data collected from research samples.
See also: Mathematics.

Probate, legal process of proving that a will is valid. Before a will can take effect, it must be shown that it is genuine, that it was the deceased's last will, that he or she signed it voluntarily and was of sound mind. Probate requires all possible heirs of the testator's property to be notified before a special hearing is held in a probate court, where objections can be lodged.
See also: Will.

Probation, alternative to prison, whereby convicted offenders are placed under the supervision of a probation officer, on condition that they maintain good behavior. The aim is to encourage reform, particularly for the young, when a spell in prison might simply reinforce criminal tendencies.

Proboscis monkey, large monkey (*Nasalis larvatus*) native to Borneo. They are herbivores (plant eaters), feeding on leaves that they shred easily with well-developed back teeth. Males may weigh up to 52 lb (24 kg) and females about half that. They stand about 21-30 in (53-76 cm) tall and live in trees near rivers, which they swim easily.

Procaine, or novocaine, pain-killing drug used as an anesthetic. Developed by German chemist Alfred Einhorn in 1905, procaine is injected into a designated area of the body to deaden nerve sensitivity prior to a surgical procedure being performed. It has been largely replaced by more effective nerve blocks in recent years but it remains popular with dentists, who inject it into the gums of patients whose teeth they are preparing to work on.
See also: Anesthesia.

Proclamation of 1763, statement issued by the British government at the end of the French and Indian Wars, establishing territorial rights for North American Native Americans. It aimed both to appease the Native Americans and to prevent land disputes, but it angered (and was in many respects disregarded by) the colonists.
See also: French and Indian Wars.

Profit, amount of money a company or individual engaged in business makes after all costs have been subtracted. Profit is the chief motivation for the establishment of all businesses in a free enterprise economic system and the goal of all employers and individuals seeking monetary gain. Profits can be increased by keeping production costs, including labor, as low as possible and employers are constantly seeking means of generating greater profits than others engaged in competing businesses and industries.

Profit sharing, incentive developed by businesses and employers to give workers a share of the extra money a company makes. It was devised to instill workers with greater company loyalty and motivate them toward higher productivity. Profit sharing provides workers with a source of income above their regular wages and may be disbursed in the form of direct cash payments, shares of company stock, or deferred payments made in lieu of pension plans.

Progeria, or Hutchinson-Gilford syndrome, rare disease that causes premature aging in children and early death. Sir Jonathan Hutchinson researched the disease in 1886 and there is no cure or treatment for it. Symptoms begin appearing by the second year of life; they include hair loss, wrinkled skin, stunted growth, and other signs of aging normally associated with older persons. Half of all progeria deaths occur by age 13 and the oldest known victim lived only to 27.

Progesterone, female sex hormone that causes changes in the womb lining necessary for the implantation of a fertilized egg.
See also: Hormone; Reproduction.

Programmed learning, teaching method whereby matter to be learned is arranged in a coherent sequence of small, clear steps (programmed), enabling the student to instruct, test, and, if necessary, correct him or herself at each step. The learning program is usually embodied in a book or booklet or adapted for use in conjunction with a teaching machine. The linear program, based on the work of psychologist B.F. Skinner, obliges the student to compare his or her own response at each step with the correct response. The intrinsic (or branching) program offers a limited choice of responses at each step. The correct response is immediately reinforced; an incorrect response obliges the student to follow a corrective subprogram leading back to the point at which the error occurred.

Progression, in mathematics, a sequence of numbers (terms) that have a direct relationship to one another. The most common types are arithmetic, which involves addition; geometric, which involves multiplication; and harmonic, which involves fractions. Each successive term in a progression is added by or multiplied by the same number all the way through the sequence. An arithmetic progression that begins with 2, 4, and 6 will continue with 8,

10, and all successive numbers that are 2 larger than the preceding number. The same principle applies to all other types of progressions.
See also: Mathematics.

Progressive Conservative Party, one of Canada's two major political parties. It is generally more conservative on most issues than Canada's Liberal party. Called the Conservative Party from its formation in 1854, it was the nation's dominant political party for nearly a century. After changing its name in 1942, the party has won only two national elections and has governed Canada only twice, in 1957-63 under John G. Diefenbaker and for six months in 1979 under Joe Clark. His Progressive Conservative-Social Credit coalition was forced to resign after losing a vote of confidence in the House of Commons on Clark's austerity budget.

Progressive education, reform movement that grew from the idea that schooling should cater to the emotional as well as the intellectual development of the child and that the basis of learning should be the child's natural and individual curiosity, rather than an enforced discipline. In the United States the movement, led by John Dewey, was most active from 1890-1950.
See also: Education.

Progressive movement, campaign for political, economic, and social reform in the United States, which began in the depression of the 1890s and ended in 1917 with U.S. involvement in World War I.
See also: Addams, Jane; Roosevelt, Theodore.

Progressive Party, name of three 20th century U.S. political organizations. Each was largely characterized by programs of social and economic reform. The Progressive Party of 1912 (better known as the Bull Moose Party) chose ex-President Theodore Roosevelt as its nominee. It left the Republican Party after the nomination of William Taft, but they were reunited during the campaign of 1916.
The Progressive Party of 1924 was formed by farm and labor leaders dissatisfied with the conservatism of the Republican administration. Its position, like that of the Bull Moose Party, was that there should be governmental control of trusts, and it upheld the right of government intervention in private wealth. Its presidential nominee was Robert La Follette, who received almost five million votes. The Progressive Party of 1948 nominated former Democratic vice president Henry A. Wallace for the presidency. The party sought better relations with the USSR and an end to the Cold War. It had support from many left-wing groups and was labeled by some a Communist-front organization. It polled little more than one million votes out of 48 million.

Prohibition, restriction or prevention of the manufacture and sale of alcoholic drinks. It refers in particular to the period from 1919 to 1933, when (by means of the 18th Amendment to the Constitution) there was a federal prohibition law in the United States. In spite of the intensive economic and group pressures that had brought it about, it soon became apparent that the law was too unpopular and too expensive to enforce. A notorious era of gangsterism followed, with a vast illegal liquor business (the activities involved were known as bootlegging) under the control of men such as Al

Capone. Prohibition was repealed (1933) by the 21st Amendment. A few U.S. states maintained local prohibition laws as late as 1966.
See also: Capone, Al; Volstead Act.

Prohibition Party, minor U.S. political party. It was founded in 1869 to prohibit the manufacture and consumption of alcohol and has fielded candidates for president and vice president in every national election since 1872. Its greatest showing was in 1892 when Gen. John Bidwell received 271,000 votes. Pressure from the party and other anti-alcohol crusaders led to the imposition of nationwide prohibition (1919-33) through passage of the 18th Amendment.

Projector, machine that passes light through film to show pictures on a screen. Lenses magnify the images on the film, showing them larger than they appear on the film itself. Projectors consist of several types—slide projectors that show still photos, movie projectors that show continuously moving film, and overhead projectors such as those used in planetariums that show images in all directions above the viewers.

Prokhorov, Aleksandr Mikhailovich (1916-), Soviet physicist awarded, with N.G. Basov and C.H. Townes, the 1964 Nobel Prize for physics for work with Basov leading to development of the maser.
See also: Maser.

Prokofiev, Sergei Sergeyevich (1891-1953), Russian composer who created a fierce, dynamic, unemotive style that later became somewhat softer and more eclectic. His works include seven symphonies, the operas *The Love for Three Oranges* (1921) and *War and Peace* (1943); *Peter and the Wolf* (1936), for narrator and orchestra; *Romeo and Juliet* (1936), a ballet; concertos for piano, violin, and cello; film scores; and chamber music.

Proletariat, name given to industrial employees as a social and economic class. In Marxist theory, the proletariat is exploited by and must inevitably overthrow the bourgeois class, made up of employers and property owners.
See also: Marxism.

Prometheus, in Greek mythology, one of the Titans and a brother of Atlas. He was sometimes said to have created humankind out of earth and water and to have stolen fire from the gods for the benefit of mankind. Zeus punished Prometheus by having him bound to a rock, whereupon his liver was devoured by an eagle.
See also: Mythology.

Promethium, chemical element, symbol Pm; for physical constants see Periodic Table. Branner, in 1902, predicted the existence of an element between neodymium and samarium. This element, promethium, was discovered by J.A. Marinsky, Lawrence E. Glendenin, and Charles D. Coryell in 1945 by fission of uranium and neutron bombardment of neodymium with neutrons. This was the first chemical identification by use of ion-exchange chromatography. Promethium is not found in the earth's crust but is obtained from nuclear reactors as a fission byproduct. Promethium-145, the most stable isotope, has a half-life longer than 17.7 years. Promethium, a metallic element, has been prepared by the reduction of the fluoride with lithium metal. It is a member of the rare-earth series of metals. Promethium isotopes are used in thickness gauges, self-luminous compounds, nuclear-powered batteries, portable X-ray sources, and auxiliary power sources.

Pronghorn, resembling an antelope (*Antilocapra americana*) the only horned animal that sheds its horn sheath and the only one with branched horns as distinct from antlers. They live in groups in arid grasslands and semi-desert of western North America, feeding on weeds and browse plants. Conservation efforts have restored numbers from an estimated 30,000 in 1924 to a present 400,000.

Proofreading, reading and correcting of printed matter prior to publication. It is done by skilled proofreaders using universally understood marks and symbols on the copy itself to indicate what corrections need to be made on the final draft. Newspapers, magazines, and printing shops employ proofreaders to check over all copy before it is published, in an effort to eliminate or minimize errors that might appear in print. Book publishing companies also use proofreaders, who mark up authors' original manuscripts as well as typeset copy (galley proofs) before they appear in book form.

Propaganda, selected information, whether true or false, designed to persuade people to adopt a particular belief, attitude, or course of action. During the 20th century all the major political ideologies have employed propaganda and made use of modern media to reach a mass audience. It plays an important role in modern warfare, and during World War II separate offices and ministries were established to promote morale and subvert the enemy. The Nazi Ministry of Propaganda, headed by Joseph Goebbels, was one of the most active. In the business world, professional propagandists—communicators in public relations and advertising—are increasingly in demand.

Propane *See:* Butane and propane.

Propeller, mechanical device designed to impart forward motion, usually to a ship or airplane, operating on the screw principle. It generally consists of two or more inclined blades radiating from a hub, and the amount of thrust it produces is proportional to the product of the mass and the fluid it acts on and the rate at which it accelerates the fluid. The inclination, or pitch, of the propeller blades determines the theoretical distance moved forward with each revolution. A variable-pitch propeller can be adjusted while in motion, to maximize its efficiency under different operating conditions; it may also be possible to reverse the propeller's pitch, or to feather it—i.e., minimize its resistance when not rotating. John Fitch developed the first marine screw propeller in 1796; John Ericsson perfected the first bladed propeller in 1837.

Propertius, Sextus (50?-16 B.C.), Roman elegiac poet, whose poems center on his love affair with his mistress Cynthia. Though often obscure, he is vivid and imaginative.

Property, social concept and legal term indicating the ownership of, or the right to enjoy, something of value; it may also be an interest in something owned by another. Under some systems such as feudalism or communism, ownership of some or all kinds of property is vested not in the individual, but in the state or its head. The U.S. Constitution establishes the individual's right to property. Common law distinguishes between real property (land and generally nontransportable goods, such as houses and trees) and personal property) (all other kinds). Financial rights, such as copyrights or patent holdings, are personal.

Property tax, money collected by state and local governments from owners of property. It is levied upon land, homes, buildings, and in some cases on farm equipment, based on a fixed percentage of the property's estimated (assessed) valuation. Monies collected from property taxes are usually used to pay for government services such as road repair, schools, and police and fire protection.
See also: Taxation.

Prophet, in the Old Testament of the Bible, a man who by special revelation proclaimed the word of God by oracles and symbolic actions; originally a seer or ecstatic. Often a scourge of the establishment, prophets were religious and social reformers who called for righteousness and faithfulness to God and pronounced judgment on the ungodly. In the early Christian Church prophecy was a recognized charisma, but soon died out except in Montanism, a heretical sect. It was revived among Anabaptists, Quakers, Mormons, and Pentecostals. In Islam Muhammad is the last and greatest prophet. Oracular prophets are found in many religions.
See also: Old Testament.

Prophylaxis, general term for the prevention of diseases. This is most often done through preventative treatments given prior to a person's contracting a disease. Vaccinations are a form of prophylaxis that build up immunities within the human body against certain types of disorders. Pasteurization of milk and milk products is another form of prophylaxis, as is proper sanitation on a community-wide scale.

Proportion, in mathematics, equality of two ratios. The numbers a, b, c, and d are said to be in proportion if $a/b = c/d$. The expression may also be written as $a:b::c:d$. The term *proportion* is useful in describing the relationship between quantities whose ratio is constant—for example, the ratio between the radius and circumference of a circle. If there are two circles with circumferences c_1, c_2 and radii r_1 and r_2 then $c_1 = 2\pi r$, and $c_2 = 2\pi r_2$. This can be written $c_1/r_1 = 2\pi = c_2/r_2$. The figures c_1, r_1, c_2 and r_2 are in proportion, and we say that the circumference of a circle is proportional to its radius.
See also: Mathematics.

Proportional representation, system of electing members to a legislature in which political parties or groups contesting the election are awarded a number of seats in the legislature more or less proportional to the number of votes they get. For instance, if 3 parties are running for seats in a 300-member legislature, and one party gets half the vote while the others roughly split the remaining half equally, the largest party would be allotted about 150 seats, the 2 others about 75 each. There are various ways of organizing such elections and of calculating the results. The system is generally used in places where there are more than 2 significant-sized parties. Supporters of proportional representation argue that it is the most democratic system, since it most accurately reflects the political desires of the population. Opponents argue that it can give unreasonable power to small groups, which can sometimes gain decisive leverage in a divided multiparty assembly.

Proslavery movement, U.S. movement to justify and expand the practice of slavery prior to the Civil War. It gained strength and prominence in the American South in direct response to the abolitionist movement that began to take hold in the northern states in the 1830s. Proslavery advocates used biblical and economic justifications for the ownership of slaves and they constituted a large and influential voting bloc in the United States Congress. The Civil War ended slavery and the proslavery movement.
See also: Abolitionism; Slavery.

Prospecting, process of searching for minerals worth exploiting economically. The simplest technique is direct observation of the local surface features characteristically associated with specific mineral deposits. This is often done by prospectors on the ground, but aerial photography is increasingly employed. Other techniques include examining the seismic waves caused by explosions (which supply information about the structures through which they have passed); testing local magnetic fields to detect magnetic metals or the metallic gangues associated with nonmagnetic minerals; and, especially for metallic sulfides, testing electrical conductivity.

Prosser, Gabriel (c.1775-1800), black American slave who planned a slave revolt in Virginia, intending to create an independent black state and to become its king. Prosser was born in Henrico County, Va., to an African woman. He was owned by Thomas H. Prosser. In the attack planned for Richmond, Virginia's capital, Prosser and his followers were to seize the arsenal and kill all whites except Frenchmen, Methodists, and Quakers. Then the rebels would proceed to take over the state. On Aug. 30, 1800, an army numbering 1,000-50,000 gathered outside Richmond. But heavy rain had washed out the bridges to the city, thwarting the army's approach. The revolt was doomed when two slaves betrayed the plot to their owner, who then informed Gov. James Monroe. Prosser and about 34 supporters were captured, tried, and hanged.
See also: Slavery.

Prostaglandin, variety of naturally occuring aliphatic acids with various biological activities including increased vascular permeability, smooth muscle contraction, bronchial constriction, and alteration in the pain threshold. Seminal fluid contains lipid-soluble substances that stimulate smooth muscle, and it has been suggested that the active principle should be called prostaglandin. Although prostaglandins are present in highest concentration in seminal fluid, they have been found in numerous other tissues, such as the kidney, iris, pancreas, lung, and brain.

Prostate gland, male reproductive gland that surrounds the urethra at the base of the urinary bladder and that secretes prostatic fluid. This organ is formed of fibrous muscular and glandular tissue. It is described as having the shape of a chestnut and as being an inverted pyramid whose base is applied to the neck of the bladder. The normal gland usually measures about

1 in (2.54 cm) from front to back, 1 1/4 in (3.18 cm) from above downward and nearly 2 in (5 cm) from side to side. The connective tissue around the gland is condensed to form a fibrous capsule. There is a groove between the neck of the bladder and the base of the prostate that contains a venous plexus. The prostate is traversed from top to bottom by the urethra. The glandulary tissue consists of secretory acini. After middle age, acini may contain concretions of secretion and desquamated cells.

The glands of the median lobe and mucosal glands constitute the glands of the inner zone, in which penile enlargement usually starts. Cancer of the prostate usually starts in the outer zone which consists of the main prostatic gland.

See also: Reproduction.

Prosthetic, mechanical or electrical device inserted into or onto the body to replace or supplement the function of a missing, defective, or diseased organ. Artificial limbs were among the first prosthetics, but metal or plastic joint replacements and bone fixations are now also available. Replacement teeth are also prosthetics. The valves of the heart may be replaced with mechanical devices, and electrical pacemakers can be implanted to stimulate the heart muscle at a set rate.

Prostitution, practice of exchanging sexual favors for material profit, usually money. Prostitution is as old as civilization and has flourished throughout history, especially in urban centers, which generate demand and provide conditions of relative anonymity. Although there is some male prostitution, the term usually refers to the practice as performed by women.

Protactinium, chemical element, symbol Pa; for physical constants see Periodic Table. Discovered in 1917 by 2 teams of scientists working independently; Otto Hahn and Lise Meitner of Germany and Frederick Soddy and John Cranston of Great Britain. It is found in the mineral *pitchblende* in minute quantities. Protactinium is a lustrous, radioactive metal, and a member of the actinide series. The element was initially prepared by decomposing its iodide in a vacuum with an electrically heated filament. The longest lived is an alpha emitter with a half-life of 32,500 years. It is a dangerous and toxic material.

Protagoras (c.490-421 B.C.), Greek Sophist, remembered for the maxim "Man is the measure of all things." A respected figure in Athens, where he spent most of life, he taught rhetoric and the proper conduct of life ("virtue"), and was appointed lawmaker to the Athenian colony of Thurii in 444 B.C. Little is known of his teaching, but he is thought to have been a relativist concerning knowledge and a skeptic about the gods, although he upheld conventional morality.

See also: Sophist.

Protective coloration, adaptation of coloration by animals, often providing a means of defense against predators. Except where selection favors bright coloration for breeding or territorial display, most higher animals are colored in such a way that they blend in with their background: by pure coloration, by disruption of outline with bold lines or patches, or by a combination of the two. The most highly developed camouflage is found in ground-nesting birds, or insects. Associated with this coloration must be special behavior patterns enabling the animal to seek out the correct background for its camouflage and to "freeze" against it. Certain animals can change their body texture and coloration to match different backgrounds: octopuses, chameleons, and some flatfishes. An alternative strategy adopted by some animals, particularly insects, is the use of shock-coloration: when approached by a predator, these insects flick open plain wings to expose bright colors, often in the form of staring "eyes," to scare the predator.

Protectorate, country that is nominally independent but surrenders part of its sovereignty, such as control over foreign policy, in return for protection by a stronger state. The degree of control and dependency varies.

Protein, high-molecular-weight compound that yields amino acid through hydrolysis. Although hundreds of different amino acids are possible, only 20 are found in appreciable quantities in proteins, and these are all alpha-amino acids. Proteins are found throughout all living organisms. Muscle, the major structural material in animals, is mainly protein; the 20% of blood that is not water is mainly protein. Enzymes may contain other components, but basically they, too, are protein. Approximately 700 proteins are known; of these, 200-300 have been studied and over 150 obtained in crystalline form. Some are very stable, while others are so delicate that even exposure to air will destroy their capability as enzymes. The best food sources for proteins are meat, fish, eggs, milk, and cheese. These foods provide all the essential aminoacids and are known as complete proteins. Vegetables and nuts do provide proteins but are not complete proteins. The absence of protein in the diet can diminish growth and reduce energy levels.

Protestant ethic, set of values that esteems hard work, thrift, duty, efficiency, and self-discipline. The Protestant ethic follows from the beliefs, identified with Calvinism, that a person's time and talents are gifts from God and that prosperity is a sign of piety and salvation. The concept of a protestant ethic was formalized by the German sociologist Max Weber in his essay, "The Protestant Ethic and the Spirit of Capitalism" (1904-5). He attributed the economic success of Protestant groups to Protestant values.
See also: Weber, Max.

Protestantism, principles of the Reformation. The name derives from the *Protestatio* of the minority reforming delegates at the Diet of Speyer (1529). Protestantism is characterized by subordinating tradition to the Bible as the basis for doctrine and practice, and stresses justification by faith, biblical preaching, and a high personal morality. In reaction to Roman Catholicism it rejects papal claims, the mass, and the worship of saints. The main original branches were Lutheranism, Calvinism, Anglicanism, and Zwinglianism, with small Anabaptist sects. Exercise of the right of privacy judgment in interpreting Scripture led to fragmentation, a trend reversed in recent decades by the Ecumenical Movement. Later Protestant churches include the Congregational churches, Baptists, Quakers, Methodists, the Moravian Church, and the Pentecostal churches.
See also: Reformation.

Protista, members of a proposed group of organisms having characteristics of both the plant and the animal kingdoms. The classification usually includes single-celled organisms that have a distinct nucleus and organelles (structures that perform specific functions): protozoans, diatoms, bacteria, and some algae. Some scientists consider multicelled fungi and seaweeds as protista. The classification was proposed by the German zoologist Ernst H. Haeckel (1866).

Proton, elementary particle having a positive charge equivalent to the negative charge of the electron but possessing a mass approximately 1,837 times as great. A member of the baryon class of elementary particles, the proton was discovered in 1919 by Ernest Rutherford. The proton is, in effect, the nucleus of the hydrogen atom. Every atomic nucleus contains at least one proton.
See also: Atom.

Protoplasm, basic substance of which all living things are made up. Mostly water, protoplasm also contains proteins, fats, and inorganic salts. It is present in all cells, usually differentiated into the nucleus and the cytoplasm. The latter is generally a transparent viscous fluid containing a number of specialized structures; it is the medium in which the main chemical reactions of the cell take place. The nucleus contains the cell's genetic material.

Protozoan, single-celled organism belonging to the phylum Protozoa. Protozoans fall into 4 classes: flagellates, sarcodines, sporozoans, and ciliates. Most are aquatic, living in fresh or salt water. Some live in plants or animals and cause serious diseases. A few protozoans contain chlorophyll and make their own food, but the majority must ingest their food. They reproduce in many ways, including undergoing fission (cell division) or budding. Protozoans tend to be solitary; a few cluster in colonies.

Protractor, semicircular device used to measure or to construct angles. The curve is usually marked in degrees, (0-180), or sometimes in mils (0-3,200). A plane protractor is used to measure angles within a plane. A spherical protractor is used in navigation and astronomy to measure spherical angles.
See also: Angle.

Proudhon, Pierre Joseph (1809-65), French social thinker. He first gained notoriety with his book *What is Property?* (1840). He advocated a society in which property would be distributed among free individuals who cooperated spontaneously outside a framework of state authority—a philosophy he called *mutualism*. In 1847 he clashed with Karl Marx, thus starting a struggle between libertarian and authoritarian views on socialism which continued long after his death.

Proust, Joseph Louis (1754-1826), French chemist who established the law of definite proportions, or Proust's law.
See also: Chemistry.

Proust, Marcel (1871-1922), French novelist whose seven-part work *Remembrance of Things Past* is one of the greatest novels of the 20th century. It was written during the period 1907-19, after Proust, who suffered continually from asthma, had retired from Parisian high society and become virtually a recluse. A semiautobiographical exploration of time, memory, and consciousness, with an underlying theme of the transcendency of art over the futility of one's best efforts, it broke new ground in the art of the novel and was enormously influential.

Provençal, or langue d'oc, Romance language developed from the Latin spoken in southern France, principally Provence. During the Middle Ages, Provençal produced a notable literature that reached its highest point with the courtly love poetry of the troubadours.

Provence, region and former province of France, embracing the lower Rhone River (including the Camargue) and the French Riviera. The chief cities are Nice, Marseilles, Toulon, Avignon, Arles, and Aix-en-Provence (the historic capital). It is a sunny and picturesque region, famous for historical associations and its fruit, vineyards, and olives. It was the first transalpine Roman province (hence the name), and later it became an independent kingdom (879-933), finally passing to the French kings in 1486.
See also: France.

Proverbs, Book of, book of the Bible's Old Testament; an example of the "wisdom literature" popular in post-exilic Judaism. Its eight sections, attributed in their headings to various authors, including Solomon, consist of numerous pithy proverbs and mostly unconnected moral maxims, probably dating between the 9th and 2nd centuries B.C.
See also: Old Testament.

Providence (pop. 156,200), capital of Rhode Island, on the Providence River at the head of Narragansett Bay. The second-largest city in New England (after Boston), Providence is an important industrial, commercial, and education center. Its port is among the busiest in New England. Its major industries include jewelry, silverware, textiles, machinery, and metal products. Brown University is located here, as are the famous Rhode Island School of Design, Bryant College, Catholic Teacher's College, Providence College, Providence-Barrington Bible College, and Rhode Island College. Providence is among the oldest cities in the United States, founded by Roger Williams in 1636 after his expulsion from the Plymouth Colony. Williams and his followers named it for "God's merciful providence" and made it a haven for religious dissenters. Toward the end of the century, Providence became a major port and commercial center. In the 18th and 19th centuries manufacturing (especially textiles) developed strongly. The city maintains a number of historic old homes and public buildings, many of which date from colonial times.
See also: Rhode Island.

Province, region governed or administered by a country, empire, or diocese. Some nations are formed by a union of provinces, while others are divided into provinces, e.g., Canada. To the Romans, a province was a conquered land ruled from Rome as a self-contained unit.

Provincetown *See:* Cape Cod; Mayflower.

Provo (pop. 263,590), a city in Utah and the seat of Utah County. Named for Étienne Provost, a fur trapper, it was founded by Mormons (1849) and incorporated in 1851. Its products include fruit, steel, and iron. Brigham Young University is in Provo.
See also: Utah.

Prud'hon, Pierre Paul (1758-1823), French painter. His best-known works are the portrait of the Empress Josephine (1805) and *Crime Pursued by Vengeance and Justice* (1808). His painting, influenced by Correggio, is soft and sensual in character.

Prune, dried plum. Certain plum varieties, especially French prune plums, are suited for prune production. The ripe fruit is dried in a dehydrator for 14-24 hours, dipped in a lye solution, and allowed to cure for at least 2 weeks.

Pruning, the cutting away of a plant's branches, shoots, buds, or roots. Pruning is done to shape a plant, increase air and light circulation among the branches, increase fruit and flower quality, remove dead, diseased, injured, or hazardous parts, retard water loss after transplanting, or renew growth. A gardener prunes certain plants according to the season and makes the cut at a prescribed place and angle.

Prussia, state in north central Europe that became the foundation of the modern state of Germany. At the height of its strength it stretched from west of the Rhine to Poland and Russia. The Baltic territory later known as East Prussia was Germanized by the Teutonic Knights in the 1200s and later became the duchy of Prussia. In 1618 it came under the rule of the Electors of nearby Brandenburg, the Hohenzollerns; and Frederick I declared himself king of Prussia in 1701. Under his successors, particularly Frederick the Great, the Prussian state expanded to become the strongest military power in northern Europe. In 1862 Bismarck became premier, and as a result of a planned series of wars and skillful diplomacy conducted under his direction, King William I of Prussia was declared Emperor of Germany in 1871. Prussia was the largest and most powerful of the states of the united Germany until 1934, when by a decree of Hitler the separate German states ceased to exist as political entities. After World War II former Prussian territory was divided among East Germany, Poland, and the USSR.
See also: Germany.

Prussian blue, category of deep-blue pigments containing ferrocyanide. It is used to color paint, enamel, lacquer, printing ink, and carbon paper. Some Prussian blue is prepared from sodium ferrocyanide that has been oxidized in the presence of sodium chlorate, sodium chromate, or other reagent. Others are made by oxidizing a mixture of ferrous sulfate and potassium ferrocyanide. Prussian blue was first made in 1704.

Prussic acid (HCN), also called hydrocyanic acid, a colorless, highly toxic, aqueous solution of hydrogen cyanide. The acid is flammable and evaporates readily. It is used in the manufacture of plastics, fumigants, and dyes. Prussic acid was first derived from the pigment Prussian blue.

Przewalski's horse, or Eastern wild horse, last remaining race of true wild horses. Of the three subspecies of *Equus przewalskii*, two—the steppe tarpan and forest tarpan—were exterminated by the middle of the 19th century. Only Przewalski's horse remained, undiscovered until 1881. Ancestors of domestic horses, they are about the size of a pony, yellow or red-brown, and with an erect mane. It is probable that they, too, are now extinct in the wild. Today it is an endangered species with less than 200 animals living in zoos and fewer than 50 living in the wild.

Psalms, Book of, collection of 150 songs in the Old Testament, used as the hymn book of Judaism since the return from exile and prominent in Christian liturgy. Metrical psalms are sung in the Reformed churches. Many psalms are traditionally ascribed to David; modern scholars date them between the 10th and 2nd centuries B.C. Their fine poetry embodies a rich variety of religious experience, both national and individual.
See also: Old Testament.

Psi particle, subatomic particle consisting of a charmed quark and an anticharmed quark bonded by their opposite electric charges and a strong nuclear force, or strong interaction. The psi particle itself has no electric charge. The psi particle, also called a J particle, was discovered in 1974 by two separate teams of U.S. physicists.
See also: Quark.

Psittacosis, infectious atypical form of pneumonia caused by *Chlamydia psittaci* and transmitted by certain birds. Human infection usually occurs by inhaling dust from feathers or excreta of infected birds; it may also be transmitted to humans by a bite from an infected bird or, rarely, by cough droplets of infected bird or, rarely, by cough droplets of infected persons. The onset may be insidious or abrupt, with fever, chills, general malaise, and anorexia. The temperature gradually rises and a cough develops, initially dry but at times becoming mucopurulent. During the second week pneumonia and frank consolidation may occur with secondary purulent lung infection. Convalescence is gradual and may be prolonged, especially in severe cases. Tetracycline is an effective treatment.
See also: Pneumonia.

Psoriasis, skin condition characterized by patches of red, thickened, and scaling skin. It often affects the elbows, knees, and scalp but may be found anywhere. Several forms are recognized, and the manifestations may vary over time in each individual. Coal tar preparations are valuable in treatment, but steroid creams and cytotoxic chemotherapy may be needed. There is also an associated arthritis.

Psychedelics *See:* Hallucinogenic drug.

Psychiatry, field of medicine concerned with the study and treatment of mental disorders, including neurosis and psychosis. Its major branches are psychotherapy, the application of psychological techniques to the treatment of mental illness where a physiological origin is either unknown or does not exist; and medical therapy, where attack is made either on the organic source of the disease or on its physical or behavioral symptoms.
See also: Mental illness.

Psychical research, field of study concerned with the evaluation of phenomena having to do with so-called extrasensory perception. So far, no scientific evidence for such phenomena has been found.
See also: Extrasensory perception; Parapsychology.

Psychoanalysis, system of psychology having as its base the theories of Sigmund Freud; also the psychotherapeutic technique based on that system. The distinct forms of psychoanalysis developed by Carl Jung and Alfred Adler are more correctly termed *analytical psychology* and *individual psychology*, respectively. Freud's initial interest was in the origins of neuroses. On developing the technique of free association to replace that of hypnosis in this therapy, he observed that certain patients could in some cases associate freely only with difficulty. He decided that this was due to repression, where memories of certain experiences being held back from the conscious mind, and noted that the most sensitive areas were in connection with sexual experiences. He thus developed the concept of the unconscious (later to be called the *id*) and suggested (for a while) that anxiety was the result of repression of the libido. He also defined *resistance* by the conscious mind to acceptance of ideas and impulses from the unconscious, and *transference*, the idea that relationships with other people or objects in the past affect the individual's relationships with other people or objects in the present.
See also: Freud, Sigmund; Psychology.

Psychological warfare, various propaganda methods directed at a nation's enemy. The objective is to demoralize the enemy's people, break their will, and discredit their leaders. Civilians, soldiers, and prisoners of war may be subjected to psychological warfare.
See also: Propaganda.

Psychology, originally the branch of philosophy dealing with the mind, then the science of mind, and now, considered in its more general context, the science of behavior, whether human or animal, and of human thought processes. Psychology is closely connected with medicine, psychiatry, and sociology. There are a number of closely interrelated branches of human psychology. *Experimental psychology* embraces all psychological investigations undertaken by the psychologist. The experiments may center on the individual or on a group, in which latter case statistics will play a large part in the research. *Social psychologists* use statistical and other methods to investigate the effect of the group on the behavior of the individual. In *applied psychology*, the discoveries and theories of psychology are put to practical use, as in industrial psychology. *Comparative psychology* deals with the different behavioral organizations of animals, including humans. *Physiological psychology* attempts to understand the neurology and physiology of behavior. *Clinical psychologists* diagnose and treat mental disorders, principally using psychological tests, psychotherapy, and behavior therapy. They also do research on psychological factors affecting mental illness.

Psychosis, any mental disorder that, whether neurological or purely psychological in origin, renders an individual incapable of distinguishing reality from fantasy. Symptoms may include delusions and hallucinations, severe mood swings, dissociation, etc. If the loss of mental capacity is progressive,

the illness is termed a deteriorative psychosis. Today, the term is less often used in psychiatric diagnosis.
See also: Mental illness; Schizophrenia.

Psychosomatic medicine, that aspect of medical treatment that considers the emotional and mental component of physical illness. Emotional and mental disturbances undermine a person's physical health. They can also make a person feel sick when there is no physical cause. Disorders linked with emotional disturbances include asthma, headache, ulcers, hypertension, neurodermatoses (chronic skin disorders), sexual dysfunction, gastrointestinal upsets, and rheumatoid arthritis, among others. A patient whose complaint is determined to be psychosomatic may be treated by a physician, psychiatrist (or other therapist), or both.

Psychotherapy, application of the theories and discoveries of psychology to the treatment of mental illness, particularly in the form of some sort of relationship between the therapist and the patient. Psychoanalysis, the technique pioneered by Sigmund Freud, was the first form of psychotherapy. Since then many others have been developed, including behavior therapy and Gestalt therapy. Most approaches to psychotherapy involve some type of support, confrontation, or interpretation. Any approach may be applied in a group setting of 5 to 12 people. Group therapy enables a therapist to serve more people, and members of a group can learn from and provide support for one another.
See also: Behavior therapy; Gestalt psychology; Psychology.

Psyllium, herb belonging to the plantain family, Plantagnaceae. *Plantango psyllium* and *P. ovata* are common species. An annual, the plant may grow 20 in (51 cm) high. It has narrow leaves, $1-2^{1}/_2$ in (2.5-6.4 cm) long, and tiny flowers along spikes. Psyllium is cultivated in southern Europe and India for the medicinal, especially laxative, properties of its seeds.

Ptarmigan, any of several birds of the grouse family that can be identified by their white wings and underparts. The willow ptarmigan and rock ptarmigan live in Arctic regions, while the white-tailed ptarmigan is found above the treeline of the Rocky Mountains. Ptarmigans turn white in winter. They have feathered toes that act as snowshoes, and they can burrow under snow for food.

PT boat, small, manueverable boat used by the U.S. Navy to torpedo enemy ships. Its full name is *patrol torpedo boat*. The PT boat was used to advantage during World War II but taken from the active list in 1959. PT boats were 77-80 ft (23-24 m) long. Powered by 3 supercharged gasoline engines, a PT boat could travel at 43 knots, or 49 mi (79 km) per hr. The near-flat hull, which allowed the PT boat to skim over smooth water, handicapped the boat in rough waves.
See also: Navy, United States.

Pteranodon *See:* Pterosaur.

Pteridophyte, class of plants that produce spores and have roots, stems, and leaves. Having vascular tissue places pteridophytes in the division, or phylum, Tracheophyta. Among other plants, the class includes ferns, horsetails, club mosses, and numerous species known from fossils. The pteridophyte's life cycle is one of alternating generations and asexual (with spores) and sexual (with egg and sperm) reproduction. Spores released from spore cases develop into a plant unlike the parent. This second form develops male and female reproductive organs. These produce eggs and sperm that unite to begin the first form of the plant. Pteridophytes that lived millions of years ago are the source of today's coal.

Pterosaur, member of a group of flying reptiles that lived 195-65 million years ago, during the Mesozoic era. The compact body had a pointed head with powerful, toothed jaws. Skin between the hindlimb and the forelimb's 4th finger served as a wing. The other 3 fingers were clawed and free for clutching. The slender hindlimbs seem to have been adapted for suspending the animal. Scientists believe that the pterosaur, besides gliding and soaring, flapped its wings. There are 2 known groups of pterosaurs: the earlier rhamphourhynchoids, the size of a sparrow; and the various sized pterodactyls. The *Pteranodon*, a pterodactyl descendant, had a wingspan estimated at up to 51 ft (15.5 m), making it the largest flying reptile.

Ptolemy, or Claudius Ptolemaeus (2nd century A.D.), Alexandrian astronomer, mathematician, and geographer. Most important is his book on astronomy, now called *Almagest* ("the greatest"), a synthesis of Greek astronomical knowledge, especially that of Hipparchus. His geocentric cosmology dominated Western scientific thought until the Copernican Revolution of the 16th century. His *Geography* gave rise to Columbus' belief in the westward route to Asia. In his *Optics* he attempted to solve the astronomical problem of atmospheric refraction.
See also: Astronomy.

Ptolemy, name used by all 15 Egyptian kings of the Macedonian dynasty (323 B.C.-30 B.C.). **Ptolemy I Soter** (367 B.C.- 283 B.C.) was one of Alexander the Great's generals. He secured Egypt for himself after Alexander's death and defended it in a series of wars against Alexander's other generals. He founded the library of Alexandria, which became a center of Hellenistic culture. **Ptolemy II Philadelphus** (308 B.C.-246 B.C.) succeeded in 285. Under him Alexandria reached its height; he completed the Pharos lighthouse and appointed Callimachus librarian. **Ptolemy III Euergetes** (c.280-221 B.C.) Succeeded in 246. He extended the empire to include most of Asia Minor, the eastern Mediterranean, and the Aegean islands. After 221 the Ptolemaic empire entered a long period of decline, gradually losing its overseas possessions. **Ptolemy XV Cesarion** ("son of Caesar"; 47-30 B.C.) ruled from 44 B.C. jointly with his mother, Cleopatra VII. On their defeat at the battle of Actium (31 B.C.), Egypt became a Roman province.
See also: Egypt, Ancient.

Ptomaine poisoning, type of food poisoning caused by spoiled foods.

Puberty *See:* Adolescence.

Public domain, in U.S. law, ownership of a property or resource by the people. In 1980 public domain or public land made up 34% of U.S. land.

Processes, plans, and creative works not protected by patent or copyright are said to be in the public domain.

Public health, organization and practice of preventative medicine within a community. Many threats to health are beyond individual control: Disease, epidemics, pollution of the air, and purity of water can only be effectively regulated by laws and health authorities. Among the strictest controls are those on sewage and waste disposal. Most advanced countries have pure-food laws controlling food purity, freshness, and additives. In the United States, these controls are the responsibility of the Food and Drug Administration. The work of individual countries in the public-health field is coordinated by the World Health Organization. Some countries have complete public-health services that provide free or low-cost medical treatment of all kinds.

Public lands, land areas owned by the U.S. government, especially those it sells or leases to individuals. The government uses public lands for parks, forests, cemeteries, wildlife refuges, federal buildings, and defense installations. Congress determines how to use or dispose of public lands; the Bureau of Land Management in the Department of the Interior administers public lands. About 762 million acres (308 million hectares) are public lands.

Public opinion, opinions held by many people on issues of local, national, or worldwide importance. Public opinion is shaped by factual information and individuals' values and emotions. It is circulated and further influenced by conversation, fora, the media, schools, public figures, and special interest groups, such as political parties, labor unions, religious organizations, and businesses. Public opinion polls survey the range of public opinion within a group. In a democratic society, government and private institutions are responsive to public opinion and divergent public opinion is permitted.

Public opinion poll, technique for measuring the range of opinions held by the general public or by specifically limited groups of people. It developed during the 1920s. Opinion polls rely on certain statistical laws that show that small, carefully chosen samples of any group can accurately represent the range of opinions of the whole group, or population. The population in question, known as the "universe," may be a general one (all voters in the United States) or a limited one (all car workers in Detroit). Accuracy depends on the care with which the sample is constructed and on the size of the sample. Since 1944 all polls have adopted the method of random selection pioneered by the U.S. Census Bureau in which each member of the "universe" has an equal chance of being questioned. Pioneers in U.S. public-opinion polling include George Gallup, Louis Harris, and Elmo Roper.

Public relations (PR), general term for fostering goodwill for a person, corporation, institution, or product without actually paying for advertisements. Practitioners of PR supply information to the media in the hope that the media will not bother to make any changes in what they want to have said. PR people suggest improvements in behavior, grooming, packaging, etc., to a client or employer. The term *public relations* is thought to have been used first by Ivy L. Lee, who styled himself an "adviser" on "public relations" as early as 1919.

Public utility, business that performs a service for the public and is subject to government regulation. Companies that supply electricity, water, and natural gas and provide sewage treatment, waste disposal, telephone service, and transportation are examples of public utilities. In Canada and Europe, the state owns the public utilities. In the United States, most public utilities are privately owned; some are owned by municipalities and counties. Government regulation assures that the public utility, a monopoly, charges a reasonable fee and supplies adequate and safe service to all who apply for it.

Public Works Administration (PWA), or Federal Emergency Administration of Public Works, a New Deal agency set up in 1933 to stimulate employment and purchasing power. Under H.L. Ickes it made loans and grants, mainly to governmental bodies, for projects which included the Grand Coulee and Bonneville dams. The PWA was phased out from 1939.

Publishing, preparation, manufacture, and distribution of printed materials. In Europe, publishing became distinct from printing and bookselling soon after the introduction of printing (15th century). By the 1800s, book publishing was an important industry. Today, large publishers are often owned by conglomerates. Many publishers specialize as to subject matter; type of book: trade, text, or reference; and means of distribution. Trade books (fiction and nonfiction) are sold to readers through stores; textbooks reach students through school purchases; reference books are sold to libraries and individuals. Some books are sold by subscription or through book clubs. In a publishing house, the steps needed to bring a manuscript to book form are carried out by separate departments: editorial, production, promotion, and distribution.
See also: Printing.

Puccini, Giacomo (1858-1924), Italian opera composer. His first international success, *Manon Lescaut* (1893), was followed by *La Bohème* (1896), *Tosca* (1900), *Madama Butterfly* (1904), and *Turandot* (uncompleted at Puccini's death, produced 1926). A lyric style and strong orchestration are characteristic of his operas, which have great dramatic and emotional power. Puccini's works are among the most popular in the operatic repertoire.
See also: Opera.

Pudding stone, kind of conglomerate rock. It consists of pebbles and gravel embedded in a fine-grained, loosely cementing matrix. The term is chiefly British.

Puebla (pop. 646,600), capital of Puebla, Mexico. The city, one of Mexico's largest, was founded in 1531. It is known for its architecture, much of which is decorated with colored tiles. Puebla's products include pottery, glass, tiles, cotton textiles, fruits, and vegetables.
See also: Mexico.

Puebla, state of Mexico, in central Mexico, near Mexico City. It produces agricultural products and textiles. Three of Mexico's highest mountains, Orizaba (Citlatltépetl), Popocatépetl, and Ixtacihuatl, are within Puebla. Its capital is the city of Puebla.
See also: Mexico.

Pueblo (pop. 123,051), city in southeastern Colorado and the seat of Pueblo County. It lies on the Arkansas River in the foothills of the Rocky Mountains. Among its products are steel, timber, and coal. It was built on the site of a frontier trading post and fort (1842).
See also: Colorado.

Pueblo, several Native American tribes living in southwestern United States (Arizona and New Mexico) in permanent villages (*pueblos*). They have the oldest and most developed pre-Columbian civilization north of Mexico. The various tribes, which include the Hopi and Zuñi, are descended from the basket makers and cliff dwellers. Pueblo Indians are noted for their handiworks; their social system and religious practices remain largely intact today.

Puerto Rico, officially the Commonwealth of Puerto Rico, island in the Caribbean Sea.
Land and climate. Puerto Rico is the smallest and easternmost island of the Greater Antilles, the other members of which are Cuba, Jamaica, and Hispaniola. It is about 950 mi (1,529 km) southeast of Miami, Florida and 550 mi (885 km) north of Caracas, Venezuela. A number of offshore islands, including Vieques, Culebra, and Mona, also belong to Puerto Rico, bringing the commonwealth's total area to about 3,515 sq mi (9,104 sq km). Along the coast is a narrow fertile plain from 1 to 12 mi (19 km) wide. In the center of the island is a chain of mountains that roughly divides it into two distinct northern and southern regions. Puerto Rico has a tropical climate, but the effects of high temperature are moderated by the trade winds. Tropical hurricanes frequently bear down on the island, especially between August and October. The capital city is San Juan. The official language is Spanish, but English is also spoken.
People. The people of Puerto Rico are a mixture of Spanish and African. Some two-thirds of the population lives in the cities of San Juan, Ponce, and Mayagüez. Most Puerto Ricans are Roman Catholic.
Economy. Puerto Rico's was formerly a single-crop economy based upon sugar, but it now depends largely upon manufacturing. Metals, chemicals, oil refining, textiles, and sugar products account for most manufacturing and provide the principal exports. Coffee, tobacco, and tourism are also important. The United States is Puerto Rico's main trading partner.
History. Puerto Rico was discovered in 1493 by Christopher Columbus. In 1508, Juan Ponce de Leòn founded a colony. The native Arawak people perished under Spanish rule and, from 1510, black African slaves were imported to work on sugar plantations. The island was ceded to the United States in 1898 following the Spanish American War. In 1917, the Puerto Ricans received U.S. citizenship. U.S. economic dominance resulted in economic dislocation and political tension. In 1952, Puerto Rico became a commonwealth in free association with the United States. Under the arrangement, Puerto Ricans remain U.S. citizens, though they cannot vote in U.S. elections and are not obligated to pay U.S. taxes. Following World War II and Operation Bootstrap, a program for strengthening the island's economy, Puerto Rico experienced increased investment that spurred economic growth and diversification. However, high unemployment coupled with a high birth rate have led large numbers of Puerto Ricans to emigrate to the United States. The island's relationship to the United States remains a political issue. Mainstream political parties are divided between those favoring statehood

and those favoring the commonwealth arrangement. A nationalist minority outside the mainstream seeks independence. The issue dominates Puerto Rico's political life.

Puff adder *See:* Adder.

Puffball, fungus of the family Lycoperdaceae. Puffballs produce a roundish fruiting body (basidiocarp) that contains spores. Before maturity, the basidiocarp is firm and edible. The dry, mature puffball often has cracks from which the powdery spores issue.

Puffer, or globe fish, fish that blows up its body like a balloon. It is found in warm and temperate seas, and some grow to 3 ft (0.91 m) long. The bodies of some puffers contain a deadly poison, tetradontoxin. In Japan they are a delicacy, but a cook has to have a license to prepare puffers, for it is necessary to remove the poison parts.

Puffin, any of several stubby seabirds of the auk family. Black or black-and-white, they are characterized by their large, laterally compressed bills, which become further enlarged and brightly patterned at the beginning of the breeding season. Puffins live in colonies on sea cliffs, nesting in burrows.

Pug, breed of toy dog. It has a squarish build, wrinkled face, short muzzle, and curled tail. Adults stand 10-11 in (2.5-2.8 cm) and weigh 13-18 lb (6-8 kg). The pug probably originated in China.

Pugachev, Emelian Ivanovich (1742-75), Cossack leader of the great Urals peasant revolt (1773-74). Claiming to be Peter III, murdered husband of Catherine II of Russia, he declared serfdom abolished and led an army of serfs and Cossacks that seized several cities and killed thousands before he was captured, sent to Moscow in an iron cage, and executed.
See also: Cossacks.

Puget, Peter (1762?-1822), British naval officer and explorer. As a lieutenant with Captain George Vancouver, he explored Puget Sound (1792) and other coastal areas of northwest North America.

Puget Sound, irregular inlet of the Pacific Ocean in northwestern Washington. It extends south about 100 mi (161 km) to Olympia and is navigable by large ships (U.S. navy yard at Bremerton). Seattle and Tacoma lie on its shores, and the state's fish and lumber industries are centered in the area. It was explored by George Vancouver in 1792 and named by him.
See also: Pacific Ocean; Puget, Peter.

Pulaski, Casimir (c.1748-79), Polish soldier, hero of the anti-Russian revolt of 1768 who, exiled from Poland, fought in the American Revolutionary War. He fought at the battles of Brandywine and Germantown. In 1778 he formed his own cavalry unit, the Pulaski Legion. He was mortally wounded at the siege of Savannah.
See also: Poland; Revolutionary War in America.

Pulitzer, Joseph (1847-1911), Hungarian-born U.S. publisher who created the Pulitzer Prizes. In 1883 he bought the New York *World* and raised the circulation tenfold in seven years by aggressive reporting (the term *yellow journalism* was coined to describe its style). In the 1890s Pulitzer was involved in a circulation war with William Randolph Hearst's New York *Journal*. He regularly ran liberal crusades. He also endowed the school of journalism at Columbia University.

Pulitzer Prizes, awards for achievement in U.S. journalism and letters, given every May since 1917 through a foundation created by the estate of Joseph Pulitzer and administered by Columbia University. There are eight cash awards for journalism ($1,000 each), five for literature ($500 each), and four traveling scholarships. An award for music was added in 1943.
See also: Pulitzer, Joseph.

Pulley, grooved wheel mounted on a block with a cord or belt passing over it. A pulley is a simple machine applying the equilibrium of torque to obtain a mechanical advantage. Thus the block and tackle is a combination of ropes and pulleys used for hoisting heavy weights. A belt and pulley combination can transmit motion from one part of a machine to another. Variable speed can be obtained from a single-speed driving shaft by the use of stepped or cone-shaped pulleys with diameters that give the correct speed ratios and belt tensions. To help prevent excessive belt wear and slipping, the rim surface of a pulley is adapted to the material of the belt used.

Pullman, George Mortimer (1831-97), U.S. industrialist and inventor of the first modern railroad sleeping car, the Pullman (patented 1864). In 1880 he built a model company town, Pullman, Ill. (now part of Chicago), later site of the Pullman Strike.
See also: Railroad.

Pullman Strike (May-July 1894), famous boycott of rolling stock of the Pullman Palace Car Co., Pullman, Ill., by E.V. Dees's American Railway Union to protest the company's wage cuts and victimization of union representatives. After the owners obtained a federal injunction the strike was broken by federal troops and the U.S. labor movement suffered a major setback.

Pulsar, short for *pulsating radio star*, a celestial radio source emitting brief, extremely regular pulses of electromagnetic radiation. Each pulse lasts a few hundredths of a second, and the period between pulses is of the order of one second or less. The pulse frequency varies from pulsar to pulsar. The first pulsar was discovered in 1967 by Anthony Hewish and S.J. Bell. The fastest pulsar yet observed has a period of 0.033 sec, emitting pulses of the same frequency in the X-ray and visible regions of the spectrum. It is likely that there are some 10,000 pulsars in the Milky Way, though fewer than 100 have as yet been discovered. It is believed that pulsars are the neutron star remnants of supernovas, rapidly spinning and radiating through loss of rotational energy.
See also: Astronomy.

Pulse, throb in the artery walls due to the beating of the heart. The walls expand when the heart contracts and contract when the heart relaxes. This

creates a wave of pressure that can be felt externally. The pulse is usually counted on the thumb side of the wrist, but it may be taken over any artery that can be felt. A doctor takes the pulse to determine if the heart is beating normally.
See also: Artery; Heart.

Puma, cougar, panther, or mountain lion (*Felis concolor*), the most wide-spread of the big cats of the Americas, occupying an amazing variety of habitats. Powerful cats, resembling a slender and sinuous lioness with a small head, they lead solitary lives, preying on various species of deer. The lifespan of a puma in the wild is about 18 years. A puma can cover up to 20 ft (6.1 m) in a bound and will regularly travel up to 50 mi (80.5 km) when hunting.

Pumice, porous, frothy, volcanic glass formed by the sudden release of vapors as lava cools under low pressure. It is used as an abrasive, an aggregate, and a railroad ballast.

Pump, device for taking in and forcing out a fluid, thus giving it kinetic or potential energy. The heart is a pump for circulating blood around the body. The steam engine was developed to power pumps for pumping out mines. Piston pumps—the simplest of which is the syringe—are reciprocating *volume displacement pumps*, as are diaphragm pumps, with a pulsating diaphragm instead of the piston. One-way inlet and outlet valves are fitted in the cylinder. Rotary volume displacement pumps have rotating gear wheels or wheels with lobes or vanes. *Kinetic pumps*, or fans, work by imparting momentum to the fluid by means of rotating curved vanes in a housing: Centrifugal pumps expel the fluid radially outward; and propeller pumps, axially forward. Air compressors use the turbine principle. *Air pumps* use compressed air to raise liquids from the bottom of wells, displacing one fluid with another. If the fluid must not come into direct contact with the pump, as in a nuclear reactor, *electromagnetic pumps* are used. An electric current and a magnetic field at right angles induce the conducting fluid to flow at right angles to both; or the principle of the linear induction motor may be used. To achieve a very high vacuum, the *diffusion pump* is used, in which atoms of condensing mercury vapor entrain the remaining gas molecules.

Pumpkin, plant (genus *Cucurbita*) of the gourd family. The genus includes winter squashes (*C. maxima* or *C. moschata*) and summer squashes, but the term *pumpkin* usually refers to the round, orange-skinned fruit of the vine *C. pepo*. The pumpkin's stringy pulp is used as food and pie filling. The seeds, which fill the pumpkin's cavity, are also eaten. At Halloween, pumpkins are carved into jack-o'-lanterns. The pumpkin probably originated in North America.

Punch and Judy, leading characters in a children's handpuppet show of the same name. Punch, descended from Pulcinella (Punchinello) of the Commedia Dell'Arte, is a hooknosed, hunchbacked, wife-beating rogue who usually ends on the gallows or in a crocodile's mouth. He is accompanied by his shrewish wife, Judy (originally called Joan), and their dog, Toby. The Devil, Baby, Hangman, Policeman, and Doctor may also appear.

Punic Wars, 3 conflicts between Carthage and Rome. Rome emerged from the Punic Wars as the dominant Mediterranean power. The **First Punic War**

(264-241 B.C.) involved a local dispute over the control of the Strait of Messina, between Sicily and Italy. Carthage, led by Hamilcar Barca, and the Sicilian town Syracuse fought well on land but yielded to Rome's greater sea power. During the **Second Punic War** (218-201 B.C.), Hannibal, the Carthagenian general, crossed the Alps into Italy. The Romans struggled to contain him and finally defeated him (202 B.C.) in Africa. Rome gained Carthage's Spanish provinces. The **Third Punic War** (149-146 B.C.) resulted from Carthage's alleged violation of the 201 B.C. treaty. Rome blockaded Carthage and sacked the city.
See also: Carthage; Hannibal; Rome, Ancient.

Punishment *See:* Capital punishment.

Punjab (Sanskrit, "five rivers"), large wheat-growing region in the northwest of the Indian subcontinent, on the upper Indus River plain. Formerly the British Indian province of Punjab, it was divided in 1947 into what became known as Punjab (Pakistan) and Punjab (India). In 1966 Punjab (India) was divided into two further provinces, Punjab and Haryana.
See also: India.

Pupa, immature stage in the development of those insects whose larval form is completely different in structure from the adult form and in which complete metamorphosis occurs. The pupa normally is a resting place in which the larval structure is reorganized to form the adult. Everything but the nervous system changes, and feeding and locomotion are suspended.

Pupfish, about 30 species of fish (genus *Cyprinodon*) belonging to the killifish family. Pupfish live in the southwestern United States and Mexico, in springs and streams. A few species can tolerate water temperatures of 108°F. (42°C) and thrive in hot springs. Some pupfish are endangered or extinct. Efforts are being made to protect the remaining species.

Pupil *See:* Eye.

Puppet, figure of a person or animal manipulated in dramatic presentations. There are hand (or glove) and finger puppets; jointed marionettes string-controlled from above; and rod puppets, often used in shadow plays. Puppetry, with which ventriloquism is associated, is an ancient entertainment, popular in many countries.

Purcell, Edward Mills (1912-97), U.S. physicist who shared the 1952 Nobel Prize for physics for his discovery of nuclear magnetic resonance (NMR) in solids.

Purcell, Henry (c.1659-95), English composer, the foremost of his time. A master of melody and counterpoint, he wrote in every form and style of the period: odes and anthems for royal occasions, many choral and instrumental works, and music for plays and masques, including his opera *Dido and Aeneas* (1689).

Pure food and drug laws, in the United States, general term for laws such as the Federal Food, Drug and Cosmetic Act (1938) prohibiting the distribution of impure foods and drugs and the false or misleading labeling of such products. The Food and Drug Administration (FDA) enforces these laws and publishes explanatory regulations.

Purgatory, in Roman Catholicism, the place where Christians after death undergo purifying punishment and expiate unforgiven venial sins before admission to heaven. Indulgences, masses, and prayers for the dead are held to lighten their suffering.

Purim (Feast of Lots), Jewish festival of the 14th day of Adar (Feb.-Mar.), a celebration of the deliverance from massacre of Persian Jews through intervention by Esther and Mordecai. The story is told in the Book of Esther.

Puritans, English reforming Protestants who aimed for a simpler form of worship expressly warranted by Scripture, devout personal and family life, and the abolition of clerical hierarchy. They stressed self-discipline, work as a vocation, and the Christianizing of all spheres of life. Most were strict Calvinists. The term was first used in the 1560s for those dissatisfied with the compromise of the Elizabethan settlement of the Church of England; under James I, after their unsuccessful pleas for reform at the Hampton Court Conference (1604), some separated from the Church of England. Archbishop Laud set about systematic repression of Puritanism, causing some to emigrate to the colonies. The English Civil War—known also as the Puritan Revolution—led to the establishment of Presbyterianism, but under Oliver Cromwell Puritan dominance was weakened by internal strife. Most Puritans were forced to leave the Church after the Restoration (1660), becoming Nonconformists. Many New England settlers were Puritans, and their influence on the colonies was profound, especially their concern for education and church democracy.
See also: Protestantism.

Purple Heart *See:* Decorations, medals, and orders.

Purus River, third-longest river in South America and a major tributary of the Amazon River. It rises in the Andes in Peru and meanders 1,956 mi (3,148 km) in a northeasterly direction into Brazil.

Pusan (pop. 3,798,100), second-largest city in South Korea, in the southeast. Having an excellent natural harbor, it is a major port and a center for commerce, shipbuilding, and the fishing industry. It is also a manufacturing and transportation center. Visitors come to its religious and historic landmarks, beaches, and hot springs. During the Korean War, it was South Korea's capital and a landing site for men and arms.
See also: Korea.

Pushkin, Alexander (1799-1837), poet, widely recognized as the founder of modern Russian literature. A sympathizer of the Decembrist Revolt, he spent his adult life in exile or under police surveillance. His poetic range included the political, humorous, erotic, lyrical, epic, and verse tales or novels like *Russlan and Ludmilla* (1820), *The Prisoner of the Caucasus* (1822), and his masterpiece *Eugene Onegin* (1833). Other works are the great drama *Boris Godunov* (1831) and such prose works as "The Queen of Spades" (1834) and *The Captain's Daughter* (1836).

Pushtuns, ethnic group comprising about one half the population of Afghanistan and one fifth the population of Pakistan. They are also called Pathans, Pashtuns, Pakhtuns, and Pukhtuns. Their language, called Pashto, Pushtu, or Pukhtu, is related to Persian. Most Pushtuns live as farmers or nomadic herders and follow Islam. The group is divided into about 40 tribes. Each consists of groups of extended families and is governed by a democratic council. Ancestors of the Pushtuns can be traced to 4000 B.C. During the Soviet invasion of Afghanistan (1979-89), guerrilla bands of Pushtuns resisted the Soviets.

Pussy willow, small tree (*Salix discolor*) particular to North America and characterized by a silky, often drooping flower cluster called a catkin, produced in the early spring.

Putnam, Israel (1718-90), U.S. patriot and general in the Revolutionary War. A veteran of the French and Indian Wars, he was prominent in the Battle of Bunker Hill, but had less success as commander of Continental forces at the Battle of Long Island.
See also: Revolutionary War in America; French and Indian Wars.

Putnam, Rufus (1738-1824), U.S. pioneer who served in the French and Indian Wars and in many of the engagements of the Revolutionary War. He emerged a brigadier general and chief engineer of the army and in 1786 helped organize the Ohio Company of Associates.
See also: Revolutionary War in America; French and Indian Wars.

Pu Yi (1906-67), as Hsuan T'ung, the last emperor (1908-12) of China. The Japanese installed him as Emperor K'ang Te of the puppet state Manchukuo (1934-45). He was captured by the Soviets and returned to China (1950), where he was imprisoned until 1959.

PVC *See:* Vinyl.

Pygmalion, in Greek mythology, king of Cyprus who carved a statue of a beautiful woman and then fell in love with it. The goddess Aphrodite brought the statue (named Galatea) to life as an answer to Pygmalion's prayer for a wife just like her, and they were married. The Pygmalion theme has been used by many authors, particularly George Bernard Shaw in his play *Pygmalion* (1913).

Pygmy, term used to denote those people whose adult males are on average less than 5 ft (1.52 m) tall. Some Kalahari desert Bushmen are of pygmy size, but the most notable pygmies are the Mbuti, or Bambuti, of the Ituri Forest, Zaïre, who, through their different blood type, skin color, thick lips, and scant body hair but thick head hair, are regarded as distinct from the surrounding peoples and were probably the original inhabitants of the region. A Stone Age people, they are nomadic hunters, living in groups of 50 to 100. Asian pygmies are generally termed *Negritos*. Peoples rather larger than pygmies are described as pygmoid.

Pyle, Ernie (Ernest Taylor Pyle; 1900-45), U.S. journalist and war correspondent. He accompanied U.S. troops to all the major fronts in North Africa
and Europe during World War II, and his popular news column won a
Pulitzer Prize in 1944. He was killed by Japanese machine-gun fire during
the Okinawa campaign.
See also: World War II.

Pyle, Howard (1853-1911), U.S. writer and illustrator of children's books,
such as *The Merry Adventures of Robin Hood* (1883) and *The Story of King
Arthur and His Knights* (1903).

Pylos (modern Greek Pilos, formerly Navarino), ancient port in the southwestern Peloponnese, Greece, site of a Mycenaean palace of the 13th century
B.C., associated with king Nestor. In the modern Greek War of Independence,
it was the site of the Battle of Navarino (1827).
See also: Greece.

Pym, John (1584-1643), English statesman. A Puritan, he led parliamentary
opposition to Charles I and organized the impeachment of the Duke of
Buckingham (1626). Dominating the Short and Long Parliaments, he narrowly escaped arrest by the king in 1642 and then arranged an alliance with
the Covenanters in 1643.

Pynchon, Thomas (1937-   ), U.S. novelist whose works, influenced by
James Joyce and Vladimir Nabokov, are noted for their ingenious wordplay
and complexity. His novels include *V* (1963), *The Crying of Lot 49* (1966),
Gravity's Rainbow (1973), a National Book Award winner, *Vineland* (1990),
and *Mason & Dixie* (1997).

Pyongyang (pop. 2,000,000), capital and largest city of North Korea. It lies
on the Taedong River in an important coal-mining area and is a major
industrial center producing iron, steel, machinery, and textiles. An ancient
settlement, it was the capital of the Choson kingdom in the 3rd century B.C.
The city was severely damaged during the Korean War.
See also: Korea.

Pyorrhea *See:* Periodontitis.

Pyramid, polyhedron whose base is a polygon and whose sides are triangles
having a common vertex. A pyramid whose base is triangular is termed a
tetrahedron (or triangular pyramid); one whose base is a regular polygon is
termed regular; one with a square base, square; one with a rectangular base,
rectangular.

Pyramids, structures built by the Egyptians and other ancient peoples as
royal tombs or temples; they are composed of square bases and 4 triangular
faces that meet at a common point, the apex. The Egyptian pyramids, erected
around 4,500 years ago, are the largest and most notable. The first pyramid
dates back to the Old Kingdom and was built by the architect Imhotep for
King Zoser c.2650 B.C. The largest pyramid was constructed for King Khufu
(reigned c.2589-c.2566 B.C.), also known as Cheops. It is 13 acres (5.3
hectares) in area and 482 ft (147 m) high. It is considered one of the Seven

Wonders of the Ancient World. Pyramidal structures were also constructed by the native peoples of Central and South America. The Mayan pyramids were characterized by level tops that were probably used as pulpits.
See also: Egypt, Ancient.

Pyrenees, mountain range between France and Spain, stretching 270 mi (435 km) from the Bay of Biscay to the Mediterranean and rising to Pico de Aneto (11,168 ft/3,404 m) in the central section. The average height is about 3,500 ft (1,067 m) and the maximum width about 50 mi (81 km). The range includes extensive forests and pasture land. Its mineral deposits include iron, zinc, bauxite, and talc, and there are sports and health resorts and a growing tourist industry.

Pyrethrum, any of a group of flowers (genus *Chrysanthemum*) that produce insect powder. Similar in appearance to the daisy, pyrethrums have stems measuring up to 1 ft (30 cm). The insecticide is developed from the powdered or dried flowers and is considered one of the least harmful to humans and animals. Kenya is the world's chief exporter of pyrethrum.

Pyridoxine *See:* Vitamin.

Pyrite, or iron pyrites (FeS_2, iron (ll) disulfide), hard, yellow, common sulfide known as fool's gold for its resemblance to gold. Of worldwide occurrence, it is an ore of sulfur that crystallizes in the isometric system, usually as cubes. It alters to goethite and limonite.

Pyromania, recurring impulse to set fire to objects or buildings.

Pyrometry, process of measuring exceedingly high temperatures through the use of a pyrometer, an instrument that can function in heat far hotter than that tolerated by ordinary thermometers. Most pyrometers measure temperature by detecting the rise in electrical resistance in a metal, by the increase in the intensity of light, or by similar electrical or radiation techniques.

Pyroxene, general term for a group of crystalline silicate minerals containing iron, calcium, and magnesium, prevalent in igneous, metamorphic, and lunar rocks. The color of pyroxenes ranges from black and brown to colorless.

Pyrrho of Elis (360-270 B.C.), Greek philosopher, the founder of skepticism. He taught that because nothing can be known with certainty, suspension of judgment and imperturbability of mind are the true wisdom and source of happiness.
See also: Skepticism.

Pyrrhus (c.318-272 B.C.), king at the age of 12 of Epirus, northwestern Greece, he served with Demetrius I of Macedonia in Asia Minor, was helped by Ptolemy I of Egypt to regain his throne, and later won and lost Macedonia. His costly victory over the Romans at Asculum (279), gave rise to the term *Pyrrhic victory*. Further campaigns in Macedonia and Sparta failed. He was killed in Argos.
See also: Greece, Ancient.

Pythagoras (c.582-507 B.C.), Greek philosopher who founded the Pythagorean school. Attributed to the school are: the proof of the Pythagorean

theorem (the suggestion that the earth travels around the sun, the sun in turn around a central fire); observation of the ratios between the lengths of vibrating strings that sound in mutual harmony, and ascription of such ratios to the distances of the planets, which sounded the "harmony of the spheres"; and the proposition that all phenomena can be reduced to numerical relations. The Pythagoreans were also noted for their concept of the soul, the life of moderation, and their interest in medicine. They exerted great influence on Plato and ancient philosophy generally.
See also: Philosophy.

Pythagorean theorem, statement that, for any right-angled triangle, the square of the hypotenuse is equal to the sum of the squares of the other two sides. The earliest known formal statement of the theorem is in the *Elements* of Euclid, but the basis of it was known long before this time.
See also: Geometry.

Pythias *See:* Damon and Pythias.

Python, Old World equivalent of the New World boa, a snake bearing small spurs as the vestiges of hindlimbs. These two groups are clearly the closest relatives of the ancestral snake type. Like boas, pythons are nonvenomous constrictors. They are found from Africa to Australia in a wide variety of habitats. All have bold color patterns in browns and yellows. The largest species, the reticulate python of Asia, reaches 33 ft (10.1 m). Pythons feed on small mammals, birds, reptiles, and frogs; the larger African species also feed on small antelopes.

Q

Q, 17th letter of the alphabet, can be traced back to the letter *koph* in the Semitic alphabet and *koppa* in ancient Greek, on through the Etruscan alphabet, taking its modern form in Latin, usually followed by *u*. As an abbreviation, a capital *Q* is used for "Quebec" and for "queen" in titles such as Q.C. (Queen's Counsel). A lower-case *q* may stand for "quart," "question," and is part of *q.v.* for the Latin phrase *quod vide* (which see), meaning "refer to."

Qadhafi, Muammar Muhammad al- (1942-   ), Libyan leader. One of a group of army officers who deposed King Idris I in 1969, he became chairman of the ruling Revolutionary Command Council and commander-in-chief of the armed forces. One of the world's most controversial heads of state, he has been vehemently anti-Israel and supported several insurgent and terrorist groups around the world. In response to his support of terrorists, in 1986 U.S. planes attacked Tripoli, destroying a military camp.
See also: Libya.

Qandahar, or Kandahar (pop. 191,300), city in southern Afghanistan, second largest Afghan city, and major international trade center. Industries include farming and fruit processing and exportation.
See also: Afghanistan.

Qatar

Capital:	Doha
Area:	4,377 sq mi
	(11,337 sq km)
Population:	697,000
Language:	Arabic
Government:	Absolute monarchy
	(emirate)
Independent:	1971
Head of gov.:	Emir
Per capita:	U.S. $11,600
Mon. unit:	1 Rihal = 100 dirham

Qatar, oil-rich emirate in Arabia. It comprises a low limestone peninsula, about 120 mi (193 km) long, that juts north into the Persian Gulf from eastern Saudi Arabia. Its 4,416 sq mi (11,337 sq km) consist of barren desert that receives under 4 in (10 cm) of rainfall a year. The only natural vegetation is scrub. Oil accounts for the majority of exports and government income. Most of Qatar's workers are employed in the oil fields; others are goat and camel herders, fishers, or pearl divers. The merchants and industrial workers live in Doha, the capital, in eastern Qatar. Industry has expanded since 1939, when an oil strike led to the growth of the Dukhan oil field in western Qatar, one of the richest in the Middle East. In 1971 Qatar ceased to be a British protectorate and became a fully independent member of the UN.

Qin dynasty, also Ch'in dynasty, era of totalitarian Chinese rule dating from 221 B.C.-206 B.C. Under the rule of Shi Huangdi, the Chinese regions and regional chiefs were unified into one central empire. The dynasty is noted for advancing national unity and for the building of China's Great Wall. *See also:* Great Wall of China; Shi Huangdi.

Quadhafi, Muammar Muhammad al- *See:* Qadhafi, Muammar Muhammad al-.

Quadrilateral, in geometry, plane 4-sided polygon. Quadrilaterals with 2 pairs of sides parallel are called parallelograms; with one pair of sides parallel, trapezoids; with no 2 sides parallel, trapeziums (the word *trapezium* is often used as a synonym of *trapezoid*). Parallelograms whose sides are all of equal length are termed rhombuses. Each side of a parallelogram is equal in length to the side parallel to it, and each interior angle is equal to the interior angle diametrically opposite it. A parallelogram whose interior angles are each 90° is a rectangle; a special case of this is the square, all of whose sides are equal. The sum of the interior angles of a quadrilateral is always 360°.

Quadruple Alliance, alliance of 4 countries. Historically, the most famous are (1) alliance among Britain, France, Austria, and the Netherlands (1718) to prevent Spain from changing the terms of the Peace of Utrecht (Spain later joined the alliance), (2) alliance among Britain, Austria, Russia, and Prussia (signed 1814, renewed 1815) to defeat Napoleon and, after his defeat and first abdication, to ensure that France abided by the terms of the 1815 Treaty of Paris, and (3) alliance among Britain, France, Portugal, and Spain (1834), supporting Queen Isabella II of Spain.

Quail, name for 2 distinct groups of game birds of the pheasant family. About 45 species of quail exist. Small ground birds of open country, quail are found on every continent except Antarctica. They feed on insects, grain, and shoots and rarely fly, even when disturbed. Quail live in groups called coveys in the fall and winter. The tiny painted quail was carried by Chinese mandarins to warm the hands.

Quaker-ladies *See:* Bluet.

Quakers, or Society of Friends, church known for its pacifism, humanitarianism, and emphasis on inner quiet. Founded in 17th-century England by George Fox, it was persecuted for its rejection of organized churches and any dogmatic creed. Many Quakers emigrated to America, where in spite of early persecution they were prominent among the colonizers. In 1681 William Penn established his "Holy Experiment" in Pennsylvania; from that point the church's main growth took place in America. The early Quakers adopted a distinctive, simple style of dress and speech; simplicity of manner is still a characteristic Quaker Trait. They have no formal creed and no clergy, putting their trust in the "inner light" of God's guidance. Their meetings for worship, held in "meeting houses," follow a traditional pattern of beginning in silence, with no set service and no single speaker. The Quakers have exercised a moral influence disproportionate to their numbers through practicing what they believe, particularly pacifism. In the United States they were prominent abolitionists and have been among the pioneers of social reform. *See also:* Fox, George; Penn, William.

Quanah, or Quanah Parker (1845-1911), North American Comanche chief and leader of a brief uprising against settlers in an effort to end their slaughter of the buffalo in Texas. Quanah was the son of Chief Peta Nokoni and Cynthia Ann Parker, who was captured as a child by the Comanches. Quanah became an advocate of education and agricultural training for members of his tribe, who moved to a reservation (1875) near Fort Sill, Oklahoma.

Quantico Marine Corps Development and Education Command, training center for U.S. Marine Corps officers at Quantico, Va. The Quantico facility houses various schools including the Basic School for Commissioned Officers, The Woman Officer School, the Command and Staff College, and training schools for communications, ordnance, and computer sciences. Quantico also has a U.S. Navy hospital and a Marine air installation. *See also:* Marine Corps, U.S.

Quantrill, William Clarke (1837-65), Confederate guerrilla leader in the U.S. Civil War. A criminal before the war, Quantrill was made a Confederate captain in 1862. In 1863, with a force of 450 men he attacked the town of Lawrence, Kans., and slaughtered 150 civilians. He was killed by Union troops while on a raid in Kentucky. *See also:* Civil War, U.S.

Quantum electrodynamics, or QED, concept in theoretical physics. It concerns the motions and relationships between charged electrical particles including electrons, positrons, and photons and their interaction with electrical and magnetic fields. QED allows highly accurate predictions of changes in the properties of these particles. Physicists Richard P. Faynman and Julian S. Schwinger of the United States and Sin-itiro Tomonaga of Japan contributed in the 1940s to the development of QED.
See also: Feynman, Richard Phillips.

Quantum mechanics, fundamental theory of small-scale physical phenomena (such as the motions of electrons within atoms). This theory was developed during the 1920s, when it became clear that the existing laws of classical mechanics and electromagnetic theory were not successfully applicable to such systems. French physicist Louis De Broglie suggested (1924) that particles have a wavelike nature, with a wavelength h/p (h being the Planck constant, and p the particle momentum). This wavelike nature is significant only for particles on the molecular scale or smaller. These ideas were developed by Erwin Schrödinger and others into the branch of quantum mechanics known as wave mechanics. Werner Heisenberg of Germany worked along parallel lines with a theory incorporating only observable quantities, such as energy, using matrix algebra techniques. His uncertainty principle (that a subatomic particle's momentum and position cannot both be accurately known) is fundamental to quantum mechanics, as is Wolfgang Pauli's exclusion principle (that each electron in an atom is in a quantum state shared by no other electron in that atom). Paul Dirac incorporated relativistic ideas into quantum mechanics.
See also: Atom; Physics.

Quantum theory *See:* Quantum mechanics.

Quapaw, North American Plains Indians of the Siouan language group. By the 17th century they had migrated from the Ohio valley to near the mouth of the Arkansas River. They relinquished most of their lands to the United States in 1818.

Quarantine, period during which a person or animal must be kept under observation in isolation from the community after having been in contact with an infectious disease. The duration of quarantine depends on the disease(s) concerned and their maximum length of incubation. The term derives from the period of 40 days that ships had to wait before their crews could disembark at medieval European ports, due to fear of their carrying plague.
See also: Epidemic.

Quark, particle believed by physicists to be the basic subunit of neutrons and protons. The quark theory was first proposed by 2 American physicists, Murray Gell-Mann and George Zweig in 1964. The theory holds that neutrons and protons consist of even simpler particles called quarks. Scientific studies have indicated evidence of quarks since 1971.
See also: Gluon; Hadron.

Quarles, Benjamin Arthur (1904-   ), U.S. historian, teacher and writer of the impact of African-American culture on U.S. history. Quarles was pro-

fessor (1939) and dean (1945-53) at Dillard Univ., and headed the department of history at Morgan State College (1953-74). His writings include
Frederick Douglass (1948), *The Negro in the Civil War* (1953), *The Negro
in the American Revolution* (1961), and *The Negro in the Making of America*
(1964).

Quarrying, excavation, from open-pit mines, of dimension stone (cut stone)
or crushed stone to be used for building projects or ornamentation. The 3
major methods of quarrying are the plug and feather method, by which rock
is loosened by applied pressure; the use of explosives; and channeling with
special machinery.

Quartering Act *See:* Revolutionary War in America.

Quartz, rhombohedral form of silica, usually forming hexagonal prisms,
colorless when pure. A common mineral (SiO_2), it is the chief constituent of
sand, sandstone, quartzite, and flint and an essential constituent of high-silica
igneous rocks, such as granite, rhyolite, and pegmatite. It also occurs as the
gems chalcedony, agate, jasper, and onyx. Quartz is piezoelectric and is used
to make oscillators for clocks, radio, and radar and to make windows for
optical instruments. Crude quartz is used to make glass, glazes, and abrasives,
and as a flux.

Quartzite, hard metamorphic rock composed of and cemented by recrystal-
lized quartz grains. The fracturing of quartzite takes place through the grains,
rather than between them, due to the extreme strength of the bonding.

Quasar, or quasi-stellar object, a starlike celestial object whose spectrum
seen telescopically shows an abnormally large red shift. Quasars may be
extremely distant objects—perhaps the inexplicably bright cores of galaxies
near the limits of the known universe—receding from Earth at high velocities
(which would account for the red shift). Quasars also show variability in light
and radio emission. (Although the first quasars were discovered by radio
astronomy, not all are radio sources. These phenomena might indicate that
quasars are comparatively small objects comparatively close to us (large and
more distant objects being unlikely to vary in this way). There are about 200
quasars in each square degree of the sky.
See also: Astronomy; Red shift.

Quasimodo, Salvatore (1901-68), Italian poet and translator of poetry
awarded the 1959 Nobel Prize for literature. During and after World War II
he turned (originally because of his opposition to fascism) from a complex,
introverted, "hermetic" style to social protest and examination of the plight
of the individual, as in *Day after Day* (1947). His first poems were collected
in *Waters and Lands* (1930).

Quaternary Period, period in geologic time, of the Cenozoic era whose
beginning is marked by the advent of humans. It has lasted about 4 million
years, up to and including the present.

Quayle, Dan (James Danforth Quayle; (1947-   ), U.S. vice president
(1989-93) with George Bush. Quayle served as U.S. senator from Indiana

(1981-89), following two terms in the House of Representatives (1976, 1978). Quayle and Senator Edward M. Kennedy of Massachusetts developed (1982) the Job Training Partnership Act .

Quebec, largest province in Canada, second-largest in terms of population. Its capital is Quebec City, one of the oldest cities in North America. About 80% of the people of Quebec are of French descent and speak French. Montreal, on the St. Lawrence River, is the second-largest French-speaking city in the world.

Land and climate. The enormous land area of Quebec can be divided into 3 well-defined regions: the Canadian Shield, the St. Lawrence Lowlands, and the Appalachian Uplands. Over 90% of the area of Quebec lies within the Canadian Shield, a rocky plateau filled with uninhabited forests, lakes, and streams. The St. Lawrence Lowlands, including the St. Lawrence River Valley, has been smoothed out by glacial action and erosion. The Appalachian Uplands, which lie partly along the New Brunswick border and partly along the U.S. border, is part of the Appalachian Chain, which runs from the Gaspe Peninsula in Quebec as far south as Alabama in the United States. Much of this region has been smoothed out by erosion to form a rolling plateau. The St. Lawrence River, which links the Great Lakes and the Atlantic Ocean, is Quebec's most important river. Numerous rivers in northern Quebec flow west into the Hudson Bay or north into the Ungava Bay. The largest lake in the province is Lake Mistassini in south-central Quebec. More than half the total area of Quebec is forested. Above the 52nd parallel, west of the Ungava Peninsula, is a tundra region. In general, the climate of Quebec is continental, with severe winters and cool to hot, humid summers. In southern Quebec, precipitation averages 35 to 45 in (889 to 1,143 mm) a year, while the Laurentian Mountains receive well over 100 in (2,540 mm) of snow per year, making skiing a popular sport.

People. Most of the population of Quebec is concentrated in a relatively narrow strip of land along the St. Lawrence River and close to the U.S. border. About 85% are urban dwellers. French Canadians, mostly descended from 17th- or 18-century settlers, constitute 80% of the population. Separate radio and television stations and newspapers exists for the French- and English-speaking communities. French was made the official language of education, business, and government by the French Language Charter of 1977. Roman Catholicism dominates the religious life of the province.

Economy. Quebec has vast supplies of raw materials and almost limitless hydroelectric power. Industries include aluminum processing, foodstuffs, textiles, chemicals, and metal products. Montreal and Quebec City are the leading manufacturing centers; ships, aircraft, and railway rolling stock are the chief products. The principal mineral products are iron ore, asbestos, and copper. Dairying is the most important branch of agriculture, and Quebec's forestry industry accounts for nearly half of Canada's wood and paper products. The development of iron ore mines in the northeast has encouraged development of a steel industry. Construction began in 1979 on La Grande Complex, on La Grande River, scheduled to be the world's second-largest hydroelectric plant.

History. The first permanent settlement in Quebec dates from 1608, when the French explorer Samuel de Champlain built a trading post at the site of Quebec City. From then until defeat by the British in the French and Indian War (1754-63), the region was controlled by the French. Since the beginning

of British rule in 1763, Quebec's history has been dominated by its effort to preserve its French identity. Its attempts to maintain its cultural identity led to prolonged conflict with "English" Canada. In 1867 Quebec became a founding province of the Dominion of Canada, and as such was given considerable autonomy. In the 1960s a French separatist movement emerged, and the Canadian government has since made several concessions to French Canadians in the field of education. When the issue of constitutional reform was raised in the early 1980s, Quebec was the focus of the debate on national unity. In 1990, an attempt was made to amend the Canadian constitution in the Meech Lake Accord, which, if approved, would yield greater autonomy and additional rights to Quebec. While the initial discussions for the amendments indicated possible ratification, the Meech Lake Accord eventually failed because a political consesus could not be reached. The failure to reach an accord has further complicated an already complex issue between English-speaking Canadians and Quebec.
See also: Canada.

Quebec (pop. 645,500), capital of Quebec province, situated on the St. Lawrence River. Founded in 1608 by Samuel de Champlain, it is Canada's oldest city. Despite British dominance since 1759, Quebec has remained essentially French, and more than 90% of its citizens claim French ancestry. Today it is a leading manufacturing center and transatlantic port. Industries include shipbuilding, paper milling, food processing, machinery, and textiles.
See also: Quebec.

Quebec, Battle of, most important battle of the French and Indian War, whose outcome transferred control of Canada from France to Britain. French troops under General Louis Joseph de Montcalm were defending Quebec City. On the night of Sept. 12, 1759, British troops under General James Wolfe silently scaled the cliffs west of the city to the Plains of Abraham. After a short, bloody battle the French fled. Both Wolfe and Montcalm were mortally wounded.
See also: French and Indian Wars.

Quebec Act, passed by the British Parliament in 1774, one of the Intolerable Acts that led to the American Revolution. It guaranteed the use of the French civil code and established religious freedom for the Roman Catholic Church in Quebec. It also extended Quebec's boundary to the Ohio and Mississippi rivers.
See also: Intolerable Acts.

Quebec, University of, also Université du Québec, largest Canadian university, founded 1969. The university has 6 campuses, in Chicoutimi, Hull, Montreal, Rimouski, Rouyn, and Trois-Riviéres. All instruction is in French.

Quebec Conference (1864), conference in the city of Quebec that laid the foundations of the Canadian Confederation. Representatives from the British provinces in North America produced a series of 72 resolutions outlining a centralized federal union. This union was desirable in that it promoted better defense and economic growth, and eased friction between French- and English-speaking groups. The Quebec Conference became the basis of the

British North America Act (1867), which created the Dominion of Canada. *See also:* Confederation of Canada.

Quebec separatist movement, various French-Canadian political factions in Quebec, Canada, which demand that French be the sole language of Quebec and that Quebec separate from Canadian rule and become an independent nation. The movement, begun in the early 1960s as the Quiet Revolution, and furthered by legislator René Lévesque and his Parti Québécois, stemmed from anger with British-centered policies, and governmental discrimination against French-speaking peoples. Despite the terrorist tactics of some groups, the separatist movement is growing in popularity. Nevertheless a popular referendum held in 1995 indicated that a majority of the electorate was against separation from Canada.

Quebracho, South American hardwood tree (genus *Schinopsis*) of the cashew family, with a high content of tannin, an extract used to tan leather. The quebracho grows mainly in Paraguay and Argentina. *Quebracho* means *ox-breaker* in Spanish.

Quechua, also Kechua or Quichua, linguistic family belonging to natives of South America. They were once part of the Inca Empire and now live mostly as peasants in the Andean highlands from Colombia to North Chile. Quechua is also the name of the family to which the official language of the Incas belonged; some 28 languages of the family are still spoken.

Queen, female monarch or the wife of a king, with all the powers allowed by the country that she rules. A queen regnant rules in her own right, by virtue of her birth; a consort is the wife of a king; and a dowager queen is the widow of a king. *See also:* Monarchy.

Queen, Ellery, pen-name and fictional hero of American detective writers Frederic Dannay (1905-82) and Manfred B. Lee (1905-72). Their successful *The Roman Hat Mystery* (1929) was followed by over 100 other novels characterized by complexity of plot. *Ellery Queen's Mystery Magazine* was founded in 1941.

Queen Anne's lace *See:* Wild carrot.

Queen Anne's War *See:* French and Indian Wars.

Queens, largest and second most populous of the 5 boroughs that make up the city of New York. Queens is located at the western end of Long Island and is linked to Manhattan by an intricate network of tunnels and bridges crossing the East River. A largely middle-class area of small homes, Queens includes such residential neighborhoods as Forest Hills, Flushing, and Kew Gardens, as well as the industrial and commercial centers of Long Island City and Astoria, directly opposite Manhattan. In the southern part of the borough are a racecourse (Aqueduct), several beaches, and the John F. Kennedy International Airport. Flushing Meadow was the site of the 1939-40 and 1964-65 World's Fairs. Queens was founded by the Dutch in 1635, became part of the British province of New York in 1683, and became part of New York City in 1898.
See also: New York City.

Queensberry rules, basic rules of modern boxing, drawn up in 1865 under the auspices of John Sholto Douglas, 8th Marquess of Queensberry, supplanting London prize-ring rules. Innovations included the use of padded gloves instead of bare fists, a 10-sec count to determine a knockout, and the division of the bout into rounds with intermissions.
See also: Boxing.

Queensland, second largest Australian state, in the northeastern region of Australia, covering 667,000 sq mi (1,727,530 sq km). Tropical and eucalyptus forests in the rugged east contrast with pasture and desert on the vast western plain. It produces sheep, nearly half of Australia's cattle, and such crops as sugarcane, wheat, cotton, and fruit. It has valuable oil and mineral deposits. Founded as a penal colony (1824-43), Queensland became a state of the Commonwealth in 1901.
See also: Australia.

Quemoy, or Chin-men, island group on the Formosa Strait off southeastern China. The islands have a combined area of about 58 sq mi (150 sq km), with 2 large islands and 12 islets. The Quemoy Islands remained a Chinese Nationalist garrison after the communist takeover in 1949.

Querétaro, state in central Mexico, on the Mexican Plateau, 6,119 ft (1,865 m) above sea level. Querétaro covers about 4,420 sq mi (11,450 sq km) of land, which includes mountainous areas, plains, and fertile valleys. Industries include farming and the mining of opals, silver, iron and copper. The Mexican constitution was drafted there (1916-17).
See also: Mexico.

Quesnay, François (1694-1774), French economist and a leader of the physiocrats. Although trained in medicine (he was physician to Louis XV), his fame rests on his essays in political economy, which first began to appear in 1756 in Denis Diderot's *Encyclopédie*, and on his *Economic Table* (1758), which influenced Adam Smith.
See also: Physiocrat.

Quetzal (*Pharomacrus mocinno*), bird in the trogon family. Compared to the cream-colored females, the resplendent quetzal males display long tails—up to 3 ft (91 cm)—and brilliant feathers colored green on their backs, gold on their heads, with deep red on their undersides. The national bird of Guatemala, the quetzal lives in countries of Central and South America as well as in Mexico.

Quetzalcóatl (Nahuatl, "plumed serpent"), ancient Mexican god identified with the morning and evening star. He is said to have ruled the pre-Aztec Toltec empire and to have invented books and the calendar. He represented the forces of good and light; whether he was an historical leader or merely mythological is not certain. The Aztec leader Montezuma II welcomed Hernándo Cortés, believing him to be descended from the god.
See also: Mythology.

Quevedo Villega, Francisco de (1580-1645), Spanish satirist, poet, and prose writer. Master of the *conseptismo* style of terse and arresting intellectual conceits, he is best known for *the Life of a Swindler* (1626), a parody of the picaresque novel, and *Visions* (1627), a bitter, fantastic view of Spanish society.

Quezon City (pop. 1,169,800), Philippine city on Luzon Island, near Manila. Once the capital of the Philippine Islands (1948-76), Quezon City is primarily a residential area. It is the seat of Ateneo de Manila University and the University of the Philippines.
See also: Philippines.

Quezon y Molina, Manuel Luis (1878-1944), Filipino statesman who played a leading role in the Philippine independence movement before becoming the first president of the Philippine Commonwealth (1935). His presidency, continued in exile after Japanese invasion, was marked by efforts to improve conditions for the poor.
See also: Philippines.

Quicksand, sand saturated with water to form a sand-water suspension possessing the characteristics of a liquid. Quicksands may form at river-mouths or on sandflats; they are dangerous because they appear identical to adjacent sand. In fact, the density of the suspension is less than that of the human body, so a person who does not struggle may escape being engulfed.

Quicksilver *See:* Mercury (element).

Quilt, bedcover made from 2 layers of cloth with an inner padding of insulating material. The layers are sewn together with plain or decorative stitching. The top cover of most quilts is made of brightly colored or patterned fabric pieces cut in geometric or fanciful shapes. Some quilts, particularly older ones, are considered folk art.

Quincy (pop. 42,554), westernmost city in Illinois, located on the Mississippi River. The development of meat packing, brewing, grain milling, and manufacturing industries and easy access to river transportation made Quincy a commercial center beginning in the 1850s. The city was the site of the sixth Lincoln-Douglas debate (1858), and is the home of Quincy College.
See also: Illinois.

Quincy (pop. 84,743), city in eastern Massachusetts, the birthplace of Presidents John Adams and John Quincy Adams and an important industrial and shipbuilding center. Situated in Boston Harbor about 8 mi (13 km) south of Boston, Quincy was incorporated in 1888. The Fore River shipyards at Quincy are among the most important in the United States. Other industries include dairy products, gears, riveting machinery, detergents, and television tubes.
See also: Massachusetts.

Quine, Willard Van Orman (1908-), U.S. philosopher and logician. He rejected the long-standing philosophical claims that analytic ("self-evident") statements are fundamentally distinguishable from synthetic (observational) statements and that the concept of synonymy (sameness of meaning) can be exemplified.
See also: Philosophy.

Quinine, alkaloid derived from cinchona bark from South America, long used in treating a variety of ailments (now rarely used). It was preeminent in early treatment of malaria until the 1930s, when atabrine was introduced. Quinine is also a mild analgesic and may prevent cramps and suppress heart rhythm disorders. Its side-effects include vomiting, deafness, vertigo, and vision disturbance.
See also: Cinchona; Malaria.

Quinsy, acute complication of tonsillitis in which abscess formation causes spasm of the adjacent jaw muscles, fever, and severe pain. Incision and drainage of the pus produce rapid relief; antibiotics are helpful; and the tonsils may be removed when the infection diminishes.
See also: Tonsillitis.

Quintana Roo, state in southeastern Mexico on the Yucatán Peninsula, whose capital is Chetumal. The state, covering an area of about 19,387 sq mi (50,212 sq km), is a flat plain covered by dense jungle, with a hot and humid climate. Population is sparse. Quintana Roo became a Mexican territory in 1902 and a state in 1974.
See also: Mexico.

Quintilian (Marcus Fabius Quintilianus; A.D. 35?-95?), Roman rhetoric teacher, whose famous 12-volume *Institutio Oratoria*, covering rhetorical techniques, educational theory, literary criticism, and morality, deeply influenced Renaissance culture.

Quirinal Hill, one of the famous 7 hills of Rome. The hill was named for Quirinus, a mythological deity, and was the habitation of the Sabines. Many temples, gardens, and a public bath were built there.
See also: Sabines.

Quirinus, in Roman mythology, god responsible for the well-being and prosperity of the community. Believed by some to be either Mars in a different bodily form, or the divine incarnation of Romulus, Quirinus lost importance after about 200 B.C.
See also: Mythology.

Quisling, Vidkun Abraham Lauritz (1887-1945), Norwegian fascist leader who assisted the German invasion of Norway (1940) during World War II and was afterward appointed premier of Norway's puppet government (1942-45) by Adolf Hitler. He was executed for treason. His name has come to mean "traitor." He had formed his own political party, the National Union, in 1936, and contacted German Nazi leaders.
See also: World War II.

Quito (pop. 1,100,800), capital and second largest city of Ecuador and oldest capital in South America. It is located just south of the equator at the foot of the Pichincha volcano, at an altitude of 9,350 ft (2,850 m). Seized from the Incas by a Spanish conquistador in 1534, it is famous for its Spanish colonial architecture.
See also: Ecuador.

Quixote, Don *See:* Don Quixote.

Qumran, village on the northwestern shore of the Dead Sea, on the West Bank of Jordan, near the caves where the Dead Sea Scrolls were found (1947). Built by Essenes (130-110 B.C.), it was destroyed by an earthquake (31 B.C.), rebuilt, and destroyed again by the Romans (A.D. 68).

Quoits, game similar to horseshoes in which 2 players alternately attempt to toss a ring (quoit) around a stake (hob or mott). The quoit is metal and has 1 rounded and 1 flat surface and weighs at least 3 lb (1.5kg). The distance between the hobs is 54 ft (16 m). Points are scored by circling or touching the hob. A game is 21 points.

Quorum, minimum number of members who must be present before an organization can legally transact business. This number, or proportion, varies with the constitution or by-laws of the organization concerned; legislative bodies usually cannot pass laws unless a majority of their members is present (but all are not necessarily voting).

Qur'an *See:* Koran.

R

R, 18th letter of the English alphabet, corresponding to the Semitic letter *resh*, meaning "head," and represented by a sign based on an ancient Egyptian picture symbol for a human head. R is *rho* in the Greek alphabet and the 17th letter of the Roman alphabet. The present form of the capital R comes from classical Latin, the small r from Carolingian script.

Ra *See:* Re.

Rabat (pop. 1,472,000), capital city of Morocco, in the north, on the Atlantic Ocean. Dating from the Phoenician civilization, the city was founded in the 12th century and presently is a governmental center. Industries include textile, brick, and cement production.
See also: Morocco.

Rabbi (Hebrew, "my master" or "my teacher"), leader of a Jewish religious congregation with the role of spiritual leader, scholar, teacher, and interpreter of Jewish law. The term originated in Palestine, meaning merely religious teacher, after the return from exile and destruction of the hereditary priest-hood (1st century A.D.).
See also: Judaism.

Rabbit, herbivorous lagomorph (gnawing) mammal (family Leporidae), usually with long ears and a white scut for a tail. Best known is the European rabbit (*Oryctolagus cuniculus*), which lives in discrete social groups in colonial burrows. Territory is defended by all members of the group, and within the group there is distinct dominance ranking. It attains maturity at three months and can breed every month thereafter.

Rabbit fever *See:* Tularemia.

Rabelais, François (1492?-1553), French monk, doctor, and humanist author. With his *Gargantua and Pantagruel* (five books, 1532-62), an exuberant mixture of popular anecdote, bawdiness, and erudition, Rabelais created a comic masterpiece that is also an important social vehicle for exploring the important issues of society: education, law, philosophy, and religion. It is considered one of the great masterpieces of world literature. *See also:* Humanism.

Rabi, Isidor Isaac (1898-1988), U.S. physicist whose discovery of new ways of measuring the magnetic properties of atoms and molecules paved the way for the development of the maser and the atomic clock. His work earned him the 1944 Nobel Prize in physics.
See also: Maser; Physics.

Rabies, or hydrophobia, acute infectious disease of mammals, characterized by irritation of the central nervous system, followed by paralysis and death. The cause is a virus often present in the saliva of rabid animals. These animals transmit the infection by biting animals or humans. In humans, the incubation period varies from 10 days to over a year. The disease commonly begins with a short period of mental depression, restlessness, malaise, and fever. Restlessness increases to uncontrollable excitement, with excessive salivation and painful spasms of the laryngeal and pharyngeal muscles. As a result, the person cannot drink (hence hydrophobia: fear of water). Rabies rarely occurs in humans if proper treatment (vaccination) is carried out immediately after exposure.
See also: Pasteur, Louis.

Rabin, Yitzhak (1922-95), late prime minister of Israel (1974-77, 1992-95) and Israeli military leader. Rabin, after distinguished service in and after World War II, commanded Israel's defense forces from 1964-67, including the Six-Day War. He served as ambassador to the United States (1968-73), as minister of labor (1974), and as minister of defense (1984-90). During his second office as premier he successfully negotiated with the PLO on peace measures in the occupied territories. For their efforts Arafat, Peres, and Rabin won the Nobel Peace Prize in 1994. Rabin was killed in 1995 by an extreme right-wing Israeli.
See also: Israel.

Rabinowitz, Soloman *See:* Sholem Aleichem.

Raccoon, stout, bearlike, nocturnal mammal (genus *Procyon*), with a distinctive black mask and five to eight black bands on the bushy tail. Raccoons are found in North and South America. They live in trees, alone or in small family groups, descending at night to forage for crayfish, frogs, and fish in shallow pools.

Raceme, type of flower cluster characterized by multiple flowers with separate short stems ranging along a common stalk (or peduncle). Racemous flowers multiply along the main stalk as it grows.

Racer, any of several species (family Colubridae) of swift North American snakes. Racers are broad-headed, varied in color, and measure from 3 1/2 ft (107 cm) to 6 ft (1.8 m) in length.

Races, human, subdivisions of the species *homo sapiens*. The concept of race provides distinctions that are useful in the scientific study of the human species, its dissemination and adaptation to various environments and conditions throughout the world. It can also provide useful clues and insights for historians and cultural anthropologists into a people's development. Like Darwin's theory of evolution, the concept of race has a history outside of science, in social and political thought and mass psychology. Racism is any ideology which assigns superiority to one group of people and inherent inferiority to others on the basis of certain physical characteristics. Both the scientific concept of race and the ideology of racism have histories.

In the West, by late medieval and modern times, all human beings were considered divisible into people of white, black, or yellow skin. A fundamental distinction was observed among humans based upon a leading physical characteristic. By the 19th century, this elementary classification was filled in with more study and research and the three basic races were held to be Caucasoid, Negroid, and Mongoloid. These distinctions were based upon observed physical differences characteristic of each group or race, including skin color, hair, stature, body proportions, skull shape, and facial features. Advances in science have significantly changed the content of the term *race*. It was discovered that the groupings are more than three and the traits that distinguish peoples are more mutable, or changeable, and more subtle than was formerly known. For example, the study of blood types has revealed not only significant differences among Europeans, Asians, and Africans, but within the group that was classified Negroid, there are significant differences among Australian Aborigines, Micronesians, and Negritos of the Philippines.

Most anthropologists now understand races as geographical and local groups and identify nine instead of three. The nine in the current classification are African, American Indian, Asian, Australian, European, Indian, Melanesian, Micronesian, and Polynesian. The geographical groups are defined by major blood types and genetic groups whereas local races are defined by more restricted gene pools. Examples of local races in Europe are the Basques and Lapps.

Human races develop as a result of evolution and in response to the environment. In addition to the obvious inherited differences, such as melanin or inner eyefolds, modern science has discovered the importance of blood types. In some races, certain blood types are dominant, and certain races are susceptible to particular blood disorders. Africans, for instance, may succumb to sickle cell anemia. But scientists have determined that the same trait in the blood responsible for the anemia also makes Africans relatively immune to malaria, suggesting an inherited trait formed by natural selection and conditioned by a specific environment. Human races are understood as less static and more in flux not only as the result of natural selection, gene mutation, and changes in which genes dominate in a group's gene pool, but also as the result of war, migrations, and intermarriage. Rather than providing any evidence for the notion of superior and inferior groups, scientific study indicates the basis for physical differences among humans and studies the remarkably wide and varied adaptations of a single highly successful species. Ideologies of race, though they claim to be scientific, are not, but they remain potent. Though not unique to the West, ideologies of race have claimed scientific authority in the West beginning with the theories of Joseph Arthur Gobineau in the 19th century and later with Huston Stewart Chamberlain,

the anti-Semitism of Nazis, and theories of the inherent racial inferiority of blacks. At bottom, all these theories of race advance the same propositions: that certain peoples are inherently superior and certain others inherently inferior, and that these qualities of superiority or inferiority are inherited, characteristic of an entire group and each of its individual members, and readily identifiable by certain physical traits. Growing and flourishing side by side with advances in modern science and claiming to be grounded in science, theories of race persist in spite of the fact that there is no scientific basis for their claims.
See also: Racism.

Rachel, in the Old Testament, daughter of Laban, wife of Jacob, and mother of Joseph and Benjamin. Rachel was one of the four Jewish matriarchs.
See also: Bible; Old Testament.

Rachmaninoff, Sergei Vassilievich (1873-1943), Russian composer and virtuoso pianist. After a successful career in Russia he left in 1917, settling in Switzerland (until 1935) and then the United States. His extensive output of piano music, symphonies, songs, and choral music incudes such popular works as *Prelude in C Sharp Minor* (1892) and *Second Piano Concerto* (1901).

Racial segregation *See:* Segregation.

Racine (pop. 84,298), industrial city of southeastern Wisconsin, situated on Lake Michigan at the mouth of the Root River. Founded in 1834, it was a major grainshipping area before the railroads were built, and it is still a depot for the dairy and agricultural products of the outlying farm areas. Racine is one of the leading manufacturing cities in Wisconsin.
See also: Wisconsin.

Racine, Jean (1639-99), French tragic dramatist. After a Jansenist education at Port Royal schools, he surpassed his rival Pierre Corneille with seven tragedies, from *Andromaque* (1667) and *Britannicus* (1669) to *Phèdre* (1677), possibly his masterpiece. His greatness lies in the beauty of his verse, expressing both powerful and subtle emotions, and the creation of tragic suspense in a classically restrained form. Racine's work are the epitome of French classical theater.

Racing, contest of speed in both individual and team competition, popular throughout history. The ancient Greek Olympics (700s B.C.) featured only a foot race. The marathon, a race of 26 mi 385 yds (42.2 km), is a test of both speed and endurance. Among the many types of races, which can involve machine operation or animals, are swimming, skiing, walking, roller skating, motorboat racing, and dog racing.
See also: Automobile racing; Track and field; Horse Racing.

Racism, belief that some races are inherently superior to others. Racism in the early 19th century was an offshoot of nationalism, placing emphasis on the differences among cultures. Also, the study of human types revealed some physical differences among the races. Despite the theories of Carolus Linnaeus and J.F. Blumenbach, that environment rather than heredity

molded intellectual development, many associated culture with race, assuming white superiority. Guided by thinkers like Joseph Arthur Gobineau (1816-82), the concept of "tribal nationalism" began to appear. It was used to justify imperialism, the imposition of colonial status on less technologically accomplished peoples, and finally the concept of the "master race" fostered by the Nazis. Horror at the mass exterminations before and during World War II, together with greater understanding through the social sciences, such as anthropology, discredited racism.
See also: Prejudice; Races, human; Segregation.

Rack, implement of torture made of a wooden structure with rollers at two ends. The rollers were wound, pulling the attached legs and arms of a victim from their joint sockets.

Rackham, Arthur (1867-1939), English artist best known for his fanciful, delicately colored illustrations for children's books, such as *Grimm's Fairy Tales* (1900), *Peter Pan* (1906), and *A Wonder Book* (1922).

Racquetball, fast-paced indoor court game played by 1-4 players with 18-in (45.7-cm) racquets and a hollow rubber ball. Played on a 4-sided handball court, racquetball basically follows the same rules as 4-wall handball.
See also: Handball.

Radar (*ra*dio *d*etection *a*nd *r*anging), system that detects long-range objects and determines their positions by measuring the time taken for radio waves to travel to the objects, be reflected, and return. Radar is used for navigation, air control, fire control, storm detection, in radar astronomy, and for catching speeding drivers. It developed out of experiments in the 1920s that were measuring the distance to the ionosphere by radio pulses. R.A. Watson-Watt showed that the technique could be applied to detecting aircraft, and from 1935 Britain installed a series of radar stations that were a major factor in winning the Battle of Britain in World War II. From 1940 the United Kingdom and the United States collaborated to develop radar. *Continuous-wave radar* transmits continuously and detects the signals received by their instantaneously different frequency. *Pulsed radar* has a highly directional antenna, alternately a transmitter or a receiver. As a transmitter, it scans the area systematically or tracks an object, emitting pulses, typically 400 per second. As a receiver, the antenna amplifies and converts echo pulses to a video signal that is displayed on a cathode-ray tube. The time-lag between transmission and reception is represented by the position of the pulse on the screen. Various display modes are used: commonest is the plan-position indicator (PPI), showing horizontal position in polar coordinates.

Radcliffe, Ann (1764-1823), English novelist remembered for her Gothic novels, notably *The Mysteries of Udolpho* (1794) and *The Italian* (1797).

Radcliffe-Brown, A(lfred) R(eginald) (1881-1955), British anthropologist and author of studies of kinship and social organization. His *Andaman Islanders* (1922; rev. 1948) was a pioneering work.
See also: Anthropology.

Radcliffe College, private liberal arts college affiliated with Harvard University, in Cambridge, Mass. Established in 1879 for women undergraduate students, Radcliffe maintains its own board of trustees while sharing faculty and facilities with Harvard.

Radian, in geometry, metric unit for measuring angles, used to simplify calculations. The radian measure of an angle is the ratio a/r; a being the length of the arc intercepted by the given angle; and r being the radius of the circle. An angle of approx. 57.3 (or 360° divided by 2 pi) = 1 radian.
See also: Angles.

Radiant energy *See:* Star; Sun.

Radiation, emission and propagation of energy through space or through a material medium in the form of waves. The term may be extended to include streams of subatomic particles—alpha-rays or beta-rays—and cosmic rays. In the case of electromagnetic radiation (light), energy is transmitted in bundles (photons). Acoustic radiation is made up of sound waves.
See also: Radioactivity.

Radiation belt *See:* Van Allen belts.

Radiation detector *See:* Geiger counter.

Radiation sickness, malaise, nausea, loss of appetite, and vomiting occurring several hours after exposure to ionizing radiation in large doses. This occurs as an industrial or a war hazard or more commonly following radiation therapy for cancer, lymphoma, or leukemia. Large doses of radiation may cause bone marrow depression, or gastrointestinal disturbance. Skin erythema and ulceration, lung fibrosis, nephritis, and premature arteriosclerosis may follow radiation, and there is a risk of malignancy.
See also: Fallout.

Radiator, device in which steam or hot water circulates and gives off heat. Through a process called convection, hot air expands and rises as surrounding cooler air is drawn in. This constant circulation of air can take place within the radiator tubing in convector radiators; radiators also heat air via direct radiation. Radiators are found in homes, offices and stores, as well as in automobiles and other engine-powered vehicles.

Radical, atom or group of atoms having an unpaired electron. Most radicals combine with other atoms to form compounds or ions, although free radicals, those remaining unbound to others, may exist briefly.
See also: Atom.

Radicalism, political philosophy whose purpose is to root out economic, political, and social injustices. Radicals may support different causes in different societies at different times. An English radical reform movement in the 18th to 19th centuries called Radicalism or Utilitarianism supported suffrage and greater democracy. In the 20th century, prodemocracy movements in Communist countries and procommunist movements under non-communist governments are referred to as groups based on radicalism.

Official radical political parties exist in some countries, but not the United States.

Radical Republican *See:* Reconstruction.

Radio, communication of information between distant points using electromagnetic radiation (radio waves). Radio waves are often described in terms of their frequency, which is measured in hertz (Hz) and found by dividing the velocity of the waves by their wavelength. Radio communications systems link transmitting stations with receiving stations. In a transmitting station a piezoelectric oscillator generates a steady radio-frequency (RF) "carrier" wave, which is amplified and "modulated" with a signal carrying the information to be communicated. The simplest method of modulation is to pulse (switch on and off) the carrier with a signal in, for example, Morse code. Speech and music enter the modulator as an audiofrequency (AF) signal from tape or a microphone, and can also interact with the carrier. The modulated RF signal is then amplified to a high power and radiated from an antenna. At the receiving station, another antenna picks up a minute fraction of the energy radiated from the transmitter, together with some background noise. This RF signal is amplified, and the original audio signal is recovered (demodulation, or detection). In point-to-point radio communications most stations can both transmit and receive messages, but in radio broadcasting a central transmitter broadcasts program sequences to a multitude of individual receivers. Because there are potentially so many users of radio communications, use of the RF portion of the electromagnetic spectrum is strictly controlled to prevent unwanted interference between signals having adjacent carrier frequencies. The International Telecommunication Union (ITU) and national agencies like the U.S. Federal Communications Commission (FCC) divide the RF spectrum into banks that they allocate to the various users.

Radio, amateur, hobby practiced throughout the world by enthusiasts ("hams") who communicate with one another on short-wave radio, by voice "phone," or by using international Morse code. In the United States, the various grades of license may be obtained by passing tests of progressively greater difficulty. Citizens' Band (CB) radio, a more informal kind of "ham" radio, became popular in the United States in the late 1970s, with a vast network of amateur radio operators.

Radioactive fallout *See:* Fallout.

Radioactivity, spontaneous disintegration of unstable atomic nuclei, accompanied by the emission of alpha particles (weakly penetrating helium nuclei), beta rays (more penetrating streams of electrons), or gamma rays (electromagnetic radiation capable of penetrating up to 4 in/100 mm of lead). In 1896, Antoine Becquerel noticed the spontaneous emission of energy from uranium compounds (particularly pitchblende). The intensity of the effect depended on the amount of uranium present, suggesting that it involved individual atoms. The Curies discovered further radioactive substances such as thorium and radium; about 40 natural radioactive substances are now known. Their rates of decay are unaffected by chemical changes, pressure, temperature, or electromagnetic fields, and each nuclide (nucleus of a particular isotope) has a characteristic decay constant, or half-life (amount

of time for half of a substance to decay). Rutherford and F. Soddy suggested in 1902 that a radioactive nuclide decays to a further radioactive nuclide, a series of transformations that ends with the formation of a stable "daughter" nucleus. A large number of induced radioactive nuclides have been formed by nuclear reactions taking place in accelerators or nuclear reactors.
See also: Radiation.

Radiocarbon, or Carbon 14, naturally occurring radioactive isotope of carbon. With an atomic weight of 14, it is heavier than ordinary carbon, which has an atomic weight of 12. Radiocarbon is produced when cosmic rays disturb nitrogen atoms in the upper atmosphere, causing them to gain a neutron and lose a proton. Radiocarbon, found in 1.1% of CO_2 (carbon dioxide) molecules, is absorbed by plants in CO_2 gas and passed on to animals and humans. Radiocarbon dating, developed in the 1940s by U.S. chemist Willard F. Libby, can calculate the age of organic matter to about 50,000 years, by comparing its remaining amount of radiocarbon to that in a contemporary radiocarbon sample. Radiocarbon breaks down by releasing particles over a period measured by the half-life (the time it takes half the isotope to decay)—5,700 years. Counting radiocarbon involves burning a portion of it to release the CO_2 gas; today a particle accelerator and a magnetic field are used to separate out the carbon 14 atoms. Artificially produced radiocarbon is used medically as a "tracer" to study biological functions. The artificial isotope was first produced (1939) in the United States by chemists Martin D. Kamen and S. Ruben.

Radiochemistry, use of radioisotopes in chemistry, especially in studies involving chemical analysis. Tracer techniques, in which a particular atom in a molecule is "labeled" by replacement with a radioisotope, are used to study reaction rates and mechanisms.

Radio Free Europe/Radio Liberty(RFE/RL), radio broadcasting networks based in Munich, Germany. It was originated in 1950 to broadcast political, social, and cultural information to people in Communist nations of Central Europe. Privately owned and run, it is supported by the U.S. government.

Radiogeology, branch of geology in which scientists measure radioactive elements in rocks, fossils, and other geological specimens to determine their age. The measurement that enables this determination is called half-life—the time it takes one-half of the atoms of a radioactive isotope to decompose and form a different isotope. Radioactivity, found in all living things, is caused by uranium and thorium and their decay products: radioactive potassium, samarium and rubidium, and raciocarbon.

Radioisotope *See:* Isotope; Radioactivity; Radiochemistry.

Radiology, in medicine, diagnosis and treatment through the use of radioactivity, gamma rays, and X-rays.

Radiosonde, meteorological instrument package attached to a small balloon capable of reaching the earth's upper atmosphere. The instruments measure the temperature, pressure, and humidity of the atmosphere at various altitudes, the data being relayed back to earth via a radio transmitter.

Radio telescope, basic instrument of radio astronomy. The receiving part of the equipment consists of a large dish that operates on the same principle as the parabolic mirror of a reflecting telescope. The signals that it receives are amplified and examined. It is possible to build radio telescopes far larger than any possible dish by using several connected dishes; this is known as an array.
See also: Jansky, Karl Guthe; Lovell, Sir Bernard.

Radio waves *See:* Electromagnetic waves; Radio.

Radish, herb (*Raphanus sativus*), relative of mustard whose edible root looks like a small white to red turnip and has a burning flavor. A native of Europe, it was introduced as a garden plant but has become a weed. Radishes are eaten raw but the related *horseradish*, not a true radish, is ground up and served as a condiment.

Radisson, Pierre Esprit (1636?-1710), French fur trader who worked for both French and British in the exploration of parts of present-day Minnesota and Wisconsin. His reports of the wealth of furs obtainable prompted the creation of the Hudson's Bay Company.
See also: Hudson's Bay Company.

Radium, chemical element, symbol Ra; for physical constants see Periodic Table. Radium was discovered by Pierre and Marie Curie in 1898. It occurs in the minerals carnotite, uraninite, and pitchblende. Radium is produced by electrolysis of its chloride. Radium is a brilliant, white, radioactive, reactive metal. It is decomposed by water and turns black in air. It is a member of the alkaline-earth metals. Its salts color a flame carmine red. Radium is radioactive and emits alpha, beta, and gamma rays. The curie (Ci), a unit of radioactivity, is defined as the amount of radioactivity that has the same disintegration rate as 1 g of radium-226 (3.7×10^{10} disintegrations/second). Radium and its compounds are used in medicine, neutron sources, and self-luminous paints. Radium is a source of the element radon.

Radon, chemical element, symbol Rn; for physical constants see Periodic Table. Radon was discovered by Friedrich E. Dorn in 1900. Radon is present in the air to the extent of one part in 10^{21} and occurs in some spring waters, such as those at Hot Springs, Ark. Radon is a colorless, odorless, and chemically inert gas. It is a radioactive byproduct of the alpha-decay of radium, thorium, and actinium and is a member of the noble, or inert gases. It is the heaviest known gas. It has been reported that fluorine reacts with radon to form radon fluoride. Radon is a radiation hazard, and remedial action is recommended for homes where the activity is greater than 4 picocuries/liter.

Raeburn, Sir Henry (1756-1823), Scottish painter. He was a lesser known portraitist than his famous English contemporary, Sir Joshua Reynolds. He painted directly on canvas with strong brush strokes and without the assistance of preliminary sketch marks. These portraits, mostly of well-to-do Scots, also were painted so that light and color produced dramatic effects.

Raffia, Asian palm (*Raphia ruffia*) whose long, tough leaf fibers are used for making baskets and tying up plants.

Raffles, Sir Stamford (1781-1826), British colonial administrator who re-founded the ruined city of Singapore (1819). He persuaded the British government to seize Java, which he governed from 1811 to 1815. His career was marked by his liberalism, especially in his opposition to slavery.
See also: Singapore.

Rafflesia, genus of parasitic Indonesian plants with the largest flower in the world, up to 1 yd (0.9 m) across. The flower lacks petals but bears broad fleshy sepals. It smells of decaying meat, which attracts flies to pollinate it. It is named for Sir Thomas Raffles, the founder of Singapore.

Raft, simple platform, usually square or rectangular, that floats on water. One of the earliest forms of water travel, rafts originally were made from logs, reeds, or animals skins tied with vines. Today they are often constructed from synthetic materials that are inflated for buoyancy. Rafts travel on water currents, often aided by the use of poles, paddles or sails; they have been used as a means to cross wide rivers, such as the Mississippi. Adventurers, including Thor Heyerdahl of Norway (1947) and William Willis of the United States (1963-64) have successfully crossed oceans on simple rafts.

Rafting, water recreation that gained popularity in the 1960s. On inflatable rafts, usually 12-16 ft (3.7-5 m) long, people travel the rapid currents, or white water, of rivers. A 6-person crew guides the raft with paddles as the passengers enjoy the ride and scenery. The Colorado River, where it cuts through the Grand Canyon, is among the most popular rafting sites in the United States.

Ragtime, style of piano playing in which the left hand provides harmony and a firm beat, while the right hand plays the melody, usually syncopated. Famous exponents of the style, which was the immediate predecessor of jazz, are Scott Joplin and Jelly-Roll Morton.
See also: Jazz.

Ragweed, or hogweed, composite weedy herb (genus *Ambrosia*) with inconspicuous flower heads. The giant ragweed, or buffaloweed, grows up to 18 ft (5.5 m) high. Ragweed pollen is an important cause of hay fever. Some ragweeds have tiny seeds, others have spiny burs that catch in hair and clothing.

Rail, family of marsh birds, including gallinules, coots or mud hens, and rails proper. Protected by their camouflage coloring, rails eat seeds, grasses, worms, and insects. These extremely slender birds are often classified by their long or cone-shaped short bills. They lay their eggs in nests built on the ground or among grass in or near a marsh. Types of rails, found throughout the world, include the water rail, land rail (corncrake), king rail, black rail, yellow rail, VIrginia rail, sora rail, and clapper rail.

Railroad, land transportation system in which cars with flanged steel wheels run on tracks of two parallel steel rails. Railroads are economical in their use of energy because the rolling friction of wheel on rail is very low; however, costs of maintenance are high, so high traffic volume is needed. Costs, rising competition and overmanning led to the closure of many minor lines in the

United States and Europe. Maintenance, signaling, and many other functions are now highly automated.

Railroads developed out of the small mining tracks or tramways built in the United Kingdom and Europe from the mid-16th century. They used gravity or horse power, and the cars generally ran on flanged rails or plateways. The first public freight railroad was the Surrey Iron Railway (1801). The modern era of mechanized traction began with Richard Trevithick's steam locomotive *New Castle* (1804). The first public railroad to use locomotives and to carry passengers was the English Stockton and Darlington Railway (1825). The boom began when the Liverpool and Manchester Railway opened in 1830 using George Stephenson's *Rocket*, a much superior and more reliable locomotive. In the 1880s track gauges were standardized at 4 ft 8 1/2 in (1.435 m), allowing various lines to use one another's rails. After ever-increasing development in the 2nd half of the 19th century, railroads began to decline in the 1920s because of competition from other forms of transportation, such as air travel, trucking, and passenger cars. The sharp increases in oil prices in the early 1970s appeared to give railroads a new lease on life; however, railroads were limited mostly to commuter lines, rather than to hauling freight. In the United States the national Amtrak system survived with the aid of federal subsidies.

Railroad, electric *See:* Electric railroad.

Railroad, model, hobby in which a miniature railroad system is developed. The model railroader, who often uses kits with to-scale (size proportionate to the original) parts, assembles and then operates the cars, tracks, signals, bridges, and other railroad equipment. Miniature towns accompanied by scenery are also developed. Carpentry, electrical skills, and imagination are involved in building and operating a model railroad. Demand for manufactured model railroad products in the United States arose after model railroads were exhibited at the Century of Progress Exposition in Chicago (1933-34). The National Model Railroad Association was formed (1935) to create standards for model railroad materials.

Railway brotherhoods, unions for railroad workers in the United States and Canada. Because railway work—originally viewed as dangerous— was uninsured, these unions formed (1863) to insure workers. The unions generally operated through collective bargaining rather than strikes, since the railroads were strictly controlled by the government. By the 1950s the unions in this brotherhood joined the American Federation of Labor and Congress of Industrial Oranizations. By 1969 the four unions of the Railway brotherhoods merged to form the United Transportation Union.

Railway Labor Act, legislation passed by the U.S. Congress (1926) to settle labor disputes in the railway and later the airline industries. This act was created to avoid strikes by the well-organized railroad unions that might jeopardize the national economy. A 60-day period after a fact-finding board is appointed is required before a strike may commence; employees may reject the board's recommendations and strike after 60 days. The federal National Mediation Board and the National Railroad Adjustment Board administer the Railway Labor Act.

See also: National Mediation Board.

Rain, water drops falling through the atmosphere, the liquid form of precipitation. Raindrops range in size up to 0.16 in (4 mm) in diameter; if they are smaller than 0.02 in (0.5 mm), the rain is called *drizzle*. The quantity of rainfall is measured by a *rain gauge*, an open-top vessel that collects the rain, calibrated in inches or millimeters and so giving a reading independent of the area on which the rain falls. Light rain is less than 0.1 in (2.5 mm) hr, moderate rain up to 0.3 in (7.6 mm) hr, and heavy rain more than 0.3 in/hr. Rain may result from the melting of falling snow or hail, but it is commonly formed by direct condensation. When a parcel of warm air rises, it expands, almost without loss of heat; thus its relative humidity rises until reaching saturation, water vapor begins to condense as droplets, forming clouds. These droplets coalesce into raindrops chiefly through turbulence and nucleation by ice particles (and also cloud seeding). Moist air may be lifted by convection, producing *convective rainfall*; by forced ascent of air as it crosses a mountain range, producing *orographic rainfall*; and by the force within cyclones, producing *cyclonic rainfall*.

Rainbow, arch of concentric spectrally-colored rings seen in the sky by an observer looking at rain, mist, or spray with his or her back to the sun. The colors are produced by sunlight's being refracted and internally reflected by spherical droplets of water. The primary rainbow, with red on the outside and violet inside, results from one total internal reflection. Sometimes a dimmer secondary rainbow with reversed colors is seen, arising from a second total internal reflection.

Rainbow Bridge National Monument, largest and one of the most perfectly arched natural bridges in the world, situated slightly north of the Arizona-Utah border in Utah's Escalante Desert. Its 278-ft (85-m) span arches 309 ft (94 m) above a deep gorge. It was made a national monument in 1916.

Rain dance, ritual Native American dance ceremony performed to induce rain. These various ceremonial dances are performed by different tribes (mainly the Pueblos) during the planting and growing seasons, to help provide rainfall necessary for good harvests. The dances are directed at spirits that control natural phenomenon.

Rain forest *See:* Tropical rain forest.

Rain gauge, instrument that measures accumulated rainfall in a specific location during a particular period. The open vessel is calibrated to measure linear units. These devices vary in type: some collect the water in an inner tube marked with measurements, some empty and simultaneously record the amount of collected rainwater, some collect and weigh falling rain. Computer analysis is used to calculate the amount of rainfall.

Rainier III (Rainier Louis Henri Maxence Bertrand de Grimaldi; 1923-), prince of Monaco since 1949. He married the U.S. actress Grace Kelly (1929-82) in 1956.
See also: Monaco.

Rainmaking, method by which cloud precipitation is increased. Modern techniques of cloud seeding create conditions within clouds in which crystals, or water drops, become heavy and large enough to fall to earth as rain. Generators or airplanes inject the bottoms of clouds with substances called seeding agents—such as ammonium nitrate and urea, silver iodide crystals, or dry ice—to begin this crystalmaking process. Rainmaking can increase an area's water supply or reduce the intensity of an approach storm.

Rain tree, or monkeypod tree (*Pithecellobium saman*), shade tree found in tropical climates of the Americas. This short tree has branches that may span 100 ft (30 m) or more. Monkeys often eat its black seed pods. The rain tree has pink to white flowers, as well as a transparent fluid—rainlike in appearance—that drips from its branches.

Rainy Lake, island-studded lake on the U.S.-Canadian border, between Minnesota and Ontario, located 125 mi (201 km) north of Duluth. It covers 350 sq mi (906.5 sq km) and forms a 56 mi (90 km) long and 5 mi(8 km) wide area flanked by rocky, pine-covered, and deeply serrated shores. It drains into the Lake of the Woods by way of the Rainy River.

Raisin, dried grape. Ripe grapes that are 20% sugar by weight are picked and then laid out in the sun to dry for 10-14 days on brown paper. Machines help stem, grade, rinse, and package the raisins. Raisins are mainly produced in California, Australia, Greece, Iran, and Turkey. A delicacy since ancient times, raisins are noted for their natural sugar content and various vitamins and minerals. Requiring no preservatives, they are eaten as is or used in cooking or baking. Thompson Seedless grapes are most commonly used; other types are Muscat of Alexandria, Black Corinth, and Sultana.

Raja, or Rajah (from Sanskrit *rjan*, "king"), Indian or Malay prince (extended to other men of rank during British rule). Higher-ranking princes were called *maharajas* (or *maharajahs*). A *raja's* wife is a *rani*.

Rajputs (Sanskrit, "kings' sons"), military and landowning caste mostly of the Rajasthan (now Rajputana) region, India. Their origins date back nearly 1,500 years. Although their influence in northern and central India has waxed and waned and at times has been considerable, since India's independence (1947) it has steadily declined.

Rake, tool with large teeth that gathers hay or leaves. As part of a tractor system, modern rakes gather large amounts of cut hay and place them in piles called windrows. Hand rakes with long handles are used to collect smaller amounts of material, usually lawn leaves. Rakes may also be used to break up top soil.

Rákóczy, Francis II (1676-1735), prince of Transylvania who led a Hungarian rising against the Habsburg Empire. Initially successful, he was elected prince (1704), but after several crushing defeats he left the country (1711) and died in exile in Turkey.
See also: Transylvania.

Raleigh (pop. 150,255), capital of North Carolina and seat of Wake County. Named for the English colonizer, Sir Walter Raleigh, it was incorporated as the state capital in 1792. The city supports a variety of light industry,

including the manufacture of chemicals, electronics, textiles, processed foods, and building products. It also serves as the marketing and distribution center for the surrounding agricultural region. Raleigh is the home of North Carolina State University, St. Augustine's College, Meredith College, and Shaw University. North Carolina Museum of Art was opened at Raleigh in 1955.
See also: North Carolina.

Raleigh, or **Ralegh, Sir Walter** (1554?-1618), English adventurer and poet, a favorite of Queen Elizabeth I. His efforts to organize colonization of the New World resulted in the tragedy of the Lost Colony of Roanoke Island, Va. In 1589 he left court and consolidated his friendship with Sir Edmund Spenser, whose *Faerie Queene* was written partly under Raleigh's patronage. Returning, he distinguished himself in raids at Cadiz (1596) and the Azores (1597). James I imprisoned him for treason in the Tower of London (1603-16), where he wrote poetry and his uncompleted *History of the World*. After two years' freedom, during which he made an unsuccessful expedition to the Orinoco River, he was executed in England under the original treason charge.

Ram *See:* Battering ram; Sheep.

Ramakrishna Paramahansa (1836-86), Indian saint whose teachings, now carried all over the world by the Ramakrishna Mission (founded in Calcutta in 1897), emphasize the unity of all religions and place equal value on social service, worship, and meditation.

Raman, Sir Chandrasekhara Venkata (1888-1970), Indian physicist awarded the 1930 Nobel Prize in physics for his discovery of the *Raman effect*: When molecules are exposed to a beam of infrared radiation, light scattered by the molecules contains frequencies that differ from that of the beam by amounts characteristic of the molecules. This is the basis for Raman spectroscopy.
See also: Physics.

Ramapithecus, prehistoric ape. Its remains were discovered in Pakistan (1932) by the U.S. anthropologist George E. Lewis. Named after a mythological Indian prince, Ramapithecus lived approximately 8 to 14 million years ago. Its remains have also been found in China, Kenya, Greece, and Hungary. In the late 1970s, scientists came to believe that Ramapithecus is most likely related to the orangutan rather than being a hominid, of the human family.
See also: Prehistoric people.

Ramayana, major Hindu epic poem, composed in Sanskrit in about the 3rd century B.C., concerning the war waged by the legendary hero Rama against Ravana, the demon-king of Lanka. Helped by Hanuman, king of the monkeys, Rama eventually rescues his wife, Sita, abducted by Ravana, and slays the demon, enabling the righteous once more to live in peace.

Rameau, Jean Philippe (1683-1764), French composer and one of the founders of modern harmonic theory. He achieved recognition with his *Treatise on Harmony* (1722) and composed some 30 operas, among them *Hippolyte et Aricie* (1733) and *Castor et Pollux* (1737).

Rameses II *See:* Ramses II.

Ramie (*Boehmeria nivea*), perennial plant of the nettle family, grown for its fiber. Native to Asia, it is now also grown in Florida. Stalks grow from 3-7 ft (1-2 m) high and produce large leaves. When the plants are mature, the fiber is stripped from the stalks, washed to remove impurities, and dried. Ramie is one of the oldest sources of fiber and is ideal for the manufacture of canvas, ropes, and nets because its strength increases when it is wet.

Ramp, or wild leek (*Allium tricoccum*), wild plant considered a member of either the amaryllis or lily family. The ramp, which smells and tastes like onion, grows in great abundance in the Midwest United States. The leaves appear in early spring, after which green-to-white tiny flowers appear.

Rampal, Jean-Pierre (1922-), French flutist. A virtuoso known for his pure luxuriant tone, he revived interest in the flute as a solo instrument.

Ramsay, Sir William (1852-1916), British chemist awarded the 1904 Nobel Prize in chemistry for his discovery of helium, codiscovery (with Lord Rayleigh) of argon, and codiscovery (with Morris Travers) of krypton, neon, and xenon.
See also: Chemistry; Helium.

Ramses II (c.1304-1237 B.C.), called "the Great," Egyptian pharaoh, 4th king of the 19th dynasty, who built hundreds of temples and monuments, probably including Abu Simbel and the columned hall at Karnak. He campaigned against the Hittites, and celebrated a battle at Kadesh (1300 B.C.) on many of his monuments, but was eventually obliged to make peace (c.1283). His long reign marked a high point in Egyptian prosperity. He may have been the Pharaoh who allowed the Hebrews to leave Egypt, as told in Exodus in the Bible.
See also: Egypt, Ancient.

Ranching, breeding and raising usually of cattle or sheep on large tracts of land; in California also the name for farms smaller than 10 acres. Ranches, called stations in Australia, exist throughout the world. Land boundaries for U.S. ranches in the West were established in the mid 1800s. Cowboys (sometimes cowhands or cowpunchers), brand young animals with the farm insignia, oversee grazing cattle, and round up and lead animals in a cattle drive to market. Sheep ranchers harvest sheered wool from sheep as well as manage the herds. Today, in addition to horses, ranchers use trucks, jeeps, and sometimes helicopters to increase production.

Rand, Ayn (1905-82), U.S. writer. Her "objectivist" philosophy—individualistic, egoistic, and capitalist in inspiration—is at the core of such novels as *The Fountainhead* (1943) and *Atlas Shrugged* (1957). She also wrote nonfiction, including *For the New Intellectual* (1961) and *Capitalism, the Unknown Ideal* (1966).

Randolph, name of a prominent Virginia family. **William Randolph** (1651?-1711) was attorney general for Virginia (1694-98). The post was also held by his son **Sir John Randolph** (1693?-1737) and his grandson **Peyton**

Randolph (1721?-75), who was also president of the 1st Continental Congress. **Edmund Jennings Randolph** (1753-1813), a nephew of Peyton, became attorney general (1776-86) and then governor (1786-88) of Virginia. At the Constitutional Convention (1787) he drafted the Virginia Plan, calling for representation in Congress to be related to state population. He did not sign the Constitution but later urged its ratification. He became the first U.S. attorney general (1789-94) and secretary of state (1794-95). **John Randolph of Roanoke** (1773-1833), great-grandson of William Randolph, entered the U.S. House of Representatives in 1799. A much-feared orator and champion of States' Rights, he led Southern opposition to the Missouri Compromise in 1820. **George Wythe Randolph** (1818-67), great-great-great grandson of William Randolph and grandson of Thomas Jefferson, became Confederate secretary of war in 1862.

Randolph, A(sa) Philip (1889-1979), U.S. African-American labor and civil rights leader. He organized the Brotherhood of Sleeping Car Porters (1925), then an all-black union, and served as its president until 1968. His influence was instrumental in the setting up of the Fair Employment Practices Committee in 1941. He became a vice president of the American Federation of Labor and Congress of Industrial Organizations (AFL-CIO) in 1955. In 1963 he directed the March on Washington for Jobs and Freedom.
See also: Labor movement; Civil rights.

Randolph, Edward (1632?-1703), British colonial agent whose reports led to the Massachusetts charter being revoked in 1684. He was secretary and registrar of the Dominion of New England (1685-9) and in 1691 became surveyor general of customs for North America.

Randolph Air Force Base, center for recruiting, assigning, and training of personnel for the United States Air Force; Air Training Command headquarters. Founded in 1930, this base is located in south central Texas, near the city of San Antonio. It occupies about 3,000 acres (1,200 hectares).
See also: Air Force, U.S.

Range, or stove, appliance that creates heat for cooking and area warming. U.S. cast iron ranges were first produced in the mid-1600s; Europeans developed ranges in the 15th century, while the Chinese invented them in the 8th century. Modern ranges provide individual cooking units on top, and one or more ovens within. They are fueled by gas or electricity; some ovens use microwaves.

Range finder, instrument used to ascertain the distance of an object from the observer. In *coincidence* range finders, used in many cameras, light from a distant object passes through two separate apertures, forming a double image that can be viewed through the eyepiece; a mirror in one aperture can be rotated by a knob until both images coincide exactly, and a calibrated scale on the knob indicates the distance of the object. In the *stereoscopic* range finder, which has mainly military uses, adjustment is made until a stereoscopic image produced by a special optical system coincides with the image of a reference mark; the range may then be read from a calibrated scale.
See also: Radar.

Rangoon *See:* Yangon.

Ranjit Singh (1780-1839), ruler of India who united many Sikhs in a great kingdom. As head of the Sikhs, a religious group of India that lives mainly in the northwest state of Punjab, he began his rule upon his father's death (1792). He conquered neighboring Indian states and overthrew Afghan control, gaining the title "Lion of the Punjab." Through treaties signed with British colonists, Ranjit kept the peace in India, although his efforts to unite all Sikhs were curtailed.
See also: India; Sikhism.

Rank, military, designation of position in the military service. Often called grade when associated with salary level and lower-level personnel, rank also refers to an officer's authority. In the U.S. titles for rank include the President as commander in chief, commissioned officers, and non-commissioned officers, which include warrent officers and enlisted personnel.

Rank, Otto (1884-1939), Austrian psychoanalyst and pupil of Sigmund Freud, best known for his suggestion that the trauma of birth is the basis of later anxiety neurosis and for applying psychoanalysis to artistic creativity.
See also: Psychoanalysis.

Ranke, Leopold von (1795-1886), German historian, one of the founders of modern historical research methodology. Professor of history at Berlin (1834-71), Ranke insisted on objectivity and the importance of original documents.

Rankin, Jeannette (1880-1973), pacifist, feminist, social reformer, and first woman elected to the U.S. Congress. She became Republican Congress-woman at large for Montana in 1917-19 and returned to the House in 1941, when she cast the only vote against entering World War II. In the 1960s she reemerged as a leader of the campaign against the war in Vietnam.

Ransom, John Crowe (1888-1974), U.S. poet and proponent of the New Criticism, which emphasized textual, rather than social or moral, analysis. Professor of poetry at Kenyon College, Ohio (1937-58), he founded and edited the *Kenyon Review* (1939-59). His poetry includes *Chills and Fever* (1924).

Rape, crime of forced sexual intercourse without the consent of the subject, who may be male or female. Statutory rape refers to sexual intercourse with someone who is under the legal age of consent (age 12-16 in the United States), is mentally defective, or does not comprehend the physical or other consequences of the act. In most societies of the world, rape is considered a serious crime. Rape crisis centers offer counseling for rape victims and encourage them to report the crime to the police. Some psychologists hold that rape is an antisocial act that is only peripherally sexual.
See also: Crime.

Rape, flowering plant in the mustard family. Rape is used for animal feed; its seed is used in the production of a cooking oil. This deep green plant, originally from Europe, has jagged leaves and clusters of tiny yellow flowers. The plant may grow up to 3 ft (91 cm) tall and may be an annual or biennial.

Raphael (Raffaello Santi or Sanzio; 1483-1520), Italian High Renaissance painter and architect. He was early influenced by Perugino, as in *Marriage of the Virgin* (1504). In Florence (1504-8) he studied the work of Michelangelo and Leonardo da Vinci, being influenced especially by the latter, and painted his famous Madonnas. From 1508 he decorated the Vatican rooms for Julius II; the library frescoes, masterly portrayals of symbolic themes, use Raphael's new knowledge of classical art. His Sistine Chapel tapestries (1515-16) and his sympathetic portraits were much imitated. Chief architect of the Vatican (from 1514), he worked at rebuilding Saint Peter's Basilica.
See also: Renaissance.

Rapid City (pop. 81,343), second-largest city in South Dakota, situated on Rapid Creek near the Black Hills. It was established when gold was found in the area in the 1870s and grew with later discoveries of uranium and other minerals. Its economy has since diversified to include marketing and processing for local agricultural and lumbering industries and the production of cement. It is the home of the South Dakota School of Mines and Technology, which has a well-known Museum of Geology.
See also: South Dakota.

Rapid Deployment Force, special U.S. military unit trained to act quickly upon command. Called the RDF, the force was founded in 1980 particularly to protect U.S. interests in oil-rich regions of the Middle East. Headquartered in Tampa, Fla., the RDF has ships and personnel stationed on the Diego Garcia Island in the Indian Ocean. The island location helps this force move swiftly when necessary to areas around the globe.

Rappahannock River, river flowing 212 mi (341 km) southeast from the Blue Ridge Mountains of Virginia to Chesapeake Bay. It is joined by its main tributary, the Rapidan, above Fredericksburg near the Salem Church Dam.

Rare earth, name for the elements scandium and yttrium and the lanthanide series, Group IIIB of the Periodic Table, occurring throughout nature as monazite and other ores. They are separated by chromatography and ion-exchange resins. Rare earths are used in alloys, including misch metal, and their compounds (mixed or separately) are used as abrasives, for making glasses and ceramics, as "getters," as catalysts in the petroleum industry, and to make phosphors, lasers, and microwave devices.
See also: Berzelius, Jöns Jakob, Baron.

Rasmussen, Knud Johan Victor (1879-1933), Danish explorer and ethnologist. From Thule, Greenland, he undertook many expeditions to study Eskimo culture, including the longest dog-sled journey known, from Greenland to Alaska (1923-24), described in his *Across Arctic America* (1927).
See also: Eskimo; Ethnography.

Raspberry, fruit-bearing bushes (genus *Rubus*), including some 200 species. European cultivated red-fruited varieties are derived from *B. idaeus*, while

North American varieties, including a number that are black-fruited, are derived from three species.

Rasputin, Grigori Yefimovich (1872-1916), Russian mystic (the "mad monk") who gained influence over the Tsarina Alexandra Fyodorovna after supposedly curing her son's hemophilia in 1905. The scandal of his debaucheries, as well as his interference in political affairs, contributed to the undermining of the imperial government in World War I. He was assassinated by a group of ultraconservatives.

Ras Tafari *See:* Rastafarians; Haile Selassie.

Rastafarians, world-wide religious group founded in Jamaica in the 1920s. Its original members, of African descent, believed that Haile Selassie (Ras Tafari)—who ruled Ethiopia 1916-74—was a messiah who would return all African descendants to the continent of Africa. Reggae music and hair worn in dreadlocks (long ropes of curls) are part of Rastafarian culture.
See also: Haile Selassie.

Rat, name for numerous species of rodents belonging to many different families, largely Muridae and Cricetidae. The brown (*Rattus norvegicus*) and black (*R. rattus*) rats are familiar farmyard and warehouse pests. A strong exploratory urge and an ability to feed on almost anything make them persistent pests; in addition, they transmit a number of serious diseases, such as typhus and plague. Rats native to the New World include wood rats or pack rats, cotton rats, and the rice rats.

Ratchet, toothed wheel that operates with a catch, or *pawl*, so as to rotate in only one direction. Typically, the toothed ratchet wheel is rotated by a handle. The pawl is curved and pivoted so that it rests on or presses against the wheel teeth. When the wheel rotates in the permitted direction, the teeth can move beneath the pawl. As soon as the rotation ceases, the pawl engages one of the wheel teeth and prevents any motion backward. A release mechanism is usually incorporated to disengage the pawl when required. The escapement in clocks and watches is an example of a ratchet.

Ratel, or honey badger, carnivorous nocturnal African mammal (genus *Mellivora*) with distinctive grayish back and black underparts. It has powerful legs and strong claws and eats almost anything, even pythons. Its fondness for honey has led to a close association with the honeyguide, a bird that directs it to bees' nests.

Rate of exchange *See:* Exchange rate.

Rationalism, philosophical doctrine that reality has a logical structure accessible to deductive reasoning and proof. Against empiricism, it holds that reason unsupported by sense experience is a source of knowledge not merely of concepts (as in mathematics and logic) but of the real world. Major rationalists in modern philosophy include Descartes, Spinoza, Leibniz, and Hegel.
See also: Age of Reason.

Rationing, method by which distribution of food and other important products are controlled. Governments usually impose rationing policies in times of large demand and short supply, such as war or severe inflation. Rationing was used in the United States, among other countries, during World War II. Coupons or a point system are allocated to families to obtain rationed products. Rationed products bought outside of the rationing system are considered black market products.

Rattan, stems from any of 200 species of climbing palm of the genus *Calamus*, family Palmaceae. The stems are strong and pliant and are used to make furniture, baskets, canes, rope, and umbrellas. Rattan palms are native to the East Indies and Africa, and some are edible or have medicinal or veterinary uses. The stems may grow to 500 ft (150 m).

Rattlesnake, any of two genera (*Crotalus* and *Sistrurus*) of pit vipers of the Americas, referring to a rattle, composed of successive pieces of sloughed-off dead skin, at the end of the tail. Rattlers have moveable fangs that fold up into the roof of the mouth when not in use and are shed and replaced every three weeks. They are extremely venomous snakes, with the diamondback rattler being the largest and most dangerous.

Ratzel, Friedrich (1844-1904), German geographer. With works such as *Anthropogeography* (1882-91), *Political Geography* (1897), *The History of Mankind* (1896-98), and *Lebensraum* (1901), he strongly influenced later German geopolitics.
See also: Geopolitics.

Rauschenberg, Robert (1925-   ), U.S. artist, an initiator of the Pop Art of the 1960s. His "combines" (collages) use brushwork along with objects from everyday life, such as pop bottles and news photos.

Rauschenbusch, Walter (1861-1918), U.S. Baptist minister, reformer, and theologian. A leader of the Social Gospel movement, he became a national spokesman for social evangelism with his *Christianity and the Social Crisis* (1907).
See also: Baptists.

Rauwolfia serpentina *See:* Reserpine.

Ravel, Maurice (1875-1937), French composer, known for his adventurous harmonic style and the combination of delicacy and power in such orchestral works as *Rhapsodie Espagnole* (1908) and *Bolero* (1928), and the ballets *Daphnis and Chloé* (1912) and *La Valse* (1920). *Gaspard de la Nuit* (1908) is among his many masterpieces for the piano, his favorite instrument.

Raven, largest member of the crow family, with a wedge-shaped tail. The common raven (*Corvus corax*) is found in the United States and in the Old World, where it appears in many European legends as a prophet of doom. Ravens eat many things but are particularly fond of carrion.

Ravenna (pop. 136,100), city in northeastern region of Italy, famous for its superb mosaics, notably in the 5th-century mausoleum of Galla Placidia and 6th-century churches (notably San Vitale and Sant'Apollinare Nuovo). Emperor Honorius made Ravenna his capital; it was seized by Odoacer in

476 and was later seat of the Byzantine exarch. It was given to the Pope in
the 8th century by the Carolingean King Pepin the Short. Papal control was
lost and not regained until the 16th century. Modern Ravenna, an agricultural
and manufacturing center, has a port and petrochemical plants.
See also: Italy.

Rawlings, Marjorie Kinnan (1896-1953), U.S. novelist. With a dramatic
change in lifestyle from urban journalist to Florida back-country resident,
she began to write fiction about life in her new home of Cross Creek. Her
novel *The Yearling* (1939) won the Pulitzer Prize for fiction. Her stories were
collected in *When the Whippoorwill* (1940). *Cross Creek* (1942), a nonfiction
book of essays, humorously describes her life on her Florida farm.

Rawlinson, Sir Henry Creswicke (1810-95), British soldier and archeologist who deciphered the cuneiform inscriptions of King Darius I of Persia.
See also: Archeology.

Ray, any of a group of more than 400 species of flat-bodied marine fish (order
Rajiformes) with a boneless skeleton made from a tough, elastic substance called
cartilage. Rays resemble sharks in having gill slits, but under the pectoral fins.
Most rays live on the sea floor and feed on smaller species. Rays eggs are fertilized
and hatched inside the female. The largest rays are the mantas, which may grow
to 22 ft (7 m) wide and weigh up to 3,000 lbs (1,360 kg).

Ray, John (1627-1705), English naturalist, who, with Francis Willughby
(1635-72), made important contributions to taxonomy, especially in *A General History of Plants* (1686-1704).

Ray, Man (1890-1976), U.S. abstract artist and photographer, a founder of
the Dada movement. He recreated several "lost" photographic techniques
and produced surrealist films.
See also: Dada.

Ray, Satyajit (1921-92), Indian film director. *Pather Panchali* (1954) was
his acclaimed debut. His many other films include *Aparajito* (1956), *The
Music Room* (1958), and *The World of Apu* (1959). He received an Oscar for
his works.

Rayburn, Sam (1882-1961), longest-serving U.S. House of Representatives
speaker (17 years from 1940) and congressman from 1913. A dedicated
Democrat, he helped build New Deal policy.

Rayleigh, John William Strutt, 3rd Baron (1842-1919), English physicist
awarded the 1904 Nobel Prize in physics for his measurements of the density
of the atmosphere and its component gases, work that led to his isolation
(with William Ramsay) of argon.
See also: Atmosphere; Physics.

Raymond, Henry Jarvis (1820-69), co-founder and editor of the *New York
Times* from 1851 who took an active part in forming the Republican Party.
He was in the House of Representatives for one term (1865-67), losing
renomination because of his moderate stand on Reconstruction.

Rayon, synthetic cottonlike fiber with a sheen. Patented in 1884 by the French inventor, Hilaire Chardonnet, it was named rayon in 1924. Rayon is produced from cellulose fiber of wood pulp or cotton. Chemicals reduce the cellulose to a thick liquid, which is forced under pressure into a metal spinneret and emerges as filaments. The filaments are twisted into silky yarn or cut and spun. Spun rayon can be treated to simulate wool, linen, or cotton. The 3 main processes for making rayon are viscose, cuprammonium, and acetate.

Razor, sharp-edged instrument used to shave hair from the skin. Razors in crude forms, such as clam shells and flints, have been used since prehistoric times. They evolved into the 3 basic types in use today. Straight-edged razors (blades 3-4 in (8-10 cm) long encased in a safety handle) and safety razors (hoe-shaped with shorter blades and protected cutting surface) manually remove hair from a lathered surface. Electric razors, powered by motors, move a series of small, sharp blades over unlathered skin. Many electric razors are "cordless," able to operate on batteries.

RCMP *See:* Royal Canadian Mounted Police.

RDX, or Research Department Explosive ($C_3H_6O_6N_6$), powerful explosive used in bombs. Discovered by Hans Henning in Germany (1899), RDX was used extensively by the air forces of both sides in World War II. Known also as hexogen and cyclonite, it is a white, insoluble, crystalline solid. RDX is produced by the action of nitric acid on a product of formaldehyde and ammonia. Its chief nonmilitary use is in blasting caps, detonators, and fuses. RDX can also be mixed with trinitrotoluene (TNT) to form a more powerful explosive known as Composition B.
See also: Explosive.

Re, or Ra, in Egyptian mythology, the sun god. Worshipped as the creator of the entire earth, Re evolved into the chief deity of ancient Egypt. Many myths and legends came to be associated with Re; early pharaohs claimed to be descended from him. Re has appeared in Egyptian hieroglyphics as the sun, lion, cat, or bird, and is symbolized by a pyramid.
See also: Mythology.

Reaction, chemical *See:* Chemical reaction.

Reactor, nuclear *See:* Nuclear reactor.

Read, George (1733-98), American Revolutionary leader. As a representative of Delaware, he signed both the Declaration of Independence and the Constitution, one of only 6 people to do so. After serving as Delaware's attorney general (1763-74) and legislator (1765-77), Read represented the state in the first 2 Continental Congresses (1774-77). At the Constitutional Convention of 1787, he was an outspoken proponent of the rights of smaller states; his efforts helped Delaware become the first state to ratify the Constitution and enter the Union. He served as one of Delaware's first 2 U.S. senators and served (1789-93) until he was named chief justice of the Delaware Supreme Court, a position he held until his death.

Reading, process of assimilating language in the written form. Initial language development in children is largely as speech and has a primarily auditory or phonetic component; the recognition of written letters, words, and sentences represents a transition from the auditory to the visual mode. In reading, vision is linked with the system controlling eye movement, so that the page is scanned in an orderly fashion. Reading is represented in essentially the same areas of the brain as are concerned with speech, and disorders of the two often occur together. In dyslexia, pattern recognition is impaired, and a defect of reading and language development results.

Reading (pop. 336,523), city on the Schuylkill River in southeast Pennsylvania. It is surrounded by rich farmland and the state's famous "Pennsylvania Dutch" colony, but it is best known as a major manufacturing center. The town was laid out in 1748 and named after the Penn family's home city in England. Reading was one of the first places in the United States to manufacture iron products and supplied cannon for the Revolution.
See also: Pennsylvania.

Reagan, Ronald Wilson (1911-   ), 40th president of the United States. Reagan's administration strengthened the U.S. military presence in Europe, increased support for anti-Communist forces in Central America, and signed a nuclear-arms-reduction treaty with the Soviet Union. It also made large cuts in federal income taxes while sharply reducing spending on domestic programs. Although Reagan's two terms brought lower unemployment and a temporarily stronger economy, social programs suffered and the federal budget deficit grew larger than ever in U.S. history.
Early life. Reagan attended Eureka (Ill.) College. After graduating in 1932, he worked as a radio sports announcer in Iowa. In 1937, he began a successful new career as a film actor. In 1940, he married actress Jane Wyman. They had one child and adopted another, but divorced in 1948. During World War II, Reagan served in the Army Air Forces (1942-45), making training films. He then returned to acting and served as president of the Screen Actors Guild (1947-52; 1959). In 1952, he married actress Nancy Davis; they had two children.
Political career. Once a liberal Democrat, Reagan became a conservative Republican. He was elected governor of California in 1966 and reelected in 1970. In 1976, he ran for the Republican presidential nomination, but lost. In 1980, Reagan did get the nomination. He and running mate George H.W.

Ronald Wilson Reagan

40th U.S. president

Born:	Tampico, Ill.; Feb. 6, 1911
Term:	Jan. 1981-Jan. 1989
Vice president:	George H.W. Bush
Political party:	Republican
Spouses:	Jane Wyman;
	Anne Frances (Nancy) Robbins
	Davis Reagan
Children:	4

Bush won a landslide victory over the Democratic incumbents, President Jimmy Carter and Vice President Walter Mondale.

President. Reagan immediately called for tax cuts combined with reductions in social and other domestic programs. Congress passed most of the proposed cuts. The business failures and higher unemployment of a recession, coupled with increased military spending, made the federal budget deficit soar and the economy weaken. Reagan's administration met with rising public criticism, particularly from blacks, women, and environmental groups. By 1984, however, the economy seemed to recover and Reagan and Bush were reelected in another landslide, defeating Democratic candidates Walter Mondale and Geraldine Ferraro. In Reagan's second term, the economy took another beating: a stock-market crash in October 1987.

Reagan faced a number of foreign-relations crises. In 1983, he sent U.S. troops to invade Grenada and to join a multinational peacekeeping force in Lebanon. In Central America, Reagan's administration supported anti-Communist forces in El Salvador and the "contras" opposing Nicaragua's government. Over the course of Reagan's two terms, U.S.-Soviet relations worsened, then slowly improved. Reagan met several times with Mikhail Gorbachev, the Soviet leader, and they signed a nuclear-arms-reduction treaty in 1987.

Dubbed "the Teflon president" for his ability to withstand criticism and scandal, Reagan's popularity remained high throughout his presidency. He survived a 1981 assassination attempt, as well as the Iran-contra affair, a major domestic crisis (1986-87). It was revealed that Reagan's administration had sold weapons to Iran in exchange for the release of hostages held in Lebanon (contradicting Reagan's public statements against dealing with terrorists), then used the money to illegally fund the Nicaraguan contras.

Retirement. When his second term ended in 1989, Reagan retired to California. In 1994 it was made public that Reagan suffers from Alzheimer's disease.

Real estate, term used to describe land and that which is attached to it, including buildings, trees, and underground resources, such as minerals or water. Real estate is generally sold by plots of ground (parcels), which are surveyed, sized, and registered with the particular governing agency for that area. Real estate properties for sale can be listed with agencies and sold by brokers or realtors, but often the owners of the property sell it themselves. The U.S. real estate industry employs about 1.8 million brokers; many more are involved in subsidiary businesses such as construction, financing (mortgage lending), appraising, and property management. In all 50 states, real estate agents must pass tests and be licensed before they can legally sell properties.

See also: Property.

Realism, in art and literature, the faithful imitation of real life; more specifically, the artistic movement which started in France c.1850 in reaction to the idealized representations of romanticism and neoclassicism, with a social dimension derived from scientific progress and the revolutions of 1848. In France the leading painters were Jean-Baptiste Corot, Gustave Courbet, Honoré Daumier, Jean François Millet, and its main literary expression was in the novels of Honoré de Balzac, Gustave Flaubert, and Emile Zola. In the United States, Thomas Eakins, Winslow Homer, and members of the Ashcan

School were realistic painters, and Stephen Crane, Theodore Dreiser, William Dean Howells, Henry James, and Frank Norris led the literary movement.

Reaper, machine for harvesting grain. The U.S. inventor Cyrus Hall McCormick's horse-drawn reaping machine (1831) consisted simply of a long knife, or cutter bar, a platform, and a rotating reel to bend the grain back against the knife and knock it onto the platform. The modern reaper, or self-binder, cuts the standing grain, binds it into sheaves with twine, and then ejects the sheaves onto the ground. Reapers are seldom used today for cutting grain, however; the harvesting of grain is done mostly with combine harvesters, machines that combine reaping and threshing.
See also: McCormick, Cyrus Hall.

Reapportionment *See:* Apportionment, legislative.

Reasoning *See:* Logic.

Rebecca *See:* Isaäc.

Rebellion of 1837-1838, 2 unsuccessful and parallel uprisings against British colonial rule in Canada, prompted by an economic depression and desire for local self-government. A subsequent report by Lord Durham, English governor general in Canada, urged the union of Upper and Lower Canada, which became law with the 1840 Act of Union.
See also: Canada.

Recall *See:* Inititive, referendum, and recall.

Receiver, in law, person, bank, or trust company appointed by a court and paid a fee to take charge of a company or a person's assets, most frequently in cases of bankruptcy. The receiver maintains existing assets in good order, since creditors will ultimately have a claim on them and may also carry on the business, collecting money that is due, paying out salaries, and dealing with suppliers.
See also: Bankruptcy.

Recession, extended period of economic decline. In the United States, a recession is defined as a drop in the gross national product (GNP) over 2 consecutive quarterly periods. During recessions, business activities such as buying, selling, and overall productivity decline, causing increases in unemployment and unpredictable fluctuations in stock markets. Until the 1970s, recessions caused prices to fall, but since then they have continued to increase despite several recessions. A sudden shortage of vital goods, such as oil and petroleum-based products, often triggers recessions and accompanying rising prices, which result in decreased consumer spending. A pattern is formed in which manufacturers decrease production to keep pace with reduced demands for their goods, and fewer workers are needed to produce those goods. Recessions are often worldwide; an extended period of recession could develop into a depression. Short-term recessions are called economic slumps.
See also: Business cycle; Depression.

Recife (pop. 1,340,000), capital of Pernambuco, state in northeastern Brazil. Located at the mouths of the Capibaribe and Berberibe rivers on the Atlantic Ocean, the city was settled by the Portuguese in 1535. The British held it briefly (1595), as did the Dutch (1630-54). In 1710 Recife became a Brazilian town, and in 1823 a city. Part of Recife is on an island; because of many intersecting waterways, is often called the Brazilian Venice. Manufactured goods include textiles, ceramics, synthetic rubber, paper and leather products, and agricultural goods. Its port exports large quantities of bananas, sugar, coffee, and cotton. Recife is an educational center with 4 universities. *See also:* Brazil.

Reciprocal trade agreement, mutual tariff reduction pact enacted between 2 or more nations. Such agreements began in response to the trend toward protectionism that prevailed throughout most of the 19th century, in which steadily increasing tariffs on imported goods hampered international trade. Bilateral trade agreements were worked out in the early 20th century, when 2 nations consented to lower import duties on certain goods they exchanged. Such pacts were later expanded to include other nations. The United States passed the first Reciprocal Trade Agreements Act in 1934; in 1947, 23 countries ratified the General Agreement on Tariffs and Trade (GATT), which reduced tariffs on specified goods by rates believed to be beneficial to all the signatory nations. Today, reciprocal trade agreements are universal, although worldwide economic conditions are continually requiring changes in the nature of these agreements. Industrially developed nations have been encouraging developing countries through modified trade agreements. *See also:* Tariff.

Reclamation, Bureau of, agency of the Department of the Interior created to administer the Reclamation Act of 1902 for reclaiming arid land by irrigation in the 16 western states. Its responsibilities were later progressively expanded.

Reconstruction, period (1865-77) when Americans tried to rebuild a stable Union after the Civil War. The deadlock inherited by President Andrew Johnson on Abraham Lincoln's death, over who should control Reconstruction, hardened with increasing congressional hostility toward restoring the South to its old position. Republicans wanted to press home the Union victory by following the 13th Amendment abolishing slavery (1865) with full civil rights for blacks, including the vote. While Congress was not in session, Johnson implemented Lincoln's policy of lenience by giving amnesty to former Confederates in return for a loyalty oath. He also condoned the Black Codes, which practically reintroduced slavery in another guise. Reconvening (1866) with a landslide victory, however, the Radical Republicans took control. Their first Reconstruction Act of 1867 divided ten southern states into five military areas, with a major general for each. Under army scrutiny, black and white voters were registered, and constitutions and governments were instituted. In 1868 six southern states were readmitted to the Union, followed in 1870 by the other four. By ratifying the 14th Amendment (1868) on black civil rights, Tennessee escaped the military phase. There were no mass arrests, no indictments for treason, and the few Confederate officials jailed were (except for Jefferson Davis) soon released. Apart from slaves, the property of the confederate leaders was untouched, although no help was

given to rescue the ruined economy. On readmission, the southern governments were Republican, supported by enfranchised blacks, Scalawags (white
Republicans), and Carpetbaggers (Northern profiteers). Constructive legislation was passed in every state for public schools, welfare taxation, and
government reform, although the governments were accused of corruption
and incompetence. The Freedmen's Bureau lasted only four years, but it did
help to found Atlanta, Howard, and Fish universities for blacks. Southern
conservatives, hostile to Radical Republican policies, turned to the Democratic Party; terrorist societies like the Ku Klux Klan crusaded against blacks
and radicals. Full citizenship for blacks, though legally assured by the 14th
and 15th (1870) amendments, was denied by intimidation, unfair literacy
tests, and the Poll Tax. The Republican Party, secure in the North, abandoned
the black cause. In 1877 when federal troops withdrew from the South, the
last Republican governments collapsed, and Reconstruction was over.
See also: Civil War, U.S.

Recorder, wind instrument related to the flute but held vertically, with a
mouthpiece that channels the airstream and without keys. Relatively easy to
play, soft and sweet in tone, it was most popular about 1600-1700 and is
again popular today. There are soprano, alto, and (with some keys) tenor and
bass recorders.

Recording industry, group of businesses that produce and sell sound recordings. The industry records primarily popular forms of music, as well as
verbal communication such as speeches and seminars. The industry began
with Thomas Edison's invention of the phonograph (1877), which pushed a
sound-sensitive needle along the grooves of a cylinder to reproduce sound.
The cylinder was replaced by flat disc—the phonograph record—in the early
1900s; this evolved into today's compact disc, which plays recorded sounds
by means of a laser beam. Invention of magnetic recording tape in the 1940s
enabled the development of cassette tapes. In the United States, the industry
employs more than 30,000 people, among them musicians, composers,
arrangers, and engineers. Most recordings today are done in studios.

Record player *See:* Phonograph.

Recreation, leisure activities that people enjoy. Recreation has become an
important aspect of modern life that often relieves stress; many businesses
and hospitals provide various forms of recreation for their workers and
patients. These activities can be passive ones, such as reading or watching
television or movies, or participatory forms ranging from hobbies and games
to strenuous amateur sports. Donation of time by volunteers to help others
is another form of recreation. Commercial recreation includes watching
sporting, cultural, and other entertainment events, or active forms, such as
tourism or visiting theme parks. State, national, and local agencies set aside
scenic or historic lands for public recreational use, usually financed through
taxes and user fees. In the United States, recreation is a multibillion-dollar
business.

Recreational vehicle (RV), temporary living quarters on wheels, used for
traveling or camping. Five basic types of RVs are in use today. Motor homes
contain an engine and living quarters, which have conveniences such as

running water and facilities for cooking, heating, and food-storage. This type includes vans adapted for overnight use. Travel trailers are not motorized and must be pulled by another vehicle, as must campers (camping trailers), which are smaller than these trailers. They have collapsible sides that can fold out to provide extra sleeping or storage space. Truck campers are adapted to fit over the bed and cab of a pickup truck. Pickup covers enclose only the bed of a pickup truck.

Rectangle, 4-sided plane figure with sides that meet at 4 right-angles. Rectangles are classified as special cases of parallelograms, in that the opposite sides are parallel and of equal length, but all 4 sides are not necessarily equal. When they are equal, rectangles are called squares. The word is derived from the Latin *rectus angulus*, meaning *straight angles*.

Rectum *See:* Colon; Intestine.

Recycling, recovery and use of waste material. Paper, aluminum cans, and glass are the most commonly recycled materials and can be used to make insulation, new cans and glass containers, and material for road construction. As concern over the earth's environment increases, recycling has emerged as an effective method for cutting down on pollution and conserving important natural resources. It has also become an increasingly vital source of material for modern industry.

Red Baron *See:* War aces.

Redbreast *See:* Robin.

Redbud, flowering tree (genus *Cercis*) of the pea family, native to North America, southern Europe, and Asia. Redbuds display their pink blossoms in early spring before their heart-shaped leaves unfold. The flowers ripen into seed pods that wild game feed on. The reddish-brown trees grow as high as 40 feet (12 m) and thrive on fertile, sandy soil. Redbuds are sometimes called Judas trees because, according to legend, Judas Iscariot hanged himself from a redbud tree after betraying Jesus.

Red cedar *See:* Juniper.

Red Cloud (1822-1909), chief of the Oglala Sioux and leader of the Native American struggle against the opening of the Bozeman Trail. The trail was closed in 1868 following the Fetterman Massacre (1866).

Red Cross, international agency for the relief of victims of war or disaster. Its two aims are to alleviate suffering and to maintain a rigid neutrality so that it may cross national borders to reach those otherwise unaidable. An international committee founded by J.H. Dunant and four others from Geneva secured 12 nations' signatures to the first of the Geneva Conventions (1864) for the care of the wounded. Aid was given to both sides in the Danish-Prussian War the same year. During World Wars I and II the Red Cross helped prisoners of war, inspecting camps and sending food and clothing parcels; it investigated about 5 million missing persons and distributed $200 million in relief supplies to civilians. The International Red Cross won the Nobel Prize in 1917 and 1944. It works through the International Committee (1880), made up of 25 Swiss citizens. Over 100 national Red Cross societies (Red Crescent in Muslim countries) carry out peacetime relief and public health work.

Red deer (*Cervus elaphus*), member of the deer family, native to Europe, Asia, and North Africa. They are named for the color of their coat, which is reddish-brown in summer, fading to grayish-brown in winter. The American elk is classified as a subspecies of red deer. Male red deer are called harts, standing 3.5-4.5 ft (1.-1.4 m) tall, weighing 250-350 lb (113-159 kg), and sporting multibranched antlers, which are shed each year. Female red deer, called hinds, are smaller than harts and do not have antlers.

Red drum *See:* Redfish.

Redfield, Robert (1897-1958), U.S. cultural anthropologist best known for his comparative studies of cultures, and for his active support of racial integration. *See also:* Anthropology.

Redfish, name for several types of popular gamefish found off the Atlantic coasts of North America. Known as red drum, channel bass, California sheepshead, red (sockeye) salmon, or by other names, the most popular types of redfish are found in the Gulf of Mexico and adjoining waterways. The gulf species are marked by a distinctive red spot near the base of the tail; they grow to 5 ft (1.5 m) long and usually weigh up to 40 lb (18 kg). Widespread restaurant demand for redfish in the late 1980s resulted in such large commercial catches that federal restrictions were imposed to protect the species.

Redford, Robert (1937-   ), U.S. actor and director, winner of the Academy Award for best director (1980) for *Ordinary People*. He made his film debut in *War Hunt* (1962), and his best-known roles include *Butch Cassidy and the Sundance Kid* (1969), *The Sting* (1973), *All the President's Men* (1976), *The Electric Horseman* (1979), *The Natural* (1984), *Out of Africa* (1985), and *Havana* (1990). Other films he directed include *The Milagro Beanfield War* (1988), *A River Runs Through It* (1993), and *Quiz Show* (1994). His Utah ranch, Sundance, is a ski resort and school for film arts.

Red fox *See:* Fox.

Redgrave, Sir Michael (1908-85), English actor. An accomplished Shake-spearean performer, Redgrave was a noted stage director and appeared in many contemporary plays and more than 50 movies, including *The Lady Vanishes* (1938), *Dead of Night* (1946), *The Importance of Being Earnest* (1952), and *The Loneliness of the Long Distance Runner* (1962). Redgrave was knighted by Queen Elizabeth II in 1959. He was married to Rachel Kempson, a popular stage actress; their daughters, Vanessa and Lynn, became famous actresses in their own right.

Red gum *See:* Sweet gum.

Red Jacket (Sagoyewatha; 1758?-1830), Seneca chief named for the red coat he wore when an English ally in the Revolution. Later an ally of the

United States in the War of 1812, he strongly opposed European customs and Christianity for his people in New York.

Redmond, John Edward (1856-1918), Irish politician. He succeeded Charles Stewart Parnell as Irish nationalist leader in the British parliament and secured the passage of the 1914 Home Rule bill. After the repression of the 1916 Easter Rising, he lost power to the revolutionary Sinn Fein movement. *See also:* Ireland; United Kingdom.

Redon, Odilon (1840-1916), French painter and engraver associated with the Symbolists. His oil paintings, usually of flowers and full of color and light, contrasted with bizarre lithographs such as *The Cyclops* (1898).

Red pepper *See:* Capsicum.

Redpoll, small bird (*Acanthis flammea*) of the finch family. Redpolls are commonly found in northern North America and migrate as far south as California and the Carolinas. Both males and females have reddish crowns; the male also has a rosy-pink breast. Adult redpolls feed on plant buds and insects. They build their nests in bushes and small trees and line them with feathers. Usually 5-7 blue speckled eggs are laid at a time.

Red River, river that rises in northern Texas and flows southeast to join the Mississippi River between Natchez and Baton Rouge, forming most of the Oklahoma-Texas boundary. Named for its red sediment, it drains about 90,000 sq mi (233,100 sq km) and is 1,222 mi (1,967 km) long.

Red River of the North, river formed at Wahpeton, N. Dak., by the junction of the Bois de Sioux and Otter Trail rivers. About 540 mi (866 km) long, it flows north as the North Dakota-Minnesota boundary and enters Manitoba, Canada, emptying into Lake Winnipeg. It drains some 43,500 sq mi (112,665 sq km) of rich wheatlands.

Red Sea, sea separating the Arabian Peninsula from the northeastern region of Africa. It extends some 1,300 mi (2,090 km) from the Bab al-Mandab strait by the Gulf of Aden in the south to the gulfs of Suez (with the Suez Canal) and Aqaba in the North. It is up to 250 mi (402 km) wide and up to 7,800 ft (2,377 m) deep.

Red shift, increase in wavelength of the light from an object (toward the red end of the visible spectrum), usually caused by its rapid recession. The spectra of distant galaxies show marked red shifts; this is usually, though far from always, interpreted as implying that they are rapidly receding from us. *See also:* Quasar.

Red snapper *See:* Snapper.

Red Square *See:* Moscow.

Redstart, bird (*Setophaga ruticilla*) of the wood warbler family. Adult males have black plumage with brilliant orange-red or salmon-red streaks; females and young birds are brown and dull yellow. They are found throughout most of North America and in winter migrate to the Caribbean region and northern South America. Eggs, usually laid in groups of 4 or 5, are creamy white with reddish-brown markings. Redstarts' diets consist mostly of insects.

Red tape, expression used to describe inaction or delay caused by official or bureaucratic inefficiency, inflexibility, or complexity, so called for the red string once used by lawyers to bind legal documents. Scottish author Thomas Carlyle (1795-1881) made the term popular.

Red tide, natural phenomenon caused by a sudden increase of microscopic reddish organisms on the surface of a body of water. Under optimum conditions, one celled organisms called dinoflagellates multiply by the millions and float on rivers, lakes, oceans, and arms of the oceans. Most red tides are harmless, but some types kill large fish and marine life by poisoning the water or using up the available oxygen supply. Why the dinoflagellate population suddenly proliferates is not completely understood, but scientists theorize that a combination of factors such as temperature, amount of sunlight, water currents, and availability of nutrients create ideal conditions for spawning. Some sea creatures feed off large numbers of the dinoflagellate colonies or eat the food the colonies thrive on, thus decreasing or ending the red tide.

Reduction, in chemistry, any process that increases the proportion of hydrogen or base-forming elements or radicals in a compound. Reduction is also the gaining of electrons by an atom, an ion, or an element, thereby reducing the positive valence of that which gained the electron.
See also: Oxidation.

Red-winged blackbird *See:* Blackbird.

Redwood (*Sequoia sempervirens*), world's tallest living tree. Growing primarily in a narrow, mountainous strip along the Pacific Ocean from northern California into southern Oregon, redwoods thrive in the region's cool, foggy climate. They are closely related to the giant sequoias that grow further inland along the western slopes of the Sierra Nevadas. Coast redwoods average 200-275 ft (61-84 m) high; the tallest measured tree in the world is a redwood standing 368 ft (112 m) along Redwood Creek in Humboldt County, Calif. Redwood trunks average 8-12 ft (2.4-3.7 m) in diameter, and the wood, resistant to decay and insects, is valued by the lumbering industry for its durability. Redwoods are also among the world's oldest living things, some trees being an estimated 3,500 years old.

Redwood National Park, area in northern California of 109,207 acres (44,196 hectares), including 40 mi (64 km) of Pacific Ocean coastline, established in 1968 to preserve groves of ancient redwood trees.

Reed, name for cosmopolitan grasses of wet ground and shallow water. They have feathery flowers, give shelter to many birds, and are used in thatching. They grow from a tangled mass of rhizomes that are hard to uproot.

Reed, John (1887-1920), U.S. journalist and radical, author of the eyewitness *Ten Days That Shook the World* (1919), which recounts the Russian

October Revolution. Reed was instrumental in the creation of the Communist Labor Party in the United States. Reed is buried in front of the Kremlin in Moscow.
See also: Russian Revolution.

Reed, Thomas Brackett (1839-1902), U.S. Republican speaker of the House of Representatives (1889-91, 1895-9) called Tsar Reed for his strong control. His "Reed Rules" (1890) are still the basis for procedure in Congress. He supported high tariffs and opposed the Spanish-American War and the annexation of Hawaii.

Reed, Walter (1851-1902), U.S. Army pathologist and bacteriologist who demonstrated (1900) the role of the mosquito *Aëdes aegypti* as a carrier of yellow fever, so enabling the disease to be controlled.
See also: Pathology; Yellow fever.

Reef *See:* Atoll; Coral.

Reference book *See:* Almanac; Dictionary; Encyclopedia.

Referendum *See:* Inititive, referendum, and recall.

Refining *See:* Metallurgy; Petroleum; Sugar cane.

Reflection, bouncing back of energy waves (e.g., light radiation, sound or water waves) from a surface. If the surface is smooth, "regular" reflection takes place, the incident and reflected wave paths lying in the same plane as, and at opposed equal angles to, the normal (a line perpendicular to the surface) at the point of reflection. Rough surfaces reflect waves irregularly, so an optically rough surface appears matt or dull, whereas an optically smooth surface looks shiny. Reflected sound waves are known as echoes.

Reflex action, automatic response of the human body to stimuli. If a part of the body such as the hand touches a hot object, it pulls away involuntarily, without conscious decision. Reflex action is caused by sensitive nerve endings transmitting messages to the brain which, in turn, sends a message about corrective action to the body part receiving the stimuli. Reflex action involves 4 stages—reception, conduction, transmission, and response—all occurring in a fraction of a second. Often the action is taken before pain is felt. Some types of reflex action can become "conditioned reflexes," in which association or anticipation, rather than actual stimulus, causes a certain reaction in the body.
See also: Nervous system.

Reformation, religious and political upheaval in western Europe in the 16th century. Primarily an attempt to reform the doctrines of the Roman Catholic church, it led to the establishment of Protestantism. Anticlericalism spread after the movements led by John Wycliffe and the Lollards in 14th-century England and by John Hus in Bohemia in the 15th century. At the same time the papacy had lost prestige due to its 70-year exile, the Babylonian Captivity at Avignon, and the 50-year Great Schism. Renaissance thought, particularly humanism, stimulated liberal views, spread by the invention of printing.

Many, like Martin Luther, criticized the low moral standards of Rome and the sale of indulgences. Luther also challenged papal authority and the accepted Roman Catholic doctrines, such as transubstantiation and celibacy, and argued strongly for justification by faith. Luther's ideas spread in Germany after the Diet of Worms (1521) and after the Peasants' War, when Luther won the support of many German princes and of Denmark and Sweden. The protest made by the Lutheran princes at the Diet of Speyer (1529) provided the term *Protestant.* The Swiss divine Huldreich Zwingli won a large following in Switzerland and southwestern Germany. He carried out radical religious reforms in Zürich, abolishing the mass. After his death (1531), John Calvin led the Swiss reform movement and set up a reformed church in Geneva. Calvin's *Institutes of the Christian Religion* (1536) had great influence, notably in Scotland, where Calvinism was led by John Knox. In France Calvin's religious followers, the Huguenots, were involved in the complex political struggles leading to the Wars of Religion (1562-98). The Protestant movement in the Low Countries was linked with the national revolt that freed the Dutch from Roman Catholic Spain. The English Reformation was initiated by Henry VIII, who denied papal authority, dissolved and seized the wealth of the monasteries, and made the Church of England autonomous. Henry remained in doctrine a Catholic, but the influence of reformers such as Nicholas Ridley and Hugh Latimer established Protestantism under Edward VI, when Thomas Cranmer issued a new prayer book (1549). There was a Roman Catholic reaction under Mary I, but in 1558 Elizabeth I established moderate Protestantism as the basis of the English Church. The religious position of Europe as a whole, however, was not settled for another century.
See also: Luther, Martin; Protestantism.

Reform bills, 3 acts of Parliament passed in Britain during the 19th century to extend the right to vote. The first (1832) abolished rotten boroughs (localities that sent members to Parliament long after their populations had disappeared) and enfranchised industrial cities, such as Birmingham and Manchester, and the propertied middle class. The second bill (1867) gave the vote to urban dwellers, and the third (1884) extended it to agricultural workers.

Reformed churches, Protestant churches arising from the Reformation that adhere to Calvinism doctrinally and to Presbyterianism in church polity and are thus distinct from the Lutheran churches and the Church of England. They grew up especially in Switzerland, Germany, France, Holland, Scotland, Hungary, and what is now Czechoslovakia. Each had its own simple formal liturgy, and all acknowledged the Reformed Confessions. There are several Reformed Churches in the United States, the largest being the Christian Reformed Church.
See also: Calvinism; Presbyterianism; Reformation.

Reformed Church in America, offshoot of the Dutch Reformed Church of the Netherlands, based on the doctrines of John Calvin. It was formed on Manhattan Island (1628) by Dutch and Walloon settlers, and received a charter from King William III of England (1696). The Reformed Church founded Hope College in Holland, Mich.; Central College, in Pella, Ia.; and Northwestern College in Orange City, Ia. It maintains seminaries in New Brunswick, N.J. and Holland, Mich.
See also: Calvin, John.

Refraction, deviation of a ray of light passing through one transparent medium to another of different density, as for instance an object that is half in and half out of water.
See also: Light.

Refractory, nonmetallic materials that can withstand high temperatures without losing their hardness. Refractory substances include magnesite, dolomite, silica, alumina, chromite, and zirconia. Firebrick or fire clay is a common refractory, using aluminum silicates and other substances to retain their original properties. Refractories are used industrially in kilns, furnaces, and crucibles, where they line or insulate the walls of these high-heat chambers or containers. Refractories are also required in nuclear power plants, where high levels of radioactivity are capable of generating intense heat.

Refrigeration, removal of heat from an enclosure in order to lower its temperature. It is used for freezing water or food, for food preservation, for air conditioning, and for low-temperature chemical processes and cryogenics studies and applications. Modern refrigerators are insulated cabinets containing a compressor, which forces a refrigerant gas, such as ammonia or freon, to pass through a condenser; losing heat through condensation, the refrigerant gas goes through refrigeration coils, where it vaporizes, removing heat from the coils, and returns as a gas to the compressor for another cycle. In another system compression is accomplished by absorbing the refrigerant in a secondary fluid, such as salt water, and pumping the solution through a heat exchanger to a generator, where it is heated to drive off the refrigerant at high pressure. Other cycles, similar in principle, using steam or air, are also used.

Refugee, or displaced person, person fleeing a native country to avoid a threat or restriction. In the 20th century refugees have created a world problem. Pogroms forced Jews to leave Russia (1881-1917). In World War I Greeks and Armenians fled Turkey. About 1.5 million Russians settled in Europe after the Russian Revolution. In the 1930s Spaniards and Chinese left their respective homelands. The World War II legacy of about 8 million refugees led to the United Nations Relief and Rehabilitation Administration, replaced in 1946 by the International Refugee Organization, which in turn was succeeded by the Office of the United Nations High Commissioner for Refugees. They resettled millions of homeless from, for example, the Korean war. Many thousand Arabs who were displaced when Israel was created in 1948 still live in Middle Eastern refugee camps and are a serious political problem. The 1971 war between India and Pakistan over Bangladesh produced 9 million refugees, most of whom subsequently settled in Bangladesh. During the 1970s thousands of refugees from Southeast Asia—the "boat people"—fled to neighboring countries, many later emigrating to the United States. The refugee population of the United States was further increased in the 1980s by boatloads of Cubans and Haitians seeking asylum or economic opportunity.

Regelation, melting of ice under pressure and refreezing when the pressure is removed. When compressed, ice changes into water; when temperature conditions are at or below 32°F (0°C), it freezes again when the pressure is taken off. A large rock on frozen water gradually sinks as the pressure melts the ice directly below it, but as the rock sinks the water refreezes around it. Glaciers undergo a slow process of regelation, melting and refreezing as they move along, in some cases pushing ice fields high up the slopes of mountains.

Regency style, English architectural and decorative style popular during the regency and reign of George IV (1811-30). It was characterized by neoclassical elegance, refinement, and the use of Egyptian and Oriental forms. John Nash was the foremost architect of the period. The term also refers to the elaborate decorative style of the French Régence (1715-23).

Regeneration, in biology, regrowing of a lost or damaged part of an organism. In plants this includes the production, for instance of dormant buds and adventitious organs. All animals possess some power to regenerate, but its extent varies from that in sponges, in which all the cells in a piece of the body, almost completely separated, will come together to build up new but smaller sponges, to that in the higher animals, in which regeneration is limited to the healing of wounds.
See also: Biology.

Regent, in monarchies, person designated to rule when the rightful ruler is absent, ill, mentally incapable of ruling, or a minor. A regent may be a single member of the nation's royal family or a council of several persons in line for the succession to the crown. Throughout the history of England and other European monarchies, regents often directed the affairs of state when a child of a deposed or deceased king succeeded to the throne; other regents ruled when the rightful monarch was in exile or judged to be mentally unstable. Prior to passage of the Regency Act in England (1937), no specific guidelines existed governing the selection of a regent, and past regents were acknowledged by common consensus. In the United States, members of governing bodies of schools, higher learning facilities, and other institutions are often called regents.
See also: Monarchy.

Reggae, popular Jamaican musical style that combines U.S. rock and soul music with calypso and other Latin American rhythms. The 1973 film *The Harder They Come* introduced reggae to the United States, where performers such as Bob Marley (1945-81) won huge audiences.

Regiment, military term for what was once the largest infantry and armored division unit in an army. Regiments today, largely administrative units not assigned to combat duty, have been replaced by more mobile units called brigades. A regiment generally has groups of battalions and squadrons under its aegis, assigned to other units called divisions. The earliest units to be called regiments were French cavalry soldiers in 1558; regiments initially recruited, equipped, and trained troops for combat. In the early United States and 19th-century Europe, each regiment usually contained 10 smaller units or companies; in the 20th century companies were phased out as war became more mechanized.
See also: Army.

Regina (pop. 175,100), capital and largest city of the Canadian province of Saskatchewan. The city, on the Trans-Canada Highway, lies in the plains of

southcentral Saskatchewan, about 100 mi (161 km) from the U.S. border. Founded in 1883 as the new capital of the Northwest Territories, it became the capital of the new province of Saskatchewan in 1905. The community originally bore the picturesque name Pile O'Bones, but was renamed Regina in honor of Queen Victoria. Major industries include steel and steel products, agricultural machinery, meat packing, and oil refining. The city is also the headquarters of the Saskatchewan Wheat Pool.
See also: Saskatchewan.

Regina Medal, children's literature award. Presented annually by the Catholic Library Association, the Regina Medal is awarded to an individual for a lifetime contribution to children's literature. Award winners do not have to be Catholic or American to receive the honor. The first winner was Eleanor Farjeon (1959). Other distinguished recipients have been Frederic Melcher (1962), Lois Lenski (1969), Beverly Cleary (1980), Dr. Seuss (1982), and Tomie DePaola (1983).

Regulators, movement in the western part of North Carolina (1764-71) that resisted extortion and oppression by colonial officials. After failing to effect reforms, they rose in revolt but were defeated at Allemance Creek (1771), and 6 leaders were hanged for treason.

Regulus, Marcus Atilius (d. c.249 B.C.), roman general captured in the first Punic War (255 B.C.). He was sent to Rome to deliver Carthage's peace terms, under parole to return if they were rejected. He nevertheless urged their rejection, returned, and was apparently tortured to death.
See also: Punic Wars.

Rehnquist, William Hubbs (1924-), U.S. jurist. After serving as assistant attorney general, he was appointed (1971) by President Richard M. Nixon to the U.S. Supreme Court as an associate justice, where he became a voice of conservatism. He was made chief justice in 1986.
See also: Supreme Court of the United States.

Reich, German term used to designate an empire. Derived from the Old High German word *rihhi*, meaning realm, the term came into widespread use during Adolf Hitler's proclamation of a Third Reich (1933-45). The First Reich was considered to be the Holy Roman Empire (9th century-1806). The Second Reich was the German empire built by Chancellor Otto von Bismarck and Kaisers Wilhelm I and Wilhelm II (1871-1919).
See also: Germany.

Reich, Wilhelm (1897-1957), Austrian psychoanalyst who broke with Sigmund Freud over the function of sexual repression, which Reich saw as the root of neurosis. He held the controversial theory that there exists a primal life-giving force called orgone energy. His design and sale of "orgone boxes" for personal therapeutic use led to his imprisonment for violating the Food and Drug Act.
See also: Psychoanalysis.

Reichstag, imperial parliament of the Holy Roman Empire and, from 1871 to 1945, Germany's lower legislative house (the upper house was called the

Reichsrat). The ruling body of the Weimar Republic, the Reichstag lacked real power under the Nazi regime.
See also: Holy Roman Empire; Weimar Republic.

Reichswehr, German term meaning "army of the state." Set up by the German republic after World War I, it had 300,000 troops until the Treaty of Versailles reduced it to 100,000. During the Wiemar Republic (1919-33), the Reichswehr developed into a training program that enabled its ranks to swell and its combat efficiency to increase after Adolf Hitler came to power. In World War II, the Reichswehr made up the core of Hitler's army, which overran most of Europe.

Reid, Whitelaw (1837-1912), U.S. journalist, ambassador to Britain (1905-12). Editor of the *New York Tribune*, (1872-1912) he was the Republican vice-presidential candidate in 1892.

Reign of Terror, period (1793-94) during the French Revolution when fanatical Jacobin reformers, including Maximilien Robespierre, Georges Jacques Danton, and Jacques René Hébert, seized control from the Girondists. They guillotined over 2,600 "counterrevolutionaries" (including Danton and Hebert, eventually) in Paris and sanctioned "Terrors" elsewhere, notably in Nantes. The Terror ended with the guillotining of Robespierre himself in 1794.
See also: French Revolution.

Reims, or Rheims (pop. 185,100), city in northern France, about 100 mi (161 km) east of Paris on the Besle River. Dating from Roman times, it is famed for its Gothic cathedral (built 1211-1430). All but two French kings were crowned in Reims (1179-1825). Center of champagne and woolen production, it also produces chemicals, machinery, and paper.

Reincarnation, or transmigration of the soul, belief that the soul survives death and is reborn in the body of another person or living thing. It is an important concept in Buddhism, Hinduism, Jainism, Sibhism. In India, reincarnation is related to the law of karma, which dictates that a person's actions in life determine the type of body the soul will enter during reincarnation.
See also: Karma.

Reindeer, deer (genus *Rangifer*) widely distributed in arctic and subarctic regions of Europe, Asia, and North America, closely related to the caribou. Reindeer stand about 3-4 ft (90-120 cm) tall and can weigh up to 400 lb (180 kg). The Lapps of northern Scandinavia have used reindeer for food, clothing, and transportation for centuries.

Reindeer Lake, natural body of water on the Manitoba-Saskatchewan border in Canada. It is a major commercial and recreational fishing site covering 2,444 sq mi (6,330 sq km). Reindeer Lake lies 1,150 ft (350 m) above sea level in a sparsely settled region near the furthest northern reaches of the coniferous forests. Once a major link in the waterborne transit route of fur trappers and traders, the lake feeds into the Reindeer River, a tributary of the Churchill River, which flows into Hudson Bay. Important lakeshore towns are Brochet, Manitoba, and Southend and Kinoosao, Sask.

Reindeer moss (*Cladonia rangiferina*), type of lichen commonly found in the Arctic. It is a principal food source for reindeer, moose, caribou, and musk oxen; in northern Scandinavia people have used it to make bread and alcohol. A short, multibranched plant that covers vast areas sufficient to feed large herds of grazing mammals, it grows more rapidly during the spring and fall months, aided by cool temperatures and high levels of humidity.

Reiner, Fritz (1888-1963), U.S. conductor, director of the Cincinnati Symphony (1922-31), Pittsburgh Symphony (1938-48), Metropolitan Opera (1948-53), and Chicago Symphony (1953-62).

Reinforcement *See:* Learning.

Reinhardt, Max (Max Goldmann; 1873-1943), Austrian theatrical director famous for his vast and spectacular productions—especially of *Oedipus Rex* and *Faust*—and for his elaborate and atmospheric use of stage machinery and management of crowds.

Relapsing fever, bacteria-transmitted ailment that may recur several times in the same person. Usually occurring in the tropics, relapsing fever is caused by spirochetes carried by lice and ticks, which thrive on unsanitary living conditions. Symptoms of the disease include fever, chills, headaches, muscular pain, and sometimes vomiting. An infected person may be violently ill for several days or a week, return to good health, but if not treated properly have a relapse—as many as 10-12 times. The body's natural defenses may successfully combat the disease for a time, but infected spirochetes still in the body may reinvade the bloodstream, causing relapses when the body's defenses weaken. Penicillin and other antibiotics combined with extensive bed rest is effective treatment.

Relativity, theory of the nature of space, time, and matter. Albert Einstein's special theory of relativity (1905) is based on the premise that different observers moving at a constant speed with respect to each other find the laws of physics to be identical, and, in particular, find the speed of light waves to be the same (the principle of relativity). Among its consequences are (1) that events occurring simultaneously according to one observer may happen at different times according to an observer moving relative to the first (although the order of two causally related events is never reversed), (2) that a moving object is shortened in the direction of its motion, (3) that time runs more slowly for a moving object, (4) that the velocity of a projectile emitted from a moving body is less than the sum of the relative ejection velocity and the velocity of the body, (5) that a body has a greater mass when moving than when at rest, and (6) that no massive body can travel as fast as, or faster than, the speed of light. These effects are too small to be noticed at normal velocities; they have nevertheless found ample experimental verification and are common considerations in many physical calculations. The relationship between the position and time of a given event according to different observers is known (for H.A. Lorentz) as the Lorentz transformation. In this, time mixes on a similar footing with the three spatial dimensions, and it is in this sense that time has been called the fourth dimension. The greater mass of a moving body implies a relationship between kinetic energy and mass; Einstein made the bold additional hypothesis that *all* energy is equivalent to mass, according to the famous equation $E = mc^2$. The conversion of mass to energy is now the basis of nuclear reactors and is indeed the source of the energy of the sun itself.

Einstein's general theory (1916) is of importance chiefly to cosmologists. It asserts the equivalence of the effects of acceleration and gravitational fields and that gravitational fields cause space to become "curved," so that light no longer travels in straight lines, while the wavelength of light falls as the light falls through a gravitational field. The direct verification of these last two predictions, among others, has helped deeply to entrench the theory of relativity in the language of physics.

See also: Einstein, Albert.

Relief, form of sculpture in which the elements of the design, whether figures or ornament, project from their background. In *high relief* the elements stand out prominently and may even be undercut; in *low*, or *bas*, *relief* they hardly emerge from the plane of the background.

Relief *See:* Welfare.

Religion, system of belief to which a social group is committed, in which there is a supernatural object of awe, worship, and service. It generally provides a system of ethics and a worldview that supply a stable context within which each person can relate to others and to the world and can understand his or her own significance. Religions are found in all societies and are generally dominant (modern secularism being an exception).Some form of religion seems to fulfill a basic human need. Some features are common to most religions: the recognition of a sacred realm from which supernatural forces operate, a mediating priesthood, the use of ritual to establish a right relationship with the holy (though ritual used to manipulate the supernatural becomes magic), and a sense of group community. Some religions have no deity as such, but are natural philosophies (e.g., Buddhism, Confucianism, and Taoism).

Religion, Wars of, French civil wars (1562-98) caused partly by conflict between Roman Catholics and Protestant Huguenots, and partly by rivalry between the French kings and such great nobles as the dukes of Guise. The worst event was the St. Bartholomew's Day Massacre (1572). The Edict of Nantes (1598) established religious freedom and concluded the wars.

See also: France.

Religious education, program of instruction in the doctrines, beliefs and practices of a given religion. This is done primarily through church-related schools or programs or religious organizations. Large sanctioned faiths, such as Roman Catholic, Protestantism and Judaism, have extensive, well-organized programs of religious education with well-qualified teachers. Smaller churches and religious sects may offer informal systems of teaching their beliefs, often in members' homes. Religious education usually uses books (primarily the Bible), visuals, and oral transmissions of doctrine. Persons planning to teach religious education must often undergo a formal program of study.

Religious festivals *See:* Holiday.

Religious life, lifestyle voluntarily chosen by persons to enhance their own spirituality. People who adopt this way of life for becoming holy and for being of the greatest service to others include monks, nuns, brothers, sisters, priests, and ministers. A religious life may be followed and practiced by individuals on their own, or within the organized framework of an established practice or religious order. Roman Catholic religious followers take vows of poverty and chastity and may belong to a religious order to practice their beliefs in a public place, such as a church. Other religions, such as Hinduism and Buddhism, sponsor monastic orders, although many Hindu and Buddhist holy men and women practice a religious life as individuals. Some Protestant faiths have established orders, but most Protestant ministers, as do Islamic and Jewish religious leaders, impart the knowledge acquired during their religious lives to their congregations.

Religious Society of Friends *See:* Quakers.

Remarque, Erich Maria (1898-1970), German-born novelist famous for his powerful antiwar novel *All Quiet on the Western Front* (1929), describing the horror of the trenches in World War I. In 1932 Remarque emigrated to Switzerland, later becoming a U.S. citizen. Other works include *Arch of Triumph* (1946).

Rembrandt (Rembrandt Harmenszoon van Rijn; 1606-69), Dutch painter and etcher. Born and trained in Leiden, he moved to Amsterdam in 1631 and achieved recognition with a group portrait, *The Anatomy Lesson* (1632). Adapting the styles of Caravaggio, Hals, and Rubens, his painting became, during 1632-42, Baroque in style, as in *Saskia as Flora* (1634), *Blinding of Samson* (1636), and *The Night Watch* (1642). The years 1643-56 were notable for his magnificent drawings and etchings, predominantly of New Testament themes, such as *The Three Crosses* (1653-61). From the mid-1650s his painting was more solemn and spiritual in mood and richer in color, as shown in portraits (*Jan Six*, 1654, *The Syndics of the Amsterdam Cloth Hall*, 1662), a series of moving self-portraits, and religious paintings like *David and Saul* (c.1658).

Remington, Frederic (1861-1909), U.S. painter, sculptor and writer chiefly known for his portrayals of the Old West, where he traveled extensively. His paintings, usually of Native Americans, cowboys, and horses, skillfully convey violent action and are notable for authenticity of detail.

Remora, warmwater fish (family Echeneidae) that feeds off other marine animals. A remora uses an oval disc at the top of its head as a suction cup to attach itself to a host animal—usually a shark, whale, sea turtle, or other large marine animal—and is carried along with them as they swim. Ranging 7 in (17 cm) to 3.5 ft (110 cm) in length, remoras enjoy a symbiotic relationship with the animals they attach themselves to, eating leftover scraps of food not eaten by the hosts while removing parasites from the hosts. Some remoras cling to the hulls of ships and boats.

Remote control, control of a system from a distance. It can range from a television set to a guided missile or satellite, over a few feet or thousands of miles. Types of remote control include radio, infrared, ultrasonic, laser, electrical, human voice, and mechanical. Radio-controlled motorboats used by the German Navy in World War I (1914-18) were the first machines operated by remote control. Today some robots are run by remote control.

Remote sensing, information-gathering process that operates independently of physical contact with the object being studied. Modern technology has developed complex forms of remote sensing through the use of electronic sensors that pick up and transmit visual images. Television is a form of remote sensing, and TV cameras are used in spacecraft to receive and translate visual data about Earth or the celestial body being studied. Satellites convey meteorologic conditions of the atmosphere or geologic conditions of the earth's surface or underground resources. Radar and sonar use sound to detect physical objects. Some sensors detect infrared (heat) rays sent out by the earth; the information is translated by computer into color images that scientists can interpret.

REM sleep *See:* Sleep.

Remus *See:* Romulus and Remus.

Renaissance (French, "rebirth" or "revival"), transitional period between the Middle Ages and modern times (1350-1650). The term was first applied by the Swiss historian Jakob Burckhardt in 1860. The Renaissance saw the Reformation challenge the unity and supremacy of the Roman Catholic Church, along with the rise of humanism, the growth of large nation-states with powerful kings, far-ranging voyages of exploration, and a new emphasis on the importance of the individual.
The origins of the Renaissance are disputed, but its first flowering occurred in Italy. In the world of learning a new interest in secular Latin literature can be detected in early 14th century, and by the middle of the century Petrarch and Giovanni Boccaccio were searching for old texts and self-consciously cultivating a prose style modeled on Cicero. They inaugurated an age of research and discovery in which the humanists ransacked the monastic libraries of Europe for old manuscripts, and scholars like Desiderius Erasmus set new standards in learning and critical scholarship. Greek was also studied, particularly after the fall of Constantinople (1453) drove many Greek scholars to the West. The invention of printing (1440) and the discovery of the New World (1492) by Columbus gave further impetus to the search for knowledge.
The Renaissance marked the end of feudalism and the rise of national governments, for example, in Spain under Ferdinand II of Aragon, in France under Francis I, in England under Henry VIII and Elizabeth. In Italy, however, independent city states engaged in fierce rivalry, providing Niccolò Machiavelli with his notorious "ideal" of a Renaissance prince. Prosperous trading provided money for the arts, and princes like Cosimo de'Medici eagerly patronized artists, musicians, and scholars. Renaissance painting and sculpture flourished in Florence and Rome with the works of Sandro Botticelli, Leonardo da Vinci, Michelangelo, and Raphael. Literary revivals occurred in England, France, and Spain; William Shakespeare and Edmund Spenser were prominent in Renaissance English literature, and some of the finest French writing came from François Rabelais and Pierre de Ronsard. In science the findings of the astronomers Nicolaus Copernicus and Galileo

Galilei were the basis of modern astronomy and marked a turning point in scientific and philosophical thought.

René of Anjou (1409-80), duke of Anjou and Provence. He inherited a claim to the kingdom of Naples (1435) but was defeated by Alfonso V of Aragon in 1442. His daughter, Margaret of Anjou, married Henry VI of England. René's court at Angers in France was a brilliant cultural center.

Reni, Guido (1575-1642), Italian baroque painter. He developed an elegant classical style, using light tones, for religious and mythological themes, such as *Aurora* (1613) and *Baptism of Christ* (1623).
See also: Baroque.

Reno (pop. 110,000), second-largest city in Nevada and a major resort and gambling center. Situated on the Truckee River, 14 mi (22.5 km) from the California state line, the city was founded in 1868 and incorporated in 1879. Legalized gambling in Nevada brings thousands of tourists to Reno every year, and liberal Nevada laws on divorce have also made Reno a well-known divorce center. The main campus of the University of Nevada is located on hills overlooking the city. Not far from Reno are Lake Tahoe and a number of other noted recreation areas.
See also: Nevada.

Reno, Marcus Albert (1834-89), U.S. Army officer during and after the Civil War. Reno was supposed to go to the aid of Colonel George A. Custer in the Battle of the Little Bighorn (1876). After Custer's defeat Reno was accused of cowardice. Reno claimed that he had been forced to retreat and was thus unable to help Custer. A military court exonerated him (1879), but one year later Reno received a dishonorable discharge for conduct unbecoming of an officer. In 1967 the Army reversed the decision and changed the record to reflect an honorable discharge.

Renoir, Jean (1894-1979), French film director, son of Pierre Auguste Renoir. His motion pictures are characterized by a sensitive feeling for atmosphere and a strong pictorial sense. *La Grande Illusion* (1937) and *The Rules of the Game* (1939) are two of his most important works.

Renoir, Pierre Auguste (1841-1919), French Impressionist painter. He started painting—with Claude Monet, Camille Pissarro, and Alfred Sisley—scenes of Parisian life, such as *La Grenouillère* (1869) and *The Swing* (1876), using vibrant luminous colors. Later he became mostly interested in figure painting, usually large female nudes set in rich landscapes. One of his best-known works is *Luncheon of the Boating Party* (1881).

Rent, in law, the price a tenant pays for the use of another's property. In economics, rent means any income or yield from something capable of producing wealth. In general usage, the term covers the monetary return from anything from real estate to cars and computers.

Reparations, term applied since World War I to monetary compensation demanded by victorious nations for material losses suffered in war. In 1919 Germany was required to pay enormous reparations to the Allies (although the United States subsequently waived all claim). After World War II, reparations were exacted from Germany and Japan.

Repeal, act of nullifying or removing a law or constitutional amendment from the books. This can be done by legislative action in several ways— either by directly stating that a certain law is repealed (express repeal) or by passing a new law that makes clear it supercedes the previous one (repeal by implication). Sometimes legislative bodies employ both types of repeal to avoid confusion. In U.S. history, the 18th Amendment (1919) that prohibited the sale and manufacture of alcoholic beverages was repealed through the enactment of the 21st Amendment (1933).

Repin, Ilya Yefimovich (1844-1930), Russian painter. His realistic paintings often expressed criticism of the Russian social order during the late 19th century.

Representative government *See:* Democracy; Republic.

Representatives, House of *See:* House of Representatives.

Repression *See:* Psychoanalysis.

Reprieve, in criminal law, the postponement of a sentence that has been imposed by the courts. The term is usually used to refer to a stay of execution when the death sentence is involved and is often granted to allow the investigation of new evidence in a case.

Reproduction, process by which an organism produces offspring. In asexual reproduction parts of an organism split off to form new individuals; the process is found in some animals but is more common in plants: e.g., the fission of single-celled plants; the budding of yeasts; the fragmentation of filamentous algae; spore production in bacteria, algae, and fungi; and the production of vegetative organs in flowering plants (bulbs, rhizomes, and tubers). In sexual reproduction, special (haploid) cells containing half the normal number of chromosomes, called gametes, are produced: in animals, sperm by males in the testes and ova by females in the ovary; in plants, pollen by males in the stamens and ovules by females in the ovary. The joining of gametes (fertilization, or conception) produces a (diploid) cell with the normal number of chromosomes, the zygote, which grows to produce an individual with genes inherited from both parents. Fertilization may take place inside the female (internal fertilization) or outside (external fertilization). Internal fertilization demands that sperm be introduced into the female—insemination by copulation— and is advantageous because the young spend the most vulnerable early stages of their life histories protected inside the mother.

Reproductive system *See:* Reproduction.

Reptile, cold blooded vertebrate with dry, scaly skin. Reptiles can be found in a wide variety of habitats, including the sea and points north of the Arctic Circle, but most live in the tropics. There are no reptiles in Antarctica. There are about 6,000 species of reptiles. They range in size from 2 in (5 cm) to 30 ft (9 m). They breathe through lungs and are cold blooded, meaning that their body temperatures vary with external conditions making it necessary for reptiles to seek conditions favorable to their metabolisms. Most reptiles lay eggs. Certain snakes and lizards retain the eggs in their bodies until the young hatch, and they are born live. The major species of reptiles are lizards and snakes, turtles, crocodilians, and tuatoras. The last are related to the now-extinct dinosaurs and live on islands off the coast of New Zealand. Lizards and snakes account for some 3,000 species, among them certain venomous types. The turtles comprise some 250 species and some are among the longest lived of all animals. Crocodilians include alligators, caymans, crocodiles, and gavials, about 20 species altogether. Most reptiles live by eating other animals and are descendants of the dinosaurs, or giant reptiles.

Reptiles, Age of *See:* Dinosaur; Prehistoric animal.

Republic (from Latin *res publica*, "thing of the people"), form of government in which the head of state is not a monarch (and today is usually a president). Popularly, the idea of a republic includes the notion of elected representation and democratic control by the people, although many present-day governments that do not meet this requirement call themselves republics. *See also:* Democracy.

Republican Party, one of the two major political parties of the United States. It is sometimes called the G.O.P., which stands for Grand Old Party, a nickname dating from the 19th century. It was founded in 1854 by dissidents of the Whig, Democratic, and Free Soil parties to unify the growing antislavery forces. Its first national nominating convention was held in 1856; J.C. Frémont was adopted as presidential candidate. Campaigning for the abolition of slavery and of polygamy in the territories, he captured 11 states. Abraham Lincoln became the first Republican president, and in spite of the unpopularity of the post-Civil War Reconstruction policies and the secession of the Liberal Republican Party in 1872, the Republicans remained dominant in U.S. politics, winning 14 out of 18 presidential elections between 1860 and 1932. In an era of scandal, the Republicans consolidated a "probusiness" and "conservative" reputation with the nomination and election of William McKinley in 1896. His successor, Theodore Roosevelt, adopted a progressive stance; he defected to the Bull Moose Party in 1912. In 1932 the Democrats swept to power, not to be dislodged until the election of the Republican Dwight D. Eisenhower in 1952. His successors, John F. Kennedy and Lyndon Johnson, were Democrats, but Richard Nixon's landslide victory in 1972 marked a zenith of party strength. The Watergate scandal shattered this, contributing to the defeat of Gerald Ford in the 1976 elections. The Republicans rallied again in 1980 to elect Ronald Reagan president and to capture control of the Senate. In 1988 the Republican George Bush was elected president. Bush was succeeded by the Democrat Bill Clinton in 1993, who had to face a Republican majority in the Congres and Senate from 1994.

Research, use of appropriate methods to discover new knowledge, develop new applications of existing knowledge, or explore relationships between ideas or events. Scientific discoveries, technological achievements, and scholarly publications are the fruits of research. Research always involves three basic steps; the formulation of a problem, the collection and analysis of relevant information, and an attempt to discover a solution or otherwise resolve the problem based on evidence.

Reserpine ($C_{33}H_{40}N_2O_9$), tranquilizing drug used to treat mild forms of hypertension (high blood pressure). Extracted from the roots of the Rauwolfia serpentina plant of India and Southeast Asia, reserpine was isolated in 1952. It came into Western medical usage to calm mental patients in 1953. For centuries, the powdered whole root had been used in India to treat the mentally ill. Since the 1960s, more effective drugs have superseded it, but low doses of reserpine are still used to relieve minor cases of hypertension.

Reservation *See:* Indian reservation; Native Americans.

Reserve Officers Training Corps (ROTC), U.S. Army recruiting project that holds courses in military leadership in schools and colleges. It grew out of the Land Grant Act of 1862 and began operating full scale under the National Defense Act of 1916. It comprises two to four years of course work and drill plus several weeks of field training. The U.S. Navy and Air Force have similar programs.
See also: Army, U.S.

Reservoir, body of water or receptacle used for storing large supplies of water. Reservoirs are most often manmade lakes, caused by damming up rivers and streams or dredging a basin into a flat stretch of land; water towers and holding tanks atop buildings are also reservoirs. Whether manmade or natural lakes, reservoirs usually supply drinking water to cities and towns, and are used to irrigate, supply power, or control flooding. Water is drawn from reservoirs through pipes (aqueducts) and in some cases is pumped hundreds of miles away.

Resin, high-molecular-weight substance characterized by its gummy or tacky consistency at certain temperatures. Naturally occurring resins include congo copal and bitumen (found as fossils), shellac (from insects), and rosin (from pine trees). Natural Resins have for the most part been replaced by synthetic resins.
See also: Resin, synthetic.

Resin, synthetic, industrial chemical compound made up of many simple molecules linked together to form large, complex molecules. Most plastics and polymers are a form of synthetic resin. Complicated chemical processes are used to convert petroleum, coal, water, air, and wood into more complex chemicals, such as alcohol, phenol, ammonia, and formaldehyde; these, in turn, are combined to form synthetic resins. The first totally synthetic resin was Bakelite, which was produced by L.H. Baekeland in 1910 from phenol and formaldehyde. The work in the 1920s of H. Staudinger on the polymeric nature of natural rubber and styrene resin, which laid the theoretical basis for polymer science, was a major factor in stimulating the extremely rapid development of a wide range of synthetic plastics and resins. Resins have a wide variety of uses in manufactured goods for which durability and flexibility are required, and are also used in paints, adhesives and coatings for cloth, metal, and paper.
See also: Plastic.

Resorcinol ($C_6H_4[OH]_2$), compound used to manufacture resins, dyes, medical products, and other chemical compounds. A phenol, it is produced by fusing benzenedisulfonic acid with sodium hydroxide (caustic soda). A key agent in commercial skin-treatment products, resorcinol is often added to external skin-treatment lotions and ointments and is an effective antibacterial, antifungal treatment. Dermatologists use it to treat acne and eczema. Resorcinol is also used to make eosin, a dye used in red ink, and is useful in photographic developers.

Resources, natural *See:* Natural resources.

Respighi, Ottorino (1879-1936), Italian composer, director (1924-26) of the Accademia di Santa Cecilia in Rome. He is best-known for tone poems, such as *The Fountains of Rome* (1917) and *The Pines of Rome* (1924).

Respiration, term applied to several activities and processes involving the exchange of gases with the environment, occurring in all animals and plants. Breathing movements, if any, and the exchange of oxygen and carbon dioxide, may be called external respiration, while energy-releasing processes at the cellular level are termed "internal respiration," or tissue respiration. Air, which contains about 20% oxygen, is drawn into the lungs (inspiration) via the nose or mouth, the pharynx, trachea, and bronchi. Expiration is usually a passive process of relaxation of the chest wall and diaphragms allowing the release of the air, which is depleted of oxygen and enriched with carbon dioxide. Exchange of gases with the blood circulating in the pulmonary capillaries occurs by diffusion across the lung alveoli. Disorders of respiration include lung disease (e.g., emphysema, pneumonia and pneumoconiosis), muscle and nerve disease (e.g., brain-stem stroke, poliomyelitis, myasthenia gravis, and muscular dystrophy, skeletal deformity, asphyxias, and disorders secondary to metabolic and heart disease. Tissue respiration involves the combination of oxygen with glucose or other nutrients to form high-energy compounds. This reaction also produces carbon dioxide and water.

Respirator, machine that aids the respiratory process in human beings, especially in extreme circumstances when a patient has difficulty breathing normally or if breathing stops altogether. Some respirators administer oxygen directly to the patient. Hospitals, mobile medical units, and other treatment facilities constantly monitor respirators to ensure proper breathing in patients hooked up to them. Portable respirators, attended by qualified personnel, may be used in a patient's home or room in an extended-care facility (nursing home). Positive-pressure respirators force or assist the flow of air into the lungs. Negative-pressure types, such as the "iron lung," create a vacuum that causes the chest to expand, thus inhaling air.

Respiratory distress syndrome *See:* Hyaline membrane disease.

Respiratory system *See:* Respiration.

Restaurant, food-and-drink facility that serves the public. Some 130 million meals are served daily in the United States 300,000 restaurants. Table-service restaurants seat patrons; they have a meal brought to them or can serve themselves at a buffet (cafeteria). Ethnic restaurants are table-service facilities that specialize in the food of a particular country or ethnic group. Other unusual (gourmet) food is sold in more highly specialized restaurants. Fast-service restaurants are characterized by large-scale production of food items, inexpensive prices, and quick service. Some provide tables but no table service for their customers. Food is ordered and paid for at a counter.

Restigouche River, river in northeastern Canada, more than 100 mi (160 km) long, forming part of the boundary between Quebec and New Brunswick. Abundant trout and salmon attract many commercial and sports fishermen to the Restigouche. The name is derived from a Native American term, translated as "the river that divides like a hand," referring to the five main branches of the river. Much of it flows swiftly through dense, sparsely inhabited wilderness before widening into a broad estuary at its mouth in Chaleur Bay, an arm of the Gulf of St. Lawrence.

Restoration, name given to the return of Charles II as king of England in 1660, after the fall of the protectorate. Coinciding with a national mood of reaction against the Puritans, the Restoration was widely popular. The Restoration period (1660 to the fall of James II, in 1688) was one of irreverent wit, licentiousness, and scientific and literary achievement. Politically, it was a period of uneasy relations between king and parliament, culminating in the Glorious Revolution (1688-89).
See also: Glorious Revolution.

Resurrection, act of God believed to restore life in perfected form to the dead. Many faiths believe resurrection—in physical or spiritual form—will come in the final days of the earth's existence when all people will stand as equals before God and be judged for their deeds in life. In Christianity, the Resurrection refers specifically to the return of Jesus after his crucifixion and the belief that his triumph over death was a spiritual redemption for all humanity. Those who follow his beliefs and practices in their own lives expect to be similarly resurrected and redeemed after their deaths. Easter is a Christian celebration of Jesus's resurrection, said to have occurred 2 days after his death on Good Friday.
See also: Religion.

Resurrection plant, one of several species of plants that curl up when dry but turn green when exposed to water. The rose of Jericho (*Anastatica hierochuntica*), a member of the mustard family, grows from seeds and, when dry, loses its leaves and curls up into a ball. The wind carries the balls, thus scattering the seeds. Another plant, also called the rose of Jericho (*Selaginella lepidophylla*), a member of the selaginella family, is most commonly found in the arid regions of the Middle East and North Africa. It reproduces by microscopic spores.

Resuscitator *See:* Respirator.

Retailing, selling of merchandise or services to the public. When a business sells at retail prices, that means it buys its goods or services from a supplier, usually a wholesaler, or directly from the factory. The business then sells the goods to consumers at a higher price designed to make a profit for the business. Specialty stores sell particular types of product and accessories, such as shoes, clothes, jewelry, or books. Department stores offer a wide variety of items in separate areas (departments) of the store. Discount stores sell their inventory at prices below normal retail prices. Supermarkets sell food and other household products. Chain stores are those under the same name or ownership in 2 or more locations. Nonstore retailing involves selling goods by mail order, telephone, vending machines, and door-to-door methods.

Retainer, in law, agreement between an attorney and client for legal representation. A retainer can be a formal or special type, in which the lawyer agrees to represent a client on a particular case, or it can be a special retainer, in which the lawyer agrees to act on behalf of the client when necessary. A retaining fee paid by a client to an attorney is also called a retainer. Once a retainer, either general or special, is agreed to, the attorney has a legal obligation to represent the client to the best of his or her abilities. The attorney cannot act on behalf of the opposing party or parties in a legal action.

Retardation *See:* Mental retardation.

Retina *See:* Eye.

Retriever, breed of sporting dog trained to search out and bring back small game shot by hunters. Easily trainable, retrievers are excellent swimmers with water-resistant coats and a highly developed sense of smell. The popular golden retriever and the Labrador retriever can also be trained as guide dogs for blind persons and the hearing-impaired. Other recognized breeds are the Chesapeake Bay, curly-coated, and flat-coated retrievers.

Reunion, volcanic island covering 970 sq mi (2,512 sq km) in the West Indian Ocean. Discovered in the early 1500s by the Portuguese, Reunion has been a French possession since 1642 and an overseas department of France since 1946. The islanders, mostly of mixed descent, are nearly all Roman Catholic and speak a Creole patois. Its products include sugar, rum, corn, and vanilla. The capital is Saint-Denis. A 36-member elected council governs the city.

Reuter, Baron de (Paul Julius von Reuter; 1816-99), German-born founder of Reuters, the worldwide news agency. He pioneered the use of the newly invented telegraph to transmit news between major European cities and, later, to other continents via underseas cables. In 1849 he set up a carrier pigeon service between Aachen, Germany, and Brussels, Belgium. In 1851 he moved to London, where he opened a telegraph office near the Stock Exchange and reported on European financial news, expanding to other types of news events. Several major daily newspapers subscribed to his supplying service, and over the years he expanded it throughout Europe and the world.

Reuters, one of the largest international news agencies, based in Britain, that distributes information to local agencies, newspapers, television, and radio to more than 150 countries. Founded by Baron de Reuter in Germany in 1849, it moved to London in 1851. Reuters expanded its coverage from financial

to general news in 1858. Today it is a trust owned mainly by the British press.
See also: Reuter, Baron de.

Reuther, Walter Philip (1907-70), U.S. labor leader, president of the
United Automobile Workers from 1946 until his death, and important labor
spokesperson. Reuther was president of the Congress of Industrial Organizations (CIO, 1952-56) and one of the architects of its merger with the
American Federation of Labor (AFL), becoming vice president of the
combined organization.

Revelation, Book of, or Apocalypse, the last book of the New Testament.
Traditionally ascribed to St. John the Apostle, it was probably written by
another John, and dated c.96. It is addressed to people being persecuted.
After 7 letters to the Asia Minor churches, it contains a series of apoca-
lyptic visions in Old Testament imagery, giving a Christian philosophy
of world history.
See also: New Testament.

Revels, Hiram Rhodes (1827-1901), pastor, educator, and first black U.S.
senator. Elected by the Republicans in Mississippi for 1870-71, he was
subsequently involved in state politics and became president of Alcorn
College, Lorman, Miss. As a minister (1845) of the African Methodist
Episcopal Church, Revels helped establish black churches and schools in the
Midwest and South.

Revenue, internal *See:* Internal revenue.

Revenue sharing, return of U.S. tax revenues to the state and local governments. The State and Local Fiscal Assistance Act of 1972, supported by
President Richard M. Nixon, appropriated $30.1 billion for this financial aid.
No conditions were attached to state uses; local governments chose from 7
broad categories. The program, representing a political revolution in the
relationship between the federal and state governments, was renewed in 1976
and 1980.

Revere (pop. 42,423), resort suburb on Massachusetts Bay, north of Boston.
Primarily a residential city, Revere has popular beach attractions, including
a dog-racing track, but little industry. Founded in the late 1620s as Rumney
Marsh, it was part of Boston (1632-1739), then Chelsea, until it became the
incorporated city of North Chelsea (1846). To honor the celebrated Boston
patriot Paul Revere, it was renamed in 1871.
See also: Massachusetts.

Revere, Paul (1735-1818), American Revolutionary hero, immortalized by
the poet Henry Wadsword Longfellow for "Paul Revere's Ride" from Boston
to Lexington (April 18, 1775) to warn the Massachusetts minutemen that the
British were coming. A silversmith and engraver, he joined in the Boston
Tea Party in 1773. During the Revolutionary War he served the new
government, designing and producing the first Continental money, casting
official seals, and supervising gunpowder and cannon manufacture. After the
War he became a prosperous merchant known for his copper and silver work,
much of which is still copied today, and his bronze bells. Revere also was

the first American to discover the method of rolling sheet copper, and constructed the first U.S. copper-rolling mill.
See also: Revolutionary War in America.

Reversing Falls of Saint John, natural wonder at the mouth of the St. John River in Saint John, New Brunswick, Canada. High tide in the Bay of Fundy at the river's mouth forces the water's current to flow backward over the falls, a 14-ft (3.7-m) drop in the river's elevation. During low tide, the river flows over the falls through a narrow gorge into the bay. But at high tide, when the water in the bay reaches its maximum level, a rushing tide (bore) sweeps in and raises the level of the river to the exact height of the drop. The rush of water backward over the falls gives the site its name.

Revivalism, in religion, emphasis on personal experience and salvation of the soul. This form of worship is often characterized by emotionally charged gospel preaching that is extemporaneous and requires audience participation. Revivalism began in Europe in the 1700s and spread quickly to North America in a series of "Great Awakenings." Prayer meetings, outdoor services, often called camp meetings, and tent meetings, or chautauquas, were practiced widely in the 1800s and early 1900s, much less so today. Itinerant preachers would travel from town to town with their entourages, set up tents, and exhort congregations to receive eternal salvation for their souls. Today, revivalism is practiced primarily by organized, denominational churches, principally Baptist and Methodist, many of whom broadcast their congregations' services to at-home audiences as well.
See also: Great Awakening.

Revolution, fundamental change in the form or nature of a government or societal way of life. A revolution can be a violent one that completely changes a form of government, such as the Russian Revolution (1917). It can also be nonviolent yet have a profound effect on the lives of people, such as the Industrial Revolution or other great changes brought on by technological innovations. Political revolutions usually occur when an outspoken leader or faction is able to capitalize on widespread dissatisfaction with an existing ruler or governing system. Some political revolutions have been nonviolent, with popular opposition forcing a decisive change, while other revolutions have resulted in large numbers of casualties and extensive property damage.

Revolutionary War in America (1775-1783), also known as the American Revolution, in which Britain's 13 North American colonies lying along the Atlantic seaboard won their independence. It was a minor war at the time that had immense consequences later—the founding of a new nation, the United States of America.
The background. Differences in life, thought, and interests had developed between England and its small colonies in America throughout the 18th century. Beginning in 1763, after the French had been defeated in the New World, Britain took steps to increase its control over the colonies and to enforce more strictly the Navigation Acts, which had been designed to regulate colonial commerce in Britain's favor. England did this in conformity with the prevailing theory of the time that colonies existed solely for the benefit of the mother country (*mercantilism*). In addition, the Proclamation of 1763, issued by King George III, limited the expansion of the American

colonies to the Appalachian Mountains. In 1764, the British Parliament, led by the king's chief minister George Grenville passed the Sugar Act, which put levies on all molasses and sugar coming into the colonies from Britain. Even more unpopular were the Stamp Act (1765) and the Quartering Act (1765), which sought to raise revenue from the colonies and force the colonists to supply living quarters for British soldiers. Outraged colonists, near rebellion, drew upon liberal ideas from England and the continent to assert the principle of no taxation without representation in the English Parliament. The meeting in 1765 in New York City of delegates from the nine colonies to protest the act (the Stamp Act Congress) was the first united action of the colonies to protest their treatment by Britain. The Stamp Act was indeed repealed, but the Declaratory Act (1766), which gave the king and Parliament full legislative authority over the colonies, and the Townshend Acts (1767), which taxed tea and other imports into the colonies, further inflamed colonials, leading to a protest in Boston, Ma. On March 5, 1770, British troops fired on the demonstrators killing five, including the black patriot Crispus Attucks (the Boston Massacre). Duties were dropped, except for tea, but the colonists still fumed. The Tea Act of 1773, designed to help the East India Company financially, aroused patriots like Samuel Adams of Boston. Colonists, disguised as Indians, raided English ships in Boston Harbor and dumped their tea overboard (the Boston Tea Party, 1773). Britain's response to the raid was a series of punitive laws called the Intolerable Acts (1774), which closed Boston Harbor until the colonists reimbursed England for the lost tea. It also restricted the Massachusetts legislature. Colonial resistance was prompt. *Committees of correspondence* were formed by patriots to exchange information, and these led to the First Continental Congress (September to October 1774) to protest the Intolerable Acts. Another congress was planned for May 1775, but by then war had begun.

Outbreak of the War. In April 1775, colonial volunteer soldiers known as *minutemen* engaged British troops at Lexington, Ma. The troops were on their way to destroy colonial arms stores at Concord, and the minutemen had been alerted to the the British action by Paul Revere and William Dawes. The Battles of Lexington and Concord were the opening shots in the war. Boston was under siege by the British, and the colonials flocking to its defense formed the Continental Army. The Second Continental Congress, meeting in Philadelphia, named George Washington as commander-in-chief of the continental forces (June 15, 1775). Two days later the British won a costly victory in Boston (the Battle of Bunker Hill) and took over the city. Washington arrived outside Boston on July 3, 1775 and began plans to retake the city. Earlier (May 1775) Benedict Arnold and Ethan Allen had captured British posts at Fort Ticonderoga and nearby Crown Point in New York. These victories secured much-needed heavy artillery for the continental forces. The guns were moved by sled to the Boston area, and by Mar. 1776, General William Howe, commander of the British army, realized he could not hold the city. He evacuated Boston on March 17 and sailed for Canada. Washington went to New York.

Declaration of Independence. Prior to open hostilities, colonists had been most concerned that their rights as English citizens were being trampled, but by 1776, the idea of complete independence from Britain was gaining support. Thomas Paine's immensely popular pamphlet *Common Sense* (published January 1776), urging the patriot cause, was a major contributing factor to the change. In June, Richard Henry Lee introduced a resolution to the Congress calling for independence; on July 2, Congress approved; and on July 4 it adopted the *Declaration of Independence*, almost exactly as drafted by Thomas Jefferson.

The War of Independence. Much hard fighting remained to make the independence real. Britain committed more troops and a large fleet to the war. By late 1776, Howe had taken New York City and driven Washington and his small, discouraged forces into winter quarters at Valley Forge, Pa. At year's end, Washington, in a stunning Christmas night (Dec. 25, 1776) surprise attack at Trenton and Princeton N.J., achieved two of the most important victories of the war. A down-and-out colonial army turned its fortunes around by dealing the best army in the world two crushing defeats. The tide also turned in the north with Arnold's major victory at Saratoga, N.Y. (Sept. 1777) over British forces under General John Burgoyne, who had advanced down New York State from Canada. The Saratoga victory helped persuade France that it could now openly commit forces to aid the embattled Americans. In 1778, it commenced operations in the West Indies, forcing Britain to spread its forces thin. With stalemate in the north, British forces concentrated on the southern states, winning victories at Savannah (1778) and Charleston (1780). The colonial cause was further damaged in 1780 by the treason of the disaffected Arnold, who had attempted to turn over a military post he commanded at West Point to the British. In 1781, General Charles Cornwallis headed an unsuccessful British campaign to take the Carolinas. He was thwarted by colonials under Nathaniel Greene and Daniel Morgan. Cornwallis turned to Virginia, where in the Spring of 1781 he was preparing to launch a campaign to conquer the south. He was ordered, however, to take up defensive positions along the Virginia coast, and prepare to return north where General Clinton feared a colonial attack on New York City. Cornwallis moved his troops to Yorktown on Chesapeake Bay. In July, Washington learned that a large French fleet, under Admiral François de Grasse, was planning to block Chesapeake Bay and trap Cornwallis's forces at Yorktown. Washington rushed his forces from New York to Yorktown to seal off Cornwallis by land. Cornwallis, besieged by colonials on land and blocked by the French from an escape by sea, surrendered to Washington on October 19, 1781. The war was essentially over.

Treaty of Paris (1782). Britain opened peace negotiations with the Americans in Paris in April 1782. An agreement was struck in November, and Congress approved it in April 1783. The treaty, which recognized the independence of the United States and established the new nation's borders, was signed on September 3, 1783.

Revolution of 1848, series of unsuccessful revolutionary uprisings in France, Italy, the Austrian Empire, and Germany in 1848. Each was relatively spontaneous and self-contained, but all had a number of common causes: the successful example of the French Revolution of 1789, economic unrest due to bad harvests and unemployment, and a growing frustration, fired by nationalist fervor, about the repressive policies of conservative politicians like Prince von Metternich and François Guizot. In 1848, a major uprising in Paris overthrew King Louis Philippe and Guizot, but it was suppressed and the Third Republic proclaimed. In Italy, during the Risorgimento, short-lived republics were proclaimed, and there was agitation to secure independence from Austria, which was itself shaken by revolutions in

Vienna, Prague, and Hungary. The demand for a representative government led to an all-German Diet in Frankfurt that failed in its efforts to unite Germany. In England there was working-class agitation (Chartism), and other European countries were also affected.

Revolver, pistol with semiautomatic action made possible by the incorporation of a revolving cylinder carrying several bullets. In 1835 Samuel Colt patented the first practical revolver. The modern revolver is based on the Colt design and is used by police and other armed forces throughout the world.
See also: Colt, Samuel.

Rexroth, Kenneth (1905-82), U.S. poet. In the 1940s and 1950s he developed a style that broke with traditional forms of poetry and became the forerunner of what is now considered the "Beat generation" of San Francisco poets and writers. His best-known works are *In What Hour* (1940), *The Dragon and the Unicorn* (1952), and *In Defense of the Earth* (1956). *The Collected Shorter Poems* (1967) and *The Collected Longer Poems* (1968) further enhanced Rexroth's literary reputation, as did a collection of his essays, *The World Outside the Window* (1987). He was also a gifted painter and translator of Chinese, Latin, and Greek poetry.

Reye's syndrome, rare disease that attacks the liver and central nervous system of children age 4-15. Of unknown cause, it is contracted by most victims following a viral illness, such as chicken pox or the flu. Aspirin use may be associated with the syndrome. Symptoms include vomiting and may progress into convulsions, disorientation, and possible brain damage and comas. Treatment is with glucose and other nutrients or with drugs and surgery when pressure within the skull reaches dangerous levels. About 3-5% of victims die. Named (1963) after Australian pathologist R.D.K. Reye, who researched it.

Reykjavik (pop. 100,800), capital of Iceland and its chief port, commercial and industrial center, and home of its cod-fishing fleet. Settled in A.D. 877, Reykjavik means "smoking bay," from the nearby hot springs that provide the city with central heating.
See also: Iceland.

Reynard the Fox, leading character in a popular medieval series of fables. Appearing first in the area between the Flanders and Germany in the 10th century, the tales, with their cunning but sympathetic hero and biting satire, became popular in France, Germany, and the Low Countries.

Reynaud, Paul (1878-1966), French statesman. After holding a number of cabinet posts (from 1930), he became premier (1940). An opponent of the Nazis, he spent World War II in prison. Afterward he held several posts and helped draft the constitution of the Fifth Republic (1958).
See also: France.

Reynolds, Sir Joshua (1723-92), perhaps the most famous English portrait painter. Ambitious and popular, he became first president of the Royal Academy of Arts (1768). He held that great art is based on the styles of earlier masters and espoused the "Grand Style." He painted nearly all his notable contemporaries, including his friend Samuel Johnson (1772). His works also include William Robertsen (1772) and Sarah Siddons as the Tragic Muse (1784). He also published influential essays on art education called *Discourses* (1769-90). Reynolds was influenced by the paintings of Anton Van Dyck, Tintoretto, Titian, Paolo Veronese, and Peter Paul Rubens.

Reza Shah Pahlavi (1877-1944), shah of Iran (1925-41). An army officer, he led a coup in 1921, becoming prime minister and later (1925) founder of the Pahlavi dynasty. He made important military, administrative, and economic reforms, but the Allies forced him to resign in World War II for refusing to allow them to use Iran as a supply route.
See also: Iran.

Rhea, large flightless South American bird of the order Rheaformes. Closely resembling the ostrich, the rhea is smaller, with larger wings, more head and neck feathers, and 3 rather than 2 toes on each foot. Rheas generally stand 5 ft (1.5 m) tall and weigh up to 55 lb (25 kg). They are plains-dwellers in the temperate region south of the equator, usually flocking together in groups of 5-30. Often found grazing with cattle, they feed on leaves, roots, and insects. The male rhea digs a hole in the ground for a nest, where several females may lay as many as 30 eggs; the male sits on the eggs until they hatch.

Rhea, in Greek mythology, wife and sister of Cronus (ruler of the Titans), daughter of Gaea (the earth) and Uranus (the sky). She became queen of the gods after Cronus defeated Uranus. She had 6 children: Zeus, Poseidon, Pluto, Hestia, Hera, and Demeter. She later helped Zeus overthrow Cronus.
See also: Mythology.

Rhee, Syngman (1875-1965), president of South Korea. A leader in the movement to win Korean independence from Japan, he was in exile in Honolulu from 1910 to 1945, serving as president of the Korean Provisional Government for 20 years. Returning to Korea after World War II, he became the first president of the Republic of Korea (South Korea) in 1948. He resigned from office in 1960 because of corruption and mismanagement by some of his appointees. He wrote *Spirit of Independence* (1904) during his imprisonment (1897-1904) for heading demonstrations for independence.

Rhenium, chemical element, symbol Re; for physical constants see Periodic Table. Rhenium was discovered by Walter Noddack, Ida Tacke, and Otto Berg in 1925. It occurs in the minerals columbite, wolframite, gadolinite, and molybdenite. It is prepared by the high-temperature reduction of ammonium with hydrogen. Rhenium is a silver-white, ductile, high-melting, dense metal. It is resistant to wear and electrical corrosion. Rhenium and its compounds are used in alloys for electrical contacts and filaments, electron tube and semiconductor applications, high-temperature thermocouples, and poison-resistant catalysts. Dmitri Mendeleev predicted this element, which he called *dwi-manganese.*

Rheostat, variable resistor used to control the current drawn by an electric motor to dim lighting. It may consist of resistive wire wound in a helix, with a sliding contact varying the effective length, or of a series of fixed resistors connected between a row of button contacts. For heavy loads, electrodes dipped in solutions can be used, the resistance being controlled by the immersion depth and separation of the electrodes.

Rhesus monkey (*Maccaca mulatta*), monkey found in southern and southeastern Asia. Its use in medical and behavioral research led to the discovery of the Rh factor, a substance found in human red blood cells. Rhesus monkeys measure 18-25 in (48-64 cm) and weigh from 9-22 lb (4-10 kg) with a tail of 7-12 in (18-30 cm). They live in deserts, farm areas, forests, mountains and swamps. They eat birds, fruit, insects, leaves, roots, and farm crops.

Rhetoric *See:* Oratory.

Rheumatic fever, feverish illness, following infection with *streptococcus* and leading to systemic disease. It occurs mainly in children age 5-15. Symptoms include skin rash, subcutaneous nodules, and a migrating arthritis. Involvement of the heart (rheumatic heart disease) may lead to palpitations, chest pain, cardiac failure, myocarditis, inflammation of the pericardium, and permanent heart damage. Treatment includes bed rest, aspirin, and steroids. Penicillin treatment of this noncontagious disease may prevent recurrence.

Rheumatism, term popularly applied to pain affecting muscles, tendons, joints, bones, or nerves, in such widely varied disorders as rheumatoid arthritis, degenerative joint disease, spondylitis, bursitis, fibrositis, myositis, neuritis, lumbago, sciatica, and gout.

Rh factor, protein substance appearing on the surface of red blood cells of most people (85% or more), capable of inducing an immune response. It was first detected in a rhesus monkey in 1940 by Karl Landsteiner and Alexander Weiner. *See also:* Landsteiner, Karl.

Rhineland, region of Germany along the Rhine River and its tributaries. From the Roman Empire through World War II, the Rhineland was strategically important; whoever controlled the river often exercised power over Western Europe. During the Middle Ages, Rhineland cities were political and religious centers of the Holy Roman Empire and, later, for the breakaway Protestant churches. For protection against raiding armies, heavily fortified castles—now tourist attractions—were built on hills overlooking the Rhine. In the Napoleonic Wars, the Franco-Prussian War, and both world wars, the Rhineland was a key battleground. Rich mineral deposits there, especially iron and coal, led to Germany's development as a world power in the late 19th and early 20th centuries. The Rhineland is still a key industrial region, and has some the world's most productive vineyards.
See also: Germany.

Rhine River, longest river in western Europe, rising in Switzerland and flowing 820 mi (1,320 km) through Germany and the Netherlands into the North Sea near Rotterdam. It is of great historical and commercial significance, being navigable by seagoing ships up to Cologne and by large barges as far as Basel. Canals link it to the Rhône, Marne, Ems, Weser, Elbe, Oder, and Danube rivers. Some of its finest scenery is along the gorge between Bingen and Bonn, with terraced vineyards, ruined castles, and famous landmarks like the Lorelei rock.

Rhinitis, most frequent of the acute upper respiratory infections, characterized by edema, swelling and widening of the blood vessels of the mucous membrane of the nose, nasal discharge, and obstruction. It can result from infections, allergic reactions, hay fever, and unknown stimuli.
See also: Cold, common.

Rhinoceros, any of 5 species of heavy land mammals (family Rhinocerotidae) characterized by one or two nasal "horn" or "horns," formed of a mass of compacted hairs. They are bulky animals with poor vision and thick, hairless skin, often falling in heavy, loose folds. They live in transitional habitats between open grassland and high forest, grazing or browsing at night on bushes or shrubs. All 5 species— the white rhinoceros (*Ceratotherium simum*), the black (*Diceros bicornus*), the Indian (*Rhinoceros unicornis*), the Sumatran (*Dicerorhinus sumatrensis*), and the Javan (*R. sondaicus*)—have been hunted for their horns to the verge of extinction.

Rhizoid *See:* Moss.

Rhizome, or rootstock, swollen horizontal underground stem of certain plants, such as ginger. The rhizome acts as an organ of perennation (ability to live over from season to season), and vegetative propagation lasts for several years. New shoots appear each spring near the scale leaves. If split, the rhizome lives on as numerous individuals.

Rhode Island, state in New England, the northeastern region of the United States; bordered by Massachusetts to the north and east, the Atlantic Ocean to the south, and Connecticut to the west.
Land and climate. Rhode Island has two main land regions. The Coastal Lowlands cover roughly half of the state's mainland, plus the islands in Narragansett Bay and all the land to the east of the bay. Low inland hills slope downward toward the coast, which is lined by sandy beaches and salt ponds. The New England Upland, covering the northwestern third of the state, is a hilly area with higher elevations than along the coast. The Providence, Seekonk, and Sakonnet rivers are saltwater arms of Narragansett Bay. Major freshwater rivers are the Pawtuxet, Pettaquamscutt, Woonasquatucket, and Potowomut. Rhode Island has many lakes, ponds, and reservoirs. Forests cover about three-fifths of the state. Rhode Island's climate is kept mild by the ocean and the waters of Narragansett Bay. Principal cities are Providence and Warwick.
Economy. Rhode Island's most important economic activity is manufacturing, followed by tourism and service industries. Chief manufactured goods are jewelry, silverware, fabricated metal products, electrical equipment, machinery, and textiles. Agriculture, of minor importance to the state's economy, is led by greenhouse and nursery products and milk. Chief crops are potatoes, hay, and apples. Mining, also of little importance, is led by construction sand and gravel.
Government. Rhode Island's present constitution was adopted in 1843. The governor serves a 2-year term. The state's legislature, called the General Assembly, consists of 50 senators and 100 representatives; all serve 2-year terms. In the U.S. Congress, Rhode Island is represented by 2 senators and 2 representatives.

Rhode Island

Capital:	Providence
Statehood:	May 29, 1790 (13th state)
Familiar names:	Ocean State, Little Rhody
Area:	1,212 sq mi (3,140 sq km); ranks 50th
Population:	987,000 (1997); ranks 43rd
Elevation:	Highest—812 ft (247 m), Jerimoth Hill;
	Lowest—sea level, along the Atlantic coast
Motto:	Hope
Flower:	Violet
Bird:	Rhode Island Red
Tree:	Red maple
Song:	"Rhode Island"

History. Algonquian peoples lived in the area before the first European explorers arrived in the early 1500s. In 1636, the first permanent white settlement was established at Providence by Roger Williams, a religious exile from the Massachusetts Bay Colony.

In following years, other seekers of religious or political freedom established settlements in the area. Relations between Indians and settlers were peaceful until the spread of settlements began forcing Indians from their lands, sparking an Indian uprising known as King Philip's War (1675-6). Rhode Island prospered in the early 1700s. Large plantations run by slave labor lined the fertile coastal plain, and trade with other colonies and nations was brisk. (Slave trade was abolished in Rhode Island in 1774.) On May 4, 1776, Rhode Island became the first of the 13 colonies to declare independence from Britain; Rhode Islanders supported the American side during the American Revolution. Rhode Island became the 13th state in 1790. From 1790, when the first water-powered spinning machines were built at Pawtucket, textile and other industries grew rapidly; urbanization also increased. During the Civil War, Rhode Island supported the Union. Industry continued to grow in Rhode Island; the state's shipyards and factories were of great importance during World Wars I and II. During the 1950s and 1960s, Rhode Island's textile industry suffered a decline as more textile manufacturers moved to the South. Rhode Island recovered somewhat in the 1980s with growth in tourism and U.S. government contracts for developing submarines.

Rhodes, or Ródhos, Greek island covering 540 sq mi (1,399 sq km), off the southwest coast of Turkey. The capital city is also called Rhodes. The island's exports include wine, fruit, and olive oil; tourism is its main industry. Rhodes was a prosperous city-state in the 3rd century B.C. At the harbor stood the Colossus of Rhodes, a statue that was one of the Seven Wonders of the ancient world.

Rhodes, Cecil John (1853-1902), English politician and business magnate who first opened up Rhodesia to European settlement. Having made a fortune in diamond mining, he founded the De Beers Mining Company in 1888 at Kimberly in South Africa. After helping bring about the British annexation of Bechuanaland (1884), he also obtained the territory to the north, later called Rhodesia (now Zimbabwe) in his honor, which he managed until 1890. Prime minister of the Cape Colony from 1890, he was forced to resign because of complicity in the Jameson raid (1896) into the Transvaal. Much of his £6 million fortune went to found the Rhodes scholarships.
See also: Rhodes Scholarship.

Rhodes, John Jacob (1916-), U.S. political leader. A lawyer in Mesa, Ariz., he was the first Republican ever elected by Arizona to the U.S. House of Representatives. He chaired the Republican House Policy Committee (1965-73) and served as House Minority Leader (1973-81), replacing Gerald R. Ford, who was chosen vice president by President Richard Nixon. Rhodes was a fiscal conservative who supported federal projects aimed at increasing Arizona's water supply.

Rhodesia *See:* Zimbabwe.

Rhodesia and Nyasaland, Federation of, British federation in central Africa created in 1953 that included Southern Rhodesia, Northern Rhodesia, and Nyasaland. In 1963 Great Britain agreed to break up the federation and give the colonies their independence, largely as a result of widespread opposition by the black majority to the white-dominated government. The new nations of Malawi, Zambia, and Zimbabwe were later formed.
See also: Malawi; Zambia.

Rhodesian ridgeback, also called African lion hound, hunting dog that originated in southern Africa. Hunters value its ability to find and hold off lions; it is also known as a good watchdog and companion. Ridgebacks are named for the ridge of hair that grows on their backs in the opposite direction from the rest of the coat, which is yellowish to reddishbrown. They have the drooping ears typical of most hounds, stand 24-27 in (61-69 cm) high, and weigh 65-75 lb (30-34 kg).

Rhodes Scholarship, award instituted (1902) at Oxford University by the bequest of Cecil John Rhodes, English politician and business magnate, for students from the Commonwealth, the United States, and Germany. The scholarship, awarded for 2 and sometimes 3 years, provides the student's university tuition and fees as well as living allowance. Elections are based on general grounds as well as on academic ability.

Rhodium, chemical element, symbol Rh; for physical constants see Periodic Table. Rhodium was discovered by William H. Wollaston in 1803. It occurs in the minerals sperrylite, iridosmine, and in some copper-nickel sulfide ores. Rhodium is a silver-white, high-melting, unreactive metal, a member of the platinum family of elements. It is one of the few substances that is not attacked by fluorine. The metal is used to harden platinum and palladium. Plated or evaporated coatings of the element have high reflectance and are used in optical instruments. Rhodium and its compounds are used in thermocouples, crucibles, electrodes, and electrical contacts and as catalysts.

Rhododendron, genus of mostly evergreen shrubs (family Ericaceae) found mainly in forests of the arctic and north temperate zones. They bear leathery dark-green leaves and, in late spring, masses of fragrant blossom. North American species include the great rhododendron, also known as great laurel or rosebay (*R. maximum*), and the mountain rosebay (*R. catawbiense*).

Rhombus, parallelogram in which the sides are of equal length but usually not at right angles to each other. Its area can be computed by using the formula $A = bh$, where b is the base and h is the height.

Rhône River, important European river, 507 mi (816 km) long, rising in Switzerland and flowing through Lake Geneva and then southwest and south through France into the Mediterranean Sea. With its tributaries, particularly the Isère and the Saône, it has a large flow of water, which has been harnessed in major hydroelectric schemes. Navigable in part, it is linked by canal to the Camargue region.

Rhubarb, name for plants (genus *Rheum*) of the buckwheat family. First cultivated in China for its purgative medicinal rootstock, it is also used for food. The pink, fleshy leaf-stalks, or petioles, sprout from underground rhizomes and bear large green leaves that can be poisonous.

Rib, in humans, one of the 24 long, flat, curved bones forming the wall of the chest.
See also: Human body.

Ribaut, or **Ribault, Jean** (1520?-65), French mariner who helped colonize Florida. On present-day Parris Island, S.C., he set up a colony in 1562. He fled to England to escape persecution as a Huguenot. In 1565 he was shipwrecked off Florida and killed by Spanish forces.

Ribbentrop, Joachim von (1893-1946), German Nazi leader, ambassador to the United Kingdom (1936-38) and foreign minister (1938-45). He helped to negotiate the Rome-Berlin Axis (1936) and the Russo-German nonaggression pact (1939) and to plan the invasion of Poland, but he wielded little influence in World War II. He was hanged for war crimes.
See also: Nazism; World War II.

Ribbon Falls, in the Yosemite Valley, one of the highest waterfalls in the world. Fed by the melting snows of the Sierra Nevadas, it drops 1,612 ft (491 m) and empties into the Merced River. In early August, the snow dries up and the falls cease. Its name derives from its ribbonlike appearance.

Ribbon worm, any of a group of elongated marine worms (phylum Nemertina), ranging in size from less than 1 in (2.5 cm) to 90 ft (27 m) long. Most live in the open sea, but some live in fresh water or on land. They all have a long proboscis, sometimes spiked and poisonous, that can be thrown out with great accuracy to capture worms and other small animals.

Ribera, Jusepe de (c.1590-1652), Spanish painter who lived after 1618 in Naples. His work, influenced by Caravaggio, combines naturalism and mysticism, as in the *Martyrdom of St. Sebastian* (1630) and *The Penitent Magdalen* (c.1640).

Ribicoff, Abraham A. (1910-), U.S. public official, widely known as a champion of consumer protection. A Democrat, he was a Connecticut representative (1949-53), governor (1955-61), and senator (1963-81). Under President Kennedy he was secretary of health, education, and welfare (1961-62).

Riboflavin *See:* Vitamin.

Ricardo, David (1772-1823), English economist, founder, with Adam Smith, of the classical school. He made a fortune as a stockbroker and then devoted his time to economics and politics, becoming a member of Parliament (1819-23). His main work, *Principles of Political Economy and Taxation* (1817), pioneered the use of theoretical models in analyzing the distribution of wealth.
See also: Economics.

Ricci, Matteo (1552-1610), Italian Jesuit missionary. He entered China in 1583, learned Chinese, and eventually won acceptance. He introduced Western mathematics, astronomy, and geography to the Chinese, and sent the first detailed reports of China to the West.
See also: Jesuits.

Rice (*Oryza sativa*), grain-yielding annual plant of the grass family (Graminae). It is grown chiefly in southern and eastern Asia, where it is the staple food of hundreds of millions of people. Rice needs hot, moist conditions to grow, which historically made it highly dependent on monsoon rainfall. Improved irrigation, fertilizers, pesticides, and the development of improved varieties have enormously increased the yield. Machinery for planting and harvesting rice is used in the United States and parts of South America, but in Asia rice farming uses hand labor. Rice has a reasonable nutrient value, but when brown rice is "polished" (to make white rice), much of its vitamin B_1 content is lost.

Rice, Elmer (1892-1967), U.S. dramatist. His plays on social themes include *The Adding Machine* (1923), an expressionist fantasy; *Street Scene* (1929), a Pulitzer Prize-winning portrait of life in a tenement; and the romantic comedy *Dream Girl* (1945).

Rice, Grantland (1880-1954), U.S. journalist known as the first famous sportswriter. Rice covered sporting events in the 1920s and 1930s and also produced poetry and his autobiography, *The Tumult and the Shouting* (1954).

Ricebird *See:* Bobolink.

Rice weevil *See:* Grain weevil.

Rich, Adrienne (1929-   ), U.S. feminist poet whose primary themes are women's issues and sexuality and the problem of human communication. Her works include *Diving into the Wreck* (1973), *Of Woman Born* (1976), *The Dream of a Common Language* (1978), *Time's Power: Poems 1985-1988*, and several volumes of selected prose.

Richard, name of three kings of England. **Richard I** (1157-99), called Coeur de Lion (the Lion Heart), was the third son of Henry II, whom he succeeded in 1189. He spent all but six months of his reign out of England, mainly on the Third Crusade. After taking Cyprus and Acre in 1191 and recapturing Jaffa in 1192, he was captured while returning to England and handed over to Holy Roman Emperor Henry VI, who held him for ransom until 1194. After a brief spell in England, he spent the rest of his life fighting against Philip II in France. **Richard II** (1367-1400), son of Edward the Black Prince, succeeded his grandfather Edward III in 1377. In his minority the country was governed by a group of nobles dominated by his uncle John of Gaunt. Richard quarreled with them but only began to assert himself after 1397; he executed his uncle the Duke of Gloucester and banished Henry Bolingbroke, Gaunt's son, and confiscated his estates. Bolingbroke returned in 1399 to depose Richard and imprison him in Pontefract castle, where he died. Bolingbroke succeeded as Henry IV. **Richard III** (1452-85), third son of Richard Plantagenet, Duke of York, and the younger brother of Edward IV, usurped the throne in 1483. The traditional picture of him as a hunchbacked and cruel ruler who murdered his nephews in the Tower has little historical backing. He instituted many reforms and encouraged trade but had little hope of defeating his many enemies gathering in France under Henry Tudor (later Henry VII). They defeated and killed Richard at Bosworth Field, ending the War of the Roses.
See also: England; United Kingdom.

Richard, Maurice (1921-   ), Canadian-born hockey player. Known for his fast skating and blistering shots, "The Rocket" was the first National Hockey League (NHL) player to score 50 goals in a 50-game season. Richard, named the NHL's most value player in 1947, played right wing for the Montreal Canadiens (1942-1960) and led them to 8 Stanley Cup championships (1944, 46, 53, 56-60). He was inducted into the Hockey Hall of Fame in 1961.

Richards, Dickinson Woodruff (1895-1973), U.S. physiologist awarded, with A.F. Cournand and Werner Forssmann, the 1956 Nobel Prize in physiology or medicine for his work with Cournand using Forssmann's catheter technique to probe the heart, pulmonary artery, and lungs.
See also: Physiology.

Richards, Ivor Armstrong (1893-1979), English literary critic. He developed with C. K. Ogden the concept of Basic English, a primary vocabulary of 850 words. His books include *The Meaning of Meaning* (with Ogden, 1923) and *Principles of Literary Criticism* (1924).

Richardson, Elliot Lee (1920-   ), U.S. lawyer and government official. After serving as assistant secretary of health, education and welfare (1957-

67), Massachusetts lieutenant governor (1965-67), attorney general (1967-69), and secretary of health, education, and welfare (1970-73), he was appointed secretary of defense and then attorney general (1973) but resigned over the Watergate Scandal. He was also ambassador to the United Kingdom (1975-76) and U.S. secretary of commerce (1976-77).

Richardson, Henry Hobson (1838-86), U.S. architect who pioneered an American Romanesque style. Among his important buildings are the Trinity Church in Boston and the Marshall Field Wholesale Store in Chicago. *See also:* Architecture.

Richardson, Samuel (1689-1761), English novelist, best known for his novels in epistolary form, especially *Pamela; or, Virtue Rewarded* (1740-41), the story of a servant girl's moral triumph over her lecherous master, and *Clarissa Harlowe* (1747-48), his tragic masterpiece, also on the theme of seduction. *The History of Sir Charles Grandison* (1753-54) portrays a virtuous hero, in contrast to the amoral hero of Henry Fielding's *Tom Jones*.

Richard the Lion-Hearted *See:* Richard.

Richelieu, Cardinal (Armand Jean du Plessis, Duc de Richelieu; 1585-1642), French cardinal, statesman, and chief minister to Louis XIII for 18 years. By a mixture of diplomacy and ruthlessness he helped make France the leading power in Europe, with a monarchy secure against internal revolt. He destroyed Huguenot power by 1628, foiled an attempt by the king's mother, Marie de Médicis, to oust him in 1630, and suppressed the plots of the Duc de Montmorency in 1632 and of Cinq-Mars in 1642, at the same time reducing the power of the nobles. In foreign policy he opposed the Habsburgs, intervening against them in the Thirty Years' War. Richelieu strengthened the navy, encouraged colonial development, and patronized the arts (founding the Académie Française). *See also:* France.

Richelieu River, river in Quebec known for its scenic beauty. It was named after Cardinal de Richelieu, prime minister of France under Louis XIII. It rises from Lake Champlain near the Vermont border and it flows about 80 mi (130 km) northward to meet the St. Lawrence River. It is used for boating and as a transportation link between New York City and Montreal.

Richfield (pop. 5,482), in central Utah, seat of Sevier County and site of various federal and state governmental agencies. Agriculture, livestock, and dairy products are its major economic activities. Located in Richfield are the offices of the Forest Service and the Bureau of Land Management. *See also:* Utah.

Richland (pop. 33,578), city in Washington and site of the U.S. Department of Energy's Hanford Atomic Energy Plant. The city's population increased dramatically as a result of The Hanford Project, created during World War II to develop nuclear weapons. In addition to the plant, economic activity also includes farming and ranching. *See also:* Washington.

Richler, Mordecai (1931-   ), Canadian writer. His novels, especially *The Apprenticeship of Duddy Kravitz* (1959) and *Cocksure* (1968), are noted for their wry wit and biting satire.

Richmond (pop. 221,900), state capital of Virginia; capital of the Confederacy (1861-65). Located at the navigation head of the James River, it is a port and a financial and distribution center, as well as being an important industrial city, with tobacco and food processing, chemicals, metals, and wood products. It has many historic buildings and sites, including the Capitol (1785), designed by Thomas Jefferson, and Hollywood Cemetery, where some 18,000 Confederate soldiers are buried. Richmond National Battlefied Park contains several Civil War battle sites.
See also: Virginia.

Richmond (pop. 74,676), Calif., major West Coast port on the northeast shore of San Francisco Bay. Richmond has more than 120 industries, including oil refining, steel fabrication, chemicals, and food processing. Settled in 1899, it has a council-manager government. Among the world's largest high-level bridges is the San Rafael-Richmond Bridge, spanning 5.5 mi (8.9 km).
See also: California.

Richmond (pop. 41,349), city in Indiana and the seat of Wayne County, located on the Whitewater River. Founded by Quakers who traveled from North Carolina in 1806, it remains a center of Quaker activity. Economic activities include metalwork and the manufacture of machine parts.
See also: Indiana.

Richmondtown, area in Staten Island, New York City, and county seat of Richmond County. Developed in 1939 as a historic site, the area includes many restored buildings dating back to the 17th century. The restoration, which is financed by the City of New York and independent sponsors, is expected to be completed in the late 1990s.

Richter, Conrad (1890-1968), U.S. writer of fiction and nonfiction known for his novels about life on the American frontier. In 1961 he won the National Book Award for his novel *The Waters of Kronos.* He is best known for his trilogy, *The Awakening Land (1940-50),* the story of a pioneer family living in Ohio; the third novel, *The Town,* won the 1950 Pulitzer Prize for literature.

Richter, Hans (1843-1916), German conductor who presented the first performance of Wagner's *Ring* cycle at Bayreuth in 1876. A Brahms specialist also, he conducted in England for many years.

Richter, Johann Paul Friedrich (1763-1825), German humorous and sentimental novelist, who wrote as Jean Paul. He achieved popularity with such works as *The Invisible Lodge* (1793), *The Life of Quintus Fixlein* (1796), and *Titan* (1800-3).

Richter scale, scale devised by C.F. Richter (1900-85), used to measure the magnitudes of earthquakes in terms of the amplitude and frequency of the

surface waves. The largest recorded earthquakes are about 8.5. A great earthquake of magnitude 8 occurs only once every 5-10 years. An increase of one unit corresponds to a tenfold increase in the size of an earthquake.
See also: Earthquake; Seismograph.

Richthofen, Manfred von (1892-1918), German aviator, nicknamed the Red Baron. Known for the daring and chivalry with which he led his squadron in World War I, he shot down about 80 opponents before being killed in action.
See also: World War I.

Rickenbacker, Eddie (Edward Vernon Rickenbacker; 1890-1973), U.S. air ace of World War I. He shot down 26 aircraft. He served as president of Eastern Airlines from 1938 to 1953.
See also: World War I.

Rickets, deficiency disease of infancy due to lack of vitamin D, characterized by poor nutrition and changes in the bones (bowleggedness, knock-knees, etc.). There is slight fever and sweating along with general symptoms.

Rickettsia, name for organisms partway between bacteria and viruses. Often borne by ticks or lice, they are responsible for a number of diseases, including typhus, scrub typhus, and Rocky Mountain spotted fever.

Rickover, Hyman George (1900-86), Russian-born U.S. admiral who brought nuclear power to the U.S. Navy. Head of the navy's electrical division in World War II, he moved to the Atomic Energy Commission (AEC) in 1947 and developed the first nuclear-powered submarine, the *Nautilus* (1954). He attained the rank of full admiral at the age of 73 and retired in 1982.

Ricksha *See:* Jinrikisha.

Ride, Sally Kristen (1951-   ), U.S. astronaut and astrophysicist. In 1983, she became the first American woman in space when she made a 6-day shuttle flight on the *Challenger*. On this and a second shuttle flight, she used the spacecraft's remote manipulator arm, a device she helped design. After the *Challenger* explosion in 1986, she was appointed to the presidential commission created to conduct an investigation.

Rideau Canal, waterway in Ontario and Canadian historic site. It serves as a link between Ottawa on the Ottawa River and Kingston on Lake Ontario. It is nearly 125 mi (200 km) long and consists of 47 locks. Completed in 1832, it was originally intended to carry military supplies from the Great Lakes region to Montreal. Instead, it was used to transport settlers.

Ridgway, Matthew Bunker (1895-1985), U.S. military leader. During World War II he led the first full-scale U.S. airborne attack in the invasion of Sicily (1943) and took part in the invasion of France (1944). He became commander of the United Nations forces in Korea (1951), supreme commander of NATO Allied Forces in Europe (1952-53), and U.S. army chief of staff (1953-55).
See also: Korean War; World War II.

Ridley, Nicholas (c.1500-55), English Protestant martyr. Under Thomas Cranmer's patronage he became a chaplain to Henry VIII and bishop of Rochester (1547) and London (1550). He helped compile the Book of Common Prayer. On the accession of the Roman Catholic Mary I (1553) he was imprisoned and burned at Oxford, with Hugh Latimer, for heresy.
See also: Book of Common Prayer; Protestantism.

Riel, Louis (1844-85), Canadian rebel leader. In 1869 he organized the *métis* (people of mixed native Canadian and French descent) of Red River, now in Manitoba, to oppose Canada's annexation of the Northwest Territories. He fled to the United States after government troops moved in (1870). In 1884 he led another Indian uprising in Saskatchewan but was captured. His execution for treason was a cause of friction between English and French Canadians.
See also: Canada.

Riemann, Georg Friedrich Bernhard (1826-66), German mathematician, whose best-known contribution is the initiation of studies of non-Euclidean geometry. Elliptic geometry is often referred to as Riemannian geometry.
See also: Geometry.

Riemenschneider, Tilman (c.1460-1531), German Gothic sculptor in wood and stone. He worked in Würzburg, where many of his works survive, and carved the marble tomb of Emperor Henry II and his wife in Bamberg Cathedral (1499-1513).

Rienzi, Cola di (1313-54), Italian popular leader. With papal support, he became "Tribune" of a popular republic in Rome (1347), but his plans for restoring the Roman Empire led to his overthrow.

Rifle, strictly, any firearm with a "rifled" bore—i.e., with shallow helical grooves cut inside the barrel. These grooves, by causing the bullet to spin, steady it and increase its accuracy, velocity, and range. The term "rifle" is more narrowly applied to the long-barreled hand weapon fired from the shoulder. Rifles are generally classified by caliber or decimal fractions or by mode of action.

Rift Valley *See:* Great Rift Valley.

Riga (pop. 875,000), capital of Latvia. Located near the Gulf of Riga at the mouth of the Daugava River, it is an important center of shipping and industry as well as the hub of Latvian cultural and political activity. The city, founded in 1201 and variously under the control of Poland, Sweden, and Russia, was incorporated into the USSR in 1940. In 1991 independent Latvian rule was restored.
See also: Latvia.

Rigel, one of the brightest stars in the galaxy. Located in the constellation Orion, it is about 50 times as large as the sun, with a diameter of about 40 million mi (64 million km). Its distance from the earth is about 900 light-years.
See also: Orion; Star.

Rigging *See:* Sailing.

Right of privacy *See:* Privacy, Right of.

Right of search, international law under which nations at war are allowed to search the vessels of neutral nations for contraband. Ships may also be searched during times of peace. Regulations regarding a ship's distance from the coast depend on the nature of the particular search. During Prohibition, some nations consented to extend the number of miles. This practice is still in effect.
See also: Contraband.

Right of way *See:* Easement.

Rights, Bill of *See:* Bill of rights.

Rights of Man, Declaration of the *See:* Declaration of the Rights of Man and the Citizen.

Right-to-work laws, laws enforced in 19 U.S. states requiring companies to maintain an "open shop" in which a person may not be prevented from working because he does not belong to a union.

Right whale *See:* Whale.

Right wing, conservative faction within a political group or party. The term derives from the custom—first used in revolutionary France—of seating nobility on the right side of the king. This convention is still used by some organizations.
See also: Conservatism.

Riis, Jacob August (1849-1914), U.S. journalist and social reformer whose book *How the Other Half Lives* (1890) drew attention to slum conditions in New York City. He worked as a police reporter on the *New York Tribune* (1877-88) and the *New York Evening Sun* (1888-99).

Riley, James Whitcomb (1849-1916), U.S. poet, known as the "Hoosier Poet." *The Old Swimmin' Hole and 'Leven More Poems* (1883) was the first of his many popular collections of humorous and sentimental dialect poems.

Rilke, Rainer Maria (1875-1926), German lyric poet. His complex, symbolic poetry is preoccupied with spiritual questioning about God and death, as in the *Book of Hours* (1905) and *New Poems* (1907-8). The poems in his later *Duino Elegies* (1923) and the *Sonnets to Orpheus* (1923) are considered his finest work.

Rillieux, Norbert (1806-94), U.S. engineer who developed an improved method of manufacturing sugar (1846). His vacuum evaporator made it possible to cheaply and effectively dehydrate sugar cane and turn it into granules.

Rimbaud, Arthur (1854-91), French poet. His vivid imagery and his "disordering of consciousness," reflected in such poems as "The Drunken Boat"

(1871), have had an enormous influence on modern poetry. He published *A Season in Hell* in 1873, after which he denounced his poetry and became an adventurer. His major collection, *Les Illuminations*, was published in 1886. Rimbaud was closely associated with the poet Paul Verlaine.

Rimsky-Korsakov, Nikolai (1844-1908), Russian composer. While still a naval officer he started teaching composition at the St. Petersburg Conservatory (1871). He wrote scores for the operas *The Snow Maiden* (1882) and *The Golden Cockerel* (1909) and a colorful symphonic suite, *Scheherezade* (1888).

Rinderpest, acute virus disease of cattle, common in North Africa and South Asia.

Rinehart, Mary Roberts (1876-1958), U.S. writer of popular detective stories, including *The Circular Staircase* (1908). She also wrote an autobiography, *My Story* (1931).

Ring, small circular band worn on the body as decoration. It is often made of metal and sometimes engraved or set with gems. Rings are most common on the fingers and ears, but are also worn on the nose or toes. Its symbolic value has been recognized throughout the ages. Rings have been used to show position or social status, designate membership in an organization, and denote friendship.
See also: Jewelry.

Ringette, sport similar to ice hockey created for women. Invented in Canada in 1963, its popularity has spread to the northern United States and some parts of Europe. Although many of its rules are similar to those of hockey, ringette does not allow body contact. Players use a bladeless stick and a hollow circular puck made of rubber.
See also: Hockey.

Ringling brothers, five U.S. brothers who created the world's largest circus. Led by John Ringling (1866-1936), they started with a one-wagon show and became Barnum & Bailey's chief rival, buying them out in 1907. The combined Ringling Bros. and Barnum & Bailey Circus was the world's largest by 1930. It remained in the family's hands until 1967.
See also: Barnum, P(hineas) T(aylor); Circus.

Ringtail, or cacomistle, member of the raccoon family found in North and Central America. About 12-15 in (30-38 cm) long, ringtails generally have grayish brown fur and long, black-and-white striped tails. They are nocturnal and subsist mainly on rodents. North American ringtails live in the deserts and forests of the West and Southwest.

Ringworm, common fungus disease of the skin of humans and animals; it may also affect the hair and nails. Ringshaped raised lesions occur; temporary baldness is seen on hairy skin, and the nails may disintegrate. Athlete's foot is ringworm of the toes, while tinea cruris is a variety that affects the groin. Treatments include topical ointments and systemic antifungal antibiotics.

Rio de Janeiro (pop. 5,336,200), second largest city of Brazil, on the Atlantic coast about 200 mi (322 km) east of São Paulo. Located in a picturesque setting, the city is a leading resort, as well as a center for the manufacture of clothing, furniture, glassware, and foodstuffs. The area was settled by the French (1555-67) and then by the Portuguese. It was the Brazilian capital from 1763 to 1960, when it was supplanted by Brasília.
See also: Brazil.

Río de la Plata, estuary formed by the Paraná and Uruguay rivers, separating Argentina and Uruguay. It flows 171 miles (275 km) southeast into the Atlantic.

Rio Grande, one of the longest rivers in North America, known in Mexico as the Rio Bravo del Norte. It rises in the San Juan Mountains in southwestern Colorado and flows 1,885 (3,034 km) southeast and south to the Gulf of Mexico at Brownsville, Tex., and Matamoros, Mexico. From El Paso, Tex., to its mouth, it forms the U.S.-Mexico border.

Rio Madeira *See:* Madeira River.

Riot, unlawful rebellion against a public authority by a group of people, involving breach of the peace, destruction of property, and/or violence. Riots are defined variously around the world, and punishment differs accordingly. Riots can be spontaneous or planned. They often break out during a protest, due to the heightened emotions of demonstrators and authorities. Although the U.S. Constitution protects the right of its citizens to group together for the purposes of peaceful dissent, such gatherings are considered riots when they involve breach of peace, destruction of property, or violence.

Riparian rights, privileges accruing to owners of land on the edges of streams, rivers, and lakes. These "water rights" allow a landowner to use the water for domestic, agricultural, or commercial purposes, usually with the provision that such use should not infringe on the rights of other riparian owners.

Ripley, George (1802-80), U.S. social reformer and critic. A transcendentalist, he founded and ran the Brook Farm community (1841-47). Later (1849-80) he became an influential literary critic with the *New York Tribune*.

Rip Van Winkle, folk tale by U.S. author Washington Irving from his collection, *The Sketch Book of Geoffrey Crayon, Gent.* (1819-20). The story concerns a cheerful but unsuccessful farmer who, while hunting in the Catskill Mountains, meets some quaintly dressed men playing ninepins. After he drinks from their keg of liquor he falls asleep and wakes to find his dog gone and his gun rusted. He makes his way home and discovers that he has slept for 20 years, his children have grown, and he has become a citizen of the United States instead of a subject of King George III. He later finds that the men he encountered were the ghosts of Henry Hudson and his crew.

Rite of passage, ceremony within a community to mark an individual's achievement of a new stage in life (e.g., birth, puberty, marriage) and consequent change of role in the community.

Rittenhouse, David (1732-96), U.S. astronomer and mathematician who invented the diffraction grating, built two orreries, discovered the atmosphere of Venus (1768) independently of Lomonosov (1761), and built what was probably the first U.S. telescope.
See also: Astronomy; Telescope.

Ritual *See:* Religion.

River, long channel of water. The ground beneath is called the bed; to either side are its banks. Rivers begin as headwaters overflowing from lakes or running down mountains as the snow melts, forming rills, brooks, and streams. The amount of river water depends on rainfall, since the river system provides the drainage for the surrounding land. The water runs downward to sea level, taking the shortest, steepest route; the river's upper course has the swiftest currents, as well as any waterfalls or rapids. The force of the current may erode the valleys or cut into rock, forming canyons. The river's lower course usually flows through a flat area called the flood plain until it reaches the mouth, the point where the river reaches the coast. The mouth may form a delta (a triangular deposit of sediment), or an estuary (a deep, wide mouth filled with fresh and salt waters). Rivers, important routes of transportation, can provide power for industry and help irrigate crops. At 4,145 mi (6,671 km), the Nile River in Africa is the longest in the world.

Rivera, Diego (1886-1957), Mexican mural painter. He painted large murals of social life and political themes throughout Mexico and in the United States, where his Marxist views aroused controversy.

River dolphin, any of four species of freshwater whales found in the waters of South America and Asia, belonging to the family Platanistidae. River dolphins differ from marine dolphins in that they have longer snouts, more teeth, poorer vision, and a lower level of activity. They measure up to 9 ft (2.7 m) long, and can be black, white, yellow, pink, gray, or brown in color.

River horse *See:* Hippopotamus.

Rivers, Larry (1923-   ), U.S. painter. He adapted the style of abstract expressionism to the popular imagery of well-known pictures and commercial advertisements, as in *Dutch Masters Series* (1963).

Riveting, joining of machine or structural parts, usually plates, by rivets. Rivets are headed bolts, usually made of steel, that are passed through the plates, a second head then being formed on the plain end by pressure, hammering, or an explosive charge. Large rivets are heated for satisfactory closing. Although riveting can be automated, it is slowly being displaced by arc welding.

Riviera, coastal region of the Mediterranean Sea in southeastern France and northwestern Italy. It is a major tourist center, noted for its scenery and pleasant climate. The Riviera's fashionable resorts include Cannes, Nice, and St. Tropez in France; Monte Carlo in Monaco; and Bordighera, Portofino, Rapallo, and San Remo in Italy.

Riyadh (pop. 1,380,000), Saudi Arabian city and seat of the Saudi royal family, about 240 mi (386 km) west of the Persian Gulf. It is an important commercial center and has rapidly expanded because of the oil trade.
See also: Saudi Arabia.

Rizal, José (1861-96), Philippine writer and patriot. His novels *The Lost Eden* (1886) and *The Subversive* (1891) denounced Spanish rule in the Philippines. His execution by the Spanish on charges of instigating insurrection led to a full-scale rebellion.

Rizzio, David (c.1533-66), Italian musician, favorite of Mary, Queen of Scots. He became Mary's secretary in 1564. Scottish nobles, including Lord Darnley, Mary's husband, assassinated him.

RNA *See:* Nucleic acid.

Roach, fish belonging to the carp and minnow family, commonly found in the lakes and rivers of Europe. Measuring from 6 to 16 in (15 to 40 cm) in length, it is yellow-green in color, with red eyes. It is often used as bait or caught for food. The name also refers to certain varieties of North American fish, notably the golden shiner.

Roach *See:* Cockroach.

Road, surfaced or unsurfaced path over which vehicles travel. Roads include streets; local and secondary thoroughfares linking rural areas and communities; primary highways, including freeways and expressways, connecting larger communities; and in the United States the Federal Interstate Highway System, a system of freeways connecting most cities larger than 50,000. The first roads appeared around 3000 B.C., soon after the invention of the wheel. Later the Chinese and Egyptians built roads, but the Romans are generally considered the first really knowledgeable road builders. In the United States, roads remained crude, unsurfaced or covered with gravel or wood planks, until the beginning of the 20th century; the invention and growing popularity of the automobile aided road development around this time. Today, the United States has almost 4 million mi (6.5 million km) of roads.

Roadrunner (*Geococcyx californianus*), large, slenderly built bird of the cuckoo family, found in arid regions in the southwestern United States and Mexico. Roadrunners fly weakly but have strong legs and run very rapidly, up to 15 mph, catching lizards and small rodents.

Roanoke (pop. 224,477), industrial, trade, transportation, and medical center, and one of the largest cities in Virginia. Roanoke comes from the Indian word *Rawenoke*, meaning *shell money*. Schools in Roanoke include Hollins College, Roanoke College, and Virginia Polytechnic Institute. The Norfolk and Western Railroad and the Appalachian Power Co. have headquarters there. Roanoke was also the childhood home of black educator Booker T. Washington. Settled in 1881 as Big Lick and renamed Roanoke in 1882, it has a council-manager form of government.
See also: Virginia.

Roanoke Island, island off the northeastern coast of North Carolina, 12 mi by 3 mi (19.3 km by 4.8 km) site of the first English settlement in North America (1585). Its economy depends on fishing and tourism.

Roaring Twenties, period of the 1920s in the United States identified with restlessness and social reform. After years of involvement with the war in Europe, the nation experienced a surge of economic prosperity that resulted in dramatic shifts in American attitudes and culture. This period, also called the Dollar Decade and the Jazz Age, inspired many in the arts to rebel against narrow-mindedness and traditional values. The period is often associated with bootleg liquor, short skirts, women smoking cigarettes, and sexual permissiveness.

Robbe-Grillet, Alain (1922-   ), French novelist, originator of the French "new novel." In works such as *The Voyeur* (1955), *Jealousy* (1957), and the screenplay for *Last Year at Marienbad* (1960), structure, objects, and events displace character and story.

Robber crab *See:* Hermit crab.

Robbins, Frederick Chapman (1916-   ), U.S. virologist who shared the 1954 Nobel Prize in physiology or medicine with J. F. Enders and T. H. Weller for their cultivation of the poliomyelitis virus in non-nerve tissues. *See also:* Physiology; Poliomyelitis.

Robbins, Jerome (1918-98), U.S. choreographer and director. He danced major roles with the American Ballet Theatre (1940-44), where he created his first ballet, *Fancy Free* (1944). With the New York City Ballet he was associate artistic director (1950-59), a ballet master after 1968, and from 1983 ballet master-in-chief (with Peter Martins). For motion pictures, television, and Broadway he choreographed and directed such·productions as *West Side Story* (1957) and *Fiddler on the Roof* (1964).

Roberts, Kenneth Lewis (1885-1957), U.S. writer and *Saturday Evening Post* correspondent. His series of popular historical novels, including *Arundel* (1930), *Rabble in Arms* (1933), and *Northwest Passage* (1937), received a special Pulitzer Prize citation (1957). He also wrote travel books.

Roberts, Owen Josephus (1875-1955), associate justice of the U.S. Supreme Court (1930-45). He was a prosecuting attorney in the Teapot Dome scandal (1924) and was involved in economic legislation in the Depression. He led the inquiry into the Pearl Harbor disaster (1941).
See also: Supreme Court of the United States.

Roberts, Sir Charles George Douglas (1860-1943), Canadian writer. His simple, descriptive poems of the Maritime provinces contributed to an emerging Canadian consciousness. Among his works are animal stories, such as *Red Fox* (1905).

Robertson, Oscar (1938-   ), U.S. basketball player. Nicknamed the "Big O" and renowned for his passing and scoring ability, Robertson played for the National Basketball Association (NBA) Cincinnati Royals (1960-70) and

Milwaukee Bucks (1971-74). His achievements include NBA Rookie of the Year (1961), 4 Most Valuable Player awards—1 regular season (1964) and 3 All-Star (1961, 64, 69), and ranking fourth on the all time regular season scoring list (26,710 career points). Robertson is the only player to average a triple-double (10 or more assists, points, and rebounds per game) for an entire season (1961-62). In 1979 he was inducted into the Basketball Hall of Fame.

Robertson, Rev. Pat (1930-   ), U.S. evangelist and politician who established the first television station for Christian broadcasting (the Christian Broadcasting Network, 1960) at Portsmouth, Va. Robertson was an unsuccessful presidential candidate in the 1988 election.

Robert's Rules of Order *See:* Parliamentary procedure.

Roberval, Sieur de (Jean François de la Rocque; 1500?-60?), French explorer who led one of the first expeditions to colonize Canada. He was named lieutenant general and viceroy of Canada by Francis I. In 1542 he and a group of 200 settlers landed in the supposedly mineral-rich territory of Newfoundland previously explored by Jacques Cartier. Many of the colonists did not survive the year, and no mineral riches were found. A later expedition also proved unsuccessful. His death was the result of murder.
See also: Canada.

Robeson, Paul (1898-1976), U.S. singer and stage and film actor. A basso, he made his concert debut in 1925 and became known for his renditions of spirituals. Son of a former slave, his most famous song was "Ol' Man River" from the musical *Show Boat* (1928). Robeson starred in the play and film of *Emperor Jones* (1925; 1933) and in Shakespeare's *Othello*. As a collegiate athlete Robeson was twice named an All-American end in football. He also starred in 3 other sports. He was also valedictorian of his class. Ostracized in the United States for his communist beliefs, he lived and sang in Europe between 1958 and 1963.

Robespierre, Maximilien Marie Isidore (1758-94), fanatical idealist leader of the French Revolution. A lawyer, he was elected as a representative of the third estate to the States-General (1789) and rose to become leader of the radical Jacobins in the National Convention (1793). He liquidated the rival moderate Girondists and as leader of the Committee of Public Safety initiated the Reign of Terror. The National Convention rose against him, alienated by his increasing power. He was arrested, summarily tried, and executed.
See also: French Revolution.

Robin, vernacular name for various unrelated species of small birds with red breasts. They include the European robin (*Erithacus rubecula*), American robin (*Turdus migratorius*), Pekin robin (*Leiothrix lutea*), and Indian robin (*Saxicoloides fulicata*). Most familiar are the European robin (robin redbreast), an insectivorous thrush noted for its beautiful song, and the American robin, a common garden and woodland bird of the United States.

Robin Hood, legendary medieval English hero. He is usually depicted as an outlaw, living with his band of followers, including Little John and Friar

Tuck, in Sherwood Forest in Nottinghamshire. He robbed the Norman overlords to give to the poor.

Robinson, Bill (1878-1949), popular U.S. dancer and entertainer, nicknamed "Bojangles." He won national and international acclaim as a musical comedy performer and was featured in numerous Broadway shows and Hollywood films, including those in which he starred with Shirley Temple. He was especially known for his "stair tap" dance, which he claimed to have invented when he danced up a staircase to receive an award from the king of England.

Robinson, Eddie (Edward Gay Robinson; 1919-   ), the most victorious coach in college football history. In 1985, Robinson guided Grambling State University to its 324th win, surpassing the record of 323 wins held by Paul (Bear) Bryant. Grambling State has captured 14 Southwestern Athletic Conference championships under Robinson and more than 200 of his players have gone on to professional football teams.

Robinson, Edwin Arlington (1869-1935), U.S. poet, known for his series of terse, sometimes bitter, verse characterizations of the inhabitants of the fictitious Tilbury Town. His *Collected Poems* (1921), *The Man Who Died Twice* (1924), and *Tristam* (1927) won Pulitzer Prizes.

Robinson, Frank (1935-   ), U.S. baseball player and manager. Known as an excellent outfielder, Robinson won the Rookie of the Year award (1956) and was the first player to be named Most Valuable Player in both the National and American Leagues (1961 and 66, respectively). He played for the Cincinnati Reds (1956-65), Baltimore Orioles (1966-71), Los Angeles Dodgers (1972), California Angels (1973-74), and Cleveland Indians (1974-76). Robinson became the first African-American manager of a major league baseball team, as player-manager of the Cleveland Indians (1975-77). He also managed the San Francisco Giants (1981-84) and Baltimore Orioles (1988). Robinson was inducted to the National Baseball Hall of Fame in 1982.

Robinson, Jackie (Jack Roosevelt Robinson; 1919-72), U.S. baseball player. A lettermen in 4 sports at UCLA, Robinson became the first African-American to be admitted into baseball's major leagues (1947). Known for his exceptional hitting and base-stealing ability, he was named Rookie of the Year and won the National League's Most Valuable Player award once (1949). Robinson played for the Brooklyn Dodgers (1947-56) and led them to a championship in 1955. He was inducted into the National Baseball Hall of Fame in 1962.

Robinson, James Harvey (1863-1936), U.S. historian. He was one of the founders of the "new history," studying the intellectual, social, and scientific development of humankind rather than only the narrow range of political events.

Robinson, Joan Violet (1903-83), British economist, writer, and advocate of Keynesian economics. A colleague of John Maynard Keynes, she worked with him to provide a new economic model based on increased government spending as a solution to depression and unemployment. Her work helped to shape the economic policies of the 1930s and has been an important influence on economic thought.

Robinson, Sir Robert (1886-1975), English organic chemist awarded the 1947 Nobel Prize in chemistry for his pioneering studies of the molecular structures of alkaloids and other vegetable-derived substances. *See also:* Chemistry.

Robinson, Sugar Ray (Walter Smith; 1921-89), U.S. boxer. Considered one of the greatest fighters of all time, Robinson won the world welterweight title (1946) and the middleweight title (1951). He retired in 1952, but returned in 1955 to regain the middleweight title. In 1958 Robinson won his fifth middleweight title, becoming the first boxer to win a divisional world championship 5 times. He retired in 1965.

Robot, mechanical device equipped with sensing instruments for detecting input signals or environmental conditions, with a calculating mechanism for making decisions, and with a guidance mechanism for providing control. *See also:* Automation.

Rob Roy (Robert MacGregor; 1671-1734), Scottish outlaw, romanticized in Sir Walter Scott's *Rob Roy* (1818). He was outlawed for cattle theft in 1712 by the duke of Montrose, whose tenants he then plundered. Hunted for many years, he surrendered in 1722 but was pardoned in 1727.

Robusti, Jacopo *See:* Tintoretto.

Rocard, Michel Louis Leon (1930-   ), French prime minister (1988-91). Rocard is a socialist who served as secretary to the Unified Socialist Party (1967-73). He was elected to 2 terms in the National Assembly (1969-73 and 1978-81) and held several government positions. Member of the European Parliment since 1994.

Rochambeau, Comte de (Jean Baptiste Donatien de Vimeur; 1725-1807), French general who commanded French troops sent to help General George Washington in the American revolution. Involved in the French Revolution, he narrowly escaped execution in the Reign of Terror. *See also:* France.

Roche, Mazo De la *See:* De la Roche, Mazo.

Rochester (pop. 245,000), large industrial city in upstate New York, on the banks of the Genesee River, near its confluence with Lake Ontario. The community was laid out by Col. Nathaniel Rochester in 1811, and it became a commercial and industrial center within 20 years. Modern Rochester is known for the manufacture of cameras and film equipment, consumer goods, and machinery and precision instruments. The city is the home of the University of Rochester and the Eastman School of Music. *See also:* New York.

Rock, hard, solid matter of the earth's crust, sometimes a combination of one or more minerals. Rock may occur close to the earth's surface or deep underground. Rocks are classified according to their origin. Igneous rock forms when magma (molten material deep within the earth) rises toward the surface and cools. Intrusive igneous rock, such as granite, results if the magma solidifies before it reaches the earth's surface. Extrusive igneous rock, such as obsidian, occurs when magma reaches the surface, as it does in a volcano eruption. Sedimentary rock, such as sandstone, gypsum, and chalky limestone, forms when sediments, or parts of other rocks, mix together and harden. These sediments can be formed by erosion, chemical action, or an accumulation of plant and animal parts. Metamorphic rock, such as marble and slate, occurs when igneous or sedimentary rocks are exposed to intensive pressure or heat and subsequently change their form. Rock is used primarily as a building material and is an important component of concrete.

Rockefeller, family of U.S. financiers and politicians. **John Davison Rockefeller** (1839-1937) entered the infant oil industry in Cleveland, Ohio, at the age of 24 and ruthlessly unified the oil industry into the Standard Oil Trust. He devoted a large part of his later life to philanthropy, creating the Rockefeller Foundation. **John Davison Rockefeller, Jr.** (1874-1960), only son of John D. Rockefeller, followed his father's business and charitable interests. He donated the land for the UN headquarters and helped found the Rockefeller Center in New York City. **John Davison Rockefeller, 3rd** (1906-78) first son of John, Jr., helped establish New York City's Lincoln Center for the Performing Arts and the United Negro College Fund. **Nelson Aldrich Rockefeller** (1908-79), second son of John, Jr., governor of N.Y. 1959-73, was appointed U.S. vice president in 1974. He sought presidential nomination in 1960, 1964, and 1968. He expanded transportation, welfare, housing, and other social services in N.Y. **Winthrop Rockefeller** (1912-73), fourth son of John, Jr., was Republican governor of Arkansas (1967-71). **David Rockefeller** (1915-   ), youngest son of John, Jr., was president of the Chase Manhattan Bank and chairman of Rockefeller University. **John Davison "Jay" Rockefeller, 4th** (1937-   ), grandson of John D. Rockefeller, Jr., became Democratic governor of West Virginia in 1977 and 1980 and was elected to the U.S. Senate in 1985.

Rockefeller Foundation, U.S. philanthropic foundation. Founded in 1913 by John D. Rockefeller, it supports research in three main areas: medical and natural sciences, agricultural sciences, and the humanities and social sciences.

Rocket, form of jet-propulsion engine in which the substances (fuel and oxidizer) needed to produce the propellant gas jet are carried internally. Working by reaction, and being independent of atmospheric oxygen, rockets are used to power interplanetary space vehicles. In addition to their chief use to power missiles, rockets are also used for supersonic and assisted-takeoff airplane propulsion, and sounding rockets are used for scientific investigation of the upper atmosphere. The first rockets—of the firework type, cardboard tubes containing gunpowder—were made in 13th-century China, and the idea quickly spread to the West. Their military use was limited, guns being superior, until military rockets were developed by Sir William Congreve (1772-1828). The 20th century saw the introduction of new fuels and oxidants, e.g., a mixture of nitrocellulose and nitroglycerin for solid-fuel rockets, or ethanol and liquid oxygen for the more efficient liquid-fuel rockets. The first liquid-fuel rocket was made by R.H. Goddard, who also invented the multistage rocket. In World War II Germany, and afterward in the U.S., Wernher von Braun made vast improvements in rocket design. Other propulsion methods, including the use of nuclear furnaces, electrically accelerated plasmas and ion propulsion, are being developed.

Rocket, model, or space model, small-scale working replica of the kind of rocket used in military and space programs. Weighing under 1 lb (0.45 km) and measuring 8-24 in (20-61 cm), these models have fuel-burning engines that allow them to travel distances of up to 2,000 ft (610 m) at a speed of 300 mph (480 kmph). Model rocketry kits are commercially available to hobbyists. Associations, clubs, and competitions exist throughout the world.

Rocket, The, first locomotive powered by steam. It was invented by George and Robert Stephenson of Britain in 1829 to provide a railway link between the cities of Liverpool and Manchester. The name derives from a response by the Stephensons to a public jibe that the locomotive was as hazardous to ride as a space rocket. The speed of *The Rocket* reached as high as 36 mph (57.9 kmph).
See also: Locomotive.

Rock festival *See:* Rock music.

Rockford (pop. 283,719), second-largest city in Illinois. It lies on the Rock River in the north-central area, about 17 mi (27 km) south of the Wisconsin state line and less than 100 mi (161 km) northwest of Chicago. Rockford is one of Illinois' major industrial centers and is known for the manufacture of machine tools, hardware, heavy earth-moving equipment, automobile parts, paint, and farm and household goods. The city is the seat of Winnebago County and the home of Rockford College (founded in 1847). Rockford was founded in 1834 at the site of a stagecoach ford and became a city in 1852.
See also: Illinois.

Rock music, the dominant popular music since the late 1950s. Rock music first emerged in the mid-1950s as rock 'n' roll, a hybrid evolving from a sophisticated blues style called rhythm and blues, which often used amplified instruments to produce a heavy beat. The first national rock 'n' roll hit—and the one that probably gave the genre its name—was "Rock Around the Clock," by Bill Haley and His Comets (1955). Rock 'n' roll's first superstar, Elvis Presley, hit on a riveting combination of harddriving rhythm and blues with country and western music. Other important performers includeed Chuck Berry and Buddy Holly. Rock 'n' roll, with its exciting beat and lyrics about school, cars, and love, was especially popular with adolescents. The impetus for the transformation of rock 'n' roll into rock music came from England, where, in the early 1960s, bands like the Beatles and the Rolling Stones remixed the original ingredients, adding new musical textures, forms, and rhythms and more sophisticated lyrics. The 1960s also saw the emergence of soul music, a product of rhythm and blues and gospel styles, which would add its sound to rock; folk rock, as in the later work of Bob Dylan; and acid rock, an attempt to reproduce musically the hallucinogenic drug experience. In the 1970s acid rock was followed by hard rock or heavy metal, which was louder and more repetitive and by eclectic mixtures of the rock sound with country, jazz, calypso, and other styles. Another 1970s innovation was disco, repetitive dance music with a rock beat. In the mid-1970s punk rock, an angry, harsh, sometimes violent style, emerged out of the postindustrial despair of working-class youth in England. Punk rock, also reflected young people's disillusionment with the so-called rock establishment and the overcommercialization of what had been a rebellious art form. The 1980s and 1990s were dominated by rock videos, short films that feature acting, dancing, and effects as well as music.

Rockne, Knute Kenneth (1888-1931), U.S. football coach. Known for his inspirational talks, and use of great speed and variety on the field, Rockne helped make football a more entertaining sport. While coaching for Notre Dame (1918-30) he achieved a record of 105 wins, 12 losses, and 5 ties, giving him a winning percentage (.881) that is the best in college football history.

Rock oil *See:* Petroleum.

Rockwell, Norman (1894-1978), U.S. illustrator, known for his realistic and humorous scenes of U.S. small town life. His work includes magazine covers for *The Saturday Evening Post* and a series of paintings of the Four Freedoms.

Rocky Mountain goat (*Oreamnos americanus*), goatlike herbivorous mammal closely related to the antelope. It is found in the coastal mountain ranges of North America. An excellent climber, it is considered to be fairly unintelligent. It has curved horns, dense whitish fur, black hoofs, and a long beard in the male of the species.

Rocky Mountain National Park, natural wild area in north central Colorado, in the heart of the Rocky Mountains. Founded in 1915, the park is dominated by Longs Peak (14,225 ft/4,345 m) and has many glaciers.

Rocky Mountains, principal range of the western region of North America. Extending from north Alaska for more than 3,000 mi (4,800 km) to New Mexico, they form the Continental Divide; rivers rising on the eastern slopes flow to the Arctic or Atlantic Ocean, and those rising on the western slopes flow toward the Pacific. Rivers originating in the Rockies include the Missouri, Rio Grande, Colorado, Columbia, and Arkansas. A relatively new system, the Rockies were formed by massive uplifting forces that began about 70 million years ago.

Rocky Mountain spotted fever, acute febrile disease caused by *Rickettsia rickettsii* and transmitted by ixodid ticks. The onset is abrupt, with severe headache, chills, and muscular pains. Fever reaches 40°C (104°F) within several days and remains high for 10 to 15 days. Untreated patients may develop pneumonia, tissue necrosis, and circulatory failure, with resulting brain and heart damage. Starting antibiotic therapy early has significantly reduced mortality, formerly about 20 percent.
See also: Rickettsia.

Rococo, 18th-century European artistic and architectural style. The term derives from *rocaille* (French, "rock work"), whose arabesque and ingenious forms are found in many rococo works. The style, characterized by lightness and delicacy, emerged c.1700 in France, finding expression in the works of François Boucher, Jean-Honoré Fragonard, and others. Some of the greatest achievements of rococo sculpture and decoration are found in the palaces and pilgrimage churches of Austria and southern Germany.

Rodent, largest order of mammals, including some 1,500 species of mice, rats, porcupines, and squirrels. Rodents have a single pair of incisors in the upper and lower jaws that continue to grow throughout life. Behind the incisors is a gap to allow recirculation of food in chewing. The cheek skin can be drawn across the gap, in front of the molars and premolars, leaving the incisors free for gnawing. Rodents are predominantly eaters of seeds, grain, and other vegetation.

Rodeo, in the United States and Canada, contest and entertainment based on ranching techniques; it derives from late-19th-century cowboy meets held to celebrate the end of a cattle drive. It usually comprises 5 main events: calf-roping, in which a mounted cowboy must rope a calf, dismount, throw the calf, and tie 3 of its legs together; steer-wrestling, in which the cowboy jumps from a galloping horse and wrestles a steer to the ground by its horns; bareback riding on an unbroken horse for 8 to 10 secs; saddle-bronc riding; and bull-riding.

Rodgers, Richard (1902-79), U.S. songwriter and composer. He collaborated with librettist Lorenz Hart on *A Connecticut Yankee* (1927), *Pal Joey* (1940), and many other Broadway musicals containing dozens of enormously popular songs. Later he teamed up with Oscar Hammerstein II on the Pulitzer Prize-winning *Oklahoma!* (1943), *South Pacific* (1949), *The King and I* (1951), and *The Sound of Music* (1959), among other shows.

Rodin, Auguste (1840-1917), French sculptor. He rose to fame in the late 1870s and in 1880 began the never-completed *Gate of Hell*, the source of such well-known pieces as *The Thinker* (1880) and *The Kiss* (1886). His works, in stone or bronze, were characterized by energy and emotional intensity, as in *The Burghers of Calais* (1884-94).

Rodney, Caesar (1728-84), American statesman. He was Delaware's delegate to the Continental Congress, signed the Declaration of Independence, and was president of Delaware (1778-82).

Rodrigo Díaz *See:* Cid, El.

Roebling, John Augustus (1806-69), U.S. engineer who pioneered modern suspension bridge design. His most famous works are the Brooklyn Bridge in New York City and a bridge at Niagara Falls (1855). He died before the completion (1883) of the Brooklyn Bridge, finished by his son Washington Augustus Roebling (1837-1926).

Roemer, Olaus (1644-1710), Danish astronomer, the first to show that light has a finite velocity. He noticed that Jupiter eclipsed its moons at times differing from those predicted and correctly concluded that the discrepancy resulted from the finite nature of light's velocity, which he calculated as 141

mi per sec (now calculated as about 186,282 mi per sec/299,792.458 km per sec).
See also: Astronomy.

Roentgen, Wilhelm Conrad (1845-1923), German physicist, recipient (1901) of the first Nobel Prize in physics for his discovery of X rays.
See also: X ray.

Roethke, Theodore (1908-63), U.S. poet who won a Pulitzer Prize for *The Waking* (1953) and a National Book Award for *Words for the Wind* (1958). Much of his imagery is drawn from nature.

Roe v. Wade, landmark decision (1973) by the U.S. Supreme Court ruling that a state may not prohibit a woman's right to have a medically initiated abortion during the first 6 months of pregnancy. A Texas waitress ("Jane Roe") began the case in 1970, when she challenged a state law that denied her a lawful abortion. The court came to this decision by determining that a fetus was not a living person and was therefore not entitled to constitutional protection.
See also: Abortion.

Rogers, Carl Ransom (1902-87), U.S. psychotherapist, who instituted the idea of the patient determining the extent and nature of his course of therapy, the therapist following the patient's lead.
See also: Psychotherapy.

Rogers, John (1829-1904), U.S. sculptor known for realistic figural groups, such as *The Slave Auction*. His extremely popular works were often mass-produced.

Rogers, Will (William Penn Adair; 1879-1935), U.S. humorist known for his homespun philosophy and mockery of politics and other subjects previously considered "untouchable." Part Irish and part Cherokee, he became famous in the Ziegfeld Follies of 1916. He wrote a syndicated column that appeared in 350 newspapers.

Rogers' Rangers, U.S. commando unit that fought on the side of the British during the French and Indian War. Led by the Loyalist Robert Rogers (1731-95), the rangers were responsible for daring raids on French settlements during the years 1758-63.
See also: French and Indian Wars.

Roget, Peter Mark (1779-1869), English scholar and physician, author of the definitive *Thesaurus of English Words and Phrases* (1852).

Rohrer, Heinrich (1933-   ), Swiss physicist, winner with Gerd Binnig and Ernst Ruska of West Germany of the Nobel Prize for physics (1986) for his contribution to the development of the scanning tunneling microscope (STM) that allows scientists to view individual atoms.
See also: Physics.

Roh Tae Woo (1932-), South Korean president (1988-92), succeeded by Kim Young Sam. Roh Tae Woo led the Defense Security Council (1979-81) under President Chun Doo Hwan. He retired from the military (1981) and organized the Summer Olympic Games held at Seoul (1988). He was active in the Democratic Justice Party before his election. In 1996, he was accused of corruption and sentenced to 17 year's imprisonment. However, in 1997 he was pardoned.

Roland, one of Charlemagne's commanders, hero of the *Song of Roland*. Ambushed by Basques at Roncesvalles in A.D. 778, he and his men were massacred because he was too proud to summon help.
See also: Charlemagne.

Roland de la Platière, husband and wife French revolutionaries. **Marie Jeanne Roland de la Platière** (1754-93) was hostess and adviser to the Girondists. Madame Roland, as she was known, became involved in a power struggle between the Girondists and the Jacobins, for which she and other leaders of the Girondists were arrested and sent to the guillotine. **Jean Marie Roland de la Platière** (1734-93) was leader of the Girondists (1791) and minister of the interior (1792-93). He committed suicide on hearing of the execution of his wife.
See also: French Revolution.

Rolfe, John (1585-1622), early English settler in Virginia who married the Indian princess Pocahontas (1614). His methods of curing tobacco made it the basis of the colony's later prosperity.
See also: Pocahontas.

Rolland, Romain (1866-1944), French writer, who won the 1915 Nobel Prize for literature. He is best known for his biographies, including *Beethoven* (1903), his pacifist articles *Above the Battle* (1915), and the novel-cycle *Jean Christophe* (1904-12).

Roller, species of bird belonging to the roller family. Flocks of rollers can be found in southern Europe during the warm season and northern Africa during the cold season. Standing at 10-16 in (25-40 cm), the roller resembles—but is not closely related to—the jay. Its name derives from the mating dance of the male, which consists of a series of airborne dives and tumbles.

Roller skating, popular source of sport and recreation. Traditional skates consist of four wheels fitted with ball bearings attached, 2 in front and 2 in back, to a shoe or to a steel platform that can be attached to a shoe. Clamp-on skates with metal wheels are generally worn out-of-doors while bootskates are most often used on rinks. For racing, wooden wheels are favored; for figure skating and roller hockey, wheels are usually made of plastic. In the late 1980s, a new type of skate, the roller blade, was introduced, with four wheels placed front to back to form a single line, or blade, of wheels.

Rolling Stones, influential rock band from Britain. Renowned for their hard-driving, blues-inspired, often sexually explicit songs, the band has influenced the course of popular music since the mid-1960s. Original band members include Mick Jagger (1943-   ), Keith Richard (1943-), Bill Wyman (1936-   ) and Charlie Watts (1941-   ). Guitarist Brian Jones left the band shortly before his death and was replaced by Mick Taylor in 1969 and then by Ron Wood in 1974. In addition to their many recordings, the Stones are known as one of the world's most exciting performance bands.

Rölvaag, Ole Edvart (1876-1931), Norwegian-born novelist, who came to the United States in 1896 and wrote in Norwegian. His trilogy *Giants in the Earth* (1927-31) is the story of Norwegian settlers in the United States.

Romains, Jules (Louis Farigoule; 1885-1972), French author and exponent of unanimism, or the collective personality. He is known for his plays and his 27-volume cycle *Men of Good Will* (1932-46).

Roman Catholic Church, major branch of the Christian church consisting of Christians in communion with the pope. It comprises the ecclesiastical organization that remained under papal obedience at the Reformation, consisting of a hierarchy of bishops and priests, with other officers such as cardinals. Roman Catholicism stresses the authority of tradition and the church (through ecumenical councils and the papacy) to formulate doctrine and regulate moral and spiritual life. Members participate in grace, mediated through the priesthood, by means of the seven sacraments. The mass is central to Roman Catholic life and worship. Doctrinally, Roman Catholic theologians emphasize the role of the Virgin Mary and the authority and infallibility of the pope. Other distinctive doctrines include clerical celibacy, limbo, and purgatory. Those held in common with the orthodox churches (but rejected by Protestants) include the invocation of saints, veneration of images, acceptance of the Apocrypha, the sacramental system, and monasticism. Since the Second Vatican Council, there has been a movement toward accommodation with the modern world, cautious dealings with the ecumenical movement, and encouragement of lay participation and vernacular liturgy. There are about 600 million Roman Catholics worldwide.
See also: Christianity.

Romance, literary term identified with fiction usually depicting idealized love. Romances typically contain nonrealistic characters and plots and use elements of fantasy or adventure. The ancient Greek romance, *Daphnis and Chloë*, written c.A.D. 200, is considered to be the first great romance. The genre reached its height in the Middle Ages with the tales of King Arthur. In the 19th century, romances contained a strong element of mystery and the supernatural.

Romance languages, one of the main groups of the Indo-European languages. It comprises those languages derived from the vernacular Latin that was spread by Roman soldiers and colonists, and that superseded local tongues. The languages include Italian, the Rhaeto-Romanic, Provençal, French, Walloon, Spanish, Catalan, Portuguese, and Romanian. The languages share a similar vocabulary and grammatical development.

Roman Circus *See:* Rome, Ancient.

Roman Empire *See:* Rome, Ancient.

Romanesque art and architecture, artistic style prevalent in Christian western Europe from c.A.D. 950 to 1200. Romanesque preceded Gothic art and architecture and is so called because its forms are derived from Roman art and architecture. The architecture, based on the round Roman arch and improvised systems of vaulting, was characterized by a massive, simple, and robust style with great vitality, particularly in the case of Norman architecture. Churches had immense towers; interiors were decorated with frescoes depicting biblical scenes. The sculptural style was varied, vigorous, and expressive, with carved, sculptured scenes on column capitals, and larger reliefs and figures on exterior portals and tympanums.

Roman Forum *See:* Forum.

Roman gods *See:* Mythology.

Romania, or Rumania, republic in southeastern Europe occupying the northeastern part of the Balkan Peninsula and bordering the Black Sea. Once part of the Roman Empire, its language is directly descended from Latin and closely resembles modern Italian. Although Romania was a communist country and a member of the Warsaw Pact, its foreign and economic policies were independent of those of the Soviet Union. Romania has worked to advance its own agriculture and industry, seeking relations with nations of the West as well as the East. Not withstanding democratization in the early 1990s the communists still hold key positions in politics and society.

Land and climate. The Carpathian Mountains are Romania's dominant geographical feature. They cross the forested southern Bukovina region and divide Moldavia in the east from Transylvania in the west. Moldavia extends east from the mountain highlands and sheltered valleys to the Prut River, forming the Moldavian "platform"—an unrelievedly flat plain covered by loess. Around Brasov, the Carpathians turn westward into the Transylvanian Alps, whose peaks reach heights of 8,347 ft (2,541 m). Beyond the Timis River, the mountain chain is continued by the Banat Mountains, which slope down to the fertile plains of the Tisza River Lowlands on the eastern edge of the Hungarian Plain. Within the arc of the Carpathians lies the Transylvania Plateau, a region of low hills, fertile valleys, and alluvial plains. At the western edge of the Carpathians, the Danube River flows south and east before swinging north to its delta, which is rich in wildlife. Between the Danube and the Carpathians are the fertile plains of Walachia. The only part of Romania south of the Danube is the Dobruja, a narrow, low-lying coastal strip that is marshy but fertile, extending into Bulgaria.

In general, Romania has a continental climate with cold, snowy winters. Winters are especially long and severe on the eastern plains and in the Dobruja. Summer temperatures average 70°F (20°C). Rainfall averages 25 in on the plains and 10 in in parts of the Dobruja. The high west-facing mountain slopes receive more than 60 in of rain and snow annually.

People. About 90% are Romanians, with Hungarian and German minorities. Over half of the population of Romania lives in town. The largest cities are Bucharest, Brasov, Iasi, Timisoara, Constantsa, Cluj-Napoca, and Galati. Bucharest is the capital city.

Economy. Over 60% of the land area of Romania is agricultural, but industry provides half of the national income. About 25% of the land is covered by forests. With large oil fields in the Prahova Valley, Romania is one of the largest producers of petroleum and natural gas in Europe. Copper, lead, coal, iron ore, and lead are mined. Principal industries are iron and steel, machi-

Romania

Capital:	Bucharest
Area:	91,699 sq mi
	(237,500 sq km)
Population:	22,395,000
Language:	Romanian
Government:	Republic
Independent:	1878
Head of gov.:	Prime minister
Per capita:	U.S. $1,480
Mon. unit:	1 Romanian leu = 100
	bani

nery, textiles, and chemicals. The main exports are oil-field equipment, furniture, agricultural machinery, and textiles.

History. Most of modern Romania was once part of ancient Dacia, thoroughly imbued with the language and culture of Rome. After the 13th century the two principalities of Moldavia and Walachia emerged, existing as dependencies of Turkey until 1829, then as Russian protectorates. United in 1861, Romania gained its independence in 1878. After World War I the Romanian-speaking province of Transylvania was acquired from Austria-Hungary. In the 1930s the country was dominated by Fascist rule; in 1941 dictator Ion Antonescu sided with the Axis powers. Overrun by the USSR in 1944, Romania became a satellite state. After King Michael's abdication in 1947 it became a republic. In the 1960s and 1970s Romania worked to establish diplomatic and economic relations with the West. In the 1980s, Nicolae Ceausescu, Romania's ruler since 1965, began a "modernization" program to industrialize urban communities. Romania's subsequent debt to Western European banks has slowed its economic growth. In December 1989, an anti-communist revolution resulted in Ceausescu's ouster and subsequent execution. On May 20, 1990 Ion Iliescu was elected president. While trying to modernize its economy, Romania has adopted harsh economic measures, which have led to continued political and social unrest.The 1996 elections ended the ex-Communists' power.

Roman numerals, system of numerical representation based on symbols invented by the ancient Romans c.500 B.C. The early Roman system—with some modification—was commonly used for simple calculations as late as the 16th century, when it was eclipsed by the Arabic system. It is used today primarily for notational and decorative purposes, and to record dates. In the Roman system, the symbols I, V, X, L, C, D, and M stand for the numbers 1, 5, 10, 50, 100, 500, and 1,000, respectively.
See also: Numeration systems.

Romanov, ruling dynasty of Russia (1613-1917). The first Romanov tsar was Michael. The last of the direct Romanov line was Peter, but succeeding tsars retained the name of Romanov, down to Nicholas II (r. 1894-1917).

Romanov, Grigoriy Vasilyevich (1923-), former USSR Communist Party official and member of the Politburo (1976-1985). He was previously a member of the Secretariat and the Presidium. Although he ostensibly quit his post for medical reasons, it is believed his removal was political. *See also:* Union of Soviet Socialist Republics.

Roman Republic *See:* Rome, Ancient.

Romans, Epistle to the, New Testament book written by Saint Paul to the Christians of Rome (A.D. 58). It presents his major statement of justification by faith, and the Christian's consequent freedom from condemnation, sin, and the law. It stresses God's sovereignty and grace. *See also:* New Testament.

Romanticism, 19th-century European artistic movement. Its values of emotion, intuition, imagination, and individualism were in opposition to the ideals of restraint, reason, and harmony promoted by classicism. The word "romantic" was first applied to art by Friedrich von Schlegel in 1798. It was later used as a label for works emphasizing the subjective, spiritual, or fantastic; those concerned with wild, uncultivated nature; and those that seemed fundamentally modern rather than classical. The evocative qualities of nature inspired poets such as William Wordsworth, Samuel Taylor Coleridge, and Alphonse Lamartine, and painters such as Joseph Turner and Caspar Friedrich. William Blake and J.W. von Goethe sought to develop new spiritual values; individualism concerned artists as disparate as Walt Whitman and Francisco Goya. The lives of Lord Byron and Frédéric Chopin seemed to exemplify the romantic myth. Among the greatest romantic composers were C.M. von Weber, Hector Berlioz, Felix Mendelssohn, Franz Liszt, and Richard Wagner.

Roman walls, walls constructed by the ancient Romans in what is now Germany, Romania, and northern England. They served to protect the Romans against invasion as well as to facilitate trade and the collection of taxes. The ruins of Hadrian's Wall, built C.A.D. 120, still exist today. It was built primarily of stone and had ditches both in front of the wall and behind. Forts and watchtowers were placed along the wall at regular intervals. *See also:* Rome, Ancient.

Romberg, Sigmund (1887-1951), Hungarian-born U.S. composer. He wrote over 70 operettas and musicals, including *The Student Prince* (1924) and *The Desert Song* (1926). He went on to write many film scores.

Rome (Italian: *Roma*; pop. 2,723,300), capital and largest city of Italy, located on the rolling plain of the Roman Campagna, 15 mi (24 km) from the Thyrrenian Sea. Rome has been a center of Western civilization for over 2,000 years. "The Eternal City" was capital of the Roman Empire and is of unique religious significance as the site of the headquarters of the Roman Catholic Church in Vatican City. Administration (of the Italian government as well as of Roma province and the region of Latium), religion, and tourism are the most important activities of modern Rome, which is also a center for commerce, publishing, movies, and fashion. A great transportation hub, the city has relatively little industry. The site of ancient Rome is the Seven Hills.

The Tiber River flows through the city, which contains many important relics of classical Rome, such as the Forum, the Colosseum, the *Domus Aurea* (Golden House), the baths of Caracalla, and the Pantheon. Rome is famous for its squares, Renaissance palaces, churches, basilicas, catacombs, and fountains. There are also many fine museums, art collections, and libraries; the Rome opera house; and the Santa Cecilia music academy, the world's oldest (1584). The University of Rome was founded in 1303.
See also: Italy.

Rome (pop. 43,826), city in Oneida County in central New York State. The location of important battles fought during the American Revolution, it is known as the site of the first raising of the American flag. The building of the Erie Canal began in Rome in 1817. Major industries are copper production and machinery. It is the home of the Griffiss Air Force base.
See also: New York.

Rome, Ancient, city-state in central Italy that grew into a vast empire. At its height, in A.D. 117, it comprised most of the known Western world. The ancient Romans made great advances in the fields of law, civil engineering, standardization in coinage and measurement, philosophy, architecture, and literature. The region was controlled by the Etruscans until Romans established an independent republic in 500 B.C. Throughout the period of the republic (500-31 B.C.), warfare was almost continuous. Under a government controlled by consuls and the senate, Rome overran central and southern Italy and defeated Carthage. Expansion continued to Greece, Asia Minor, Syria, Palestine, and Egypt, Gaul, and England. From about 100 B.C., Rome began to move steadily toward disaster. Civil wars arose from conflicts between senatorial factions, and between rich and poor. The army leaders Pompey and Julius Caesar arose to form the first Triumverate with Crassus. After the assassination of Caesar, Caesar's nephew Octavian defeated Antony and became the first emperor of Rome, renaming himself Augustus. For more than 200 years (27 B.C.-A.D. 180) the empire flourished. The establishment of trade routes throughout the empire lead to the spread of new ideas, particularly Christianity. From about A.D. 200 the period was characterized by internal strife and barbarian raids. Under Constantine I (emperor 306-337) the capital was moved to Byzantium (renamed Constantinople), and Christianity was officially recognized. At the beginning of the fifth century, the empire was divided into East and West, and a period of barbarian invasion and vandalism followed.

Rommel, Erwin (1891-1944), German field marshal, named the "Desert Fox" for his tactical genius as commander of the Afrika Korps (1941-43). His advance ended with the battle of El Alamein (1942). He commanded Army Group B in northern France when the Allies landed in Normandy (1944). He was implicated in the July 1944 plot to assassinate Hitler. Given the choice of suicide or trial, he took poison.
See also: World War II.

Romney, George (1734-1802), English portrait painter, rival of Sir Joshua Reynolds in late-18th-century London. Influenced by classical sculpture, he tended to flatter his subjects, among whom was Lady Emma Hamilton.

Romulo, Carlos Pena (1901-85), Filipino journalist and statesman. His World War II broadcasts during the Japanese occupation of the Philippines were known as "The Voice of Freedom." He won a Pulitzer Prize (1941) and was ambassador to the United States and president of the UN general assembly (1949-50).
See also: Philippines.

Romulus and Remus, mythical founders of Rome (by tradition in 753 B.C.), twin sons of Rhea Silvia, descendant of Aeneas, by the god Mars. Abandoned as infants, they were suckled by a she-wolf until adopted by a herdsman. After a long rivalry, Remus was killed by Romulus, who became the first king of Rome and was later worshiped as the god Quirinus.
See also: Mythology; Rome.

Romulus Augustulus (b. c.A.D. 461), last Western Roman emperor (475-6), puppet of his father Orestes. The end of the Western Roman Empire dates from his overthrow by Odoacer.
See also: Rome, Ancient.

Rondo, musical form in which a main theme is repeatedly stated between two contrasting sections. The rondo generally consists of five or seven parts and has a fixed pattern (ABACA or ABACABA). It was frequently used by composers of the late 18th and early 19th centuries as the last movement of a larger work. Wolfgang Amadeus Mozart and Franz Josef Haydn often concluded their symphonies with a rondo section.

Ronsard, Pierre de (1524-85), French "Prince of Poets," leader of the influential group of poets called Pléiade. Best known as a lyric poet, as in *Sonnets for Hélène* (1578), he also wrote lofty *Hymnes* (1556) on more public subjects and an epic, *La Franciade* (1572).

Ronstadt, Linda (1946-   ), U.S. singer. Ronstadt began her musical career with the rock group Stone Poneys (1967). She achieved solo success and starred as Mabel in the Broadway production and film of *The Pirates of Penzance* and sang the lead in Puccini's *La Bohème* in New York (1983). In 1993 she received a Grammy Award for best country singer.

Roof, cover for the top of a building. A roof encloses and protects a building from the elements, and helps drain water from rainfall. Large beams (often called joists), timbers, and rafters support a roof. Metal, concrete, or composite materials are used to build a roof or smaller roofing units called shingles. Flat and lean-to roofs consist of designs of one flat plane. Roofs in which the design consists of two joined flat planes are the gable roof and its inverted design, the butterfly roof. The hip, gambrel, and mansard roofs are more sophisticated designs, in which more than two flat planes are joined at various angles. The design of the roof and the choice of roofing materials are based on the function of the building as well as the climate.

Rook (*Corvus frugilegus*), European bird in the crow family. The rook is about 18 in (45 cm) long. A purple gloss on the black back, white skin next to the bill, and gray to white feathers on the face of an adult are its distinguishing features. It eats insects, worms, and grain. Some rooks native to Europe do not migrate while others in more northern locations migrate south in winter. Rookeries are enormous groupings of rooks—often in the hundreds—that gather during the mating season.

Roosevelt, Eleanor (1884-1962), U.S. humanitarian, wife of Franklin Delano Roosevelt, and niece of Theodore Roosevelt. Active in politics and social issues (notably for women and minority groups), she was a UN delegate (1945-53, 1961) and coauthored the Universal Declaration of Human Rights. Her many books include *This Is My Story* (1937) and *On My Own* (1958).
See also: Human Rights, Declaration of.

Roosevelt, Franklin Delano (1882-1945), 32nd president of the United States. Roosevelt was elected to four terms, more than any other U.S. president, and led the nation through two major crises: a severe depression and a global war. His flexible, experimental approach to politics enabled him to lead the U.S., with widespread support of the people, through one of the most formative periods in U.S. history.
Early life. Roosevelt was born into a wealthy New York family and brought up—as was his fifth cousin, Theodore Roosevelt—in a restricted social circle that was the closest to an aristocracy the United States ever had. Educated at home until age 14, he attended private school and Harvard, from which he graduated in 1903. Roosevelt entered Columbia Law School in 1904 and passed the bar in 1907. In 1905, he married Anna Eleanor Roosevelt (known by her middle name), a distant cousin who was Theodore Roosevelt's niece. The couple had six children.
Politics. Roosevelt served as a Democrat in the N.Y. Senate (1910-13), then as assistant secretary of the Navy (1913-21), gaining a national reputation as a capable administrator. In 1920, he ran for vice president with presidential candidate James M. Cox. They lost to the Republican ticket of Warren G. Harding and Calvin Coolidge.
While on vacation in Aug. 1921, Roosevelt suffered a severe attack of polio, which partially paralyzed his arms and legs. His mother urged him to retire, but his wife and his secretary, Louis Howe, encouraged him to work to regain some use of his limbs—and reenter politics. He did both. Roosevelt was elected governor of New York in 1928 and 1930. In 1932, he ran for president against incumbent Herbert Hoover. Roosevelt promised a "New Deal" to bring the nation out of its worsening depression, but it was Hoover's unpopularity that most helped Roosevelt win the election.
President. By the time Roosevelt took office in 1933, the U.S. economy was near collapse. More than 13 million people were unemployed, many farmers and city workers were homeless, and thousands of banks were closing daily. Two days after his Mar. 4 inauguration, Roosevelt ended a run on the banks by declaring a "bank holiday." He closed all banks, then had the Treasury Dept. examine their books and resupply funds where possible. Public confidence was restored by the time the banks reopened. On Mar. 9, Congress met in a special session to pass Roosevelt's call for emergency legislation. On Mar. 12, he gave the first of his many "fireside chats"—radio addresses to the nation, explaining his policies. Four days later, he began sending his New Deal proposals to Congress, beginning the "Hundred Days" in which many new programs were established to rebuild the economy and put people back to work. Among Roosevelt's ground-breaking New Deal programs were the

---

Franklin Delano Roosevelt

32nd president of the United States	
Born:	Hyde Park, N.Y.; Jan. 30, 1882
Term:	Mar. 1933-Apr. 1945
Vice presidents:	John N. Garner; Henry A. Wallace; Harry S. Truman
Political party:	Democratic
Spouse:	Anna Eleanor Roosevelt Roosevelt
Children:	6
Died:	Warm Springs, Ga.; Apr. 12, 1945

Agricultural Adjustment Administration (AAA), which paid farmers to voluntarily reduce production in order to raise prices; the National Recovery Administration (NRA), which included minimum wages and maximum hours for workers; the Civilian Conservation Corps (CCC), which put young men to work in reforestation and other public works; and the Tennessee Valley Authority (TVA), a model for interstate conservation projects of the future. The New Deal also brought in the Wagner Act of 1935, which aided labor; the Work Projects Administration (WPA), a massive new relief program; and a tax-reform bill, social-security act, and youth administration act. In 1936, Roosevelt won reelection in a landslide. However, the economy was not yet under control. When the Supreme Court nullified some New Deal acts, Roosevelt attempted to "pack" the court with additional justices who would support him, but Congress denied him that power. Full economic recovery came only with the war. Until 1937, Roosevelt had paid relatively little attention to foreign affairs. Then World War II broke out in Europe in 1939. In 1940, Roosevelt was reelected to a third term, promising to keep the nation out of war. But on Dec. 7, 1941, Japan struck the U.S. fleet at Pearl Harbor, Hawaii, in a surprise attack. Four days later, the U.S. was at war with Japan, Germany, and Italy. Roosevelt, who directed the immense U.S. war effort and conferred with Allied leaders, was elected to an unprecedented fourth term in 1944. But he did not live to see the war's end. He died suddenly on Apr. 12, 1945, of a cerebral hemorrhage.

Roosevelt, Nicholas J. (1767-1854), U.S. engineer who, at the request of Robert Fulton and Robert Livingston, built and operated the *New Orleans*, the first Mississippi paddle-wheel steamer (1811).

Roosevelt, Theodore (1858-1919), 26th president of the United States. Widely known as "Teddy" or "T.R.," he was one of the most popular, colorful, and controversial presidents, and the youngest (at 42) ever inaugurated. He also was a prolific writer.
Early life. Roosevelt was born into a well-to-do family. A sickly child, he built up his strength through strenuous exercise. In 1880, he graduated from Harvard University and married Alice Hathaway Lee. Roosevelt became involved in Republican politics and served in the N.Y. State Assembly (1882-84). In 1884, his wife died soon after the birth of their child; his mother died the same day. Roosevelt gave up his political career and moved to Dakota Territory to become a rancher and to write. In 1886, Roosevelt

---

Theodore Roosevelt

26th president of the United States

Born:	New York City, N.Y.; Oct. 27, 1858
Term:	Sept. 1901-Mar. 1909
Vice president:	Charles W. Fairbanks (Mar. 1905-Mar. 1909)
Political party:	Republican
Spouses:	Alice Hathaway Lee Roosevelt;
	Edith Kermit Carow Roosevelt
Children:	6
Died:	Oyster Bay, N.Y.; Jan. 6, 1919

---

returned to New York, married Edith Kermit Carow (the couple had five children), and built his famous home at Sagamore Hill.

Politics. Roosevelt reentered politics, losing a race for mayor of New York City (1886), and serving on the U.S. Civil Service Commission (1895-97), as president of the Board of Police Commissioners (1897-98), and as assistant secretary of the Navy (1897-98).

During the Spanish-American War, Roosevelt led the 1st Volunteer Cavalry Regiment, known as the Rough Riders. In Cuba in 1898, he led a victorious U.S. attack up Kettle Hill in the battle of San Juan Hill. Returning home a national hero, he was elected governor of New York (1898-1900), then was persuaded to run as vice president in President William McKinley's 1900 reelection campaign. The McKinley-Roosevelt ticket won. On Sept. 6, 1901, McKinley was shot by an assassin; eight days later he died, and Roosevelt became president.

President. Roosevelt, long known as a reformer, used his executive power to control the growing industrial and financial monopolies and regulate the railroads. His "trust buster" administration broke up the powerful Northern Securities Co. and other big-business trusts (monopolies). Roosevelt also intervened in a dangerously stalemated coal strike. Returned to the presidency by a wide margin in the 1904 election, he won passage of the 1906 Hepburn Act to prevent abuses in railroad-shipping rates, and of the 1906 Pure Food and Drug Act, which began U.S. regulation and inspection of foods, drugs, and medicines. He also added about 150 million acres to the national forests, established the U.S. Forest Service (1905), and created other conservation programs.

Roosevelt pursued an aggressive foreign policy. He issued the "Roosevelt Corollary" (1904) to the Monroe Doctrine, warning European nations against intervening in Latin American affairs while reserving that right for the U.S. He pushed the U.S. to build the Panama Canal and sent the U.S. fleet around the world (1907-1909) to show off its strength. In 1905, he helped mediate peace between Russia and Japan, which won him the Nobel Peace Prize.

Retirement. Roosevelt chose not to run for reelection. After his handpicked successor, William Howard Taft, took office in 1909, Roosevelt went big-game hunting in Africa. In 1912, he returned to politics, forming the "Bull Moose" (Progressive) party and losing a bid for the presidency. Retiring to private life, he remained interested in world affairs, opposing U.S. isolationism in World War   I.

Roosevelt, Theodore, Jr. (1887-1944), U.S. politician, explorer, soldier, and author; son of President Theodore Roosevelt. He participated in the founding of the American Legion (1919). As a politician, he was a representative in the New York Assembly, assistant secretary of the Navy in the 1920s, and governor of Puerto Rico (1929-32). As an explorer he traveled through Asia for the Field Museum and subsequently wrote about his experiences. He wrote other books, including *Colonial Policies of the United States* (1937). As a soldier he served as a commander in both world wars; he died in France during World War II.

Roosevelt Campobello International Park, jointly administered by the United States and Canada, covers about 2,700 acres (1,090 hectares) on Campobello Island, southwest New Brunswick, Canada.

Root, quantities that when taken a designated number of times will result in a specific quantity. Some roots are the second (square) or third (cube) time a number is designated; for example, the square of 25 is 5, because the root 5 is designated twice: 5 x 5 = 25. Similarly the cube of 27 is 3, because the root 3 is designated three times: 3 x 3 x 3 = 27. The number of times a root is designated is called its index. In algebra, the number that may stand for *x* and satisfy the equation is also called a root.
See also: Algebra; Factor.

Root, part of a plant that absorbs water and nutrients and anchors the plant. Water and nutrients enter a root through minute root hairs sited at the tip of each root. There are two main types of root systems; the taproot system, in which smaller secondary and tertiary roots branch out from a strong main root; and the fibrous root system, in which a mass of equal-sized roots are produced. In plants such as the sugar beet, the taproot may become swollen with stored food material. Adventitious roots anchor the stems of climbing plants, such as ivy. Epiphytic plants such as orchids have roots that absorb moisture from the air. The roots of parasitic plants such as mistletoe and dodder absorb food from other plants.

Root, Elihu (1845-1937), U.S. statesman. He reorganized the command structure of the army as war secretary (1899-1904) under President William McKinley, and as Theodore Roosevelt's secretary of state (1905-9) he oversaw administration of the new possessions won from Spain. A champion of the League of Nations and the World Court, he won the 1912 Nobel Peace Prize. He was a New York Republican senator (1909-15).

Root, John Wellborn (1850-91), U.S. architect, member of the Chicago School. Along with the architect Daniel Hudson Burnham, he was a leader in technical innovations and design of early skyscrapers. The use of heavy, load-bearing mason walls and iron frame interior supports were used to construct the Montauk Block office building (1881-82) and the Rookery (1885-88). The Monadnock Building (1889-91) is still the highest building with load-bearing walls and a steel interior frame. The Rand McNally Building (1889-90) used a steel-frame construction, still important in modern architecture. Root also designed the tallest building in the world for its time, the 22-story Masonic Temple (1890-92).
See also: Architecture; Burnham, Daniel Hudson.

Rope, thick, strong cord made from twisted lengths of fiber. It can be made from manila hemp, henequen, sisal, true hemp, coir (coconut palm fiber), flax, jute, and cotton. Synthetic fibers, particularly nylon and polyesters, are used for lighter and more durable rope. Other ropes, such as for suspension cables in bridge building, are made from wire.

Rorem, Ned (1923-   ), U.S. composer of melodic art-songs whose texts are drawn from the works of 20th-century U.S. poets. His *Air Music* won the 1976 Pulitzer Prize. He has published 5 volumes of diaries (1966-78).

Rosario (pop. 1,096,300), city in east-central Argentina on the Paraná River. The third largest city in the country, it developed as a shipping and processing center for the many food products from the Pampa, the fertile plains of Argentina, which Rosario borders to the east. Water and railway transportation make Rosario an important inland port city. Chemical, textile, and metal manufacturers as well as petroleum refiners are also located here. Founded in 1730, it became an important city in the 1800s when the Pampas began developing agricultural products.
See also: Argentina.

Rosas, Juan Manuel de (1793-1877), Argentine dictator, governor of Buenos Aires province (1835-52), who built up a private army of *gauchos* (cowboys). Bribery, force, expansionism, and continuous revolt marked his rule, which nevertheless contributed to Argentine unification.
See also: Argentina.

Roscius, Quintus (Quintus Roscius Gallus; d. 62 B.C.), Roman actor of such renown that "Roscius" was long a compliment for actors.

Rose, popular name for various woody shrubs and vines of the genus *Rosa*, with tough thorns and colorful flowers. There are some 100 wild rose species native to the Northern Hemisphere, but only 9 have been involved in the breeding of the hundreds of varieties now available. In many cultivated varieties the stamens become petaloid, producing double flowers. The rose family contains many important cultivated plants, including the apple, cherry, plum, and strawberry.

Rose, Ernestine Potowski (1810-92), advocate for women's rights. Born in Poland, she lived in the United States for more than 30 years before retiring to England. In New York State, she fought for and won legislation that allowed women the control of properties they had obtained before marriage (1848). Along with Elizabeth Cady Stanton and Susan B. Anthony, she founded the National Suffrage Association (1869), a group that fought for women's rights—including the right to vote. She was also an active abolitionist and prohibitionist.
See also: Women's movements.

Rose, Pete (1941-   ), U.S. baseball player. Known for his aggressiveness, he earned the nickname "Charlie Hustle." He holds the all time major league record for hits (4,256) and was named the National League's Most Valuable Player in 1973. He played several positions while a member of the Cincinnati Reds (1963-78), the Philadelphia Phillies (1979-83) and the Montreal Expos

(1984). In 1984, Rose returned to the Reds as a player-manager for 3 years, after which he continued to serve as manager until 1989, when he was suspended (later banned for life) from baseball for alleged gambling on baseball games.

Roseau (pop. 11,000), capital city of Dominica, one of the Windward Islands in the Caribbean Sea. It is a port city, located on a river by the same name. Its exports include spices and lime products. Before its independence (1978), Dominica was ruled by the British (1759-1978) after the original European colonization by the French (mid-17th century).
See also: Dominica.

Rose chafer, or rose bug (*Macrodactylus subspinosus*), beetle found in the eastern and central regions of the United States. The rose chafer feeds on and destroys rose, grape, and apple blossoms. It measures about 1/3 in (8 mm) long, is light brown to gray, and has long legs with tiny spines. Special cultivating techniques used by commercial growers, cloth coverings used by home gardeners, and insecticides used by both help rid plants of these beetles.

Rosecrans, William Starke (1819-98), Union general in the U.S. Civil War. After early successes in West Virginia and Mississippi, he was given command of the Army of the Cumberland (1862) but was heavily defeated at the Battle of Chickamauga (1863) and relieved of command.
See also: Civil War, U.S.

Rosefish, or Norway Haddock, important food fish of the family Scorpaenidae. The orange-to-red colored rosefish is abundant in the North Atlantic, especially between the New England coast and Greenland. It is also plentiful off the North Atlantic coast of Europe. It may grow up to 2 ft (61 cm) in length.

Rosemary (*Rosmarinus officinalis*), evergreen shrub of the mint family, found in southern Europe and western Asia. It has blue flowers and grayish leaves and produces a pungent, refreshing perfume.

Rosenberg, husband and wife, the only U.S. citizens put to death in peacetime for espionage. **Julius** (1918-53) and **Ethel** (1915-53) were convicted in 1951 for passing atomic secrets in World War II to the USSR, then a U.S. ally. They were electrocuted on June 19, 1953.

Rosenberg, Alfred (1893-1946), Nazi propagandist and newspaper editor, early associate of Adolf Hitler. In his *Myth of the 20th Century* (1930) he outlined a theory of Nordic racial superiority that was used to justify Nazi anti-Semitism and German world conquest. After the Nuremberg Trials, he was executed for war crimes.
See also: Nazism; Propaganda.

Rosenquist, James Albert (1933-   ), U.S. painter who turned his early billboard-painting career into a style of art. His gigantic images of movie stars, such as Kirk Douglas, and objects of cultural impact, such as *F-111*, put him in the vanguard of pop art.
See also: Pop art.

Rose of Jericho *See:* Resurrection plant.

Rose of Lima, Saint (1586-1617), born in Lima, Peru, first canonized saint in the New World (1671) and patron saint of South America.

Rose of Sharon, or Althaea (*Hibiscus syriacus*), shrub in the mallow family. The rose of Sharon, a native of Asia, is abundant in North American gardens. It is grown indoors in pots and often transplanted to the outdoors. The late purple through white and blue blooms of September are about 3 in (8 cm) wide. This shrub often reaches a height of 12 ft (3.7 m).

Rosetta Stone, inscribed basalt slab, discovered in 1799, that provided the key to Egyptian hieroglyphics. About 4 ft (1.2 m) long and 2.5 ft (0.75 m) wide, it is inscribed with identical texts in Greek, Egyptian demotic, and Egyptian hieroglyphs. Found near Rosetta, Egypt, the stone is now in the British Museum.
See also: Egypt, Ancient; Hieroglyphics.

Rose window *See:* Stained glass.

Rosewood, any of a genus (*Dalbergia*) of trees in the pea family. All species are located in tropical climates. Rosewood from Honduras and Brazil, in particular, is valuable in the commercial manufacture of fine furniture and musical instruments. The color ranges from a deep brown to purple, with attractive blackish streaks and grain markings. When cut, rosewood has a scent similar to that of garden roses.

Rosh Ha-Shanah (Hebrew, "head of the year"), Jewish New Year, observed on the 1st and 2nd days of the 7th Jewish month, Tishri (Sept.-Oct.). It is considered the Day of Judgment, when each person's fate is inscribed in the Book of Life. On Rosh Hashanah the *shofar* (ram's horn) calls Jews to 10 days of penitence ending with Yom Kippur.
See also: Yom Kippur.

Rosin, resin derived from certain pine trees from North America and Europe. A distilling process makes the resin collected from live trees usable in the manufacture of various products, from paints and paper sizing to adhesives and inks. String bows and dance shoes are treated with dried rosin to prevent slipping. Rosins range in color from black to deep red amber, and yellow. The cluster and scotch pines of Europe and the longleaf and loblolly pines of the United States produce most resins for rosin. Three main types of rosin include gum, wood, and sulfa.
See also: Resin.

Ross, Betsy (1753-1836), U.S. seamstress who is said to have made, to George Washington's design, the first U.S. flag (1776).

Ross, George (1730-79), colonial politician and lawyer from Pennsylvania. He was a signer of the Declaration of Independence (1776) while a member of the Continental Congress (1774-77). He helped write the Constitution for Pennsylvania (1776) and also served as a member of the Pennsylvania assembly (1768-76). His last political post was as one of Pennsylvania's admiralty judges (1779).

Ross, Harold Wallace (1892-1951), founder (1925) and lifetime editor of the *New Yorker* magazine. Originally conceived as basically by and for New Yorkers, the magazine won national prestige and has had an enduring effect on American journalism and literature.

Ross, John (1790-1866), Cherokee chief and, from 1839, chief of the united Cherokee nation. He opposed the U.S. government's attempt to move his people west of the Mississippi River, but in 1838 he was forced to lead them to Oklahoma on a difficult journey known as the "trail of tears."

Ross, Nellie Tayloe (1876-1977), U.S. public official. Elected to succeed her husband, who had died, she was the first woman governor (Wyoming, 1925-27). She was director of the U.S. Mint (1933-53).

Ross, Sir James Clark (1800-62), British polar explorer who reached a point farther south (78°10'S) than any explorer until 1900. He made a number of Arctic expeditions, some with his uncle, Sir John Ross, and with William Parry. He located the north magnetic pole in 1831. In the historic 1839-43 Antarctic expedition, he discovered the Ross Sea and Victoria Land. *See also:* Antarctica.

Ross, Sir John (1777-1856), British explorer whose first, unsuccessful expedition in search of the Northwest Passage was made in 1818 with James Ross and William Parry. In a return voyage (1829-33), he discovered and surveyed Boothia Peninsula, the Gulf of Boothia, and King William Island. *See also:* Northwest Passage.

Ross, Sir Ronald (1857-1932), British physician awarded the 1902 Nobel Prize in physiology or medicine for his investigations of the *Anopheles* mosquito in relation to the transmission of malaria.

Ross Dependency, section of Antarctica on the Ross Sea. Science personnel are located on bases here. The base established by the U.S. explorer Richard E. Byrd in 1928 is also here. This New Zealand-administered dependency covers about 160,000 sq mi (414,000 sq km) of land uninhabited except for the bases. An ice shelf takes up approximately 130,000 sq mi (337,000 sq km). McMurdo Sound is also found within its borders. *See also:* Antarctica.

Rossellini, Roberto (1906-77), Italian film director. His *Open City* (1945), partly made up of footage of the Italian resistance during World War II, established him as a leader of the neorealist movement. Among his other films are *General della Rovere* (1959), *The Rise of Louis XIV* (1966), and *Socrates* (1970).

Rossetti, two leading English artists, brother and sister. The poems of **Christina Georgina Rossetti** (1830-94) range from fantasy (*Goblin Market*, 1862) to religious poetry. Her brother, **Dante Gabriel Rossetti** (1828-82), was a founder of the Pre-Raphaelites. His paintings, of languid, mystical beauty, depict subjects from Dante and medieval romance. He excelled as a poet, notably in his love sonnets.

Rossini, Gioacchino Antonio (1792-1868), Italian composer best known for his comic operas, especially *The Barber of Seville* (1816). The dramatic grand opera *William Tell* (1829), with its famous overture, was his last opera.

Rosso, Il (Giovanni Battista di Iacopo di Gasparre; c.1495-1540), Italian painter, one of the founders of mannerism. *The Deposition* (1521) exemplifies the elongated figures, hectic color, and emotionalism of his paintings.

Rostand, Edmond (1868-1918), French dramatist, best known for his play *Cyrano de Bergerac* (1897), which led a romantic revival.

Rostock (pop. 246,000), city in eastern Germany, located on the Baltic Sea and the Warnow River. It is an important port city through which ships, machinery, and supplies for the petroleum industry are transported. Founded in 1218, it became an important member of the medieval Hanseatic League. The University of Rostock (1419) is also located here.
See also: Germany.

Rostov-on-Don, or Rostov (pop. 1,025,000), important city in Russia, near the Sea of Azov on the Don River. Rostov-on-Don is known mainly for farm products, coal, and farm machinery. Founded in 1780, it is an active port and railway center, as well as an industrial city at the foot of the Caucasus Mountains. It is also the site of a World War II battle (1942) in which German forces defeated the Soviet army, until the city was retaken by the Soviets a year later.
See also: Russian Federation.

Rostropovich, Mstislav Leopoldovich (1927-   ), Soviet cellist, who has had works created for him by many composers. From the mid-1970s he and his wife, the soprano Galina Vishnevskaya, lived outside the USSR. He became conductor of the National Symphony Orchestra, Washington, D.C., in 1977. In 1990 he returned to Russia.

Roszak, Theodore (1907-81), U.S. sculptor. Best known for his sinister, birdlike figures in steel and bronze, he also designed the 45-ft (14 m) spire of the Massachusetts Institute of Technology chapel.

Rot, the name given to several fungi and bacteria that destroy plants. Root rot attacks various root crops, sugarcane, and peas. Brown rot is either a cup fungus or a bacterial attack on tobacco, peas, and beans. Black rot attacks cabbages and cauliflower heads.

Rotary engine, internal-combustion engine that uses rotors instead of pistons. The most important parts of this type of engine are the triangle-shaped rotor and the chamber. The movement of the rotor keeps the chamber divided into three sections in which different stages of the combustion process occur. Depending on the engine, there may be several rotors, each containing its own chambers. The rotary engine works on a four-stroke cycle of induction, compression, combustion, and exhaust. In the induction stage a mixture of

air and gas enters the chamber. The mixture is then compressed in the second stroke of the cycle. The mixture is then ignited by spark plugs in the combustion stroke. This creates gases which cause the rotor to move. The exhaust stroke forces the burnt gases to leave the engine. Although it consists of fewer parts than equally-powered piston engines, it emits more pollution and burns more fuel. At low speeds, but not high speeds, it emits a loud noise. Felix Wankel of Germany created the most popular rotary engine design in the 1950s.
See also: Internal combustion engine.

Rotary International, worldwide service organization, consisting of members from various professions and businesses. The organization originally met in a rotating basis at the homes of its members in Chicago, where it was founded (1905) by Paul P. Harris. The club provides scholarships and business exchanges as well as health programs in communities around the world. It has member clubs in over 150 countries.

Rotary wing aircraft *See:* Helicopter; V/STOL; Autogiro.

ROTC *See:* Reserve Officers Training Corps.

Rotenone, naturally occurring insecticide. This substance is extracted from the root of the tropical derris and cube plants. Harmless to humans and other warm-blooded animals, it poisons cold-blooded animals, especially insects. Rotenone protects garden plants and vegetable crops from insect destruction and protects farm animals from certain parasites, such as fleas.
See also: Insecticide.

Roth, Mark (1951-), U.S. professional bowler. He set the record for the highest average, 221.662, in 1979. Roth's achievements include winning a record 8 Professional Bowlers Association (PBA) titles (1978), and the U.S. Open and Touring Players Championship (1984). A member of the PBA since 1970, Roth was selected as Player of the Year 4 times (1977-79, 84).

Roth, Philip (1933-), U.S. writer. His protagonists agonize between a traditional Jewish upbringing and modern urban society. He became recognized with the novella and stories in *Goodbye Columbus* (1959). His best-known novel is *Portnoy's Complaint* (1969), a hilarious, bitter account of sexual frustration. Among his other works are the novels *The Ghost Writer* (1979), *Zuckerman Unbound* (1981), and *The Anatomy Lesson* (1983), later reissued in a single volume as *Zuckerman Bound* (1985), and an autobiography, *The Facts* (1988). Roth received a Pulitzer Prize for *American Pastoral* (1998).

Rothko, Mark (1903-70), U.S. painter, a leading abstract expressionist. On large canvases he used rich and somber colors to create designs of simple, lightly painted rectangular shapes.

Rothschild, family of European Jewish bankers who wielded considerable political influence for nearly two centuries. The founder of the house was **Mayer Amschel Rothschild** (1743-1812), who established banks at Frankfurt, Vienna, London, Naples, and Paris, with his sons as managers. The financial genius who raised the business to dominance in Europe was his son **Nathan Mayer Rothschild** (1777-1836), who handled Allied loans for the campaign against Napoleon. His son, **Baron Lionel Nathan de Rothschild** (1808-79), was the first Jewish member of the British Parliament.

Rotifer, or wheel animal, microscopic roundworm only a fraction of an inch long. Rotifers are plentiful in fresh water, a few live in the sea, and others live in damp moss. They may be fixed in one place or able to swim. At the head end is the "wheel organ," a delicate ring of rapidly beating hairs that is used for movement or feeding.

Rotterdam (pop. 602,100), commercial and industrial seaport in South Holland province, second largest city in the Netherlands, and the largest harbor in the world. Site of the Europoort industrial and harbor complex, it lies at the center of an extensive canal system connecting with other parts of the Netherlands, the German Rhine ports, and the river Ruhr. Major industries include shipyards and oil refineries.
See also: Netherlands.

Rottweiler, large work dog, ancestor to the Doberman pinscher. This strong, muscular dog stands up to 27 in (69 cm) at the shoulder and weighs up to 90 lb (41 k). It is a short-haired black dog with brown markings at the legs, chest, neck, and face. In Roman times, these dogs guarded herds for the army; in medieval times, they served as guard dogs. They are named for the German town, Rottweil, in which they were developed as a breed.

Rouault, Georges (1871-1958), French artist known especially for his intense religious paintings such as *The Three Judges* (1913). Influenced by medieval stained glass work, he developed a distinctive style with the use of thick black outlines around primary colors.

Rouen (pop. 105,500), city and major port on the Seine River, industrial and commercial center, capital of historic Normandy and of today's Seine-Maritime department, northwestern France. Joan of Arc was burned at the stake here, and Champlain and La Salle sailed from Rouen to explore the New World.
See also: France.

Rough Riders (1st Regiment of U.S. Cavalry Volunteers), unit comprising cowboys, miners, and college athletes among others, organized by Theodore Roosevelt and Leonard Wood (commander of the unit) at the outbreak of the Spanish-American War (1898). They fought mainly in Cuba and are renowned for their success at San Juan Hill.
See also: Spanish-American War.

Roulette, game of chance. The roulette wheel is divided into a series of small compartments, alternatively black and red, numbered 1 to 36 with an additional zero (the U.S. game sometimes has two zeros). A croupier spins the wheel and releases into it a small ivory ball. Players bet on where the ball will settle.

Roumania *See:* Romania.

Roundheads, derogatory name for Puritans in the Parliamentary forces in the English Civil War (1642-8). Many wore their hair closely cropped, in sharp contrast to their royalist opponents, called Cavaliers.
See also: Puritans.

Round Table, table at which the medieval King Arthur and his knights sat. The actual table is claimed as an artifact that can be seen in the remains of a castle in Winchester, England. The 15th-century author Sir Thomas Malory wrote about the Round Table knights in his book *Le Morte d'Arthur*. The Round Table knights also were mentioned in the 12th-century French history *Le Roman de Brut* by Wace of Jersey. The shape of the table (with 12 positions) supposedly allowed for equal status of all the knights. A position left purposely vacant *(Siege Perilous)* was left for the knight who would eventually recover the cup—holy grail—from which Jesus drank at the Last Supper. Sir Galahad became the occupant of that seat and, according to the legend, captured the holy grail along with Sir Bors and Sir Perceval. The knights of the Round Table included, among others, Sir Gawain, Lancelot, Ban, Gareth, Bedevere, Ector, Launfal, Palomides, and Sagramore. One of the major figures in the legends of the knights of the Round Table was the sorcerer Merlin who, according to one legend, had the table constructed for Uther, King Arthur's father.
See also: Arthur, King.

Roundworm, or nematode, any of more than 10,000 species of worms making up the phylum Nematoda, found in terrestrial, freshwater, and marine forms. All roundworms are long and thin, tapering at each end, and are covered with a complex cuticle. The internal organs are suspended within a fluid-filled cavity pseudocoeom. The free-living and plant-parasitic forms are usually microscopic, but animal-parasitic species may reach up to 3.5 ft (1.07 m). Rotifers, and horsehair worms are in the same phylum.

Rous, Francis Peyton (1879-1970), U.S. physician. He shared (with C.B. Huggins) the 1966 Nobel Prize in physiology or medicine for his discovery (1910) of a tumor-causing virus in chickens.

Rousseau, Henri (1844-1910), self-taught French primitive painter much admired by Gauguin, Picasso, and others. Rousseau is known mainly for his portraits, landscapes, and jungle paintings, such as *The Sleeping Gypsy* (1897) and *The Hungry Lion* (1905).

Rousseau, Jean-Jacques (1712-78), Swiss-born French writer, philosopher, and political theorist. Greatly influenced by Denis Diderot, Rousseau first gained fame from his essay *Discourse on the Sciences and the Arts* (1750), an attack on the arts as a source for the increased wealth of the rich and an instrument of propaganda. In his *Discourse on Inequality* (1755), he professed the equality and goodness of "natural man" and asserted that the golden age of humanity occurred before the formation of society, which bred competition and the corrupting influences of property, commerce, science, and agriculture. *The Social Contract* (1762), influential during the French Revolution, claimed that when human beings formed a social contract to live in society, they delegated authority to a government; however, they retained sovereignty and the power to withdraw that authority when necessary. On

education, Rousseau suggested, in his didactic novel *Emile* (1762), that rather than imparting knowledge, education should build on a child's natural interests and sympathies, gradually developing his or her potential. For the last 10-15 years of his life, Rousseau fought mental illness (persecution mania) and lived in seclusion. *Confessions* (1782), written shortly before his death, describes Rousseau's romantic feelings of affinity with nature. He was an influential figure of the French Enlightenment and of 19th century romanticism.
See also: Age of Reason.

Rousseau, Théodore (1812-67), French landscape painter, a leader of the Barbizon school. His scenes of wooded landscapes at sunset include *Coming out of the Fontainebleau Woods* (c.1850).
See also: Barbizon school.

Roussel, Albert Charles Paul Marie (1869-1937), French composer. His music was based on contrapuntal rather than tonal construction, varying in style from *The Feast of the Spider* (1912) to *Padmavati* (1918).

Rowan, Carl Thomas (1925-), U.S. journalist and statesman. He was the first member of the National Security Council who was of African American descent. He headed the U.S. Information Agency (1964-65). Rowan has also served as ambassador to Finland (1963-64) and deputy assistant secretary of state for public affairs (1961-63). As a journalist he worked for the *Minneapolis Tribune* (1948-61) and the *Chicago Daily News* (1965-78); he has been a columnist at the *Chicago Sun-Times* since 1978. Rowan received Sigma Delta Chi national journalism awards in 1954, 1955, and 1966.

Rowing, propelling a boat by means of oars operated by hand. In sport there are 2 types: sculling, in which each member of the team (2, 4, or 8 people) uses 2 oars, and sweep rowing, in which each has 1. In the United States competitive team rowing is known as crew. For speed, the craft (shells) are long, narrow, and light. The team may be steered by a coxswain, who also sets the rhythm and speed for the crew's strokes. The first recorded race was held on the Thames River, London (1716). The annual Oxford-Cambridge race (England) began in 1829, and the Yale-Harvard race in 1852.

Rowland, Henry Augustus (1848-1901), U.S. physicist and engineer. He developed the concave diffraction grating in which lines are ruled directly onto a concave spherical surface, thus eliminating the need for additional mirrors and lenses. He also determined the mechanical equivalent of heat and of the ohm.

Rowlandson, Thomas (1756-1827), English caricaturist. His satirical work is a valuable record of contemporary English life. It includes *The English Dance of Death* (1815-16) and illustrations for *The Tour of Dr. Syntax in Search of the Picturesque* (text by William Combe, 1812-21).

Roxas y Acuña, Manuel (1894-1948), Philippine politician. He was a member of the Japanese-sponsored Philippine puppet government in World War II while aiding the Philippine underground. He became the 1st president

(1946-48) of the Republic of the Philippines, leader of an administration marked by corruption.
See also: Philippines.

Roy, Gabrielle (1909-   ), French-Canadian novelist noted for her portrayals of poor urban workers in *The Tin Flute* (1947) and *The Cashier* (1955). Some of her novels, such as *Street of Riches* (1957), are set in the isolated rural landscape of her native Manitoba.

Royal Canadian Mounted Police (RCMP), Canadian federal police force. It was formed in 1873 as the Northwest Mounted Police to bring law and order to the new Canadian territories. In 1874, the persistence and determination of the 300 men on the force became legendary: "The Mounties always get their man." In 1920 it absorbed the Dominion Police and received its present name and duties. The Royal Canadian Mounted Police serves as a provincial police force in the nation's provinces (excluding Ontario and Quebec).
See also: Canada.

Royal Gorge, canyon created by the Arkansas River in south-central Colorado, also known as the Grand Canyon of the Arkansas. It is about 10 mi (16 km) long, with steep granite walls rising more than 1,000 ft (305 m) above the river. The highway bridge over the gorge, with a main span of 880 ft (268 m), is the highest suspension bridge in the United States.

Royal Household of Great Britain, those who administer the private business and court life of the monarchy of Great Britain. Many of these positions, established in the Middle Ages, are hereditary. Today these offices are ceremonial. Over the centuries British monarchs have adjusted the roster of royal attendants. Among the many positions, the lord chamberlain administers ceremonial affairs and is head of the Royal Household; the lord steward governs financial matters of the Royal Household; and ladies of the bedchamber, ladies in waiting, and the mistress of the robes are the Queen's attendants.

Royal palm, tree (genus *Roystonea*) in the palm family, found in the southeastern United States, the West Indies, and Central America. Royal palms have column-shaped trunks with feathery palm fronds gathered at their tops.

Royce, Josiah (1855-1916), U.S. philosopher, a major proponent of idealism. Influenced by Hegel and Schopenhauer, his philosophy emphasized will and purpose rather than intellect, as expressed in *The World and the Individual* (2 vols., 1901-02). Among his other major works was *The Problem of Christianity* (2 vols., 1913), in which he developed his metaphysic of interpretation and community.
See also: Idealism.

Ruanda-Urundi, Belgium-supervised United Nations territory (1946), which later became the independent nations of Rwanda and Burundi (1962). Pygmies called Twa, a Bantu people called Hutu (or Buhutu), and Watusi are the native inhabitants of this area. The Germans laid claim to Ruanda-Urundi in the late-19th century. The Belgic gained a mandate here through the League of Nations (1923). This area is bordered by Zaïre to the west, Uganda to the north, and Tanzania to the east. Lake Tanganyika borders Burundi to the south.

Rubaiyat, collection of quatrains written by Omar Khayyám, an 11th century Persian poet, and translated to English by Edward Fitzgerald (1859). The oldest known manuscript of the original is housed at the Bodleian Library, Oxford and is dated 1460. *The Rubaiyat* views sensual pleasure as the purpose of life, and it heavily influenced post-Victorian English poetry.

Rubber, elastic substance; that is, one which quickly restores itself to its original size after it has been stretched or compressed. Natural rubber is obtained from many plants, and commercially from *Hevea brasiliensis*, a tree native to South America and cultivated also in southeast Asia and West Africa. A slanting cut is made in the bark, and the milky fluid latex, occurring in the inner bark, is tapped off. The latex—an aqueous colloid of rubber and other particles—is coagulated with dilute acid, and the rubber creped or sheeted and smoked. Natural rubber is a chain polymer of isoprene, known as caoutchouc when pure; its elasticity is due to the chains being randomly coiled but tending to straighten when the rubber is stretched. Known to have been used by the Aztecs since the 6th century A.D., and first known in Europe in the 16th century, it was a mere curiosity until Goodyear invented the process of vulcanization. Synthetic rubbers have been produced since World War II. Some latex (natural or synthetic) is used as an adhesive and for making rubber coatings, rubber thread, and foam rubber. Most, however, is coagulated, and the rubber is treated by vulcanization and the addition of reinforcing and inert fillers and anti-oxidants, before being used in tires, shoes, rainwear, belts, hoses, insulation, and many other applications.

Rubber plant, any of several plants, including the Ceará tree, Pará rubber tree, and guayule, that are sources of latex, a milky fluid used to make rubber. The India rubber fig (*Ficus elastica*), a popular house plant native to India and the East Indies, was once grown for its gum, which was made into erasers.

Rubella, or German measles, contagious viral disease that presents little danger unless contracted in the first trimester of pregnancy, when it may cause serious damage to a fetus. The disease, whose symptoms include rash and fever, usually affects children and young adults. Vaccination against rubella has proven effective.

Rubens, Peter Paul (1577-1640), Flemish artist, one of the greatest baroque painters. Influenced by Tintoretto, Titian, and Veronese, he developed an exuberant style depending on a rich handling of color and sensuous effects. His workshop, an organization of skilled apprentices and talented associates, completed an impressive body of work, designed by Rubens (who also added the final touches) but largely developed by others. These works include portraits and mythological, allegorical, and religious subjects such as *Raising of the Cross (1610), Descent from the Cross* (1611), *History of Marie de Médicis* (1622-25), *Judgment of Paris (c.1638),* and portraits of his wife. His works influenced many artists.
See also: Baroque.

Rubicon, Italian stream, famous for the crossing made by Julius Caesar in 49 B.C. As commander of Roman troops in Gaul, Caesar crossed this stream—once the border between Rome and Gaul—in reaction to the order for him to give up his power. Today the saying "to cross the Rubicon" indicates that something irreversible has occurred. In 49 B.C. this crossing eventually led to the rule of Rome by Julius Caesar.
See also: Caesar, (Gaius) Julius.

Rubidium, chemical element, symbol Rb; for physical constants see Periodic Table. Rubidium was discovered spectroscopically by Robert Bunsen and Gustav Kirchhoff in 1861. It occurs in lepidolite and several other minerals. The element is prepared by reducing the chloride with calcium. Rubidium is a silver-white, soft, low-melting, reactive metal of the alkali metal group. It can be liquid at room temperature and ignites spontaneously in air. Rubidium and its compounds are used in ion propulsion systems, vapor turbines, thermoelectric generators, batteries, photo cells, and special glasses.

Rubinstein, Anton Gregor (1829-94), Russian piano virtuoso and composer. In 1862 he founded the St. Petersburg Conservatory, where he was director 1862-67 and 1887-91. His brother, Nicholas Grigoryevich Rubinstein (1835-81), also a pianist, founded (1864) and served as director of the Moscow Conservatory.

Rubinstein, Arthur (1889-1982), Polish-born U.S. pianist who remained at the top of his profession for over 70 years. He was well known for his interpretations of Chopin.

Ruby, deep-red gemstone, a variety of corundum colored by a minute proportion of chromium ions, found in Upper Burma, Thailand, and Sri Lanka. Synthetic rubies, used to make ruby lasers, have been produced by the Verneuil flame-fusion process (1902).

Rudolf I (1218-91), German king, elected in 1273, who established the Habsburg dynasty by gaining control of Austria and Styria. The Diet of Augsburg (1282) invested his two sons with these duchies.

Rudolf II (1552-1612), king of Bohemia and Hungary. He succeeded his father Maximilian II as Holy Roman Emperor (1576-1612). His religious persecutions and a Hungarian rebellion led to his replacement by his brother Matthias.
See also: Holy Roman Empire.

Rudolph, Paul (1918-), U.S. architect, connected with Yale University (1958-65). He rejected the international style to experiment with externally visible ducts, a futuristic parking facility, and stacking mobile-home frames. His campus buildings include a controversial art-and-architecture building.
See also: Architecture.

Ruff (*Philomachus pugnax*), bird in the sandpiper family. The term *ruff* refers to the male, while the term *reeve* refers to the female. The male measures about 12 in (30 cm) long and the female measures 10 in (25 cm) long. Both ruff and reeve are gray in appearance during the winter months. In spring, when courtship begins, the male displays a cluster of feathers on his head and neck of red, brown, black, and white feathers. The male uses these feathers in an elaborate courtship performance. Mostly an inhabitant of Europe and Asia, the ruff has been spotted in North America.

Ruffed grouse (*Bonasa umbellus*), bird in the grouse subfamily, Tetraoninae, in the family Phasianidae. When the grouse beats it wings in the air, a loud drumming sound is created that can be heard far away. These birds, which measure up to 17 in (43 cm) long, display a white neck collar of thick feathers on an otherwise brownish body. In winter their legs grow thick feathers for warmth, and their feet develop webs for walking on top of the snow. They reside in the forests of North America. The ruffed grouse is the state bird of Pennsylvania.

Ruffin, Edmund (1794-1865), U.S. planter, father of soil chemistry in the United States. A strong supporter of slavery and secession, Ruffin is said to have fired the first shot on Fort Sumter, S.C., at the outbreak of the Civil War. He committed suicide rather than submit to the U.S. government. A noted agriculturalist, he pioneered crop rotation and founded the *Farmer's Register* (1833).

Rugby, ball game that originated (1823) at Rugby School in England during a soccer match. Somewhat similar to soccer and American football, rugby is played in two 40-minute halves on a field 75 yd (69m) wide by 160 yd (146 m) long. Goal lines are 100 yd (101 m) apart and there are 2 in-goals (equivalent to end zones in football). Each side, comprised of 15 in amateur play and 13 in Rugby league, attempts to move the oval, leather-covered ball beyond the opponents' goal; kicking, carrying, and passing the ball (to the side or rear) is permitted, as is tackling. Blocking, however, is not. Little protective equipment is worn and play is almost continuous.

Rugs and carpets, thick, heavy fabric, most often used as a floor covering. Carpet weaving with sheep's wool was first highly developed in the Near East. By A.D. 600 Persian carpets were internationally famous. Their vivid, long-lasting dyes came from natural materials, e.g., bark and roots. Persian designs influenced the 16th-and 17th-century carpets of India's Mogul courts and the beautiful Chinese carpets produced from the 14th to 17th centuries. Carpet weaving spread in the West, particularly in the 17th century, via France, Belgium, and England. Oriental carpets were woven on looms, still the basic technique of carpet making. But as of 1841, power-driven looms began to mechanize the industry. Classifications of carpets include Oriental, chenille, velvet, hooked, European handwoven, straw, and rag.

Ruhr, important coal-mining and industrial region in Germany, east of the Rhine River, between the valleys of the Ruhr and Lippe rivers. It has more than 30 large cities and towns including Düsseldorf, Essen, Gelsenkirchen, and Dortmund.
See also: Germany.

Ruhr River, river and tributary of the Rhine River in Germany. Through reservoirs and lakes created by dams, this river furnishes water for a densely populated industrial area of Westphalia. The river flows through the industrial Ruhr Valley for over 140 miles before it joins the lower Rhine.

Ruisdael, or **Ruysdael, Jacob van** (1629-82), celebrated Dutch landscape painter and etcher. A great influence on English and French landscapists for 2 centuries, he favored a new heroic-romantic style in which small human beings were dwarfed by forests, stormy seas, and magnificent cloudscapes. His works include *Wheatfields* and *Jewish Cemetery*.

Ruiz Cortines, Adolfo (1891-1973), Mexican president (1952-58). During his presidency, corruption was curbed and the March to the Sea to aid the maritime industry was initiated; in addition, the implementation of widespread irrigation boosted agricultural productivity and women were given the vote.

Rules of order *See:* Parliamentary procedure.

Rumania *See:* Romania.

Rumba, or rhumba, ballroom dance of Afro-Cuban origin popular in the 1930s and 1940s. The dancers take 3 steps to each bar, 2 fast side steps and 1 slow forward step in 4/4 time. The rumba is noted for the dancers' side-to-side hip motions with the torso erect and the knees relaxed. Rumba music is performed chiefly with percussion instruments.

Rumford, Benjamin Thompson, Count (1753-1814), U.S.-British scientist best known for his recognition of the relation between work and heat (inspired by observation of heat generated by friction during the boring of a cannon). He played a primary role in the founding of the Royal Institution (1799).

Rumi, Jalal-ed-Din, or **Jalal-ud-Din** (1207-73), Sufi poet and mystic of Persia. His major work was the *Mathnawi*, a poetic exposition of Sufi wisdom in some 27,000 couplets.

Ruminant, any of a group of even-toed, hoofed mammals (e.g., giraffes, camels, goats, cows) that regurgitate and rechew their food after swallowing it. They feed by filling one compartment (the rumen) of a 3- or 4-chambered stomach with unmasticated food; the food is mixed with fluid which creates a soft pulp (cud or bolus), and then is regurgitated, rechewed, and sent to the other stomach chambers for digestion.

Rummy, group of card games, all of which, including gin rummy and canasta, are variants on a set of fundamental rules. Rummy is derived from the Spanish game of *conquian* and was called "rum" (queer) poker by the English. Basic rummy was devised about 1895. The object of the game is to lay down as many sets, or melds, of cards as possible; the first player to get rid of all the cards in his hand is the winner. Melds may consist of 3 or 4 cards of the same value in different suits, or sequences of 3 or 4 cards in the same suit.

Rump Parliament, in English civil war, remaining members of Parliament after "Pride's Purge" (led by Col. Thomas Pride) ejected all opposition to

Oliver Cromwell's army (1648). These 60 members created a high court that tried King Charles I and had him executed (1649), abolished the House of Lords and monarchy, and established a ruling Council of State. The Rump Parliament itself was dissolved (1653) by Cromwell in his consolidation of power.
See also: Cromwell, Oliver.

Rumsfeld, Donald Henry (1932-   ), powerful U.S. politician and businessman. He served in the House of Representatives (1963-69). He worked for the Nixon administration, including an appointment as ambassador from the United States in Brussels, Belgium, for the North Atlantic Treaty Organization (NATO). During the administration of President Gerald Ford, he served as chief of staff (1974) and secretary of defense (1975-77). He was involved in Middle Eastern negotiations through appointment by President Ronald Reagan (1983-84). In business, he has headed G.D. Searle & Company (1977) and has been a member of the William Blair & Company investment bank (1985-).

Rundstedt, Karl Rudolf Gerd von (1875-1953), German field marshal. In World War II he was the leader of army groups in Poland, France, and Russia; military ruler of France and commander on D-Day (June 6, 1944) on the western front and during the Battle of the Bulge.
See also: World War II.

Runes, characters of a pre-Christian writing system used by the Teutonic tribes of northern Europe from as early as the 3rd century B.C. to as late as the 10th century A.D. and sometimes after. The three distinct types are Early, Anglo-Saxon, and Scandinavian. The Runic alphabet is sometimes known as Futhork for its first six characters.

Running, pastime and popular sport since ancient times. Running can be divided into 3 basic classes: sprinting, middle-distance running, and long-distance running. Sub-classes include relay racing, steeple-chasing, and cross-country running. Sprints, fueled by continuous bursts of speed, generally cover distances of 100, 220, and 440 yds (91, 201, and 402 m). At peak speed a champion sprinter may reach 26 mph (42 kmph). The mile (1.6093 km) is the traditional middle-distance race for British and U.S. runners. In long-distance running, defined as 2 miles (3.2 km) and farther, the emphasis is on endurance and pace. The marathon (26 mi, 385 yd/42.2 km) is a popular long-distance race run annually in many cities worldwide.

Runnymede, or Runnimede, meadow in Surrey, South England, on the southern bank of the Thames River. Here (or at nearby Magna Carta Island), King John conceded the barons' demands embodied in the Magna Carta (1215).
See also: Magna Carta.

Runyon, Damon (1884-1946), U.S. journalist and writer. His entertaining stories of tough-talking gangsters, Broadway actors, and the sporting underworld are written in the colorful vernacular of New York City. *Guys and Dolls* (1931), the first of several collections, became the basis for the successful musical (1950).

Rupert's Land, vast, mineral-rich region of northwest Canada granted to the Hudson's Bay Company in 1670 by Charles II. Named for Prince Rupert (first governor of the company), it comprised the basin of Hudson Bay. In 1818, the United States acquired the portion south of the 49th parallel. In 1869-70, the remainder of the land was sold back to Canada. *See also:* Hudson's Bay Company.

Rupture *See:* Hernia.

Rural Electrification Administration (REA), U.S. Department of Agriculture agency that helps provide loans and expertise for electric and telephone development in rural communities. Established by President Franklin Delano Roosevelt (1935), this agency loans money mainly to organized state cooperatives. Both state and federal regulations determine the stipulations of the individual loans. The Congress yearly determines the monies available and interest rates for the REA. In the beginning, about 10% of rural farms had electricity and about 30% had modern telephone service. REA loans have helped increase those percentages to almost 100%.

Rush, tall, grasslike plant (of various genera) in the family Juncaceae, found in marshes, on lake edges, and in paths and ditches. The green stem of the rush bears small scales, which are the leaves, and near the tip is a tuft of brownish or greenish flowers. Rushes are used for floor mats, chair seats, and baskets. The stems, when peeled of their outer covering, are used as wicks.

Rush, Benjamin (1745-1813), U.S. physician and political leader. Signer of the Declaration of Independence and member (1776-77) of the Continental Congress, he established the first American antislavery society and was treasurer (1797-1813) of the U.S. mint (Philadelphia). Among his scientific accomplishments, he was the first professor of chemistry in the colonies (College of Philadelphia), established (1786) the first free dispensary in the United States, and was a pioneer in psychiatry. He held the conviction that insanity is a disease. His *Medical Inquiries and Observations upon the Diseases of the Mind* (1812) was the first U.S. book on psychiatry. *See also:* Psychiatry.

Rush-Bagot Convention (1817), negotiations, after the War of 1812, between U.S. diplomat Richard Rush and the British minister to Washington, Sir Charles Bagot, which agreed to mutual U.S.-British disarmament on the Great Lakes. *See also:* War of 1812.

Rushdie, Salman (1947-   ), British writer and critic born in India. Rushdie has written both non-fiction and novels. His fiction often combines fantasy and folklore with realism. His works include *Grimus* (1975), *Midnight's Children* (1981), *Shame* (1983), *Jaguar Smile: A Nicaraguan Journey* (1987), and *The Satanic Verses* (1988), an allegorical novel that so offended Muslims that he was condemned to death by the Ayatollah Khomeini and forced into hiding. Rushdie has since published *Haroun and the Sea of Stories* (1990). He received the Aristeion prize for *The Moor's Last Sigh* (1996).

Rushmore, Mount *See:* Mount Rushmore National Memorial.

Ruska, Ernst August Friedrich (1906-88), German physicist and teacher, winner, with Gerd Binnig of Germany and Heinrich Rohrer of Switzerland, of the Nobel Prize (1986) for inventing the electron microscope, allowing scientists to study single atoms. He was named director of the Institute of Electron Microscopy at the Fritz Haber Institute of the Max Planck Society (1955).
See also: Microscope; Physics.

Rusk, Dean (1909-94), U.S. politician and educator. He was secretary of state (1961-69) in both the Kennedy and Johnson administrations, and he was outspoken against the Vietnam War. Serving the state department, he worked for the United Nations and the implementation of both the Marshall Plan and North Atlantic Treaty Organization after World War II. As an educator he has served as president of the Rockefeller Foundation (1952), a "distinguished fellow" at that same institution, and as professor of law at the University of Georgia since 1970.

Ruskin, John (1819-1900). English art critic, writer, and social reformer. The first volume of his *Modern Painters* (1843) championed J.M.W. Turner over the old masters; the subsequent 4 volumes (1846-60) expanded his views of the principles of true art, based on integrity and morality. He went on to apply these ideas to architecture in *The Seven Lamps of Architecture* (1849), which stimulated a Gothic revival, and *The Stones of Venice* (1851-53). *Unto This Last* (1860), first of his "letters" to workmen, began his attacks on laissez-faire philosophy. *Sesame and Lilies* (1865) continued to address social and political issues, offering such social reforms as nationalization of education and organization of labor that came to be widely accepted.

Russell, prominent family in British politics. The first member to gain national fame was **John Russell** (c.1486-1555), created first earl of Bedford for helping Edward VI to quell a 1549 rebellion. The family fortune, including Woburn Abbey, Bedfordshire, was acquired during this period. **Francis Russell** (1593-1641), fourth earl, built the square of Covent Garden (c.1631) and was active in Parliament's effort to contain the power held by Charles I. **William Russell** (1613-1700), fifth earl, was a parliamentary general in the Civil War. He was created first duke of Bedford in 1694, partly because of the fame, as a patriotic martyr, of his son **Lord William Russell** (1639-83), first notable Whig in the family. The title of Lord John Russell, first earl Russell, was inherited by his grandson **Bertrand Russell**. **Hastings William Sackville Russell** (1883-1953), a pacifist, defended some of Adolf Hitler's policies in World War II. **John Robert Russell** (1917-   ) is journalist and farmer in South Africa. In 1955 he turned his land at Woburn into a public park.

Russell, Bertrand (1872-1970), British philosopher, mathematician, and man of letters. Initially a subscriber of idealism he broke away in 1898 and eventually became an empiricist. His most important work was relating logic and mathematics. Russell endeavored to reduce all mathematics to logical principles. His results appeared in *The Principles of Mathematics* (1903) and, in collaboration with A.N. Whitehead, *Principia Mathematica* (3 vols.,

1910-13). This work particularly influenced mathematics' set theory, logical positivism, and 20th-century, symbolic logic. Russell was a vehement pacifist for much of his life, especially during World War I and after, in the "ban the bomb" movement, and in his active opposition in Europe to U.S. involvement in Vietnam in the 1960s. His views twice earned him prison sentences (1918, 1961): during the former he wrote his *Introduction to Mathematical Philosophy* (1919). His other works include *Marriage and Morals* (1929), *Education and the Social Order* (1932), *An Inquiry into Meaning and Truth* (1940), *History of Western Philosophy (1945), and popularizations such as The ABC of Relativity* (1925), as well as his *Autobiography* (3 vols., 1967-69). He received the 1950 Nobel Prize for literature and founded the Bertrand Russell Peace Foundation.

Russell, Bill (1934-   ), U.S. basketball player and coach. Known for strong rebounding and shot blocking, the 6-ft 10-in (208-cm) center is considered one of the best players of all time. Russell's achievements include winning 6 Most Valuable Player awards—5 regular season (1958, 61-63, 65) and 1 All-Star (1963), and being named an All-Star 11 times. He played in the National Basketball Association (NBA) for the Boston Celtics (1956-68) and led them to 11 NBA championships (1957, 59-66, 68, 69). Russell became the first major-league head coach of African American descent in U.S. professional sports (1966) as player-coach of the Boston Celtics. He was inducted into the Basketball Hall of Fame in 1974.

Russell, Charles Marion (1864-1926), U.S. cowboy painter, sculptor, and author. He translated his great love for the West into his many canvases of frontier life, horses, Native Americans, and cattle camps, usually set in Montana.

Russell, George William (1867-1935), Irish poet, nationalist, mystic, and painter, known by the pseudonym A.E. A theosophist, he was, with W.B. Yeats, a leader of the Celtic Renaissance and a cofounder of Dublin's Abbey Theatre.

Russell, Henry Norris (1877-1957), U.S. astronomer. His theory of stellar evolution led to the construction of the Hertzsprung-Russell diagram, work done independently of Ejnar Hertzsprung, showing the relation between a star's brightness and color. He also determined the chemical-element content of the solar atmosphere and analyzed the spectra of various chemical elements.
See also: Astronomy.

Russell, Lillian (Helen Louise Leonard; 1861-1922), U.S. singer, actress, and flamboyant beauty of the "Gay Nineties." She became a star in the show *The Great Mogul* (1881). She married 4 times, but her affair with "Diamond Jim" Brady spanned 40 years.

Russell, Lord John (1792-1878), British political figure, leader of the British reform movement. As a member of the House of Commons, he helped bring about the repeal of the Test and Corporation acts, which enabled Protestants who did not belong to the Church of England to participate in politics for the first time. He also helped extend the right to vote to more

Russian Federation

Capital:	Moscow
Area:	6,592,850 sq mi (17,075,400 sq km)
Population:	146,861,000
Language:	Russian
Government:	Federal presidential republic
Independent:	1991
Head of gov.:	Prime minister
Per capita:	U.S. $2,240
Mon. unit:	1Rouble = 100 kopecks

middle-class men through the Reform Bill of 1832. Russell later served as prime minister (1846-52, 1865, 1866).
See also: United Kingdom.

Russell, Richard Brevard (1897-1971), influential U.S. Democratic senator (1933-71) from Georgia. Governor of Georgia (1931-33), he was twice candidate for the presidential nomination. As a senator he served as chairman of the Armed Services Committee, the Appropriations Committee, and as president *pro tempore*.

Russell Cave National Monument, location of artifacts related to pre-Columbian man in northeastern Alabama. This cave offers information about ancient peoples, from a fire built about 9,000 years ago to evidence of human habitation from 3 to 4 centuries ago. As part of the National Parks System, it was made a national monument in 1961.

Russia *See:* Union of Soviet Socialist Republics; Russian Federation.

Russian, chief official language of Russia, member of the East Slavic Indo-European languages (Byelorussian and Ukrainian diverged c.1300). Russian is written in the 33-character Cyrillic alphabet introduced in the 800s by Christian missionaries. By combining colloquialism with the formal Church Slavonic, the poet Pushkin did much to shape modern literary Russian, which is based on the Moscow dialect.

Russian Federation, or Russia, largest country in the world. Its 6,592,850 sq mi (17,075,400 sq km) cover Asia's north and a major part of eastern Europe. The capital is Moscow. The federation consists of 21 republics, one autonomous province, 10 autonomous regions, and 55 dependent provinces. After the disintegration of the USSR in 1991 the federation replaced the Russian Federal Soviet Republic (RSFSR) and is considered to be successor to the USSR. (For history before 1991, see Union of Soviet Socialist Republics). Boris Yeltsin, who was president of the RSFSR since 1990, kept his position and replaced Gorbachev. Yeltsin faced severe economic crises and political division with respect to the future development of the country.

The political division culminated in the temporary occupation of the Russian White House in 1993. Economic and political liberalization progressed slowly, and by the mid-1990s communism regained popularity. In March 1998, president Yeltsin dismissed the entire government, due to the fact that the economy had not improved. Yeltsin proposed Sergej Kirijenko as the new prime minister, the duma accepted after considerable protests.
See also: Union of Soviet Socialist Republics.

Russian literature, fiction, poetry, prose, and religious writings written in the Russian language. Throughout its history, Russian literature has been characterized by a deep concern for moral, religious, and philosophical problems.
Early literature. The Byzantine influence that accompanied Russia's conversion to Christianity in the late 900s A.D. also caused Church Slavonic to be adopted as the language of religion and literature. Church Slavonic was used in the Balkans and Russia as the language of secular and religious writings and served in much the same way as Latin did in the West. The earliest writings were primarily the works of clergymen and were religious in content and didactic in purpose although the *chronicles*, records of historic events attributed to the friar Nestor, were nonreligious and had some literary quality. More important than these were the *blyiny*, oral folk lays with a mixture of pagan and Christian themes, that sometimes attained the level of epic poetry. The finest piece of early Russian literature was *The Song of Igor's Campaign* (c. 1187, author unknown), describing an unsuccessful campaign by a Russian prince against an Asian tribe, the Polovtsians.
Beginning of modern Russian literature. Western influence became important in the 17th century when numerous translations appeared and the first theater in Russia was established (1662). The most notable writer of the period was the conservative priest Avvakum (martyred 1682), who opposed the changes in the ritual of the Russian Orthodox Church in the 1650s that led to the great schism. Under Tsar Peter I (the Great), European influence increased, the Russian alphabet was revised, and Russian works were printed in the vernacular. A monk, Simeon Polotsky, introduced a rigid syllabic system of verse, whereby each line of poetry contained a fixed number of syllables with regularly placed pauses. Prince Antioch Kantemir (1703-44) wrote verse satires supporting Peter the Great's reforms, using the syllabic system. Mikhail Lomonosov, a trained scientist, was a noted writer and poet. He was most noted as the founder of modern Russian literature and a precursor of classicism. In his odes, he used the new tonic form of versification (regular patterns of stressed and unstressed syllables) which was more suitable to Russian than the strict syllabic system, and he thereby changed the nature of Russian prosody.
Classicism in Russian literature. Inspired by Lomonosov and influenced by Western models, Russian writers such as Alexander Sumarokov mixed European style with Russian themes. This is especially true of his fables and his plays, which helped begin Russian drama. His *Khorev* (1747) was the first classical tragedy in Russian. The plays of Denis I. Fonzivin (1745-92) mixed satire with more realistic concerns while the outstanding poet of the period, Gavril R. Derzhavin, wrote odes praising Catherine and ridiculing the vices of the court around her, as in his "Ode to Felitsa" (1783). Toward the end of the 18th century, Ivan A. Krylov (1768-1844) wrote many fables, some of them adapted from Aesop and La Fontaine, but most were original.

Romanticism in Russian literature. Vasili Zhukovsky and Konstantin Ba-
tyushkov were the leading poets of the preromantic period. In the 1820s, a
new group of poets introduced the Golden Age of Russian poetry. The
greatest of these was Alexander Sergeyevich Pushkin (1799-1837), who
wrote the remarkable historical play *Boris Godunov* in 1825. Other poets of
the age included Yevgeny Baratynsky, Baron Anton Delvig, and Wilhelm
Kuchelbecker. By the end of the romantic period, Russian writers turned
more to social criticism, even under the strict censorship of Tsar Nicholas I.
Among these were Mikhail Lermontov, whose *A Hero of Our Times* (1840)
was the first psychological novel in Russian literature. The poet Fyodor
Tyutchev wrote pessimistic verse, as exemplified in his "A Vision" (1829)
and "Holy Night" (1849). The most important writer of this time was Nikolai
Vasilyevich Gogol (1809-52). He is best known for his socio-political satires,
such as his famous play *The Inspector General* (1836), still performed in
many countries today.

Realism in Russian literature. Around mid-19th century began the period
of great Russian novels, which attempted to depict Russian life, customs, and
politics in a realistic manner. Ivan Turgenev's *A Sportsman's Sketches*
(1852) and *Fathers and Sons* (1862) showed his interest in social themes and
particularly in character analysis, as did his gentle comedy *A Month in the
Country* (completed 1850). Count Leo Tolstoy (1828-1910), one of the
greatest of Russian novelists, expanded the form to include deep philosophical probing as well as realistic depictions of Russian life and people, as
exemplified in his two great works *War and Peace* (1869) and *Anna
Karenina* (1875-77). The other great Russian novelist of the period, Fyodor
Dostoevsky (1821-81), wrote novels of extraordinary psychological pene-
tration. Among his most famous works are *Crime and Punishment* (1866),
The Possessed (1871-72), and *The Brothers Karamazov* (1879-80). Toward
the end of the century, the playwright and short story writer Anton P.
Chekhov (1860-1904) portrayed Russian life with a kind of lyric realism in
such plays as *Uncle Vanya* (1899), *The Three Sisters* (1901), and *The Cherry
Orchard* (1904). Prefiguring the Russian Revolution was the playwright and
novelist Maxim Gorki (1868-1936) whose works depicted the terrible plight
of the Russian poor and downtrodden. His most famous play is *The Lower
Depths* (1902).

Russian literature in the 20th Century. The unsettled times before and
during the revolution in 1917 spawned new literary trends like symbo-
lism, as exemplified in the poets Alexander Blok and Andrey Bely.
Post-symbolist poets included Anna Akmatova and Osip Mendelstam,
and futurists found a strong voice in the remarkable poet Vladimir
Mayakovsky. Boris L. Pasternak was also associated with the futurists,
but is most known for his lyric poetry and his later novel *Doctor Zhivago*
(begun 1948, published 1957) for which he won the Nobel Prize. The
terrible years of Stalin's repressive rule took a toll on Russian literature,
but in the 1960s a new generation of writers moved to reassert liberal
ideas. Among them are Yevgeny Yevtushenko and Andre Voznesensky
(poets) and prose writers Vasily Aksyonov and Vasily Shukshin. Alexander Solzhenitsyn, an outspoken critic of communism, wrote about the
Stalin repression (*The Gulag Archipelago, 1918 to 1956*, published in the
West from 1973 to 1976). He was exiled, but with the changes in Russia
in the late 1980s, the banishment was revoked. It is hoped that a more
liberal Russia will encourage a free and creative literature.

Russian Orthodox Church *See:* Union of Soviet Socialist Republics; Eastern Orthodox Church.

Russian Revolution, momentous political upheaval that changed the course of world history. It destroyed the autocratic tsarist regime and culminated in the establishment of the world's first Communist state, the Soviet Union (1922). Its roots lay in the political and economic backwardness of Russia, the chronic poverty of most of the people, and rising discontent in the middle and lower classes.

The Revolution of 1905. On "Bloody Sunday," Jan. 22, troops fired on a workers' demonstration in St. Petersburg. Widespread disorders followed, including mutiny on the battleship *Potemkin* and a national general strike organized by the St. Petersburg *soviet* (workers' council). These events, coupled with the disastrous Russo-Japanese War, forced Nicholas II to grant civil rights and set up an elected duma (parliament) in his October Manifesto. Repression continued until late in World War I, during which Russia suffered severe reverses.

The **February Revolution (1917).** Food shortages and strikes provoked riots and mutiny. A provisional government under the progressive Prince Georgi Lvov was set up, and Nicholas II abdicated.

The **October Revolution (1917).** The Bolsheviks, led by V.I. Lenin, staged an armed coup. Moscow was seized, and the remnants of the provisional government were arrested. The constitutional assembly was dispersed by Bolshevik ("Red") troops, and the Cheka (political police) was set up. A Council of People's Commissars was established, headed by Lenin and including Leon Trotsky and Joseph Stalin. In the civil war (1918-20), the anticommunist "Whites," commanded by A.I. Denikin, A.V. Kolchak, and P.N. Wrangel were defeated. Russian involvement in World War I ended with the Treaty of Brest-Litovsk. The tsar and his family were murdered at Ekaterinburg (July 1918), and the new Soviet constitution made Lenin and the Communist (formerly Bolshevik) Party all-powerful.
See also: Communism; Marxism; Lenin, V.I.

Russian wolfhound *See:* Wolfhound.

Russo-Finnish wars, conflicts during World War II. The first, the Winter War (1939-40), arose from rejection of Russian demands for military bases in Finland, territorial concessions, and the dismantling of the Mannerheim line, Finland's defense system across the Karelian Isthmus. When the Russians attacked (Nov. 30), the Finns unexpectedly threw them back. But in Feb. 1940 the Mannerheim line was broken and Finland signed the Peace of Moscow (March 12), surrendering about 10% of its territory. In the Continuation War (1941-44), Finland fought alongside Nazi Germany, and was forced to pay reparations to the USSR and to lease it the Porkkala Peninsula (returned in 1956).
See also: World War II.

Russo-Japanese War (1904-05), culmination of rivalry in the Far East between powers who sought expansion at the expense of the decaying Chinese empire. Russia occupied Manchuria during the Boxer Rebellion and coveted Korea, dominated the region and refused to share with Japan its position of influence. As a result, the Japanese attacked the Russian naval base of Port Arthur (now Lüshun, China), defeated the Russians at Mukden (now Shenyang) in Manchuria, and destroyed the Russian Baltic fleet in the Battle of Tsushima. Mediation by U.S. president Theodore Roosevelt ended the war in the Treaty of Portsmouth (1905). Russia ceded territory to Japan, recognized Japan's dominance in Korea, and returned Manchuria to China. Russia's disastrous defeat was one immediate cause of the 1905 Russian Revolution.

Russo-Turkish wars (1697-1878), conflicts resulting in Russian expansion into Ottoman territory. The first Russian success was the capture of Azov by Peter I (the Great) in 1696; it was subsequently recaptured (1711) by the Turks and lost again (1739). The 2 earliest major wars (1768-74, 1787-92), the first was declared by Sultan Mustafa III with France's encouragement, were against Catherine the Great. Allied with Austria, Russia gained the rest of the Ukraine, the Crimea, an outlet to the Black Sea, and the straits, and adopted the role of protector of Christians in the declining Ottoman Empire. Western concern over this major gain came to be known as the Western Question. Russia won Bessarabia in the war of 1806-12 and rose to the height of its power in the war of 1828-29. When Russia next pressured the Turks, France and Britain intervened, defeating Russia in the Crimean War (1853-56). The Congress of Paris, which ended that war, marked a major setback for Russia in the Middle East. The last war (1877-78), which began with an anti-Turkish uprising (1875), brought more territory to Russia in the Treaty of San Stefano. Alarmed Western powers revised the treaty in the Congress of Berlin (1878). Russia and Turkey were opponents again in World War I.
See also: Ottoman Empire.

Russwurm, John Brown (1799-1851), Jamaican-born U.S. abolitionist who led a "back to Africa" movement in the 1820s and eventually settled in Liberia (1829). He founded (1827) and edited *Freedom's Journal*, the first black-owned U.S. newspaper.
See also: Abolitionism.

Rust, brownish-red substance that forms on the surface of iron or steel when exposed to oxygen in the air. Rust both corrodes and weakens metal. It is brittle and easily flakes off the metal. Rust can be prevented by coating metal objects with heavy greases or spray-on plastics.
See also: Oxidation.

Rust, in botany, fungi of the order Uredinales and the plant diseases they cause. Rusts infect their hosts by forming orange or red spots, their spore-bearing organs, on their host's leaves. Some rusts are heteroecious: they alternate between host plants of 2 different species (e.g., the cedar rust, which infects apple and cedar trees). One crucial rust fungus (*Puccinia graminis*) attacks grain crops, causing black-stem rust of wheat. Rusts also attack ornamentals, fruits, and vegetables.

Rustin, Bayard (1910-87), U.S. civil rights activist and pacifist. He helped found the Southern Christian Leadership Conference and was chief organizer of the 1963 civil rights march on Washington.
See also: Civil rights.

Rutabaga, also called Swedish turnip, plant in the mustard family. Both its leaves and yellow root are used for food. The rutabaga root is harvested late in the autumn, when it is larger and stronger than the white turnip, a similar root vegetable. The leaves are harvested in early summer, before they become spongy and bitter.

Ruth, Babe (George Herman Ruth; 1895-1948), U.S. baseball player. Known as the first great power hitter in the major leagues, he is second on the all time home run list (714). Originally an outstanding pitcher (won 94 games, lost 46 for his career), Ruth was switched to the outfield and became a prolific hitter (.342 career average). Ruth's achievements include hitting 60 home runs in one season (1927), winning the American League Most Valuable Player award (1923), and leading the majors in home runs 11 times (1918-21, 23-24, 26-29, 31). He played for the Boston Red Sox (1914-20), New York Yankees (1920-34) and Boston Braves (1935). Known as The Bambino, he led the Yankees to 4 World Series championships (1923, 27, 28, 32) and was among the first group of players inducted into the National Baseball Hall of Fame (1936).

Ruth, Book of, name of Old Testament book in the Bible. It focuses on the love and loyalty of Ruth, described as a descendant of King David and the royal family of Israel. As a widowed non-Israelite, she gave up her home in Moab to follow Naomi, her mother-in-law, to Bethlehem. There, after working to secure a life for both herself and Naomi, she married Boaz, a kinsman to Naomi. Through the sacrifice and effort of Ruth, an Israelite family line continued. This Old Testament book, completed c. 2,500 years ago, is appreciated for its vivid characterization of Ruth and for its literary qualities.
See also: Bible; Old Testament.

Ruthenia, region in western Ukraine, southwest of the Carpathian Mountains, covering 4,940 sq mi (12,800 sq km). Formerly part of Hungary, then of Czechoslovakia (from 1919), it was ceded to the USSR (1945). The region came under independent Ukrainian rule in 1991. Uzhgorod is capital of this mountainous and densely forested region.
See also: Ukraine.

Ruthenium, chemical element, symbol Ru; for physical constants see Periodic Table. Ruthenium was discovered by Karl Klaus in 1844. It occurs in nature associated with native platinum and also with copper-nickel ores. It is obtained in commercial quantities from the mineral pentlandite. The element is prepared by the reduction with hydrogen of the oxychloride. Ruthenium is a hard, lustrous, white metal and is a member of the platinum group of elements. It is used to harden other metals and improve their wear-resistance and resistance to corrosion. It is also a versatile catalyst.

Rutherford, Ernest (1871-1937), New Zealand-born English physicist. He taught at McGill University (Montreal, 1898-1907) and the University of Manchester (1907-19); in 1919 he became director of the Cavendish Laboratory, Cambridge. In studying uranium he discovered and named alpha and beta radiation. For his theory concerning the radioactive transformation of atoms he was awarded the 1908 Nobel prize in chemistry. In 1911 he

proposed his nuclear theory of the atom, on which Bohr based his celebrated theory years later. In 1919 Rutherford announced the first artificial disintegration of an atom. His work was commemorated (1969) by the naming of rutherfordium, a chemical element.
See also: Atom; Physics.

Rutherfordium *See:* Element 104.

Rutile, mineral (TiO_2) found in the United States, Brazil, Europe, Australia, and India. It is a red to brown or black crystal. The titanium of this titanium-oxide mineral is refined for use as pigment in white paint. Porcelain as well as coating for welding rods are also colored with rutile.

Rutin, yellow pigment used as a medicine to treat problems in the circulatory system. Found in such plants as tobacco, rue, and buckwheat, among others, rutin helps make weak capillaries strong.

Rutland (pop. 18,436), second largest city in southwestern Vermont. The area of Vermont surrounding Rutland has an economic base in tourism, especially through the ski industry and other recreation derived from the region's forests, water resources, and mountains. The region contains some industry and marble quarries.
See also: Vermont.

Rutledge, family of U.S. politicians. **John Rutledge** (1739-1800) was a U.S. politician and jurist. Active in South Carolina politics, he was twice delegate to the Continental Congress (1774-76, 1782-83) and a delegate to the 1787 Federal Constitutional Convention. He helped frame South Carolina's constitution (1776) and was governor from 1779 to 1782. Rutledge served as associate justice of the U.S. Supreme Court (1789-91), but George Washington's nomination of him for chief justice (1795) was not confirmed by the Senate. His brother **Edward Rutledge** (1749-1800) was delegate to the Continental Congress (1774-76), a signer of the Declaration of Independence, and South Carolina governor (1798-1800).

Rutledge, Ann (c.1813-35), daughter of an innkeeper at New Salem, Ill., where Abraham Lincoln lived 1831-37. Her early death deeply grieved Lincoln, but stories of a romance or even engagement are probably incorrect.

Ruwenzori Range, east-central African mountain range between Uganda and Zaïre. These mountains, slightly north of the equator, rise to a snowy height of 16,763 ft (5,109 m) at Margherita Peak on Mount Stanley. The range was given its present name by the European explorer Henry Stanley (1889). In ancient times it was named Mountains of the Moon by the geographer Ptolemy. These non-volcanic mountains consist of glaciated masses of crystalline rock. The range has deep chasms and deeply carved river valleys. The rainfall and snow melt from these mountains are considered a source of the Nile River.

Ruysdael, Jacob van *See:* Ruisdael.

Rwanda

Capital:	Kigali
Area:	10,169 sq mi
	(26,338 sq km)
Population:	7,956,000
Language:	French, Kinyarwanda,
	English
Government:	Presidential republic
Independent:	1962
Head of gov.:	Prime minister
Per capita:	U.S. $180
Mon. unit:	1 Rwandese franc =
	100 centimes

Rwanda, small independent republic in east-central Africa. It is one of the most densely populated counties in Africa.

Land and climate. The land of Rwanda is dominated by the Rift Valley Highlands. From the high volcanic Virunga Mountains in the northwest, the land falls away southeastward in a series of steeply sloping flat-ridged hills. The forests that once covered these hills have been largely cleared for farming. Marshy plains form the bottoms of the deep, intersecting valleys. In the west, the land rises sharply from Lake Kivu. Chief rivers include the Nyabarongo, the Kagera, the Akanyaru, and the Ruzizi. Because it lies on high plateaus, Rwanda has a cool climate.

People. The population is comprised of three main ethnic groups: 85% are Bantu farming people known as the Hutu, 14% are a pastoral people known as the Tutsi, and a small percentage are the Twa, a pygmy people who live by hunting. The people live mostly in small villages. Kigali is the capital and largest center.

Economy. Agriculture and mining provide nearly 80% of the gross national product. The chief crops are coffee, pyrethrum, and tea. Efforts are being made to expand production. Agricultural output is insufficient to provide enough food for the people.

History. The earliest inhabitants of Rwanda, the Twa pygmies, were long ago driven into the forests by the Hutu, who came from the Congo. In the 16th century the Hutu were conquered by the tall, cattle-rearing Tutsi. The Tutsi established a feudal state and remained in control until 1959, when the Hutu liberation party known as Parmehutu set up a republican regime that was later recognized by the United Nations. The country was granted full independence in 1962. An attempted invasion of Rwanda from Burundi was bloodily repulsed in 1963. Military leaders took control of the government in 1973, and Major General Juvenal Habyarimana declared himself president. While he at first filled cabinet posts with military leaders, he gradually replaced them with civilians during the 1970s. With civilian rule restored under the new constitution of 1978, Habyarimana was elected president. Habyarimana's death in 1994, resulting from an aircrash, led to a violent and bloody strife between the two ethnic groups. In 1997 Rwandan troops played an important role in the ousting of president Mobutu of Zaire (Congo).

Ryan, Nolan (1946-　), U.S. baseball player. Known for his blazing fastball (clocked at a record 100.8 mph/161.3 kmph), he is considered one of the greatest pitchers of all time. At the end of the 1990 season, Ryan had 302 career wins and held the records for career strikeouts (5,308), strikeouts in a single season (383 in 1973), and career no-hitters (6). He pitched his seventh no-hitter early in the 1991 season. Ryan played in the major leagues for the New York Mets (1966-71), California Angels (1972-79), Houston Astros (1980-88), and Texas Rangers (1989-　).

Ryan, Thomas Fortune (1851-1928), U.S. financier and businessman. With an initial fortune made as a stockbroker, he went on to buy and sell businesses mostly involved in transportation, insurance, and banking. He amassed one of the greatest fortunes in U.S. history, valued at more than $200 million. His prosperous company, Metropolitan Traction Company, was established after he acquired the newly built New York City subway lines (1886). A later company, Consolidated Tobacco Company, was dissolved by order of the government (1911) when it was judged to be a monopoly.

Ryder, Albert Pinkham (1847-1917), U.S. painter, noted for his darkly poetic landscapes, seascapes, and allegorical scenes such as *Toilers of the Sea* (1884), *The Flying Dutchman* (1890), and *The Race Track* (1895). Ryder's body of work (only about 160 canvases) is considered among the finest of American art.

Rye (*Secale cereale*), grain of the grass family, hardiest of all cereal crops. It can grow in poor, sandy soils in cool and temperate climates. Most rye is used for human consumption, e.g. pumpernickel and light-colored rye bread or to make gin and whiskey, but rye grain and middlings (a by-product of milling) are also fed to livestock and used for cattle pasturage. The leading producer of rye is the USSR. If rye is infected with ergot, a poisonous fungus, it becomes unsafe for use.

Rykov, Aleksei Ivanovich (1881-1938), Russian communist leader. Active in the October Revolution (1917), he was Soviet Premier (1924-30) after Lenin's death. Opposed to Stalin's policies, he was dismissed from office until he recanted (reinstated 1931-36). Due to involvement in an assassination plot against Stalin, he was executed after a show trial.
See also: Russian Revolution; Union of Soviet Socialist Republics.

Ryukyu Islands, archipelago, of approximately 1,850 sq mi (4,790 sq km), forming a 650-mi (1,050-km) arc between Japan and Taiwan. Dividing the East China and Philippine seas, the 100-plus islands comprise 3 groups: the Amami Islands in the north; the central Okinawa Islands, including Okinawa; and the Sakishima Islands in the south. Many have coral reefs and some have active volcanoes. Climate is subtropical; the economy is supported by agriculture and fishing. The Ryukyus became part of Japan in 1879; they passed to the United States after World War II. The northern islands were returned in 1953, and the remainder in 1972.

Ryun, Jim (1947-　), U.S. athlete who set world records for middle-distance running. In 1966 he ran the mile in 3 minutes 51.3 seconds and 880 yards in

1 minute 44.9 seconds; in 1967 he ran 1,500 meters in 3 minutes 33.1 seconds. He also broke his own mile-run record by 0.2 seconds.

Ryzhkov, Nikolai Ivanovich (1929-   ), former prime minister of the USSR (1985-91). He left office when the restructuring of the Soviet government reduced the scope of the position. After his admittance into the Communist Party (1956), he rose through the ranks of the government, becoming deputy minister of heavy machinery (1975), chairman of the Soviet economic planning commission, called Gosplan (1979), Secretariat of the Central Committee involving economic concerns (1982), then full member of the Communist Party Politburo (1985). In 1991 he was a presidential candidate but lost the elections.
See also: Union of Soviet Socialist Republics.

R/x, symbol used on medical prescriptions. It is believed to have evolved from the Latin word recipe (meaning take), or from the ancient symbol for Jupiter that when placed on a prescription became a plea for hasty remedy. tan Traction Company, was established after he acquired the newly built New York City subway lines (1886). A later company, Consolidated Tobacco Company, was dissolved by order of the government (1911) when it was judged to be a monopoly.

Ryder, Albert Pinkham (1847-1917), U.S. painter, noted for his darkly poetic landscapes, seascapes, and allegorical scenes such as *Toilers of the Sea* (1884), *The Flying Dutchman* (1890), and *The Race Track* (1895). Ryder's body of work (only about 160 canvases) is considered among the finest of American art.

Rye (*Secale cereale*), grain of the grass family, hardiest of all cereal crops. It can grow in poor, sandy soils in cool and temperate climates. Most rye is used for human consumption, e.g. pumpernickel and light-colored rye bread or to make gin and whiskey, but rye grain and middlings (a by-product of milling) are also fed to livestock and used for cattle pasturage. The leading producer of rye is the USSR. If rye is infected with ergot, a poisonous fungus, it becomes unsafe for use.

Rykov, Aleksei Ivanovich (1881-1938), Russian communist leader. Active in the October Revolution (1917), he was Soviet Premier (1924-30) after Lenin's death. Opposed to Stalin's policies, he was dismissed from office until he recanted (reinstated 1931-36). Due to involvement in an assassination plot against Stalin, he was executed after a show trial.
See also: Russian Revolution; Union of Soviet Socialist Republics.

Ryukyu Islands, archipelago, of approximately 1,850 sq mi (4,790 sq km), forming a 650-mi (1,050-km) arc between Japan and Taiwan. Dividing the East China and Philippine seas, the 100-plus islands comprise 3 groups: the Amami Islands in the north; the central Okinawa Islands, including Okinawa; and the Sakishima Islands in the south. Many have coral reefs and some have active volcanoes. Climate is subtropical; the economy is supported by agriculture and fishing. The Ryukyus became part of Japan in 1879; they passed to the United States after World War II. The northern islands were returned in 1953, and the remainder in 1972.

Ryun, Jim (1947-), U.S. athlete who set world records for middle-distance running. In 1966 he ran the mile in 3 minutes 51.3 seconds and 880 yards in 1 minute 44.9 seconds; in 1967 he ran 1,500 meters in 3 minutes 33.1 seconds. He also broke his own mile-run record by 0.2 seconds.

Ryzhkov, Nikolai Ivanovich (1929-   ), former prime minister of the USSR (1985-91). He left office when the restructuring of the Soviet government reduced the scope of the position. After his admittance into the Communist Party (1956), he rose through the ranks of the government, becoming deputy minister of heavy machinery (1975), chairman of the Soviet economic planning commission, called Gosplan (1979), Secretariat of the Central Committee involving economic concerns (1982), then full member of the Communist Party Politburo (1985). In 1991 he was a presidential candidate but lost the elections.
See also: Union of Soviet Socialist Republics.

R/x, symbol used on medical prescriptions. It is believed to have evolved from the Latin word recipe (meaning take), or from the ancient symbol for Jupiter that when placed on a prescription became a plea for hasty remedy.

S

S, 19th letter in the alphabet, corresponding to the Semitic letter *sin*, meaning *tooth*, represented by a rounded W shape derived from an ancient Egyptian symbol for *tusk*. Phoenicians squared off the curves; Greeks turned the resulting sign on its side (as *sigma*); and, as the 18th letter of the Roman alphabet, S assumed its present form. S is used as an abbreviation for such words as south and sulfur.

Saadi, or **Sadi**, (1184-1292), Persian lyric poet. This Sufi writer is best known for 2 ethical works: his masterpiece *Gulistan* (*The Garden of Roses*, 1258) and *Bustan* (*The Orchard*, 1257), both blending prose and poetry.

Saadia ben Joseph (882-952), known as Saadia Gaon, leading figure in medieval Judaism. He was head of the Academy at Sura, Babylonia, and orthodox champion against the ascetic Karaites. He wrote a Hebrew grammar and lexicon, an Arabic translation of the Bible, created the *siddur*, or prayer book, and the *Book of Beliefs and Opinions* (933).
See also: Judaism.

Saar, or **Saarland**, state in southwest Germany, 991 sq mi (2,567 sq km), bordering France. Its capital is Saarbrücken. It is a major coal-mining, iron, and steel region whose control has historically alternated between France and Germany. After World War I, it was administered by France under the League of Nations. It was reunited with Germany after a plebiscite (1935), occupied by France after World War II, and instated as a German state in 1957.
See also: Germany.

Saarinen, 2 modern architects, father and son. **Eliel Saarinen** (1873-1950), the leading Finnish architect of his day, designed the influential Helsinki railroad station (1905-14). In 1923 he emigrated to the United States, where

he designed numerous structures in the Midwest, including the Gateway Arch in St. Louis, Mo. **Eero Saarinen** (1910-61) collaborated with his father (1938-50). His outstanding works include the General Motors Technical Center in Warren, Mich. (1951-5); Massachusetts Institute of Technology's circular chapel and concrete-dome auditorium (1955); and the Trans World Airline Terminal in New York City. He also designed Dulles International Airport in Chantilly, Va., which was completed posthumously.
See also: Architecture.

Saavedra Lamas, Carlos (1880-1959), Argentinian lawyer and statesman. As Argentina's foreign minister (1932-8), he presided over the conference that ended the Chaco War (1935). He won the 1936 Nobel Peace Prize.
See also: Argentina.

Sabah, formerly North Borneo, state in the Federation of Malaysia, on the northern tip of the island of Borneo, Malay archipelago. It lies on the South China and Sulu seas, with Kalimantan (Indonesian Borneo) to the southwest and Brunei to the west. Sabah and Sarawak (also on the island of Borneo) became British protectorates in 1882 and then crown colonies in 1946. In 1963 they joined the newly formed Federation of Malaysia. Sabah's capital is Kota Kinabalu. It has a tropical climate and is largely mountainous (highest peak, Mt. Kinabalu, 13,432 ft/4,094 m). Main exports are timber, rubber, and copra (dried coconut).
See also: Malaysia.

Sabatier, Paul (1854-1941), French chemist who shared with Victor Grignard the 1912 Nobel Prize in chemistry for his work on catalyst action in organic syntheses; especially his discovery that finely divided nickel accelerates hydrogenation.
See also: Chemistry.

Sabbath, seventh day of the Hebrew week. The Jews observe it as the day of rest laid down in the Fourth Commandment to commemorate the Creation. It starts at sunset on Friday and ends at sunset on Saturday. Christians adopted Sunday as the Sabbath to commemorate the Resurrection.
See also: Judaism.

Sabbatical year, among ancient Jews every seventh year was a year of rest for the land, ordered by the law of Moses. Crops were to be unsown and unreaped, and debtors were to be released. Today a professor's sabbatical is for rest or research.

Saber-toothed cat, either of 2 genera of extinct cats of the Cenozoic: *Smilodon* of North America and *Machairodus* of Europe and Asia. Slightly smaller than lions but similar in build, saber-toothed tigers had enormous upper canines, up to 10 in (254 mm) long, which they probably used as daggers to pierce the skin of their prey.

Sabin, Albert Bruce (1906-   ), U.S. virologist best known for developing an oral poliomyelitis vaccine, made from live viruses (1959).
See also: Poliomyelitis.

Sabine River, in northeast Texas, rises in Hunt County and flows about 360 mi (580 km) east and southeast to form the southern part of the Texas-Louisiana boundary. Near its mouth on the Gulf of Mexico it widens into Sabine Lake.

Sabines, ancient people of the Sabine Hills (Apennines) in central Italy, northeast of Rome. The legend of the abduction of the Sabine women by the Romans is fictitious, but there were numerous Roman-Sabine wars. Though there were Sabines in Rome from the earliest times, they became Roman citizens c.268 B.C. and disappeared as a separate people.

Sable (*Martes zibellina*), carnivorous fur-bearing mammal related to the martens. Sable live on the ground of coniferous forests, now restricted to parts of North Asia. About 20 in (508 mm) long, they prey on small rodents.

Sable Island, small north Atlantic island about 95 mi (150 km) southeast of Nova Scotia, Canada. The island, about 24 mi (38 km) long and 1 mi (1.6 km) wide, consists of sand dunes and is surrounded by *shoals* (sand bars). Before modern radar-aided navigation it was a serious navigational hazard and was known as the "graveyard of the Atlantic." Lighthouses were established in 1873, and it is now the site of a Canadian weather station. The island is partly covered by grasses and shrubs and inhabited by birds and, since the 18th century, wild horses.

Sac *See:* Sauk.

Sacagawea, or **Sacajawea** (1787?-1812?), guide and interpreter (1804-5) for the Lewis and Clark expedition. Sacagawea means "Bird Woman." A member of the Shoshone tribe, she was captured by a hostile tribe and sold to Toussaint Charbonneau, who became interpreter for the expedition. Her help was invaluable in obtaining supplies from the Shoshone.
See also: Lewis and Clark expedition.

Saccharides, or carbohydrates, chemical compounds composed of simple sugar or sugars in combination, including table sugar, starch, and cellulose. Saccharides, fats, and proteins are the 3 main classes of food. *Monosaccharides*, including glucose ($C_6H_{12}O_6$), are sugars that cannot be further digested to yield simpler sugar molecules. *Disaccharides*, including sucrose or table sugar ($C_{12}H_{22}O_{11}$), are composed of 2 linked monosaccharide molecules. *Polysaccharides*, including starch and cellulose, are complex molecules consisting of many linked monosaccharides.

Saccharin, calorie-free sweetening agent, much sweeter than sucrose, normally used in its soluble sodium salt form. Not absorbed by the body, it is used by diabetics and in low-calorie dietetic foods.
See also: Artificial sweetener.

Sacco-Vanzetti case, famous legal battle (1920-21) that polarized opinion between U.S. liberal-radicals and conservatives. In 1921, Nicola Sacco and Bartolomeo Vanzetti were found guilty of murdering a paymaster and his guard in South Braintree, Mass. When arrested, they were armed and gave false statements, many say out of fear of deportation due to their alien status.

By 1927, opponents of the verdict claimed that there had been insufficient evidence, and that the trial had been unduly influenced by the fact that Sacco and Vanzetti were aliens, anarchists, and draft evaders. The supreme court of Massachusetts and the governor ruled that the trial was fair. The 2 were executed on Aug. 22, 1927, preceded by demonstrations around the world. Public debate continued for years.
See also: Anarchism.

Sachs, Hans (1494-1576), most popular German poet and dramatist of his time, one of the Meistersingers, and by trade a shoemaker. His prolific output included "The Nightingale of Wittenberg" (1523), which honors Martin Luther. Sachs was the model for a leading character by the same name in Richard Wagner's *Die Meistersinger (1868)*.

Sachs, Julius von (1832-97), German botanist. Sachs studied plant metabolism and respiration, the role of minerals in plant nutrition, and the location of chlorophyll within plant cells. His *The Textbook of Botany* (1868) and *History of Botany* (1875) are among the most comprehensive and influential books in the field of botany.
See also: Botany.

Sachs, Nelly (1891-1970), German-born Swedish poet who fled Nazi Germany in 1940. Her poems deal with the sufferings and destiny of her Jewish people (*O the Chimneys*, 1967). She shared the 1966 Nobel Prize for literature with S. Y. Agnon of Israel.

Sackville, Thomas, 1st Earl of Dorset, (1536-1608), English statesman and poet. He was coauthor (with Thomas Norton) of the first English blank-verse tragedy, *Gorboduc* (1561). He is also noted for his poems "Induction" and "Complaint of Buckingham" in the collection *A Myrrovre for Magistrates* (1559-63). Sackville was raised to peerage status in 1567 and also had the dubious distinction of announcing the death sentence to Mary, Queen of Scots (1586).

Sackville-West, Victoria Mary (1892-1962), English poet, novelist, and biographer, associated (like her husband, Sir Harold Nicolson) with the Bloomsbury Group. Her works include the poem *The Land* (1926) and the novels *The Edwardians* (1930) and *All Passion Spent* (1931).

Sacrament, in Christian theology, visible sign and pledge of invisible grace, ordained by Jesus Christ. The traditional 7 sacraments (first listed by Peter Lombard) are baptism, Holy Communion, confirmation, penance, ordination, marriage, and extreme unction, of which only the first two are accepted as sacraments by many Protestants. In Roman Catholic theology the sacraments, if validly administered, convey grace objectively to the believing recipients; Protestants stress the joining of Word and sacrament and the necessity of faith.
See also: Christianity.

Sacramento (pop. 382,800), capital city of California since 1854, and seat of Sacramento County, at the confluence of the Sacramento and American rivers in central California. Its economy is based primarily upon the business

of government, military manufactures, and agriculture, for which it is a shipping, marketing, and processing center. Its history dates back to 1839, when John Sutter established a colony there on a land grant from Mexico. After the discovery of gold at nearby Sutter's Mill, Sacramento became a boom town.
See also: California.

Sacramento River, longest tributary in California, rising in the Klamath Mountains in the north, flowing southwest for about 380 mi (610 km) to join the San Joaquin River in the Central Valley, before exiting at San Francisco Bay. It is navigable for large vessels as far as Sacramento, 67 mi (108 km) upstream, the major port and largest city on the river. Shasta and Keswick are the chief dams of the Sacramento, which contributes its water to the Central Valley Project (irrigation for the southern part of the state).

Sacrifice, cultic act found in almost all religions, in which an object is consecrated and offered by a priest in worship to a deity. It often involves the killing of an animal or human being and thus the offering up of its life; sometimes a communion meal follows. Sacrifice may also be seen as the expiation of sin, the sealing of a covenant, or a gift to the god that invites blessing in return. Ancient Israel had an elaborate system of sacrifices (chief being that of Passover) that ceased when the Temple was destroyed (A.D. 70). In Christianity, Jesus' death is viewed as the one perfect and eternal sacrifice for sin.
See also: Religion.

Sadat, Anwar el- (1918-81), president of Egypt (1970-81). An army officer, he was active in the coup that overthrew King Farouk in 1952. As vice president, he became president on Nasser's death, expelling Soviet military advisers. His war with Israel and support of an Arab oil boycott against the West (both 1973) were followed by a policy reversal. Establishing close ties with the United States, he took initiatives leading to an Egyptian-Israeli peace treaty (1979). He shared the Nobel Peace Prize with Menachem Begin in 1978. Sadat was assassinated by a group of Muslim army officers.
See also: Egypt.

Saddle, seat to support a rider on the back of an animal. Most horse saddles are leather and are held in place by a girth (strap) passing underneath the horse. Two stirrup-leathers (straps) support the stirrups in which the rider places his or her feet. The English saddle is light, almost flat, and often used by jockeys and horse-show riders. The Western saddle is heavier, has a raised frontal horn to which a lariat may be attached, and is most often used by cowhands and rodeo riders.

Sadducees, Jewish sect active in Judea, Palestine, during the 1st century B.C. and active until the destruction of the Second Temple in Jerusalem, A.D. 70. The sect, associated with priests and the upper class, claimed the Old Testament alone as the source of Jewish law. With their dismissal of Jewish Oral Law they dismissed the beliefs in immortality, resurrection, and angelic beings, beliefs all held by the opposing Pharisee sect.
See also: Sanhedrin.

Sade, Marquis de (Comte Donatien Alphonse François de Sade; 1740-1814), French soldier and writer. He proposed that the existence of sexual deviation and criminal acts prove they are natural. He was charged with many sexual offenses and spent much of his life in prisons, writing sexually explicit romances, e.g., *Justine* (1791). He lived his last 11 years in Charenton lunatic asylum. The word *sadism* (infliction of pain to attain sexual pleasure) was named for him.

Sadi *See:* Saadi.

Safdie, Moshe (1938-   ), Israeli architect. His best known project is Habitat, a modular housing project designed for Expo '67, the 1967 Montreal exposition, and later reproduced in Israel, New York City, Puerto Rico, and the Virgin Islands. Other designs by Safdie include the Yeshivat Porat Joseph Rabbinical College in Jerusalem (1971-79) and the National Gallery of Canada in Ottawa (1988). Safdie became a Canadian citizen in 1959.
See also: Architecture.

Safety, protection from harm, injury, or loss. In a modern, technological society the risks of injury or accidental death caused by machines are very high. Every year in the United States there are over 100,000 deaths from accidents and around 50 million people are injured severely enough to require medical attention. This works out to 1 accidental death every 5 minutes and an injury every 3 seconds. Apart from the immense personal suffering these figures represent, the cost to the economy is enormous. The prevention of accidents is a major concern of all governments.

Safety lamp, oil-burning lamp used in coal mines that indicates the presence of explosive methane gas without igniting it. Designed in 1815 by English chemist Sir Humphry Davy, it uses a double wire gauze cylinder to enclose the flame, preventing heat from escaping and causing an explosion. In the presence of firedamp, the methane-air mixture commonly released in coal mining operations, the flame burns with a blue center, warning miners to leave the mine immediately. The safety electric lamps now used to light mines are designed so that if the bulb is broken the current shuts off, thus preventing ignition of firedamp. But although electric lamps are safe, they do not indicate the presence of the gas, and Davy lamps are still used to warn miners of the danger.
See also: Mining.

Safety valve, relief device that automatically opens to allow excess pressure to escape. Sealed by a compressed spring or a weight, it is held open until the pressure has fallen by a predetermined amount. Safety valves are used on all pressurized vessels (e.g., steam boilers) to prevent explosion.

Safflower, thistlelike herb (*Carthamus tinctorius*) that grows in most warm regions. Safflowers are grown by farmers for the oil and meal that can be made from the seeds. Safflower oil has uses in medicine and is used to make varnishes. The safflower's bright red flowers are used as a substitute for true saffron dye.

Saffron, purple-flowered Asian crocus (*Crocus sativus*) of the iris family; also, the yellow dye extracted from it. The orange-yellow stigmas of its pistils yield saffron powder, which is used for flavoring food and in medicine and perfume.

Saga, epic narrative, in prose or verse, of Old Norse literature (11th to mid-14th century). Subjects of sagas range from history (*Sturlungasaga*) to histories of mythical heroes (*Volsungasaga*) or families (*Njala*). One of the greatest saga authors was Snorri Sturluson, whose *Heimskringla* (1230) traced the history of the kings of Norway.

Sagan, Carl Edward (1934-96), U.S. astronomer, educator, and popular science writer. From 1968 a professor at Cornell University, he worked on NASA space probe projects and conducted research into the possibility of extraterrestrial life. He helped popularize science through his public television series *Cosmos* (1980). Sagan's books include the Pulitzer Prize-winning *The Dragons of Eden* (1977) and the novel *Contact* (1985).
See also: Astronomy.

Sagan, Françoise (Françoise Quoirez; 1935-), French novelist best known for the precocious and highly successful *Bonjour Tristesse* (1954), written when she was 18, and *A Certain Smile* (1956), both of which deal with the disillusion of gilded youth. In 1984 her memoires *Avec Mon Meilleur Souvenir* were published.

Sage, aromatic herb or shrub of the mint family. There are several North American species, including the crimson and purple sages of California and the lyre-leaved sage of New England. Cultivated sages include bright-flowered ornamentals known by their scientific name, *salvia*. The common garden sage (*Salvia officinalis*), native to Southern Europe and Asia Minor, has grayish leaves that are used to make tea and as a seasoning.

Sage, Russell (1816-1906), U.S. financier who amassed a fortune from the wholesale grocery, railroad, and other businesses. From his $70-million estate, his widow used $10 million to establish the Russell Sage Foundation (1907) to better U.S. social conditions.

Sagebrush, small aromatic shrub (genus *Artemisia*) of the composite family, native to the plains and mountains of western North America. These deciduous shrubs grow anywhere from 2 to 12 ft (0.6 to 3.7 m) high and have white or yellow flowers. Sagebrush is unrelated to true sage. It is the state flower of Nevada.

Sagebrush State *See:* Nevada.

Saginaw (pop. 77,508), city in southern Michigan, seat of Saginaw County, located on the Saginaw River about 85 mi (137 km) northwest of Detroit. The original settlements of Saginaw (1820) and East Saginaw (1849) were expanded to form the city (1889). A fur trade center from the early 19th century, it was also a lumber center until the lumber supply was exhausted in the late 19th century. The city now manufactures automobiles and machinery and processes sugar beets and other agricultural products. The

Saginaw River connects the city with Saginaw Bay, part of Lake Huron. *See also:* Michigan.

Sago, starch derived from the coontie or sago palm. The starch is found in the fibrous tissue at the base of the tree's stem. Sago is used to make sago flour, one of the principal foods of East Indian people.

Saguaro, or giant cactus (*Cereus giganteus* or *Carnegiea gigantea*), large member of the cactus family native to the deserts of the U.S. Southwest and Mexico. The plant uses a shallow, wide network of roots to collect moisture, which it then stores in the ribbed, spiny trunk, 1-2.5 ft (30-76 cm) in diameter. The plant may reach the age of 150-200 years, growing to a height of nearly 40 ft (12 m) and occasionally up to 60 ft (18 m). The white night-blooming flowers form at the ends of the trunk and the large branches in late spring, attracting bats, birds, and insects. The red, egg-shaped fruit is eaten by humans and desert animals.

Sahara Desert, largest desert in the world, covering about 3,500,000 sq mi (9,065,000 sq km) of North Africa from the Atlantic Ocean to the Red Sea, about 3,000 mi (4,830 km) by 1,200 mi (1,930) north to south. The terrain includes sand hills, rocky wastes, tracts of gravel, and fertile oasis. The central plateau, about 1,000 ft (305 m) above sea level, has mountain groups (Ahagger, Aïr, and Tibesti), some of which rise well over 6,000 ft (1,829 m). Rainfall averages from less than 5 in (12.7 cm) to 10 in (25 cm) annually (dry periods may last for several years), and temperatures may soar higher than 135°F (57°C) and plunge below freezing at night. Natural resources include oil, iron ore, natural gas, and phosphates. Also underground are vast aquifers holding water thought to date from the Pleistocene epoch.

Sahel, semiarid region south of the Sahara Desert, extending across north-central Africa from Senegal in the west to Ethiopia in the east. The land supports a grazing and agricultural economy with savanna-type grassland and scrub. Rainfall is 8-16 in (20-40 cm) annually, from June to August. A severe drought (1967-74) caused mass migration and the starvation of hundreds of thousands of people.

Saigon *See:* Ho Chi Minh City.

Sailfish, food and game fish of the family Istiophoridae, related to the marlin and swordfish. The sailfish has a pointed beak on the snout and a high, wide dorsal fin sail. Averaging 6 ft (180 cm) in length and 60 to 100 lb (27 to 45 kg), they feed on fish and squid and are highly prized by anglers for their fighting qualities.

Sailing, popular pastime or sport involving the navigation of a boat powered primarily by wind. The earliest known sailing vessels evolved in the Mediterranean region, particularly among the Upper Nile dwellers of ancient Egypt. These sailboats had a mast with 1 sail hung from a fixed yardarm. The Chinese developed the movable yardarm, which allowed vessels to sail with the wind across their bows as well as before the wind. In recent history, boats of varying lengths, with multiple sales and masts, gather to compete with other like vessels. The most prestigious of these races is the *America's*

Cup, an international series of races begun in 1851 and dominated by the United States until 1983. Major competitors include the USSR, Australia (winner of the Cup in 1983), and Great Britain. Boats often used for racing include schooners and ketches (2 masts/5 sails) and yawls (2 masts/4 sails). Recreational cruises are often one-design boats, 16-23 ft (4.88-7.01 m) long, such as the Star, Mercury, Comet, Lightning, and Snipe.
See also: America's Cup.

Saint, in Christian theology, person preeminent for holiness. The term was used in the New Testament to refer to all the faithful. It is now used to designate those recognized by a church as occupying an exalted position in heaven and being worthy of veneration due to martyrdom, holiness of life, miracles during life or after death, or a popular cult. All angels are saints, and the Virgin Mary is chief among them. Feast days in the Anglican, Orthodox, and Roman Catholic liturgies commemorate those canonized with sainthood.
See also: Christianity.

Saint Andrews (pop. 16,000), town in eastern Scotland on the North Sea, in the district of Fife, between the firths of Forth and Tay. The University of St. Andrews is Scotland's oldest (founded 1411). The town, known as the birthplace of golf, is home to the Royal and Ancient Golf Club (founded 1754).
See also: Scotland.

Saint Augustine (pop. 11,985), city, seat of St. John's County, on the Atlantic coast of northeast Florida. The oldest city in the United States (founded 1565), its strategic location was coveted and often fought over (Sir Francis Drake attacked it first in 1586). It did not become part of the union until 1821 (inc. 1824). Today it is a tourist center with light industry and 2 national monuments: the Castillo de San Marcos (1672-96) and Fort Matanzas (1742).
See also: Florida.

Saint Bartholomew's Day, Massacre of, the killing of French Huguenots (Protestants) by Roman Catholics, beginning in Paris on Aug. 24, 1572. Jealous of the influence of the Huguenot admiral Coligny on her son King Charles IX, Catherine de Médicis plotted to assassinate him. When this failed, Catherine, fearing Huguenot reaction, persuaded Charles to order the deaths of all leading Huguenots. On the morning of St. Bartholomew's Day thousands were slaughtered. Despite government orders to stop, the murders continued in the provinces until October. The Wars of Religion (1562-98) resumed as a result.

Saint Bernard, breed of large, stout dog developed as a rescue dog at the Alpine monastery of St. Bernard, Switzerland, in the 17th century. It measures up to 30 in (76 cm) at the shoulder and 180 lb (82 kg), and has a white and red or white and brown coat. Its acute sense of smell has helped it locate people buried in snow and makes it a valued guide dog.

Saint Bernard Passes, routes through the Alps. The Great St. Bernard (8,100 ft/2,469 m) links Martigny, Switzerland, with Aosta, Italy. The Little

Saint Christopher and Nevis

Capital:	Basseterre
Area:	101 sq mi
	(262 sq km)
Population:	42,000
Language:	English
Government:	Parliamentary
	monarchy
Independent:	1983
Head of gov.:	Prime minister
Per capita:	U.S. $5,170
Mon. unit:	1 East Caribean dollar
	= 100 cents

St. Bernard (7,177 ft/2,188 m) connects France's Isère Valley with Aosta.
See also: Alps.

Saint Christopher and Nevis, officially St. Christopher-Nevis, Caribbean
island state of the British West Indies, in the Leeward Islands. The area is
101 sq mi (262 sq km); the capital is Basseterre, on Saint Christopher
(commonly known as Saint Kitts). Discovered (1493) by Columbus, the
islands were awarded to Britain (1783) after struggles with France. Autonomy in internal affairs was granted in 1967, followed by full independence
in 1983. In 1998 a referendum was held on Nevis, at which occasion votes
for independence dominated.

Saint Clair, Arthur (1743-1818), U. S. soldier and politician. He served in
the Revolutionary War and in 1787 became president of the Continental
Congress, then first governor of the Northwest Territory (1787-1802). His
military career ended with defeat by Native American tribes in 1792.
Unpopular as governor, he was removed from office in 1802.

Saint Cloud (pop. 190,921), city in central Minnesota, seat of Stearns
County, located on the Mississippi River about 70 mi (110 km) northwest of
Minneapolis. Named for a French city, it was a fur-trading center and a stage
coach terminus from the mid-1850s. Its granite quarries were opened in 1870,
and the city is still a center for the granite industry. Other industry includes
the manufacture of optical lenses, railroad cars, and refrigeration equipment.
It is the home of St. Cloud State University.
See also: Minnesota.

Saint Croix, largest island of the U.S. Virgin Islands. It is a tourist center
and markets sugarcane and rum.
See also: Virgin Islands.

Saint Denis, Ruth (Ruth Dennis; 1878?-1968), U.S. dancer, choreographer,
and teacher, whose work strongly influenced modern dance. Deeply interested in ethnic and U.S. dances, music visualizations, and Hindu and other
Eastern philosophies, she staged her first major success, the solo *Radha*, in

1906. She and her husband, Ted Shawn, ran the influential Denishawn School and widely touring Denishawn Company (both, 1915-32).
See also: Shawn, Ted.

Sainte-Anne-de-Beaupré, village and Roman Catholic shrine in Montmorency County, southern Quebec, Canada, on the St. Lawrence River near the mouth of the Ste.-Anne River. The village was first settled in 1650. A chapel was built there in 1658 by shipwrecked French sailors who believed they were saved from death by their prayers to Saint Anne, patron saint of sailors. There were subsequent reports of miracle cures in the area, and the village became a pilgrimage center. A basilica was built as a shrine in 1876 and rebuilt after a fire destroyed it in 1922.
See also: Quebec.

Saint Elias Mountains, part of the Pacific Coast Ranges, in eastern Alaska and the southwestern Yukon Territory, Canada. The range is extremely rugged, with many high peaks; Canada's Mount Logan (19,524 ft/5,951 m) and Alaska's Mount St. Elias (18,008 ft/5,489 m) are the second and fourth highest peaks in North America. Its ice fields are the most extensive outside of the polar ice caps.

Saint Elmo's fire, glowing electrical discharge seen at the tips of tall, pointed objects—e.g., church spires, ship masts, and airplane wings—in stormy weather. The negative electrical charge of the storm clouds induces a positive charge on the prominent structures. The impressive display is named (corruptly) for St. Erasmus, patron of sailors.

Saint-Exupéry, Antoine de (1900-44), French aviator and author. After serving in the French Army Air Force (1921-23), he flew commercial routes between France, West Africa, and South America. Most of his writing gives accounts of his flying experiences (*Southern Mail*, 1928) and the philosophical and spiritual meaning he found in its challenges (*Wind, Sand and Stars*, 1939). His most famous work, however, is the fantasy *The Little Prince* (1943). Saint-Exupéry flew reconnaissance missions during World War II, disappearing over Europe on one such mission in 1944.

Saint-Gaudens, Augustus (1848-1907), U.S. sculptor famed for his heroic public monuments, including Abraham Lincoln (Lincoln Park, Chicago), the Robert G. Shaw monument on the Boston Common, and the equestrian statue of General William Sherman (Central Park, N.Y.C.).

Saint George Island *See:* Pribilof Islands.

Saint George's (pop. 7,500), capital, chief port, and industrial center of Grenada, in the West Indies. Originally settled by the French in 1650 at a location near present-day St. George's, the current site was established in 1705. In 1783 control of the town, on the southwestern coast, passed to the British, who soon made it the government headquarters for all of the Windward Islands. A center of tourism, St. George's gained its independence in 1974.

Saint-Germain, Treaty of, treaty signed by the United States and other World War I Allies and the Republic of Austria in France (1919-20), limiting Austrian powers and redistributing some of the lands of the Austro-Hungarian Empire. The treaty resulted in the complete independence of Poland, Czechoslovakia, and Hungary, and the creation of the independent state of Yugoslavia. Austria's army and war industry were restricted, and the country was required to pay reparations to the Allies. The treaty's provision prohibiting the unification of Austria and Germany was violated by Adolf Hitler in 1938.
See also: World War I.

Saint Helena, British island (47 sq mi/122 sq km) in the South Atlantic Ocean, 1,200 mi (1,931 km) west of Africa. Discovered by the Portuguese in 1502, its capital is Jamestown, where Napoleon I died in exile in 1821. With Tristan da Cunha and Ascension, it comprises the British dependency of St. Helena.

Saint Helens, Mount *See:* Mount Saint Helens.

Saint James's Palace, former royal residence (1698-1837), London, England, situated in Pall Mall. Royal gatherings are still held here and foreign ambassadors to Britain are received at its court.

Saint John (pop. 76,381), city in eastern Canada, located in southern New Brunswick on the Bay of Fundy, at the mouth of the St. John River. It is one of the only 2 ice-free ports of Canada's Atlantic coast and is New Brunswick's center of transportation, commerce, and industry, including large shipyards, oil and sugar refineries, and pulp and paper mills. Originally a French trading post (1631-35), it passed between French and English control until 1758, when the English became the permanent rulers. The growth of the city escalated rapidly when the United Empire Loyalists arrived from the United States in 1783. Known as Paar Town, the city was incorporated as St. John 2 years later.
See also: New Brunswick.

Saint John River, tributary (418 mi/673 km long) that rises in northwestern Maine and flows northeast to New Brunswick, where it makes up about 80 mi (129 km) of the U.S.-Canadian border. The river then turns south and east, flowing through New Brunswick to empty into the Bay of Fundy at St. John. It is famous for its "reversing falls," made possible by exceptionally high Fundy tides.

Saint John's (pop. 96,216), largest city and capital of Newfoundland, Canada, situated on a well-protected harbor near the Grand Banks. The site was discovered by John Cabot in 1497 and is believed to have been settled shortly after. The city's key location has made it into an important docking port for fishing boats from around the world. St. John's stands as Newfoundland's chief cultural, educational, and commercial center.

Saint-John's-wort, name generally given to over 400 species of low shrubs of the family Hypericaceae, native to temperate and tropical regions. The flowers, which include both wild and cultivated varieties, are generally yellow, with 5 petals.

Saint Joseph (pop. 83,083), city in northwest Missouri, located on the east bank of the Missouri River about 55 mi (88.5 km) northwest of Kansas City. Saint Joseph was a frontier town, established in 1826 by a French-Canadian trapper, Joseph Robidoux. It became famous as the starting station for the pony express in 1860. The modern city is a distribution center for the meat-packing industry and other regional farm products and manufactures drugs and chemicals, paper products, and other goods.
See also: Missouri.

Saint Kitts *See:* Saint Christopher and Nevis.

Saint Laurent, Louis Stephen (1882-1973), prime minister of Canada (1948-57). Internationally, St. Laurent played an important role in the founding of the United Nations (1945). As prime minister he strengthened Canada's position in the Commonwealth of Nations and was instrumental in founding the North Atlantic Treaty Organization (NATO). Domestically, he achieved the incorporation of Newfoundland as a Canadian province in 1949.
See also: Canada.

Saint Lawrence River, largest tributary in Canada, flowing 744 mi (1,197 km) northeast from Lake Ontario to the Gulf of St. Lawrence. It forms 120 mi (193 km) of the U.S./Canadian border. Canalized as part of the Saint Lawrence Seaway, it serves as the chief outlet for Great Lakes shipping (although it is closed from mid-December to mid-April due to ice).

Saint Lawrence Seaway and Great Lakes Waterway, U.S./Canadian inland waterway for oceangoing vessels connecting the Great Lakes with the Atlantic Ocean, and comprising a system of natural waterways, canals, locks, dams, and dredged channels (including the Welland Ship Canal) 2,342 mi (3,769 km) long. A joint venture between the United States and Canada, it was completed in 1959.

Saint Louis (pop. 383,700), city in eastern Missouri, on the Mississippi River. Founded as a fur-trading post by the French in 1764, it was ceded to Spain in 1770, reverting briefly to the French before passing to the United States as part of the Louisiana Purchase in 1803. The city expanded rapidly after the War of 1812 and became a major inland port, transportation center, and market. Products include beer, machinery, chemicals, and basic metals. St. Louis' Gateway Arch (630 ft/192 m high), designed by Eero Saarinen, is the city's most famous landmark. It is also known for its symphony orchestra and Washington University.
See also: Missouri.

Saint Lucia, independent West Indies island nation (238 sq mi/616 sq km) in the Windward Islands in the Caribbean Sea.
Land and Climate. St. Lucia, 27 mi (43 km) long and 14 mi (23 km) wide, is of volcanic origin with 1 active volcano. The terrain is hilly, with Morne Gimie reaching 3,145 ft (959 m), and the interior is covered with tropical rain forests. The average annual temperature is 79°F (26°C).
People. Most of the inhabitants are of black African heritage. Roman Catholicism is the religion of nearly 90% of the population, and English is the official language. However, a French patois is widely spoken.

Saint Lucia

Capital:	Castries
Area:	238 sq mi
	(616 sq km)
Population:	152,000
Language:	English
Government:	Parliamentary
	monarchy
Independent:	1979
Head of gov.:	Prime minister
Per capita:	U.S. $3,370
Mon. unit:	1 East Caribean dollar
	= 100 cents

Economy. Small-scale agriculture is the principal economic activity, with bananas, coconuts, cocoa beans, oil, and citrus fruits grown for export. Industry, including food processing, electrical components, and garments, is being diversified to include an ambitious oil complex and free-trade zone. Although tourism is growing, imports exceed exports by 200%, and the country is heavily dependent upon foreign aid.

History. Though the island was probably sited by Columbus in 1502, the Carib were able to prevent several settlement attempts by the British and French from the early 17th century until 1803, when the island was ceded to Britain. St. Lucia was part of the West Indies Federation from 1958 until it was dissolved in 1962. Full independence from Britain was granted in 1979. It has a parliamentary government.

Saint Mark, Basilica of, cathedral in Venice, Italy, named for the city's patron saint. Originally Romanesque, it became an outstanding example of Byzantine architecture through alterations made from the 12th century on. It is built in the form of a Greek cross surmounted by 5 large domes (1 in the center, the others on the 4 arms of the cross). The richly constructed and sculptured west façade, facing the Piazza San Marco, has Gothic additions. Its famous 4 bronze horses were taken from Constantinople in 1204.

Saint Marys River, river on the border between Ontario and Michigan that drains Lake Superior, then flows less than 70 mi (110 km) to empty into Lake Huron. The river is part of the St. Lawrence and Great Lakes Waterway, which links the Great Lakes with the Atlantic Ocean. The St. Marys Rapids near Lake Huron make the river impassable for large boats; these are diverted to the Sault Ste. Marie (or Soo) Canals. Saint Marys River is a source of hydroelectric power.

Saint Moritz (pop. 5,263), alpine resort town in southeastern Switzerland, Graubünden (Grisons) canton. The original Roman settlement dates from 50 B.C. The town became a resort in the 19th century, and was home to the 1928 and 1948 Winter Olympics. Saint Moritz is located in the region where Romansh, an Italic language (of Latin derivation) and one of Switzerland's official languages, is spoken.

Saint Nicholas, Feast of, festival on Dec. 6 in honor of a 4th-century bishop of Asia Minor. Saint Nicholas, later known also as Santa Claus, is patron saint of children, and the festival is celebrated as a children's holiday, with rewards and punishment according to the children's behavior. Although Santa Claus became identified with Christmas, the Feast of Saint Nicholas continues to be celebrated by some on Dec. 6.

Saint Patrick's Cathedral, largest U.S. Roman Catholic cathedral, seat of the New York Archdiocese. The Gothic Revival structure was designed by James Renwick and built between 1858 and 1879. It is located on 5th Avenue and 50th Street, New York City.

Saint Patrick's Day, March 17, celebrated as the anniversary of the death (c.A.D. 461) of Patrick, Ireland's patron saint. The Irish celebrate the day by wearing leaves of shamrock (Ireland's national flower) or green-colored items of clothing and by staging colorful parades.

Saint Paul (pop. 270,230), capital of Minnesota and seat of Ramsay County, located in the eastern part of the state on the Mississippi River. St. Paul and neighboring Minneapolis together form the Twin Cities. The site was occupied by U.S. Army Fort St. Anthony from 1819; the settlement of St. Paul was established in 1840 and became an important commercial port and fur-trading center. Railroad lines reached the city by the 1860s, extending to Puget Sound, on the west coast, by the 1890s. While the more industrial Minneapolis flourished, St. Paul suffered an economic decline starting in the 1920s, but it has undergone extensive redevelopment since the mid-1960s. Cultural assets now include 2 major performance centers (Landmark Center, 1978; Ordway Music Theatre, 1984) and the St. Paul Chamber Orchestra. *See also:* Minnesota.

Saintpaulia *See:* African violet.

Saint Petersburg (pop. 249,900), city on the central west coast of Florida, situated on the Pinellas peninsula opposite Tampa, on Tampa Bay of the Gulf of Mexico. Native Americans lived in the area since 5000 B.C. It was explored by the Spanish in the 1500s, but was first settled by European Americans in the 1840s. Russian-born Peter A. Demens, who built the railroad that connected the settlement to central Florida (1888), named the city for his birthplace. The location and unusually sunny climate have made the city a major resort and retirement community since the early 1900s. Major attractions include yacht races and spring training camps for professional baseball teams. Eckerd College and St. Petersburg Junior College are located in the city. *See also:* Florida.

Saint Petersburg *See:* Leningrad.

Saint Peter's Church, or Saint Peter's Basilica, church in Vatican City, Rome. The world's largest Christian church, it is built over the tomb thought to hold the remains of St. Peter, the first pope. The original church was built by the emperor Constantine the Great in the 4th century A.D. but demolished by Pope Julius II in the 16th century to make way for the new building.

Among the successive architects to be involved in the creation of the current church were Donato Bramante, who developed the original design on the shape of a Greek cross (from 1506); Michelangelo Buonarroti, who created the great dome (from 1547); and Carlo Maderno, who added the façade and altered the overall proportions to arrive at the shape of a Latin cross (1607-14). The church was dedicated in 1626, but further work continued, most notably by Gian Lorenzo Bernini, who created the great elliptical piazza in front of the church (completed 1667) as well as much of the interior detail. The church measures nearly 700 ft (210 m) long and is 450 ft (137 m) at its widest. The nave (main aisle) is 150 ft (46 m) high, while the dome is over 400 ft (120 m) high.

Saint Pierre and Miquelon, groups of French islands in the Atlantic Ocean, south of Newfoundland. The capital is Saint Pierre. First visited in the 17th century by Breton and Basque fishermen, the islands' ownership was long disputed between France and England. They became France's in 1814 and are now an overseas department, electing a deputy and senator to parliament. Fisheries (for cod and others), fox- and mink-farming, and tourism are important industries.

Saint-Saëns, Camille (1835-1921), French composer. He wrote many large-scale symphonies, piano concertos, symphonic poems, operas, including *Samson et Dalila* (1877), and such short works as *La Danse Macabre* (1874), and *Carnival of the Animals* (1886).

Saint-Simon, Comte de (Claude Henri de Rouvroy; 1760-1825), French philosopher and early socialist. According to his theories, voiced in *The New Christianity* (1825) and other influential writings, all people would be treated as economic equals—no wealth would be inherited, everyone would work, and compensation would be commensurate with labor. He believed that science could be used to create a fair and harmonious society. Saint-Simon fought on the side of the colonies in the American Revolution.
See also: Socialism.

Saint Sophia *See:* Hagia Sophia.

Saint Thomas, mountainous, heavily cultivated, tropical island (32 sq mi/83 sq km) of the U.S. Virgin Islands, West Indies, in the westernmost part of the Lesser Antilles in the Caribbean Sea. The economy rests on tourism but includes cattle-raising and meat-packaging. St. Thomas was settled by the Danish in 1672. The islanders have been U.S. citizens since 1927 and are administered by the U.S. Department of Interior. They are governed by a locally elected governor and senate.

Saint Vincent and the Grenadines, island nation in the West Indies, part of the Windward Islands in the Caribbean Sea, part of the British Commonwealth. *Land and climate.* The principal island, St. Vincent (133 sq mi/344 sq km), is of volcanic origin, with a forested, mountainous spine running down the center of the island. It reaches 4,000 ft (1,219 m) at Soufrière, an active volcano peak that erupted in 1979, causing extensive crop damage and the evacuation of 20,000 people. The 5 small, main islands of the Grenadines extend to the southwest. The climate is tropical.

St.Vincent and the Grenadines

Capital:	Kingstown
Area:	150 sq mi
	(389 sq km)
Population:	120,000
Language:	English
Government:	Parliamentary monarchy
Independent:	1979
Head of gov.:	Prime minister
Per capita:	U.S. $2,280
Mon. unit:	1 East Caribean dollar = 100 cents

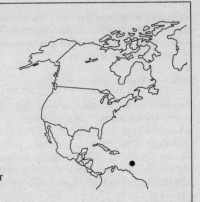

People. The majority of the inhabitants are descendants of slaves brought from Africa. Most of the population belongs to the Roman Catholic church; the official language is English.

Economy. Agriculture provides all exports, principally arrowroot and bananas, followed by spices and cacao. The small industrial sector mostly processes food crops. Tourism is also important.

History. St. Vincent was discovered by Christopher Columbus in 1498. Although both Britain and France subsequently contested control of the island, it was left largely to the Carib Indians until 1797 when, following a war with both the French and Caribs, the British deported most of the Indians. Full independence was achieved in 1979.

Saint Vitus's dance *See:* Chorea.

Saipan, island, capital of the Northern Mariana Islands and headquarters of the U.S. Trust territory of the Pacific Islands. It is mountainous and fertile. Copra, bananas, and breadfruit are important crops.
See also: Northern Mariana Islands.

Sake, or saki, alcoholic drink made from fermented rice. It is Japan's national beverage and contains 12-16% by volume of ethanol.

Sakhalin (formerly Saghalien), Russian island off the coast of eastern Siberia, in the Sea of Okhotsk, north of the Japanese island of Hokkaido. It measures about 600 mi (970 km) long and 16-100 mi (26-160 km) wide, and contains coal and iron deposits and lumber. Fishing and fur trading are also important economic activities. Ownership of the island, which was originally discovered by the Dutch, was disputed by Japan and Russia—from 1905 it was divided between the 2 countries. The Ainu people were the original inhabitants; Soviet colonization dates from the discovery of oil in 1931. By 1951 Japan had given up all claims to the island.

Sakharov, Andrei Dmitriyevich (1921-90), Soviet physicist and human-rights proponent. He played a prominent part in the development of the first Soviet hydrogen bomb (1948-56). He subsequently advocated worldwide nuclear disarmament (for which he was awarded the 1975 Nobel Peace Prize) and became a leading Soviet dissident. His subsequent banishment (1980) to the city of Gorki provoked international protest. He was pardoned in 1986. *See also:* Nuclear weapon.

Saki *See:* Munro, Hector Hugh.

Saladin (1138-93), Muslim ruler and warrior who fought against the Crusaders. He united the Shiite and Sunnite Muslims in 1171 and thus became sultan of Egypt and Syria. In 1187 he led the capture of Jerusalem from the Christians. The Third Crusade that followed resulted in a lengthy siege of the city (1189-91). Saladin finally surrendered to England's King Richard I and entered into a truce ceding coastal lands to the Christians and giving pilgrims access to Jerusalem. Saladin was a noted patron of learning and the arts.
See also: Crusades.

Salamander, tailed amphibian (order Vrodela) related to frogs and toads. Salamanders' weak limbs, which are not used for locomotion to any great extent, are small and can regenerate. These mostly nocturnal creatures range in size from under 6 in (15 cm) to 5 ft (1.5 m) and are abundant in damp areas of the northern temperate zone. Some species are aquatic, most are terrestrial, and a few are arboreal. Salamanders feed on insects and other invertebrates.

Salamis, or Koulouri (Greek, "baker's crescent"), Greek island in the Saronic Gulf (arm of the Aegean Sea between Attica and the Peloponnisos), about 10 mi (16 km) west of Athens. The rocky, crescent-shaped island, 37 sq mi (95 sq km) in area, supports little agriculture, and most residents now work in the shipping industry or in businesses in Athens. In the Battle of Salamis (480 B.C.), fought at sea by the Persians and the Athenians, Themistocles led the Greeks to a decisive victory.

Salazar, António de Oliveira (1889-1970), dictator of Portugal (1932-68). He reorganized public finances as finance minister (1926, 1928), and achieved certain modernizations as premier. Education and living standards, however, remained almost static, and political freedom was restricted, both at home and in Portugal's African colonies, where he actively suppressed revolts. A stroke in 1968 led to his replacement as premier.
See also: Portugal.

Salem (pop. 278,024), capital and third-largest city of Oregon, in the fertile Willamette Valley about 50 mi (80.5 km) south of Portland. Founded in 1840 by Methodist missionaries, it was the territorial capital in the 1850s and became the state capital when Oregon was admitted to the Union in 1859. Salem is a food-processing and distribution center. Willamette University, founded as Oregon Institute in 1842, is the oldest university in the Pacific Northwest.
See also: Oregon.

Salem (pop. 38,264), manufacturing city in northeast Massachusetts, seat of Essex County, on an inlet of Massachusetts Bay. Founded in 1626, it soon became a major port, crucial for trade with China. Today tourists appreciate it as the site of witchcraft trials (1692), and as the birthplace of Nathaniel Hawthorne, whose home has been preserved. Other sights include Pioneer Village, a reproduction of a 1630 settlement, and the House of the Seven Gables (1668), about which Hawthorne wrote his novel of the same name. *See also:* Massachusetts.

Salem, Peter (1750?-1816), former black slave, American Revolutionary soldier. Salem obtained his freedom by enlisting in the colonial army. He distinguished himself at the Battle of Bunker Hill, near Boston, June 17, 1775, saving the colonial troops from surrender by shooting British Major John Pitcairn, thus giving the troops time to retreat.
See also: Bunker Hill, Battle of.

Salem witchcraft trials, trials held in Salem, Massachusetts Bay Colony, in 1692, as a result of hysteria. The accusations of innocent townspeople began when 3 young girls claimed possession by the devil. The special court sentenced 19 men and women to death by hanging and imprisoned about 150 more. The witch hunt was brought to a halt and those imprisoned were freed in 1693. Samuel Sewall, one of the 3 judges, apologized publicly, and the colony's legislature made payments to families of those who were executed. In Arthur Miller's play *The Crucible* (1953) the events in Salem were used to symbolize the persecution of individuals as alleged communists by Senator Joseph McCarthy's House Un-American Activities Committee.
See also: Sewall, Samuel.

Salerno (pop. 147,500), city and tourist center in Campania, on the Gulf of Salerno in southern Italy. Founded by Romans in 197 B.C., it was occupied by the Norman conqueror Robert Guiscard in 1076 and was the site of a fierce beach battle between the Allies and Germans in World War II. Salerno's medical school, founded in the 9th century and at its peak in the 12th, was the first of its kind, with teachings influenced by the leading Mediterranean cultures.
See also: Italy.

Sales, Saint Francis de *See:* Francis de Sales, Saint.

Salic law, from the 14th century, law to prevent women and those descended from female lines from inheriting the throne and other titles and offices. It was not part of the Germanic *Lex Salica* (laws regarding the penal code and succession to property), as it is sometimes mistaken to be. Salic law was used into the 19th century in France and Spain, where it was rescinded for Queen Isabella II.

Salicylic acid ($C_7H_6O_3$), white crystalline solid made from phenol and carbon dioxide. It is used in medicine against calluses and warts and to make aspirin and dyes. Its sodium salt is an analgesic and is used for rheumatism.
See also: Aspirin.

Salinas de Gortari, Carlos (1948-), president of Mexico (1988-94). As secretary of planning and the budget in the cabinet of President Miguel de la Madrid Hurtado, Salinas managed Mexico's economy from 1982 to 1987. He was elected on the ticket of the ruling party, the Institutional Revolution-

ary Party (PRI), to succeed Madrid. In 1995 he left for the United States. He was suspected of being involved in political murders. In 1996, thousands of Mexican farmers blamed him for the 1994 financial crisis and wanted him imprisoned.
See also: Mexico.

Salinger, J(erome) D(avid) (1919-   ), U.S. author. His only novel, *The Catcher in the Rye* (1951), became one of the most popular postwar books, and its adolescent hero, Holden Caulfield, was accepted as a spokesperson of his generation. Salinger's short stories include *Nine Stories* (1953) and *Franny and Zooey* (1961).

Salisbury, or New Sarum (pop. 102,500), town in Wiltshire, southern England, 80 mi (130 km) southwest of London. The original town of Old Sarum was rebuilt as New Sarum when it became a bishopric in the 13th century; Salisbury's main tourist attraction, its cathedral, dates from this time. The famous prehistoric stone circle known as Stonehenge lies 7 mi (11 km) north.
See also: England.

Salish, group of Native American tribes of the U.S. Northwest and British Columbia, Canada. Two groups are distinguished. The Coast Salish, including the Quinault and Tillamook, traditionally lived by salmon fishing and hunting and gathering. The Interior Salish, including the Flathead, Spokan, and Wenatchee, lived east of the Cascade and Coast Range mountains. Those living nearest the Pacific were culturally much like the Coast Salish, while those living farther east lived much like the Plains tribes, hunting on horseback. At the time of the arrival of European settlers, many were fur trappers and traders. Most of those Salish living in the United States were moved to reservations in the mid-19th century. The Coast Salish now work largely in the fishing industry and in urban occupations, while Interior Salish are farmers, ranchers, and loggers.

Saliva, watery secretion of the salivary glands, partly controlled by the parasympathetic autonomic nervous system, that lubricates the mouth and chewed food and begins the breakdown of starches in the digestive process. There are 3 sets of salivary glands: the parotid, submaxillary, and sublingual. Saliva contains mucin, water, salts, some gamma globulins (proteins), and ptyalin (a starch-splitting enzyme) and is secreted in response to food in the mouth or by conditioned reflexes such as the smell or sight of food.

Salivary glands *See:* Saliva.

Salk, Jonas Edward (1914-95), U.S. physician and microbiologist. He is best known for developing the first poliomyelitis vaccine, made from killed viruses (1952-54). He served as director of the Salk Institute for Biological Studies at the University of California, San Diego (1963-75). From 1986 he worked on a vaccine against AIDS.
See also: Poliomyelitis.

Salmon, large, silver, soft-finned game and food fish of the family Salmonidae. Salmon are born in fresh water, spend most of their lives in the ocean, and return to fresh water to breed. The most commercially important salmon is the Pacific salmon (genus *Oncorhynchus*), of which there are 5 species. The largest is the chinook, which reaches up to 100 lb (45 kg); the blueback is the source of most canned salmon. The Atlantic salmon (*Salmo salar*), endangered due to overfishing and pollution, lives in the North Atlantic and reaches only 15 lb (6.8 kg), feeding on crustaceans and small fish. All salmon return to their natal streams to breed, spawning in the sand or gravel of the stream bed.

Salmonellosis, common type of food poisoning caused by the *Salmonella* bacteria. Poultry, milk, eggs, and egg products often carry the bacteria. Salmonellosis is usually confined to the intestines, where it causes nausea, abdominal pain, diarrhea, and fever. Treatment includes rest, replacement of body fluids and, in severe cases, the use of antibiotics.
See also: Food poisoning.

Salome (fl. 1st century A.D.), daughter of Herodias and stepdaughter of Herod Antipas (governor of Galilee), described in the New Testament (Matthew 14:6-12, Mark 6:22-28). She is said to have danced for Herod, for which she was granted a wish. At the urging of her mother, Herodias, she requested the head of the imprisoned John the Baptist. Oscar Wilde's play *Salome* (1893), which gives an erotic interpretation of these events, formed the basis for Richard Strauss's opera (1905). Another biblical Salome, possibly mother of the apostles James and John, appears in Mark 15:41 and 16:1.
See also: Bible; New Testament.

Salomon, Haym (1740-85), Polish-born U.S. financier, patriot, founder of the first Philadelphia synagogue. Salomon was active in the Polish independence movement before emigrating to New York in 1772. He was a major financial supporter of the American Revolution, lending large sums of money to the colonial government, giving money outright to equip troops, and making interest-free loans to Thomas Jefferson and other prominent statesmen. He was twice arrested and imprisoned for treason by the British (1776, 1778). Salomon challenged the Pennsylvania rule that civil servants swear belief in the New Testament, a rule that was later changed.

Salon, reception hall or drawing room often used for gatherings of society figures, intellectuals, politicians, or artists and their work. Salons can also be fashion establishments offering products or services to customers.

Salonika (pop. 396,300), port city in northern Greece, on the Salonika Gulf, established c.316 B.C., by the Macedonian king Cassander. Known as Thessaloniki in Greek, the city is now an industrial center producing textiles, soap, tobacco, minerals and leather products. It is also the second most important home of modern Greek culture, after Athens.
See also: Greece.

Salpiglossis *See:* Painted-tongue.

Salsify, or oyster plant (*Tragopogon porrifolius*), purple flowering plant of the composite family whose edible root has a flavor similar to oysters.

SALT *See:* Strategic Arms Limitation Talks.

Salt, common name for sodium chloride (NaCl), a chemical compound with an equal number of sodium ions (+) and chlorine ions (−). It is found in seawater and in solid deposits (rock salt, or halite). Pure salt forms colorless-to-white odorless cubic crystals. An essential in the diet of humans and animals, salt is most familiarly used to flavor food. It is also used in much larger quantities to preserve hides in leathermaking, to manufacture soap, as a food curative and preservative, to keep highways ice-free in winter, and in the manufacture of sodium, chlorine, and sodium hydroxide.

Salt, chemical, compound that is formed by a chemical reaction between an acid and a base. When a base totally neutralizes the acid with which it combines, a normal salt results. If neutralization is less than total, an acid salt or basic salt is produced. Table salt (sodium chloride) is a simple salt, a compound of a metal and a non-metal. When simple salts combine with other simple salts, double salts result.

Salter, Susanna Madora (1860-1961), first woman to be elected mayor of a U.S. town (Argonia, Kans.; 1887). Opponents of Prohibition had nominated Salter, a Woman's Christian Temperance Union officer, as a joke.

Salt Lake *See:* Great Salt Lake.

Salt Lake City (pop. 1,100,000), capital of Utah, seat of Salt Lake County, on the Jordan River in north-central Utah, near the Great Salt Lake. Founded in 1847 by Brigham Young, who led a band of Mormons from persecution, it is the world center of the Church of Jesus Christ of Latter-Day Saints. The city surrounds the Temple (1853-93) at its center. It is a commercial and industrial center for minerals, electronics, oil refining, and chemicals. Other sights include the State Capitol (1914) and the Brigham Young Memorial (1897).
See also: Utah.

Salton Sea, large saline lake in southeastern California. Until flooded by the Colorado River in 1905, it was a depression, known as the Salton Sink, 280 ft (85 m) below sea level. It now covers 370 sq mi (958 sq km) and is 232 ft (71 m) below sea level.

Saltpeter, or potassium nitrate (KNO_3), chemical compound occurring as a colorless crystal or white powder. It is found in limestone caves or can be produced by combining potassium chloride with sodium nitrate. It is used for explosives, matches, fertilizer, and to preserve food.
See also: Explosive.

Salts, any of various chemical salts used as agents for cleansing the intestines or as laxatives. Epsom salt, Glauber's salt, and Rochelle salt are examples.

Saluda Dam, large, earth-filled dam on the Saluda River, near Columbia, S.C. The dam, completed in 1930, is 211 ft (64 m) high and 8,650 ft (2,637 m) long.

Saluki, lean, fast-running working hound first bred c.5000 B.C. in Arabia and Egypt to hunt gazelle. The dog has long, silky ears and weighs about 60 lb (27 kg); it stands 23 to 28 in (58 to 71 cm) high at the shoulders. Its colors are light tan, white, brown, or black and tan.

Salute, formal greeting to honor another person, flag or nation, done by raising the hand to the head, by firing guns or presenting arms. Salutes can include dipping of flags, tilting of airplane wings or raising a clenched fist or outstretched palm. Salutes are used mostly in the military or to show respect to a visiting dignitary.

Salvador, or Bahia (pop. 2,056,000), third largest city in Brazil, after São Paulo and Rio de Janeiro. An Atlantic port, Salvador's main industries include food and tobacco processing, textile manufacturing, petrochemical production, and oil exploration equipment. Its exports include cacao, fruit and fruit juices, petroleum, sugar, tobacco and vegetable oils. Founded in 1549, Salvador is the home of the University of Bahia, the Catholic University, and the city's 16th-century cathedral.
See also: Brazil.

Salvage, in maritime law, either the rescue of life and property (a ship and its cargo) from danger on water or the reward given by a court to those who effect a rescue (called *salvors*). Under the law of the sea, it is the duty of a ship's master to go to the aid of an imperiled vessel. If life or property are saved, the owner of the rescue ship, the master, and the crew share in the salvage award. These awards are generous in order to encourage sailors and shipowners to risk their lives and property in rescue operations.
See also: Flotsam, jetsam, and lagan.

Salvation Army, nonsectarian, Christian organization founded in London as the Revival Society by William Booth (1865). In 1878 the mission became the army, with Booth as general. Under strict, quasimilitary discipline, the members seek to strengthen Christianity and help the poor and destitute. The army now operates 8,000 centers in the United States alone. Its official journal is *War Cry*.

Salvia, any of various plants (genus *Salvia*) of the mint family, that thrive in tropical climates. Some are used as food seasonings, others for ornamental purposes. The 700 species of woody plants vary in size and height and produce flowers of many colors, including brilliant reds, blues, whites, yellows, and violets. Salvia originates in Brazil.

Salween River, or Salwin River, river in eastern Burma, originating in eastern Tibet and flowing south 1,500 mi (2,400 km) to empty into the Bay of Bengal. A gorge makes the river largely unnavigable, but the Salween is important agriculturally, providing irrigation and flowing through a fertile delta.

Salzburg (pop. 143,900), historic city in central Austria, on the Salzbach River. The birthplace of Wolfgang Amadeus Mozart, it is world famous for its annual music festival (begun 1917).
See also: Austria.

Samaria, city in ancient central Palestine built by King Omri c.800 B.C. as the capital of northern Israel; also, the region surrounding the city. It fell to Assyria c.722 B.C. and to Alexander the Great in 331 B.C.. John Hyrcanus destroyed Samaria in 120 B.C., but it was rebuilt by Herod the Great. Samaria is the traditional burial site of St. John the Baptist.

Samaritans, members of a religious sect residing in the ancient district of Samaria, central Palestine. Originally non-Jewish colonists from Assyria, the Samaritans intermarried with the Israelites and accepted the Jewish Torah. However, they were not socially accepted—hence the significance of the Good Samaritan in Luke's Gospel.

Samarium, chemical element, symbol Sm; for physical constants see Periodic Table. Samarium was discovered spectroscopically in 1879 by Paul Émile Lecoq de Boisbaudran in the mineral samarskite. It is found in the minerals monazite and bastnasite, which are commercial sources. It is present to the extent of 1% in misch metal. The metal is prepared by reducing the oxide with barium. Samarium is a silvery, reactive metal. Ion-exchange and solvent extraction techniques have led to much easier isolation of the so-called rare-earth elements. An alloy of samarium with cobalt is used to make a permanent magnet with the highest resistance to demagnetization of any known material. Samarium and its compounds are used in carbon-arc lighting applications, permanent magnets, special glasses, and organic catalysts and as a neutron absorber in nuclear reactors.

Samarkand (pop. 370,000), city in and former capital of Uzbekistan, central Asia. One of the world's oldest cities, Samarkand was a stopover on the ancient trade route between China and the Middle East. In 329 B.C. it was conquered by Alexander the Great. In the 8th century it was taken by the expanding Arab empire, and by the 9th century it had become a center of Asian Islamic culture. It was destroyed by Genghis Khan in 1220. Rebuilt, it became the capital of Tamerlane's empire in the 14th and 15th centuries. The Uzbeks conquered it in the 1500s, and surrendered it to the Russians in 1868. After 123 years of Russian rule government returned to Uzbekistan. Today its industries include cotton and silk goods, wine, tea, and radio and automotive parts.

Samnites, ancient tribe of the mountains of southern Italy who fought 3 wars with the Romans (343-341 B.C., 316-304 B.C., 298-290 B.C.) before being conquered and almost totally destroyed. In 80 B.C. the Romans completely suppressed the remaining Samnites in the Social War, and the few survivors blended into Roman culture.

Samoa, chain of 10 islands and several islets in the South Pacific, midway between Honolulu and Sydney. Volcanic and mountainous, their total area is about 1,200 sq mi (3,108 sq km.). The people are mostly Polynesians. The soil is fertile, producing cacao, coconuts, and bananas. The climate is tropical. Savai'i (the largest), Upolu, and the other Western islands constitute independent Western Samoa. The capital is Apia, on Upolu. American Samoa consists of the eastern islands: Tutuila, the Manua group, and the Rose and Swains islands. The capital is Pago Pago, on Tutila. Discovered by the Dutch in 1722, Samoa was claimed by Germany, Great Britain, and the

United States in the mid-19th century, but in 1899 the United States acquired sole rights to what is now American Samoa.
See also: American Samoa; Western Samoa.

Sámos, one of the Sporades islands, southeastern Greece, in the Aegean Sea, separated from Turkey by the Sámos Strait. The island, 184 sq mi (476 sq km), yields crops of olives and grapes. For a time under Turkish control, it became part of Greece in 1913. It was the birthplace of the mathematician and philosopher Pythagoras and is known as the home of Aesop, the semilegendary creator of fables.

Samoset (1590?-1655), Pemaquid chief who welcomed, assisted, and became a staunch friend of the Plymouth Pilgrims. In 1625 Samoset presented John Brown with 12,000 acres of Pemaquid land for the colonists' use and settlement.
See also: Massasoit.

Samothrace, mountainous Greek island in the northeastern Aegean Sea. About 70 sq mi (180 sq km) in area, Samothrace has hot springs, clay deposits, and one high mountain, the Fengári, near its center. Its many Hellenistic artifacts and ruins date back to the 4th century B.C. Industries today include sponge fishing and sulfur production.

Samoyed, strong working dog of northern Siberia used to pull sleds and oversee reindeer herds. Its heavy white or cream colored coat protects it from severe weather and moisture. It weighs 35-65 lb (15.9-29.5 kg) and stands 19-23.5 in (48.3-59.7 cm) high at the shoulder. The Samoyed people of Siberia developed the breed thousands of years ago.

Sampras, Pete (1971-), U.S. tennis player, youngest ever to win the men's singles title in the United States Open tennis tournament (1990). He is known for his powerful serve, one-handed backhand, and serve-and-volley style of playing. In July 1998, Sampras won the Wimbledon tournament for the fifth time.

Sampson, Deborah (1760-1827), schoolteacher from Plympton, Mass., who disguised herself as a man to fight in the Revolutionary War. Wounded twice before her identity was discovered, she was given an honorable discharge by Gen. George Washington. The U.S. Congress granted her a military pension in 1805.
See also: Revolutionary War in America.

Sampson, William Thomas (1840-1902), U.S. admiral, commander of the North Atlantic Squadron in the Spanish-American War.

Samson, in the Bible, hero in ancient Israel known for his extraordinary strength, which came from his long hair. During Israel's war with the Philistines, Samson killed a thousand Philistines with the jawbone of an ass. His love for a Philistine woman, Delilah, became his downfall when she learned the secret of his strength and cut his hair as he slept. Samson was captured and imprisoned. When his hair grew back, he tore down the pillars of the temple, killing both himself and the Philistines inside.
See also: Bible.

Samuel, Books of, Old Testament books (known to Catholics as 1 and 2 Kings) that tell of the statesman, general, and prophet Samuel (11th century B.C.). He united the tribes under Saul and chose David as Saul's successor. *See also:* Bible; Old Testament.

Samuelson, Paul Anthony (1915-), U.S. economist, adviser to Presidents John F. Kennedy and Lyndon B. Johnson, and winner of the 1970 Nobel Prize in economics. His widely used college textbook, *Economics* (1948), has been translated into 21 languages. *See also:* Economics.

Samurai, hereditary military class of Japan. From A.D. 1000 the samurai dominated Japan, though after 1600 their activities were less military than cultural. They exerted influence through bushido, a code that demanded feudal loyalty and placed honor above life. The class lost its power in the reforms of 1868. *See also:* Shogun.

Sana (pop. 427,185), capital and largest city of Yemen, in southern Arabia on a high inland plain. The city, a trade center for grapes and other crops as well as the economic, political, religious, and educational center of Yemen, is linked to the Red Sea port of Hodeida by road. Sana, which is shaped like a figure eight and surrounded by a wall 20-30 ft (6-9 m) high, is noted for the architectural splendor of the Bab al-Yaman (Yemen Gate) and the 7-story Republican Palace, as well as some 50 mosques. Originally a pre-Islamic settlement, it was subsequently ruled by the Ethiopians (6th century) and the Ottoman Turks (17th century and 1872-1918) before Yemen's independence (1918). *See also:* Yemen.

San Andreas Fault, break in the earth's crust running 600 mi (965 km) from Cape Mendocino, northwestern Calif., to the Colorado desert. It was the sudden movement of land along this fault that caused the San Francisco Earthquake of 1906. The fracture, and the motion responsibile for this and other quakes, is a result of the abutment of the eastern Pacific and North American plates. *See also:* Earthquake.

San Antonio (pop. 966,400), city in south-central Texas, seat of Bexar County, on the San Antonio River 150 mi (241 km) north of the Gulf of Mexico. Founded in 1718 by the Spanish, who built a series of missions in the area over the next 13 years, it was an important settlement in early Texan history. Captured (1835) by the Texans during the Texas Revolution, its Alamo was attacked by Mexicans in 1836. It is one of the largest military centers in the United States and the site of a major medical complex. Its manufactures include clothing, chemicals, and processed food; San Antonio is well known for its artists' colonies, museums, and historical sites. *See also:* Texas.

San Blas, 4 tribes of about 20,000 Native Americans living on the San Blas Islands off the eastern coast of Panama. The most heavily populated of the tribes is the Cuna. San Blas still practice traditional customs. About 7 out of 1,000 San Blas are albinos.

Sánchez, George Isidore (1906-72), U.S. educator and spokesman for educational reform in the Spanish community. He advocated that schools in Spanish-speaking communities offer bilingual classes, using Spanish-speaking teachers and teaching subjects in Spanish. His book *Forgotten People: A Study of New Mexicans* (1940) is a classic sociological study. Sanchez received a doctorate in education from the University of California at Berkeley in 1934. He was a professor of Latin-American education at Texas University.
See also: Education.

Sand, in geology, collection of rock particles with diameters in the range 0.125-2.0 mm. It can be graded according to particle size: fine, medium, coarse, and very coarse. Sands result from erosion by glaciers, winds, or ocean or other moving water. Their chief constituents are usually quartz and feldspar. Sand's uses include making bricks, cement, glass, and concrete.

Sand, George (Amandine Aurore Lucie Dupin; 1804-76), French novelist. Her novels, at first romantic, later socially oriented, include *Indiana* (1832) and *The Haunted Pool* (1846). Her life-style—coupled with her ardent feminism—caused much controvery. Her lovers included Frédéric Chopin and Alfred de Musset. Her memoirs, *The Story of My Life* (1854-55), provide a graceful justification of her views.

Sandalwood, any of several parasitic trees of the family Santalaceae (especially *Santalum album*), native to India, whose timber exudes a fragrant odor; also, the wood obtained from the trees. Sandalwood oil is used in perfumes and medicines.

Sandbur, or bur grass, any of several species of prickly weed (genus *Cenchrus*) that grow in wasteland. Sandbur is native to the western United States. The prickly fruits cause painful wounds when they catch onto flesh.

Sandburg, Carl (1878-1967), U.S. poet and biographer who won Pulitzer prizes for *Abraham Lincoln: The War Years* (1940) and *Complete Poems* (1951). He left school at 13 and at 20 fought in the Spanish-American war. While a journalist in Chicago, he wrote vigorous earthy free verse, as in *Chicago Poems* (1916) and *Smoke and Steel* (1920). He was also a notable folk-song anthologist.

Sand dollar (*Echinarachnius pama*), marine invertebrate animal that lives in the sand in shallow coastal waters. It has a thin circular body about 2-4 in (5-10 cm) wide. The sand dollar has tiny, movable spines that it uses to dig and crawl. It feeds on aquatic organisms that it finds in the sand.

Sanderling, shorebird (*Calidris alba*) belonging to the snipe and sandpiper family. It stands about 8 in (20 cm) high. Sanderlings breed on Arctic beaches and migrate south in winter to sandy beaches everywhere. They feed on small shellfish and insects that wash up on the shore. Their feathers are rust or gray on the upper parts and pure white underneath.

Sand fly, any of various minute, biting, 2-winged flies (families Psychodidae, Simuliidae, and Ceratopogonidae) found in the southern United States and the tropics. Sand flies are a major health hazard. They carry several diseases, including kalazar.

Sandhill crane *See:* Crane.

Sandia National Laboratories, nuclear weapon research laboratory located in Albuquerque, N. Mex. Sandia researches, engineers, and produces all components of nuclear weapons systems, except explosives. Its technicians design and produce arming and firing systems and safety systems that prevent weapon use by unauthorized persons. Founded in 1945, Sandia employs 8,400 people. It is operated by American Telephone & Telegraph (AT&T) for the U.S. Department of Energy.
See also: Nuclear weapon.

San Diego (pop. 1,148,00), city in southern California; seat of San Diego County, located on the Pacific Coast close to the Mexican border. A center for oceanography, culture, medicine, and research, its natural harbor houses a great navy base, a large fishing fleet, and lumber and shipbuilding yards. Its heavy industries include aircraft, missiles, and electronics; its economy is also supported by tourism and convention business. San Diego was explored and claimed in 1542 by Spain, who later built (1769) the Presidio (historic fort) and the first of Father Junípero Serra's missions. It is also the site of the Cabrillo National Monument, an enormous zoo, and a well-known aquatic park.
See also: California.

San Diego Naval Base, center of operations for many Pacific-based fleet commands. Established in 1917, the base is a training and supply center and has an antisubmarine-warfare school, a hospital, and a recruiting station. The 11th Naval District Headquarters is located there.
See also: Navy, United States.

Sandiford, Lloyd Erskine (1937-), prime minister of Barbados since 1987. Deputy prime minister, minister of education, and leader of the House of Assembly, he assumed the post of prime minister on the death of predecessor Errol W. Barrow. Previously he served as minister of education and community development (1967-75) and minister of health and welfare (1975-86).
See also: Barbados.

Sandinistas, leftist Nicaraguan revolutionary movement that overthrew the Somoza family dictatorship in 1979. Named after César Sandino, a Nicaraguan patriot and guerrilla leader of the 1920s, it assembled a broad coalition in the country to defeat Anastasio Somoza and his hated Civil Guard. After the revolution the Sandinista National Liberation Front (FSLN) ruled through a 5-man junta.
See also: Nicaragua.

San Domingo *See:* Santo Domingo.

Sand painting, highly developed art form among the Navajo and Pueblo peoples of the southwestern United States, used in connection with rites of healing. Painting designs are made from crushed, colored sandstone. When the painting is completed, the person needing healing sits on it and has sand from it applied to his or her body. When the ritual is completed, the painting is destroyed.

Sandpiper, any of several small to medium-sized wading birds forming part of the family Scolopacidae and found in all parts of the world. Most are slim birds with long straight bills and dull brown, gray, or white plumage. Among the species found in North America are the spotted sandpiper (*Actitus macularia*) and the upland sandpiper (*Bartramia longicauda*).

Sandstone, sedimentary rock consisting of consolidated sand, cemented after deposition by such minerals like quartz, calcite, or hematite or set in a matrix of clay minerals. The sand grains are chiefly quartz. Sandstone beds may bear natural gas or petroleum, and they are commonly aquifers (water-bearing). Sandstone is quarried for building and crushed for use as an agglomerate.

Sandstorm, storm in which wind drives masses of coarse sand through the air a few feet above the ground. Sandstorms are powerful agents of erosion and can damage crops.

Sand verbena, low-growing summer annual plant (genus *Abronia*) native to western North America. The plants have fragrant pink, white, or yellow flowers and grow best in open, sunny places and light soils. There are about 25 species of sand verbena.

Sanford, Maria L. (1836-1920), one of the first female professors in the United States. A leading educator of African Americans, Native Americans, and exceptional students, she taught at the University of Minnesota for 30 years.

San Francisco (pop. 728,900), western California city and seaport on the Pacific coast, on a peninsula between the Pacific and San Francisco Bay. Its economy is based on shipping and shipbuilding, with exports of cotton, grain, lumber, and petroleum products. It is also the financial, cultural, and communications center for the Northwest Coast. The city, noted for its cosmopolitan charm, has many tourist attractions including cable cars, Chinatown, Fisherman's Wharf, the Nob Hill mansions, and Golden Gate Park. There are several museums, art galleries, and a famous opera house. Founded by the Spanish (as Yerba Buena) in 1776, the city passed into U.S. hands in 1846 and was named San Francisco (1847). The gold rush (1848) soon attracted thousands of settlers to the area, which grew even more during World War II when the city served as an embarkation and supply point for the Pacific theater. Parts of the city were rebuilt after the earthquake of Apr. 18-20, 1906, and more recently, the earthquake of 1989, which occurred on the 84th anniversary of the 1906 quake and measured from 3.3-5.4 on the Richter scale.

San Francisco Conference, conference (April-June 1945) to set up the UN. The conference was sponsored by the United States, Great Britain, the USSR, and China and attended by 50 nations.
See also: United Nations.

San Francisco-Oakland Bay Bridge, series of connected suspension bridges that join Oakland, California to Buena Yerba Island and Buena Yerba Island to San Francisco. Over 8 mi (13 km) long, it is one of the longest constructed spans over water in the world. Each part of the full span consists of a 2-tiered suspension bridge. In addition, a tunnel and a viaduct lead to Oakland. The earthquake of 1989 collapsed part of the bridge, built in the 1930s.

Sanger, Frederick (1918-), British biochemist awarded the 1958 Nobel Prize in chemistry for his work on proteins, particularly for first determining the complete structure of bovine insulin (1955). He shared the 1980 Nobel Prize in chemistry with Paul Berg and Walter Gilbert of the United States for research on nucleic acids (DNA), the carriers of genetic traits. His work helped develop a process for analyzing the structure of DNA. Sanger is one of a handful of people to receive 2 Nobel prizes.
See also: Biochemistry; DNA.

Sanger, Margaret (1883-1966), U.S. pioneer of birth control and feminism who set up the first birth-control clinic in the United States (1916), founded the National Birth Control League (1917), and helped organize the first international birth-control conference (1927).
See also: Planned Parenthood Federation of America.

Sanhedrin, supreme Jewish legislative and judicial court in Roman times. Some scholars hold that there were two Sanhedrin, one religious and one political. Jesus was tried by the religious Sanhedrin while Saints Peter, John, Stephen, and Paul appeared before it on charges of religious error. It ceased to exist in Jerusalem after the Romans put down a rebellion by the Jews in A.D. 66-70.

Sanitation, field of public health dealing with environmental control and the prevention and control of disease. In the United States, government agencies establish and enforce laws that promote a healthful environment.
Sanitation activities include food processing and distribution, to prevent contamination of food products through various stages of handling; water and sewage treatment, to treat bacteria, viruses, etc. in water and to remove solid wastes and harmful chemicals from sewage that would contaminate the lakes, rivers, and other bodies of water (and their inhabitants) that receive it; solid waste disposal, also known as refuse disposal, to prevent environmental damage and the fostering of disease; and measures to control air pollution, rodents, and noise.

San Jacinto, Battle of, decisive engagement (Apr. 21, 1836) in the war for Texan independence. It was won by General Sam Houston, whose troops, though outnumbered, surprised and defeated the Mexicans under General Antonio López de Santa Anna, thereby establishing Texas as an independent republic.
See also: Texas.

San Joaquin River, river in central California rising from the junction of 2 forks in the Sierra Nevada, south of Yosemite National Park. It flows 350 mi

(563 km) southwest,then northwest across the San Joaquin Valley to reach the Pacific at Suisun Bay (eastern arm of San Francisco Bay). The very fertile San Joaquin Valley and the Sacramento River Valley to the north together constitute the Central Valley, a rich agricultural region. The 2 rivers have a joint delta east of Suisun Bay.

San José (pop. 296,600), capital and largest city of the Central American nation of Costa Rica. It is a center for government, industry, and finance, and is the location of the nation's largest agricultural market. San José is situated at the center of the country in a valley. It was founded by Spanish settlers in the mid-18th century.
See also: Costa Rica.

San José (pop. 801,300), western Californian city (incorporated 1850) about 50 mi (80 km) southeast of San Francisco in the Santa Clara Valley, the seat of Santa Clara County. The economy has long been centered around fruit processing; since World War II heavy industry has also been developed, including aerospace, chemical and electronics firms. San Jose State College (founded 1857) is the oldest state-run college of California. Founded in 1777, San Jose was the first state capital of California (1849-52).
See also: California.

San Jose scale (*Aspidiotus perniciosus*), insect in the armored scale family. Although small as a pinhead, this insect causes mass destruction to a wide variety of trees and their fruit. The wind blows the scales from tree to tree, and upon arrival, they begin to eat a tree's sap. Native to China, they have been found throughout the United States and Canada since their discovery in the San Jose area of California around 1880. Oil spray and natural enemies such as the Chinese ladybird beetle help protect trees from this insect.
See also: Scale insect.

San Juan (pop. 434,800), capital and chief port of Puerto Rico on the northeastern coast of the island. Ponce de León named its bay (Puerto Rico) in the early 1500s, prior to the founding of the city in 1521. The city, which has retained its colonial atmosphere, is known for its fine beaches and exceptional harbor. It is now a trade center producing sugar, rum, metal products, textiles, and furniture, and has a strong tourist industry. Among its landmarks is El Morro castle (begun 1539).
See also: Puerto Rico.

San Juan Hill, Battle of *See:* Spanish-American War.

San Marino, one of the world's smallest republics and possibly the oldest state in Europe, southwest of Rimini, Italy. Built on 3 peaks of Mount Titano, its townships include San Marino (the capital) and Serravalle. Tradition reports that San Marino was founded as a refuge for persecuted Christians in the 4th century. A.D. The area is 24 sq mi (61 sq km). San Marino's chief sources of income are tourism and the sale of postage stamps. The republic is governed by 2 captains-regent assisted by a 60-member council of state.

San Marino

Capital:	San Marino
Area:	24 sq mi
	(61 sq km)
Population:	25.000
Language:	Italian
Government:	Republic
Independence:	1203
Head of gov.:	President
Per capita:	14,400
Mon. unit:	1 Italian lira = 100
	centesimi

In 1992 San Marino joined the UN. It has access to the EU by means of a customs union with Italy.

San Martín, José de (1778-1850), Argentine patriot and hero of South American struggles for independence. Under his military leadership, Argentina fought successfully for its independence from Spain (1812). San Martín also, with the aid of Bernard O'Higgins, freed Chile (1817-18) and helped Simón Bolívar gain independence for Peru (1821-22). San Martín was born in Argentina but raised mainly in Spain, where he was educated as a professional soldier. After the struggles for South American independence were fought and won, he went to Europe (1824).
See also: Argentina; Chile; Peru.

San Quentin, California's oldest prison, opened in 1852. Its normal capacity is 2,700 inmates, but it has held as many as 3,900 prisoners. Located about 10 mi (16 km) from San Francisco, San Quentin is a maximum security prison for prisoners convicted of violent crimes. The prison administration provides counseling, education, and work-release programs.

San Salvador (pop. 497,600), capital and largest city of El Salvador, about 25 mi (40 km) from the Pacific Ocean. Because it is situated in a volcanic region, it has suffered many earthquakes. The city was founded in 1525 by Spanish explorer, Pedro de Alvarado. It is now a trade center, producing textiles, tobacco and soap.
See also: El Salvador.

Sanskrit, classical language of the Hindu peoples of India and the oldest literary language of the Indo-European family of languages. Some early texts date from 1500 B.C., including the Vedic texts. Vedic Sanskrit was prevalent roughly 1500-150 B.C., classical Sanskrit roughly 500 B.C.-A.D. 900. Sanskrit gave rise to such modern Indian languages as Hindi and Urdu and is distantly related to the Celtic, Romance, and Slavonic languages.

Santa Ana (pop. 239,000), second-largest city in El Salvador. It is a major coffee processing center with one of the world's largest coffee mills. Its other industrial activities include sugar milling, brewing, and the manufacture of cotton textiles, footwear, and furniture.

Santa Anna, Antonio López de (1794-1876), Mexican general and dictator who tried to suppress the Texan revolution and fought U.S. troops in the Mexican War. He helped establish Mexican independence (1821-29) and became president (1833). When the Texan settlers revolted against his tyranny (1836), he defeated them at the Alamo but lost the battle of San Jacinto (1836), was captured, and had to resign. He gained and lost the presidency 3 further times (1841-44, 1846-47, 1853-55). He spent most of his final years in exile.
See also: Mexico.

Santa Claus, Christmastide bearer of gifts to children. The jolly fat man who is transported by flying reindeer and drops presents down chimneys is a comparatively recent (19th-century) legend derived from St. Nicholas (introduced as *Sinter Klaas* to the New World by Dutch settlers), whose feast day (Dec. 6) is a children's holiday. A drawing by cartoonist Thomas Nast is believed to have helped fix the image of a rotund, white-bearded Santa Claus in the popular imagination after such a figure was described in Clement Moore's 1822 poem, "An Account of a Visit from St. Nicholas."
See also: Christmas.

Santa Fe (pop. 117,043), capital of New Mexico and seat of Santa Fe County, in the north-central part of the state on the Santa Fe River. The elevation of about 7,000 ft (11,265 km) above sea level provides a bracing climate. Tourism is the major source of income, with the Spanish colonial architecture and numerous cultural attractions drawing many visitors. Santa Fe was founded in 1609-10 as capital of the large but unsettled Spanish territory known as New Mexico. It was under Spanish and Mexican authority until the Mexican War, after which it was ceded to the United States (1846). In the 19th century it was the western terminus of the important wagon route known as the Santa Fe Trail.
See also: New Mexico.

Santa Fe Trail, overland trade route between the western part of Missouri and Santa Fe, N.M., in use from its opening (1821) until the coming of the Santa Fe Railroad (1880). Manufactured goods passed west, furs and bullion, east.

Santa María *See:* Columbus, Christopher.

Santayana, George (1863-1952), Spanish-born U.S. philosopher, writer, and critic. He was an influential writer on aesthetics in books like *The Sense of Beauty* (1896). In *The Life of Reason* (1905-06) he emphasized the importance of reason in understanding the world, but was skeptical of what one can really know. *Skepticism and Animal Faith* (1923) suggests a relationship between faith and knowledge.

Santiago (pop. 4,600,000), capital and principal industrial, commercial, and cultural city of Chile, on the Mapocho River. Industries include textiles, foodstuffs, and iron and steel foundries. It was founded in 1541 by Pedro de

Valdivia. Numerous earthquakes destroyed most of the colonial buildings, and Santiago is now a modern city with parks and wide avenues.
See also: Chile.

Santiago (pop. 278,600), second-largest city in the Dominican Republic, lying on the Yanque del Norte River. Santiago is a distribution center for cacao, coffee, fruits, sugar cane, and tobacco, and manufactures cigars, cigarettes, dolls, and clothing. It was founded c. 1500 by Bartholomew Columbus, a brother of Christopher Columbus.
See also: Dominican Republic.

Santiago de Cuba (pop. 405,000), second-largest city in Cuba, founded in 1514 by Diego de Velazquez de Cuellar, and capital of Oriente province. The center of Cuba's mining industry, Santiago is also a shipping center for iron, manganese, sugar, coffee, and tobacco. The Morro Castle is one of its landmarks.
See also: Cuba.

Santo Domingo (pop. 1,410,000), capital and chief port of the Dominican Republic, at the mouth of the Ozama River. Its official name was Ciudad Trujillo (1930-61). Founded by Columbus's brother Bartholomew (1496), it is the oldest continuously inhabited European settlement in the Western Hemisphere, with a university dating from 1538. It was the site of the first Church in the New World.
See also: Dominican Republic.

Santo Domingo, University of, oldest university in the Western Hemisphere, located in the Dominican Republic. It was established by Pope Paul III in 1538 as the Univ. of St. Thomas Aquinas. A lay institution since 1815, the university offers courses in agronomy, architecture, business, engineering, law, medicine, philosophy, and veterinary medicine. It has an enrollment of about 50,000 students.

Santos (pop. 428,500), one of Brazil's major port cities, and the world's leading coffee port. Cotton, sugar, bananas, castor oil, beef, oranges, hides, and manufactured goods are also exported. Its industries include sawmills, canneries, and the manufacture of candy, soap, soft drinks, and canvas. Santos has two airports and a railroad link to São Paulo.
See also: Brazil.

Santos-Dumont, Alberto (1873-1932), aviation pioneer in both lighter-than-air and heavier-than-air machines. Born in Brazil of wealthy parents, he was educated in France, where he spent most of his life. His "Demoiselle" (Grasshopper) monoplane was the forerunner of the modern light plane. He was awarded the Deutsch-Archdeacon Prize (1906) for the first observed power flight in Europe. Depressed over the use of aircraft in war, Santos-Dumont took his own life.
See also: Aviation.

Sanzio, Raffaello *See:* Raphael.

Saône River, waterway of eastern France. The Saône flows some 268 mi (431 km) and connects with the Rhône River at Lyon. The industrial city,

São Tomé and Príncipe

Capital:	São Tomé
Area:	372 sq mi
	(964 sq km)
Population:	150,000
Language:	Portuguese
Government:	Republic
Independent:	1975
Head of gov.:	Prime minister
Per capita:	U.S. $350
Mon. unit:	1 Dobra = 100 cêntimos

Chalon-sur-Saône, lies on its banks. It is navigable for 233 mi (375 km) and has 30 locks. Barge traffic is heavy along its lower course.

São Paulo (pop. 9,480,400), largest city and industrial center of Brazil; capital of São Paulo state, it lies 225 mi (362 km) southwest of Rio de Janeiro. Founded in 1554, it grew rapidly with the development of the coffee industry in the 1880s (it still sends coffee to the port of Santos), and its other industries are diverse. It is the site of 4 universities and numerous cultural institutions.
See also: Brazil.

São Tomé and Príncipe, republic in the Gulf of Guinea, off the west coast of Africa, comprising 2 main islands and several islets; total area is 372 sq mi (964 sq km). The capital, São Tomé, lies 190 mi (306 km) west of Libreville, Gabon.
Land and climate. São Tomé Island accounts for almost 90% of the country's area and holds about 90% of its population. The land (volcanic rock) slopes downward to fertile volcanic soil on the east coast. Forests grow near the west shore. Príncipe is similar in land pattern. The islands have a tropical climate.
People and economy. The country depends heavily on cocoa for its income. Copra, coconuts, palm kernels, bananas, and coffee are also important exports. Most of the inhabitants are of mixed African and Portuguese ancestry.
History. Discovered in the 1400s by the Portuguese, the islands achieved independence in 1975. The withdrawal of skilled Europeans after independence seriously disrupted the former plantation economy. In 1991 a multi-party system was introduced. In 1995 a group of army officers attempted a coup. After the US and France had terminated their aid and the EU had threatened to do the same, the old government returned within a week.

Sap, in botany, the watery fluid in the stems and roots of plants. There are two kinds of sap. One consists of water and dissolved minerals and travels from the roots of the tree to the leaves, moving through a layer in the stem and trunk called the xylem. The other consists of water carrying dissolved plant foods, moving from the leaves to other parts of the plant for storage. It passes through a layer called the phloem.

Sapir, Edward (1884-1939), U.S. anthropologist, poet, and linguist, whose most important work was on the relation between language and the culture of which it is a product. He suggested that one's perception of the world is dominated by the language with which one articulates it.
See also: Anthropology.

Sapodilla, evergreen tree (*Achras zapota*) found in tropical America; also, the fruit of the tree. The bark and fruits contain a milky latex (chicle) that is collected in Central America to provide the raw material for chewing gum. When ripe, the flesh of the fruit is brown and has the consistency of a pear.

Saponin *See:* Soapberry.

Sapphire, any gem variety of the mineral corundum (except those that are red, which are called ruby); blue sapphires are best known, but most other colors of the spectrum are included. The highest-quality sapphires come from Kashmir, Burma, Thailand, Sri Lanka, and Australia. Synthetic stones made by flame-fusion are used for jewel bearings, phonograph styluses, etc.

Sappho (6th century B.C.), Greek poet born in Lesbos. Surviving fragments of her work, mainly addressed to young girls, are among the finest classical love lyrics. The terms *sapphism* and *lesbianism*, meaning female homosexuality, derive from Sappho and Lesbos.

Sapporo (pop. 1,704,100), capital of Hokkaido, the northernmost island of Japan. Laid out in 1871 with wide, tree-lined boulevards intersecting each other at right angles, Sapporo serves as the island's manufacturing and cultural center, and its products include hemp cloth and rubber goods. Sapporo was the site of the Winter Olympics of 1972.
See also: Japan.

Saprophyte, plant that gets its food from dead and decaying material. Saprophytes do not carry out photosynthesis. Most fungi, including molds, mildews, and rusts, are saprophytes. Their fine threads creep over the food, secreting digestive juices and absorbing the resulting solution. Some flowering plants, such as the pinesap, are known as saprophytes, but in fact they rely on a fungus in their roots to absorb food from dead leaves.
See also: Fungi.

Sapsucker, bird of the woodpecker family. Sapsuckers drill neat rows of holes in the bark of trees and lick up the sap that oozes out, but their main food is insects, which they catch in the air or on trees. The 3 North American sapsuckers are the widely distributed yellow-bellied sapsucker (*Sphyrapicus varius*), and the red-breasted (*S. ruber*) and Williamson's sapsucker (*S. thyroideus*) of the Western and Pacific states.

Saracens, Muslims who invaded parts of the Christian world in Asia, Africa, and Europe from the 600s to the 1000s. They consisted of people of Palestine

and Syria, the Arab Moors, and the Seljuks. The term *Saracen* was first used by Greek and Roman writers to describe wandering Arab tribes.
See also: Muslims.

Saragossa (pop. 594,400), industrial and trading center located in northeast Spain. The city has metalworks, sugar refineries, chemical plants, and factories that manufacture electrical equipment, farm machinery, and furniture. The city's name comes from Caesarea Augusta, the name that Roman Emperor Augustus gave it in 25 B.C.
See also: Spain.

Sarah *See:* Ishmael; Isaac.

Sarajevo (pop. 415,600), capital and cultural center of Bosnia and Hercegovina. It retains a strong Muslim character and is famous for its many Muslim mosques. Austrian Archduke Francis Ferdinand was assassinated at Sarajevo in 1914, precipitating World War I. During the civil war that started in the early 1990s Sarajevo was badly damaged and social and economic life virtually came to a stand still.
See also: Bosnia and Hercegovina.

Saranac Lakes, group of lakes in the Adirondack Mountains of northeastern New York. The region of these glacial lakes is a popular recreation area. The 3 lakes are Upper Saranac (8 mi/13 km long, 2 mi/3.2 km wide), Middle Saranac or Lake Saranac (3 mi/4.8 km long, 1 mi/1.6 km wide), and Lower Saranac (5 mi/8 km long, 1 mi/1.6 km wide).

Sarasota (pop. 277,776), city in southwestern Florida, on the Sarasota Bay of the Gulf of Mexico. Founded in the 1880s, it has become a popular tourist spot. It is home to New College of the Univ. of Southern Florida and to the Mote Marine Laboratory. From 1927 to 1960 it was also the winter home of the Ringling Brothers and Barnum & Bailey Circus.
See also: Florida.

Saratoga Springs (pop. 23,906), city in eastern New York, in the southeastern foothills of the Adirondack Mountains. A flourishing resort since the 19th century, its tourist attractions include mineral springs, thoroughbred racing, and the Saratoga Performing Arts Center, summer home of the New York City Opera, New York City Ballet, and Philadelphia Orchestra. It is also home to Skidmore College.
See also: New York.

Saratov (pop. 909,000), one of the chief ports on the Volga River. Petroleum, natural gas, and power from the Balakovo hydroelectric station form the basis of oil-refining and chemical industries. Manufactures of this industrial complex include machinery, machine tools, ball bearings, flour milling, and consumer products.
See also: Union of Soviet Socialist Republics.

Sarawak, state of Malaysia on the northwestern coast of Borneo. It has a tropical climate, and much of its area, 48,050 sq mi (131,582 sq km), is covered by a primary rain forest. Sarawak became self-governing and joined

Malaysia in 1963 after having been occupied by the Japanese during World War II. For 100 years prior to this, Sarawak was governed by an Englishman, James Brooke, and his heirs. The people of Sarawak are Dyaks, Malays, Melanaus, and Murits. Its products include sago palm, timber, rubber, pepper, coconuts, and camphor.
See also: Malaysia.

Sarazen, Gene (Eugene Saraceni; 1902-   ), U.S. golfer. He won the Professional Golfers Association (PGA) tournament in 1922, 1923, and 1933; the U.S. Open in 1922 and 1932; and the British Open in 1932. He also played 6 times in the Ryder Cup competition between U.S. and British players. Sarazen's outstanding 235-yd (215-m) shot helped win him the 1935 Masters tournament.

Sarcoidosis, chronic disease characterized by fibrous and inflammatory nodules principally affecting lymph glands, skin, lungs, and bones, but arising in any tissue of the body. The cause of the disease is uncertain.
See also: Lymphatic system.

Sarcoma, form of tumor derived from connective tissue, usually of mesodermal origin in embryology. It is often distinguished from cancer because its behavior and natural history may differ, although it is still a malignant tumor. It commonly arises from bone (*osteosarcoma*), fibrous tissue (*fibrosarcoma*), or cartilage (*chondrosarcoma*). Excision is required, though radiation therapy may be helpful.

Sarcophagus, stone coffin. The ancient Egyptians were probably the first to use sarcophagi for the burial of kings and important persons. Some were shaped like small houses, others like human forms with facial features. The best-known modern examples of sarcophagi include those built for George Washington in Mt. Vernon, Napoleon Bonaparte in Paris, the duke of Wellington in London, and V.I. Lenin in Moscow.

Sardine, name for the young of members of the herring family, particularly the European sardine, or pitchard (*Sardina pilchardus*). Sardines get their name from the fact that they were originally caught near Sardinia. They are usually preserved in oil and canned as food.

Sardinia, Italian island in the Mediterranean, 120 mi (193 km) to the west of mainland Italy and just south of Corsica. It is a mountainous area of 9,301 sq mi (24,090 sq km), with some agriculture on the coastal plains and upland valleys. Wheat, olives, and vines are grown, and sheep and goats raised; fish and cork are also exported. Zinc, antimony, and lead are extracted from the ancient mines, and tourism is growing in importance. The island is an autonomous region of Italy, with its capital at Cagliari.

Sardinia, Kingdom of, kingdom founded in 1720 when the Treaty of London awarded the island of Sardinia to Savoy. The kingdom included Sardinia, Savoy, Piedmont, and Nice. Napoleon annexed Sardinia to France in 1802, but it was restored after his defeat in 1815, and Genoa and Liguria were added to it. In 1861 Victor Emanuel II was proclaimed king of a united Italy that included Sardinia.

Sardis, capital of the ancient kingdom of Lydia. Its remains go back to at least 1300 B.C., but it may be even older. It was the first city to mint gold and silver coins. Destroyed by an earthquake in A.D. 17, Sardis was later rebuilt. It was destroyed and rebuilt several times until its final destruction by the Sassanian Persians c. A.D. 615.

Sardonyx, form of the mineral quartz. It is one of the less expensive gemstones. Found in Brazil, Uruguay, and India, sardonyx has bands of reddish-brown and white. It is used in rings and cameos.

Sargasso Sea, oval area in the North Atlantic, of special interest as the spawning ground of American eels, many of whose offspring drift across the Atlantic to form the European eel population. Bounded on the east by the Canaries Current, on the south by the North Equatorial Current, and on the west and north by the Gulf Stream, it contains large masses of seaweed.

Sargent, John Singer (1856-1935), U.S. painter famous for his many flattering portraits of high-society figures in the United States and United Kingdom. A master of the brushstroke, he is distinctive for his treatment of texture. One of his most notable works, *Madame X* (1884), showing the alluring Parisian Madame Gautreau, created a furor that obscured the painting's brilliance.

Sargon of Akkad, king who founded the first great empire in history c. 2300 B.C. An outstanding military leader and administrator, he was the first king to maintain a permanent army. Sargon built a magnificent capital city called Akkad in central Mesopotamia. He reigned for 56 years.
See also: Mesopotamia.

Sark, one of the Channel Islands and the smallest self-governing unit in the United Kingdom. Located in the English Channel, 22 miles (35 km) off the coast of France, it has an area of 2 sq mi (5 sq km).

Sarney, José (1930-   ), Brazilian politician, president (1985-90). He served as governor of the state of Maranhao, 1965-70, was elected vice president in 1985, and assumed the presidency in Apr. 1985 upon the death of President Tancredo Neves. His Cruzado Plan was an effort to control Brazil's severe inflation and foreign debt.
See also: Brazil.

Sarnoff, David (1891-1971), Russian-born U.S. radio and television pioneer. Starting his career as a telegraph messenger boy, he became president of RCA and later founded NBC, the first commercial radio network (1926).

Saroyan, William (1908-81), U.S. author known for combining patriotism with emotional idealism. Among his many works are *The Daring Young Man on the Flying Trapeze* (1934), a collection of short stories; the novel *The Human Comedy* (1943); and the play *The Time of Your Life* (1939). He won the Pulitzer Prize for the latter but turned it down because he disapproved of literary awards.

Sarton, May (1912-   ), U.S. writer. Her books include the poetry collections *Inner Landscape* (1939) and *Halfway to Silence* (1980), the novels *The Bridge of Years* (1946) and *The Magnificent Spinster* (1985), and the journals *Recovering* (1980) and *May Sarton: A Self Portrait* (1986). Sarton has taught at Harvard University and Wellesley College.

Sartre, Jean-Paul (1905-80), French philosopher, novelist, and playwright, exponent of existentialism. His writings reflect his vision of the human being as master of his or her own fate, with each life defined by a person's actions: "Existence precedes essence." His works include *Being and Nothingness* (1943); the novels *Nausea* (1938) and *The Roads to Freedom*, a trilogy (1945-49); and the plays *The Flies* (1943) and *No Exit* (1944). Sartre founded the review *Les Temps Modernes* in 1945. A close associate of Simone de Beauvoir and a Communist who spoke eloquently for the left, his influence was international. In 1964 he refused the Nobel Prize for literature.
See also: Existentialism.

Saskatchewan, 1 of the 3 prairie provinces of Canada. The principal wheat-growing province, it produces about one-third of the nation's wheat. It is also a rich source of minerals such as potash and petroleum. Most of Saskatchewan's resources are processed within the province.
Land and climate. Saskatchewan can be divided into 2 major portions: the Canadian Shield, which covers the northern third of the province; and the plains and lowlands, which make up the southern two-thirds. The Canadian Shield is a rough, rocky, mineral-rich terrain that contains many lakes, swamps, and small streams. The plains and lowlands are mostly flat or gently rolling, with black, fertile soil. Most of the province's 20,000 lakes are found north of Prince Albert. The largest is Lake Athabasca, about two-thirds of which lie in the northwest corner of Saskatchewan, the rest in the province of Alberta. The principal river is the Saskatchewan. Divided into the South Saskatchewan and the North Saskachewan, the 2 branches join just east of Prince Albert and flow eastward into the province of Manitoba. Much of the province, especially the northern half, is covered by forests. Numerous commercial forests include valuable supplies of spruce, poplar, and pine. Saskatchewan's inland location gives it a continental climate. Winters are cold, with average January readings of 10°F (–12°C) in the southwest and –23°F (–31°C) in the northeast. Average July temperatures range from 57°-67°F (14°-19°C). Precipitation is light; most of it falls during the growing season, which in the south lasts about 100 days.
People. The population of Saskatchewan is concentrated in the southern half of the province, which has become markedly urban. Today over 75% of the people live in communities of more than 1,000 inhabitants. Over 25% live in the 2 largest cities, Saskatoon and Regina, the capital. Saskatchewan is the only province in which the people have a variety of ethnic inheritances, rather than a majority of French or British.
Economy. The economy of the province is heavily dependent on farming. Wheat is the main crop; barley, rye, and flax also are grown. Since the discovery of oil and the development of service-supply industries, agriculture has declined in relative importance. Service industries now account for 50% of the total gross domestic product. Food processing and distribution as well as the manufacture of farm machinery are increasing in importance. The province also produces a significant proportion of Canada's crude oil.

Oil refining and steel manufacturing can be found in Regina and other northern cities. Lignite coal, mined since the 1880s, has been strip-mined since 1956.

History. It is believed that the first people to inhabit the land of Saskatchewan were the Paleo-Indians, who came from Asia 20,000-30,000 years ago. European-American traders from the Hudson's Bay Company first arrived in 1690. The region was explored some 40 years later by Sieur de la Verendrye. After the purchase of the Northwest Territories by the new Dominion of Canada in 1870, farming settlements spread; they grew rapidly after Saskatchewan joined the Confederation and became a province in 1905. The Great Depression and World War II brought hardship and discontent that led to the formation of the Cooperative Commonwealth Federation (1944-64). In the 1970s and 1980s, petroleum and petroleum-based industries brought new wealth and prosperity to the province.

See also: Canada.

Saskatchewan River, river system in the provinces of Alberta and Saskatchewan, Canada. The North Saskatchewan flows east 760 mi (1,223 km) from the glaciers of the Rocky Mountains. The South Saskatchewan flows east 550 mi (885 km) from the combined waters of the Bow and Oldman rivers. The rivers then join and flow 340 mi (547 km) to empty in Lake Winnipeg, Manitoba. The river system, first explored by Henry Kelsey (1690), became an important fur trade route. It is now important in the irrigation of southern Alberta and as a source of hydroelectric power. Among the cities lying on the Saskatchewan River and its tributaries are Edmonton, Calgary, Saskatoon, and Prince Albert.

Saskatoon (pop. 210,000), largest city of the province of Saskatchewan, on the South Saskatchewan River, western Canada. Founded by John Lake and members of the Temperance Colonization Company in 1883, it was joined to the Canadian Pacific Railway in 1890. It is now a major trading center, and has stockyards and other agriculture-related industry. The economy is also supported by oil refineries and, since the 1950s, potash mining.

See also: Saskatchewan.

Sassafras, tree (*Sassafras albidum*) of the laurel family, found in the eastern half of North America. In the northern states it is usually little more than a shrub, but it grows to 100 ft (30.5 m) in the south. Oil of sassafras, used to flavor foods and perfume soap, is extracted from its bark and roots. Sassafras tea is also made from the roots.

Sassoon, Siegfried (1886-1967), English poet and novelist. Decorated for bravery in World War I, he wrote bitterly satirical poetry such as *The Old Huntsman* (1917) and *Counter Attack* (1918), which shocked the public with their graphic portrayal of trench warfare, their attacks on hypocritical patriotism, and their pacifist conclusions. His novels include *Memoirs of a Fox-Hunting Man* (1928).

Satellite, in astronomy, celestial object that revolves with or around a large celestial object. In our Solar System this includes planets, comets, asteroids, and meteoroids, as well as the moons of the planets, although the term is usually restricted to this last sense. Of the dozens of known moons, the largest

is Callisto (Jupiter IV); the smallest, Phobos (the inner moon of Mars). The earth's moon is the largest known satellite relative to its parent planets; indeed, the earth-moon system is often considered a double planet.
See also: Astronomy.

Satellite, artificial, object placed in orbit as a satellite. First seriously proposed in the 1920s, they were impracticable until large enough rockets were developed. The first artificial satellite, Sputnik 1, was launched by the USSR on Oct. 8, 1957, and was soon followed by a host of others, mainly from the USSR and the United States, but also from the United Kingdom, France, Canada, West Germany, Italy, Japan, and China. These satellites have many scientific, technological, and military uses. Astronomical observations (notably X-ray astronomy) can be made unobscured by the atmosphere. Studies can be made of the radiation and electromagnetic and gravitational fields in which the earth is bathed and of the upper atmosphere. Experiments have been made on the functioning of animals and plants in space (with zero gravity and increased radiation). Artificial satellites are also used for reconnaissance, surveying, and meteorological observation, as navigational aids (position references and signal relays), and in communications for relaying television and radio signals. Manned satellites, especially the historic Soyuz and Mercury series, have paved the way for space stations, which have provided opportunities for diverse research and for developing docking techniques; the USSR Salyut and U.S. Skylab projects are notable. The basic requirements for satellite launching are determined by celestial mechanics. Launching at various velocities between that required for zero altitude and the escape velocity produces an elliptical orbit lying on a conic surface determined by the latitude and time of launch. To reach any other orbit requires considerable extra energy expenditure. Artificial satellites require a power supply—solar cells, batteries, fuel cells, or nuclear devices; scientific instruments; a communications system to return encoded data to earth; and instruments and auxiliary rockets to monitor and correct the satellite's position. Most have computers for control and data processing, thus reducing remote control to the minimum.
See also: Satellite.

Satie, Erik (Eric Alfred Leslie Satie; 1866-1925), French composer and pianist. Satie was the philosophical leader of "Les Six," a group of French composers including Darius Milhaud, Arthur Honneger, and Francis Poulenc who rejected the impressionist style of Claude Debussy and Maurice Ravel. He was deliberately eccentric, rejecting convention and popular acceptance. He best-known works include the ballet *Parade* (1917) and pieces for solo piano. His *Gymnopédies* (1888) for solo piano were made famous in their orchestrated version by Debussy.

Satinwood, East Indian tree (*Chloroxylon swietenia*) or shrub of the citrus family. Their wood is very hard and is used for inlays on furniture. West Indian satinwood, or yellow wood, so-called for its color, is found in Florida, as is wild lime, a close relative.

Satire, in literature or cartoons, on stage or screen, use of broad humor, parody, and irony to ridicule a subject. More serious than burlesque, it often contains moral or political criticism. In literature, classical satirists Aristophanes, Horace, and Juvenal were followed by such writers as Rabelais, Daniel Defoe, Jonathan Swift, Voltaire, Oscar Wilde, and Mark Twain.

Sato, Eisaku (1901-75), prime minister of Japan (1964-72). A Liberal-Democrat, he presided over the reemergence of Japan as a major economic power and was active in foreign affairs. He won the 1974 Nobel Peace Prize for work on deterring the proliferation of nuclear weapons.

Saturation, in chemistry and physics, term applied to a state in which further increase in a variable above a critical value produces no increase in a resultant effect. A saturated solution will dissolve no more solute, an equilibrium having been reached. Raising the temperature usually allows more to dissolve; cooling may produce supersaturation, in which sudden crystallization depositing the excess solute occurs if a seed crystal is added. In organic chemistry a saturated molecule has no double or triple bonds and so does not undergo additional reactions.

Saturn, in early Roman mythology, god of fertility and planting, eventually identified with the Greek god Cronus as father of Jupiter, Juno, Ceres, Pluto, and Neptune. In ancient Rome he was honored in the Saturnalia festival, a period of revelry and gift-giving starting Dec. 17, during which business, school, and war were suspended.
See also: Mythology.

Saturn, second-largest planet in the Solar System, the sixth from the sun. Until the discovery of Uranus (1781), Saturn was the outermost planet known. It orbits the sun in 29.46 years at a mean distance of 886.7 million mi (1.427 billion km). Saturn has the lowest density of any planet in the Solar System, less than that of water, and may contain over 60% hydrogen by mass. Its total mass is about 95 times that of the Earth. Saturn has 17 known satellites; the largest, Titan, about the same size as Mercury, has a cold nitrogen atmosphere with traces of methane and other gases. Other major satellites include the Mimas, Enceladus, Tethys, Dione, Rhea, Iapetus, Phoebe, and Hyperion. The most striking feature of Saturn is its ring system, composed of countless tiny particles of ice and rock. Three or four major ring divisions are visible from Earth; space probes (1980, 1981) revealed the rings to consist of hundreds of narrow ringlets. The rings are about 10 mi (16 km) thick.
See also: Planet; Solar System.

Saturnalia, in ancient Rome, festival honoring Saturn, god of fertility and planting. The annual festival, which started Dec. 17, originated as a 2-day celebration of the winter planting, but became a week-long period of feasting and gift-giving, the cessation of business and a brief time of freedom for slaves. Its observances are thought to have eventually been absorbed into the celebration of Christmas. "Saturnalia" has become a generic term for any period of wild revelry.
See also: Saturn.

Satyr, in Greek mythology, male spirit of the forests and mountains, often shown as part man and part goat, with hooves, tail, and pointed ears.

Companions of Dionysus, satyrs played an important part in his festivals. *See also:* Mythology.

Saucer, flying *See:* Unidentified flying object.

Saudi Arabia, desert kingdom occupying most of the Arabian Peninsula of southwestern Asia.
Land and climate. Parts of the frontiers of Saudi Arabia have yet to be accurately determined. Estimates of the country's area vary from about 830,000 sq mi (2,149,700 sq km) to 927,000 sq mi (2,400,930 sq km). It is bordered on the north by Jordan, Iraq, and Kuwait; on the east by the United Arab Emirates, the Persian Gulf, and Qatar; on the south by Oman, Yemen, and Southern Yemen; and on the west by the Red Sea and the Gulf of Aqaba. Most of the country is desert. Rising steeply from the narrow, barren Red Sea coastal plain are the western highlands of the Hejaz in the north and the Asir Highlands bordering Yemen in the south. Eastward sloping desert plateaus of sand and rock cover the interior of the country. The Rub al Khali (Empty Quarter) is a great, southern sand desert of some 250,000 sq mi (647,500 sq km). The An Nafud, the northern sand desert, covers almost 25,000 sq mi (64,750 sq km). In the east, the Hasa Lowlands, mostly sand or gravel, fall away gradually to the sands, lagoons, and occasional coral reefs along the Persian Gulf. There are oases where date palms, tamarisks, and acacias grow, but there are neither lakes nor rivers. The coastal regions have an oppressively humid climate. The interior deserts are hot and dry, and summer temperatures in some areas exceed 120°F (49°C). In winter, however, frosts are common on the plateaus and in the mountains. Some desert areas go without rain for several years in succession.
People. The people of Saudi Arabia are almost entirely Arab. Riyadh, the capital, the Red Sea port of Jiddah, and the Muslim holy cities of Mecca and Medina are the main centers. Islam is the state religion: 80% of the people belong to the Sunni branch of Islam.
Economy. Saudi Arabia's rich oil fields, discovered in 1936, represent nearly one-fifth of the world's known reserves, and the oil and natural gas industry dominates the economy. The Arabian American Oil Company (Aramco) is chiefly responsible for oil operations in Saudi Arabia, although other U.S. and some Japanese concerns also have concessions. Since 1974, Saudi Arabia has held 60% of the ownership of these foreign concessions. Petro dollars are used for industrial development, especially oil refining, ambitious irrigation projects, and foreign investments. Saudi Arabia also produces limestone, gypsum, and salt. Its chief crops are sorghum, dates, wheat, barley, coffee, citrus fruits, and millet.
History. In the 7th century, the formerly disparate Semitic nomadic tribes of the Arabian Peninsula were united for the first time under Islam. In succeeding centuries rival sheikdoms rose and fell. In the 1500s Arabia came under the Ottoman Turks as part of the Ottoman empire. Between 1750 and 1800 the fundamentalist Wahabi sect led by the Saudi rulers of Dariya reconquered most of the Arabian Peninsula. Modern Saudi Arabia was founded by Ibn Saud, who, between 1902 and 1932, conquered Hijd and the Hejaz, joining them with Hasa and Asir and establishing a hereditary monarchy. Ibn Saud died in 1953 and was succeeded by Saud IV, who was deposed in 1964. King Faisal succeeded to the throne and reigned until his assassination in 1975. He was succeeded by King Khalid, who began programs of industrialization

Saudi Arabia

Capital:	Riyadh
Area:	865,000 sq mi
	(2,240,000 sq km)
Population:	20,786,000
Language:	Arabic
Government:	Islamic absolute
	monarchy
Independent:	1932
Head of gov.:	King
Per capita:	U.S. $7,040
Mon. unit:	1 Saudi riyal = 100
	halalah

and social welfare before he died in 1982; he was followed by the current monarch, King Fahd. Saudi Arabia, through its oil wealth, has considerable political influence in the Middle East and has supported Arab countries and the Palestinians in their conflict with Israel. At the same time, as an ally of the United States, Saudi Arabia also has been something of a moderate voice in the region. Saudi Arabia asked for U.S. military assistance and joined forces with the U.S. and other allies in the Persian Gulf War against Iraq (1990-91). Saudi Arabia plays a major role in the Organization of Petroleum Exporting Countries (OPEC). In 1995, the border conflict with Yemen was solved.

Sauk, or Sac, Native American tribe of the Algonquian language group. Encountered by the French near Green Bay, Wis. (1667), they later lived along the Mississippi River, hunting and farming. Many took part in the Black Hawk War (1832) rather than move west, but they were eventually resettled in Oklahoma and Iowa.

Saul, first king of Israel (1000 B.C.). The son of Kish of the tribe of Benjamin, he was annointed by Samuel after the tribes decided to unite under a king. His reign was generally successful, but he killed himself after a defeat by the Philistines. His rival, David, succeeded him. (1 Sam,10-31.)

Sault Sainte Marie (pop. 80,900), French settlement founded (1668) on the north bank of the St. Mary's River, which connects Lakes Superior and Huron. Sault is French for "rapids", which provide hydroelectric power for the city and the iron and steel, pulp, paper, and lumber industries. An international railway bridge linking the cities of Sault Ste. Marie in Michigan and Ontario was built in 1887. A U.S. canal and a Canadian canal were constructed in 1895 to link the St. Lawrence and Great Lakes Waterway.

Saurischian *See:* Dinosaur.

Sauvé, Jeanne Mathilde (1922-), first woman to serve as Speaker of the House of Commons (1980-84) and governor general (representative of the British monarch; 1984-89) of Canada. Sauvé worked for UNESCO (from

1950) and as a journalist and broadcaster (1952-72) before being elected to the House of Commons (1972). She served under Prime Minister Pierre Trudeau as minister of state for science and technology (1972), of the environment (1974), and of communications (1975).

Savanna, tropical grassland of South America and particularly Africa, lying between equatorial forests and dry deserts.

Savannah, name of 2 historic U.S. steamships. The first *Savannah* was the first steamship to cross the Atlantic (1819), sailing from Savannah, Ga. to Liverpool, England in 24 days, powered by sails as well as steam. The second, built by the U.S. government and launched in 1959, was the first nuclear-powered cargo ship. This 595.5-ft (195-m)-long ship, which can carry 60 passengers and 9,400 tons of cargo, proved commercially impractical.

Savannah (pop. 147,000), port city in southeastern Georgia near the mouth of the Savannah River, seat of Chatham County. The town was established by James Oglethorpe when he founded Georgia colony in 1733. Its capture (1864) ended General William T. Sherman's march to the sea during the Civil War. In addition to being a major Southern port, Savannah has become a center for agricultural trade and for the production of wood pulp and paper. The city is home to several colleges, and a U.S. Army training center for helicopter pilots is located nearby. Since 1955 it has attracted tourists with its restored historic buildings.
See also: Georgia.

Savannah River, river forming the Georgia-South Carolina border, arising from the confluence of the Tugaloo and Seneca rivers and flowing southeast into the Atlantic Ocean. The 314-mi (505-km) river is used for flood control and hydroelectric power. It is navigable by oceangoing vessels for about 23 mi (37 km) and by smaller vessels for about 230 mi (370 km), as far as Augusta, Ga.

Savings and loan association (S&L), or thrift institution (formerly, building and loan association), U.S. financial institution that accepts private savings of depositors, investing them primarily in home mortgages. Such institutions, the first of which was founded in Pennsylvania in 1831, originally were *mutual*, that is, owned and operated by the depositors. They are now predominantly *capital-stock* institutions, owned and operated by stockholders. They operate under federal and state charters, with deposits insured by the Savings Association Insurance Fund (SAIF). Many S&L's failed during the Great Depression of the 1930s. In the 1980s a combination of deregulation, mismanagement, criminal conduct, competition for depositors' funds from commercial banks and other financial institutions, and loan defaults due to recession resulted in a major crisis in the industry. It is estimated that the costs to taxpayers to "bail out" the S&L's will total $500 billion.
See also: Federal Home Loan Bank Board.

Savings bank, financial institution that encourages saving by individual depositors, paying them interest or dividends, while providing funds to borrowers, who pay interest. In the United States savings banks originated in the early 19th century as charitable nonprofit institutions. Such institutions, which are concentrated in the northeast, are now mostly nonprofit *mutual saving banks*, run by a board of directors. They now provide the additional service of *negotiable order of withdrawal* (NOW) accounts, which function like checking accounts.

Savings bond, interest-bearing bond issued to an individual by the government in specific denominations, functioning as a loan to the government for a fixed term. U.S. savings bonds were first issued to raise money during World War I. Series E, issued from 1941 to 1979, helped finance World War II. The current Series EE is issued in denominations from $50 to $10,000, sold for 50% of face value. Bonds reach maturity (come due) in 12 years. While earlier bonds had fixed interest rates, government savings bonds since Nov. 1982 have market-based rates. U.S. savings bonds are issued by the Department of the Treasury.

Savonarola, Girolamo (1452-98), Italian religious reformer. A friar of the Dominican order living in Florence, he was a powerful and outspoken critic of the Church, preaching against the corruption of the court of Pope Alexander VI and predicting that the Church would be punished. When he refused the pope's order to present himself in Rome, he was forbidden to preach (1495), the violation of which order led to his excommunication (1496). Savonarola remained unrepentant, and he was tried by an ecclesiastical court and executed by civil authorities.

Savoy, powerful dynasty of northwestern Italy that at times ruled portions of Italy, France, and Switzerland. It was founded in the 11th century by Humbert, whose holdings were in the regions of Savoy and Piedmont. Savoy holdings extended into France and Switzerland by the 15th century. Its control in Italy expanded in the 18th and 19th centuries, helping to consolidate rule of the peninsula, and a member of the family, Victor Emmanuel II, became king of Italy in 1861. Victor Emmanuel II was succeeded by his son Humbert I, who was assassinated (1900), Victor Emmanuel III, who abdicated after World War II, and Humbert II, whose brief reign ended (1946) when Italy became a republic.
See also: Italy.

Saw, cutting tool consisting of a flat blade or circular disk, having on its edge a row of sharp teeth of various designs, usually set alternately. The first true saws (copper and bronze) were used in Egypt c.4000 B.C., but only with the use of steel did they become efficient. Hand saws include the crosscut saw for cutting wood to length, the backsaw for joints, the coping saw for shaping, and the hacksaw for cutting metal. Power saws include circular saws, band saws (with a flexible endless steel band running over pulleys), and chain saws.

Sawfish, any of a family (Pristidae) of sharklike fish having "saws" of cartilage set with 2 rows of teeth on their snouts. Sawfish are found in all warm seas and may swim up rivers. The common sawfish of the Gulf of Mexico swims up the Mississippi. Sawfish can grow up to 30 ft (9 m) in length. They use the saw to dig up shellfish or to kill small fish. Although they are reported to be docile, fishers treat them with considerable respect.

Sawfly, insect related to the wasps. Sawflies often have striped bodies. They are harmless to humans, although they do serious damage to plants. They have a long, tubular egg-laying organ with which they drill holes in the leaves of plants or in wood to lay their eggs. The larvae, which look like caterpillars, eat the plants' tissues.

Saw Maung (1928-), president of the Union of Myanmar (Burma, 1988-92). Armed forces chief of staff and a close associate of former ruler Ne Win, he led the coup that placed him in office, ousting President Maung Maung. He then abolished parliament and formed the National Unity Party.
See also: Myanmar.

Saxifrage, any of a genus (*Saxifraga*) of small rock plants whose leaves grow in a rosette at the base of the stem and whose flowers grow in clusters at the tip of the stem. Many of them produce a small bulb at the base of each leaf. The usual place to find saxifrages is in crevices and ledges of rocky cliffs in cold and temperate regions of the Northern Hemisphere. Several species are native to the United States, including the early saxifrage (*S. virginiensis*) and the umbrella plant (*S. peltata*).

Saxons, Germanic people who, with the Angles and the Jutes, founded settlements in Britain from A.D. 450 supplanting the Celts. The 3 peoples eventually formed the Anglo-Saxon kingdom. From modern Schleswig (northern Germany) the Saxons also spread along the coast to northern France before being conquered by Charlemagne (804).

Saxony, state in eastern Germany. Saxony was established as a duchy in the late 9th century. Its size and boundaries shifted as it was broken up and then reestablished as Electoral Saxony (1356). From 1697 to 1763 the elector of Saxony was also king of Poland; during this time the state and its capital city of Dresden were an important center of culture. Saxony was made a kingdom by Napoleon I (1816), but upon his defeat half of its lands became part of Prussia. After World War II Saxony became part of East Germany but was abolished as a political unit by the Communists. In 1990, with the reunification of Germany, Saxony was reestablished as a state.

Saxophone, brass musical instrument, classified as a woodwind since its sound is produced by blowing through a reed. Patented by the Belgian Adolphe Sax in 1846, the saxophone exists in soprano, alto, tenor, and baritone forms; the bass is rare. Sometimes used in the symphony orchestra, the saxophone is better known for its important role in jazz, where it is a leading solo and ensemble instrument.

Sayers, Dorothy (1893-1957), English writer of detective stories and creator of the popular, impeccably aristocratic and erudite Lord Peter Whimsey. He is the hero of some 16 books, beginning with *Whose Body?* (1923). Sayers also wrote religious essays and dramas.

Scabies, infectious skin disease caused by a mite (*Sarcoptes scabiei*) that burrows under the skin, often of the hands or feet; it causes an intensely itchy skin condition that is partly due to allergy to the mite. The disease is spread through contact. Treatment is with ointments.

Scalawag, in U.S. history, derisive term employed by Southern Democrats for Southern whites who cooperated with Republican Reconstruction governments after the Civil War. Although some scalawags sought personal gain, many sought to bring about educational and social reforms, including laws beneficial to blacks. The Southern Democrats gradually regained control in the 1870s.
See also: Reconstruction.

Scale, weighing, instrument for measuring weight. *Balance scales*, which date to about 2500 B.C. and are still in use, measure an unknown quantity by balancing it against established weights. *Mechanical scales*, which date from the 18th century, use beams, springs, or pendulums to convert the measurement of weight into a precise reading on a graduated scale. For example, *spring scales*, including the ordinary bathroom scale, measure weight according to the tension created when the weight stretches or compresses a spring. *Electronic scales*, which have been in commercial use since the 1950s, convert the force exerted by the weight into an electronic signal.

Scale insect, any of various small insects of the order Homoptera (especially family Coccidae) with a flattened body covered by a layer, or "scale," of waxy secretion. There are more than 2,000 species. They live on plants, and many are serious pests. The *cottony cushion scale* did immense damage to the Californian orange plantations after its introduction from Australasia. The *elm scale* kills trees. Other scale insects are collected for their secretions. The dye cochineal is obtained from a scale insect, and the lac insect used to be collected by the millions—its "scale" turned into shellac.

Scalia, Antonin (1936-), U.S. Supreme Court justice, appointed 1986 by President Ronald Reagan. Scalia practiced law in Cleveland and taught at the Univ. of Virginia and Chicago law schools. He then served as U.S. assistant attorney general in the 1970s, and as judge of the U.S. Court of Appeals for the District of Columbia 1982-86. Scalia, who is known for his politically and socially conservative views, his advocacy of judicial restraint, and a narrow interpretation of the Constitution, is the first associate justice of the Supreme Court of Italian descent.
See also: Supreme Court of the United States.

Scallop, bivalve mollusk (family Pectinidae) distinguished by a shell whose valves are rounded, with a series of ribs radiating across the surface in relief. Scallops are used for food. Unique among bivalves, scallops swim extremely well, propelled by jets of water expelled in snapping the shell shut. There are about 300 species. Chief among the commercial species is the common bay scallop (*Argopecten irradians*), found in North America.

Scandinavia, region of northwestern Europe. Geographically it consists of the Scandinavian peninsula (about 300,000 sq mi/777,000 sq km), occupied by Norway, Sweden, and Denmark. Because of close historical development, Finland, Iceland, and the Faeroe Islands are also covered by the term in matters of language, culture, peoples, and politics.

Scandinavian literature, literature of Scandinavia (Denmark, Norway, and Sweden) and usually including Finland and Iceland, from the end of the

Viking Age (c.1100) to the present. The peoples of Scandinavia speak closely related North Germanic languages, except those of Finland, whose language is related to Hungarian. Early literature of the 12th and 13th centuries captured works of the oral tradition in writing. These included heroic ballads of Denmark and Sweden, Icelandic poetry collected in the *Poetic Edda*, and heroic *sagas* of Iceland and Norway. There followed a period during which most writing was in Latin and was technical or religious. Literature in the vernacular and about everyday life reemerged in the 18th century, including writings of Swedish poet Carl Michael Bellman and Danish playwright Johannes Ewald. The interest in folk tales shown by the romantic movement of the early 19th century is evident in the epic poem *Kalevala* (1835; derived from Finnish legend), collections of tales in Norway, and the original tales of Hans Christian Andersen in Denmark. Other writers of the romantic movement were Norway's Bjørnstjerne Bjørnson (*A Happy Boy*, 1860) and Finland's Aleksis Kivi (*Seven Brothers*, 1870). Henrik Ibsen of Norway and August Strindberg of Sweden were playwrights of the realist movement of the late 19th century who had international influence. The modern period includes writings of Knut Hamsun of Norway (*Hunger*, 1890) and Selma Lagerlöf of Sweden (*Gösta Berling's Saga*, 1891), and more recently, Isak Dinesen of Denmark (*Winter's Tales*, 1942) and Nobel Prize winners Sigrid Undset of Norway (*Kristin Lavransdatter* trilogy, 1920-22) and Pär Fabian Lagerkvist of Sweden (*Barabbas*, 1950).

Scandium, chemical element, symbol Sc; for physical constants see Periodic Table. Scandium was discovered in 1876 by Lars Nilson in the minerals euxenite and gadolinite. It occurs in nature in over 800 mineral species in minute amounts. Scandium is obtained from thortveitite or uranium mill tailings. It is prepared by reducing the fluoride with calcium metal. Although not a member of the rare earth series of metals, it is chemically similar and often considered with them. It is a soft, silvery, reactive metal resembling yttrium and the rare-earth metals (more than aluminum or titanium), and is often associated with tin and zirconium. It is used to produce high-intensity lights. Scandium-46 is used as a radioactive tracing agent. Scandium is the ekaboron predicted by Dmitri Mendeleev (1869).

Scapegoat, in the Old Testament (Leviticus 16:8), goat designated by the Jewish high priest on Yom Kippur (Day of Atonement) to bear the sins of the people and to be sent out into the wilderness. Similar practices existed in ancient Greece and Rome. By extension, the term also refers to a person or group unfairly blamed for the ills of others.
See also: Old Testament.

Scar, mark resulting from the healing of a wound or disease process in a tissue, especially the skin. Also called a cicatrix. The presence of excessive scar tissue is called a keloid.

Scarab, family (*Scarabaeidae*) of beetles that includes the dung beetles, chafers, and dor beetles. Most of the 20,000 species are scavengers of decaying organic matter, especially dung, or they feed on the foliage and roots of growing plants, as do the chafers, many of which may become agricultural pests.

Scarlatti, name of 2 Italian composers of the baroque period. **Alessandro Scarlatti** (1660-1725) was a leading musical scholar, teacher, and composer of hundreds of church masses, cantatas, and oratorios, as well as more than 100 operas. Although few of his works are now performed, he is important for innovations in harmony, thematic development, and the use of instruments. His son **Domenico Scarlatti** (1685-1757) also composed operas and church music but is known for his many brilliant sonatas for harpsichord. An influence upon Franz Joseph Haydn and W.A. Mozart, he is still widely played.
See also: Baroque.

Scarlet fever, infectious disease caused by certain strains of streptococcus. It is common in children and causes sore throat with tonsillitis, a characteristic skin rash, and mild systemic symptoms. Penicillin and symptomatic treatment are required. Scarlet fever occurs in epidemics; some infections are followed by rheumatic fever or nephritis.
See also: Impetigo.

Schacht, Hjalmar Horace Greeley (1877-1970), German financier and banker. He helped halt post-World War I inflation in Germany and was finance minister (1934-37) and Reichsbank president (1923-30; 1933-39). Conflict with Goering and Hitler led to imprisonment in a concentration camp. He was acquitted at the Nuremberg Trials (1946).
See also: Germany.

Schaller, George Beals (1933-), U.S. zoologist and advocate for the protection of endangered species. Schaller's field research includes studies of the daily life and environment of lions and mountain gorillas of East Africa and giant pandas of China. He is author of *The Year of the Gorilla* (1964), *The Deer and the Tiger* (1967), and *The Serengeti Lion: A Study of Predator-Prey Relations* (1972), for which he won the 1973 National Book Award for the sciences. In 1972 he became research associate and coordinator at the Center for Biology and Conservation, New York Zoological Society. In 1980 Schaller, another U.S. conservationist, and a group of Chinese scientists went on a World Wildlife Fund mission in China to locate and rescue pandas.
See also: Zoology.

Schally, Andrew Victor (1926-), Polish-born U.S. medical researcher who shared the 1977 Nobel Prize in physiology or medicine with Rosalyn S. Yalow and Roger C. L. Guillemin for the discovery and synthesis of hormones produced by the hypothalamus. The analysis of these hormones, which control body chemistry, had a revolutionary effect on the study of brain functioning.
See also: Hypothalamus.

Schapiro, Meyer (1904-), Lithuanian-born U.S. art historian and critic. One of the most highly regarded and influential art scholars in the United States, he taught for many years at Columbia Univ. Among his books are *Romanesque Art* (1977) and *Modern Art: 19th and 20th Centuries* (2 vols., 1978-9). He also wrote important essays, e.g., "The Nature of Abstract" (1937) and "Leonardo and Freud" (1956).

Schawlow, Arthur (1921-   ), U.S. physicist who did pioneering work in the 1950s that led to the construction of the first laser. He shared the 1981 Nobel Prize in physics with Nicolass Bloembergen (of the United States) and Kai M. Siegbahn (of Sweden) for contributions to the development of laser spectroscopy.
See also: Laser.

Schechter v. United States, Supreme Court decision (1935) that ruled unconstitutional the 1933 National Industrial Recovery Act (NIRA), an important part of President Franklin D. Roosevelt's New Deal program. The Schechter Poultry Co. had been convicted of violating an NIRA code regulating interstate commerce. The Court ruled that the NIRA delegated too much legislative power to the U.S. president.
See also: National Recovery Administration.

Scheele, Carl Wilhelm (1742-86), Swedish pharmacist and chemist. He was the discoverer of chlorine and isolated oxygen, although credit went to English scientist Joseph Priestley, who published findings before Scheele. He also isolated many acids, and made significant discoveries regarding nitrogen and manganese, conducting his experiments in the restricted environment of the apothecaries where he was employed.
See also: Chemistry; Chlorine.

Schelde River, important navigable waterway of northwestern Europe. Rising in northwestern France, it flows 270 mi. (434.5 km) north and northeast to Antwerp, Belgium, then northwest, as the East Schelde and West Schelde rivers, through the Netherlands to the North Sea. There are canal links to the Rhine and Meuse rivers.

Schelling, Friedrich Wilhelm Joseph von (1775-1854), German philosopher. Influenced by Baruch Spinoza, J.G. Fichte, and others, he developed a concept of an absolute unity of mind and matter toward which all history and nature progressed. Although once a close friend of G.W.F. Hegel, he became an opponent and rival. His view of art as the union of the natural and the spiritual influenced Samuel Taylor Coleridge, Schelling's contemporary and an English poet and philosopher.
See also: Philosophy.

Scherzo (Italian, "joke"), light, lively musical composition. The term most often refers to a movement in 3/4 meter (usually the third) of a sonata, symphony, or similar composition of the late 18th or 19th century; it developed from the minuet but was characterized by a much faster tempo and, frequently, a display of rhythmical humor and surprise (especially in the works of Ludwig van Beethoven). Some light vocal and instrumental compositions of the Baroque period, as well as some dramatic piano pieces by Frederick Chopin and Johannes Brahms, were also named scherzo.

Schiele, Egon (1890-1918), Austrian artist. A leader of the Austrian expressionists, he was influenced by the French impressionists and by Austrian artist Gustav Klimt. His paintings exhibit decorative qualities and a strong sense of line, but also an eroticism and emotional intensity that the public sometimes found disturbing. He is best known for self-portraits and paintings of nude or partly clothed women.

Schiller, Johann Christoph Friedrich von (1759-1805), German playwright, poet, writer on philosophy, history, and aesthetics. Schiller's highly successful early plays, including *The Robbers* (1781) and *Don Carlos* (1787), articulated his violent opposition to tyranny. In Weimar he became professor at the Univ. of Jena (1789) and married writer Charlotte von Lengefeld. At this time he also began his important friendship with Johann Wolfgang von Goethe, with whom he shared many values and ideas. In 1787 Schiller began writing historical works, as well as works on philosophy and aesthetics, heavily influenced by Emmanuel Kant. He and Goethe also edited the literary magazines *Horen* and *Musenalmanach*. Some of his most important works were historical dramas, including *Wallenstein* (1798-99), *Mary Stuart* (1800), and *William Tell* (1804). He also translated works of Shakespeare and Racine. Schiller is acknowledged to be a leading figure of German literature, second only to Goethe. Beethoven used Schiller's poem "Ode to Joy" (1785) as the text for the final movement of his Ninth Symphony.

Schipperke (Flemish; "little skipper"), Belgian breed of dog once used to guard canal barges. Descended from the Leauvenaar, a black sheep dog, it is a short, stout dog, often tailless, with a foxlike head and a thick black coat, standing 12-13 in (30.5-33 cm) and weighing about 15 lb (7 kg).

Schirra, Walter Marty, Jr. (1923-), U.S. astronaut, 1959-69. Schirra, whose parents were both stunt fliers, attended the U.S. Navel Academy and flew combat missions in the Korean War. In 1959 he became one of the 7 original U.S. astronauts. In his first mission in the Mercury space program, Oct. 3, 1962, he circled the earth 6 times in *Sigma 7*. He and Thomas P. Stafford piloted Gemini 6 in the first space rendezvous (with Gemini 7, Dec. 15, 1965) and was command pilot for Apollo 7 (Oct. 11-22, 1968). Schirra retired from the Navy and the space program and entered private business in 1969.

Schism, Great *See:* Pope.

Schist, common group of metamorphic rocks that have acquired a high degree of schistosity, i.e., the parallel arrangement of sheety, or prismatic, minerals resulting from regional metamorphism. Schistosity is similar in nature and origin to cleavage in slate but is coarser. The major constituents of most schists are either mica, talc, amphibole, or chlorite.

Schistosomiasis, or bilharziasis, parasitic disease caused by the schistosome, a type of flatworm. The disease is usually acquired by bathing in infected water. The schistosome larvae enter the body through the skin and live in the blood as parasites. As adults they lay eggs that cause infection and destroy the kidneys, liver, and other organs. The disease can ultimately cause death. It afflicts more than 200 million people in Africa, Asia, and Latin America.

Schizophrenia (formerly called dementia praecox), type of psychosis characterized by confusion of identity, hallucinations, delusion, and illogical

thought. The 3 main types of schizophrenia are catatonia, in which the individual oscillates between excitement and stupor; paranoid schizophrenia, which is similar to paranoia except that the intellect deteriorates; and hebephrenia, which is characterized by withdrawal from reality, bizarre behavior, delusions, hallucinations, and self-neglect.
See also: Psychosis.

Schlesinger, name of 2 famous 20th-century U.S. historians. **Arthur Meier Schlesinger** (1888-1965) is best known for his U.S. history *The Rise of the City, 1878-1898* (1933) from the series he edited, *A History of American Life*. He stressed the cultural, social, and economic context of history. **Arthur Meier Schlesinger, Jr.** (1917-), his son, won Pulitzer prizes for both *The Age of Jackson* (1945) and *A Thousand Days* (1966), the latter written after a period as special assistant to President John F. Kennedy.

Schleswig-Holstein, state in northern Germany, 6,046 sq mi (15,660 sq km) bordering Denmark. The capital, Kiel, lies at the eastern end of the Kiel Canal, which links the North and Baltic seas. The main economic activities are dairy farming, fishing, shipbuilding, and engineering. Schleswig was a Danish fiefdom from the 12th century. Holstein came under Danish control in the 15th century. Disputes with the German states led to the Austro-Prussian War in 1864. Prussia annexed these 2 Danish duchies in 1866. North Schleswig was reunited with Denmark in 1920.

Schliemann, Heinrich (1822-90), German archeologist, best known for his discoveries of Troy (1871-90) and Mycenae (1876-78).
See also: Archeology.

Schmalkaldic League, alliance of German Protestant states during the Reformation, formed in 1531 for defense against the Catholic Holy Roman emperor Charles V. Member states included Hesse, Saxony, Brunswick, Anhalt, Mansfeld, Magdeburg, Bremen, Strassburg, and Ulm. The Protestants were defeated in 1547 in the War of the Schmalkaldic League, but the subsequent Peace of Augsburg (1555) gave Lutheran churches the right to exist.
See also: Reformation.

Schmidt, Helmut (1918-), chancellor of West Germany (1974-82). A Social Democrat, he was party floor leader in the Bundestag (1962-69), defense minister (1969-72), and finance minister (1972-74). He succeeded Willy Brandt as chancellor when the latter resigned amid a spy scandal. In a continent plagued with economic difficulties, Germany under Schmidt remained stable and prosperous. However, violent radical groups asserted themselves in the early 1980s, and he stepped down after losing a confidence vote in 1982. Since 1983 he is editor in chief of the German newspaper Die Zeit.

Schmitt, Harrison Hagan (1935-), geologist, astronaut, politician. Schmitt joined the National Aeronautics Space Administration (NASA) as an astronaut in 1964. In Dec. 1972 he flew on the Apollo 17 lunar-landing mission, becoming the first U.S. scientist to fly in space and, with Eugene A. Cernan, spent 3 days on the surface of the moon. He was elected to the

U.S. Senate in 1976 as a Republican from New Mexico, and became a staunch backer of President Ronald Reagan; however, he lost the 1982 election. In 1989 President George Bush named him to serve on an 8-member commission on government ethics.
See also: Astronaut.

Schnauzer *See:* Giant schnauzer; Miniature schnauzer; Standard schnauzer.

Schnitzler, Arthur (1862-1931), Austrian playwright. He wrote about love and the personality basis of racism, particularly anti-Semitism, in the Vienna of Sigmund Freud. His work included *Anatol* (1893), *Playing with Love* (1896), and *Merry-Go-Round* (1897).

Schoenberg, Arnold (1874-1951), German composer, theorist, and teacher who revolutionized music by introducing serial, or 12-tone, music. His string sextet *Transfigured Night* (1899), with harmonic clashes, was followed by the declaimed songs of *Pierrot Lunaire* (1912) and experiments in whole-tone and finally 12-tone music, culminating in his unfinished opera *Moses and Aaron* (1930-51). Schoenberg emigrated to the United States in 1933.

Schofield, John McAllister (1831-1906), U.S. Union general in the Civil War, from 1864 commander of its Army of the Ohio in the Atlanta Campaign. He was secretary of war (1868-69) and commander of the U.S. Army (1888-95).
See also: Civil War, U.S.

Scholarship, grant-in-aid awarded to a student. In the United States scholarships are awarded by schools, states, the federal government, and private organizations on the basis of financial need, for scholastic excellence or ability or athletic prowess, to aid special groups such as those with particular disabilities, or to encourage students to enter particular fields of study. Under the Servicemen's Readjustment Act (GI Bill of Rights), World War II veterans were given federal tuition grants and stipends to attend college or vocational school; similar acts were passed for veterans of the Korean and Vietnam wars. Rhodes and Fulbright scholarships are among the important awards for U.S. students to study abroad.

Scholasticism, philosophical system of medieval Church teachers, or scholastics, who applied philosophic (primarily Aristotelian) ideas to Christian doctrine. They held that although reason was always subordinate to faith, it served to increase the believer's understanding of what was believed. Typical scholastic works are the commentary on an authoritative text and the *quaestio*, in which the writer sets out opposing authorities and then reconciles them in answering a question. St. Thomas Aquinas's *Summa Theologica* consists of a systematically constructed series of *quaestiones*. The influence of Aristotle on medieval thought was enormous but was not available in the West until a Latin translation appeared in the 13th century.

Schongauer, Martin (1450?-91), German painter and engraver. He was one of the first engravers to use copper plates, and his delicate, skillful work influenced Albrecht Dürer and other German artists. His works include the engravings *The Death of the Virgin Mary* and *Christ Bearing the Cross*, the painting *The Virgin in the Rose Arbor* (1473), and the mural in Breisach, *Last Judgment* (c.1491).

School, institution whose primary purpose is to impart knowledge. The most numerous and the most important kinds of schools are those used to educate the young, from early childhood to early adulthood, preparing them for the roles they will play in society, the economy, and in political life. Schools provide students with knowledge, from the basics of reading, writing, and reasoning, to the most sophisticated branches of the arts and sciences. Schools also reflect society and transmit its values and norms.

Before the 1800s in the West, education was reserved for a relatively privileged few. Among the Assyrians, Babylonians, and Egyptians, organized knowledge was largely dominated by priests. Much of what was known was deliberately kept secret and obscure to enhance the power and prestige of a privileged few. Masters of arts and crafts passed on their techniques directly from one generation to the next; the process of teaching and learning was more restricted, personal, and direct. The ancient Greeks marked a significant departure from this approach. Politically independent, socially mobile, free of the dominance of a priesthood, they used their own senses and reason to question what they saw and heard. The spirit of free, rational inquiry among the Greeks led to a free exchange of ideas, the growth of rival world views, the gathering of organized bodies of knowledge, the appearance of the Western world's first teachers for hire, and the first schools open to free inquiry. Education was still a privilege, but the Greeks made learning a goal in its own right and the mark of a truly free individual. The Romans were deeply influenced by Greek practice and ideals.

After the fall of the Roman Empire, education at first declined and then was revived and transformed by the Christian church. It was no longer necessary to educate citizens but to preserve and spread the faith. What little education there was took place in monasteries and was almost wholly religious. Over the centuries, bodies of knowledge accumulated and new needs had to be met. Busy with war and politics, the aristocracy could not read or write, but they needed clerks; in the early days they used men trained by the church. In time, education moved from the monastery schools to schools in the great cathedrals that developed into universities. The upper classes began to cultivate and patronize learning and schools.

In the Renaissance, from the 14th to the 16th centuries, scholars recovered and began to read the works of Greeks and Romans and aspired to their learning and level of culture. Education and the schools began to break away from the church and its priesthood. The Renaissance was followed by the Protestant Reformation and the invention of the printing press. The former challenged the authority of the Roman church, the latter made books available to all who could read, leading to profound changes in education and in schools. The modern state, modern commerce and finance, the rise of a more complex urban society dominated by the middle class and the advent of modern science and technology revolutionized education and schools. Learning was no longer a luxury, privilege, or virtue; it had become a necessity. School systems were established, theories of education were developed, and the modern profession of teaching had its beginnings.

In the United States today, in addition to pre-schools and kindergartens, there are elementary schools, many of them public; middle schools; junior public high schools; and public high schools. Education generally proceeds on a two-track system—vocational or academic. For higher education, students may go on to community college, three-quarters of which are public, or to one of the nation's colleges and universities. There are also many schools for advanced training and retraining of highly skilled professionals, as well as correspondence schools, night schools, and special and vocational education schools.

In the United States, schools are run by elected school boards of education or by local boards composed of parents and teachers. Schools deal with questions of curricula, libraries and censorship, and teachers and their qualifications, as well as questions of the separation of church and state that arise over school prayer and religious instruction. Fundamental issues of conflicting moral values and public health must be addressed in dealing with drugs in the schools. In the universities, corporate and government grants providing badly needed funds for scientific research often generate controversy. In the United States, Japan, Africa, and Europe, schools and particularly colleges and universities not only are places for study and research, but also play vital roles in their relation to the leading issues in their societies.

Schopenhauer, Arthur (1788-1860), German philosopher, noted for his doctrine of the will. In *The World as Will and Idea* (1819), his main work, he argued that will is the ultimate reality, but advocated the negation of will to avoid suffering. He encouraged the contemplation of philosophy and the arts as a haven of relief from the insatiable strivings of will. Schopenhauer's ideas influenced Friedrich Nietzsche and modern existentialism.
See also: Philosophy.

Schrieffer, John Robert (1931-), U.S. physicist who shared with Leon Cooper and John Bardeen the 1972 Nobel Prize in physics for their work on superconductivity.
See also: Superconductivity.

Schrödinger, Erwin (1887-1961), Austrian-born Irish physicist and philosopher of science who shared with Paul Dirac the 1933 Nobel Prize in physics for his discovery of the Schrödinger wave equation, describing the wavelike behavior of electrons, which is of fundamental importance in studies of quantum mechanics. It was later shown that his theories of wave mechanics were equivalent to the matrix mechanics theories of Werner Heisenberg.
See also: Quantum mechanics.

Schubert, Franz Peter (1797-1828), Viennese composer. He wrote nine symphonies, of which the Fifth (1816), Eighth (1822), and Ninth (1828) are among the world's greatest. He is also famous for his piano pieces and chamber music (especially his string quartets), but above all for his over 600 *lieder* (songs). In addition to individual lieder such as "The Erl King" and "The Trout," he wrote song cycles, among them *The Maid of the Mill* and *Winter's Journey.*

Schulz, Charles Monroe (1922-   ), U.S. cartoonist, creator of "Peanuts." The "Peanuts" series, which Schulz began in 1950, is about young children but appeals to adults as well in its benign humor and insight into human foibles. The characters of the comic strip, including the insecure Charlie

Brown, the bossy Lucy, and the beagle Snoopy, have become the subjects of television programs, an Off-Broadway play, and many books and greeting cards. The comic strip appears in thousands of newspapers throughout the world.
See also: Cartoon.

Schuman, Robert (1886-1963), French politician. Prime minister (1947-48) and foreign minister (1948-52), he launched the Schuman Plan, which resulted in the European Coal and Steel Community, precursor of the European Economic Community.
See also: France.

Schuman, William (1910-92), U.S. composer. His symphonies, chamber music, ballets, and operas are known for their rhythmic vivacity and their debt to jazz. His cantata *A Free Song* won the first Pulitzer Prize in music (1943). He was president of the Juilliard School of Music (1945-62) and of Lincoln Center for the Performing Arts (1962-69).

Schumann, Clara (1819-96), German pianist and composer. The daughter of the important piano teacher Friedrich Wieck, she became a well-known soloist and the first to perform entirely from memory. She married pianist and composer Robert Schumann over strenuous objections of her father, and became one of the chief exponents of his piano compositions. After her husband's death in 1856 she continued performing widely, touring frequently to England. A close friend of Johannes Brahms, she also was one of the main interpreters of his compositions. In her later years she was active as a piano teacher, heading the piano department of the Frankfurt Conservatory (1878-92). Her compositions include a piano concerto, smaller piano compositions, songs, and cadenzas for Beethoven's 3rd and 4th piano concertos.

Schumann, Robert (Alexander) (1810-56), German composer and critic, a leader of the romantic movement. His early work, until 1840, comprises inspired piano pieces (e.g., *Symphonic Études, Papillons*). He then turned his attention to music for orchestras (e.g., *Piano Concerto in A Minor*, 1841-45), achieving great heights of emotional intensity, and to songs, uniting voice and piano in beautiful classical compositions. He was an ardent advocate for and influence on new composers, such as Brahms and Chopin. In the 1840s he began to show signs of mental illness and, after a suicide attempt in 1854, was placed in an asylum, where he remained until he died.

Schumpeter, Joseph Alois (1883-1950), Moravian-born U.S. economist. Schumpeter emigrated to the United States in 1932, when he joined the faculty of Harvard University. His major works were on the importance of entrepreneurs (*The Theory of Economic Development*, 1911) and the inevitability of business cycles and the unequal distribution of wealth (*Capitalism, Socialism, and Democracy*, 1942) in the healthy capitalist economy.
See also: Economics.

Schurz, name of German-born U.S. couple prominent in public life. **Carl Schurz** (1829-1906) came to the United States after fighting in the 1848-49 revolution in Germany. An antislavery activist, he was a supporter of

Abraham Lincoln and later a brigadier general in the Civil War. He served in the U.S. Senate as a Missouri Republican (1869-75), helped found the Liberal Republican Party, and was secretary of the interior (1877-81). Schurz wrote biographies of Henry Clay (1887) and Abraham Lincoln (1889). He was editor of the *New York Evening Post* and *The Nation* in the early 1880s, and chief editorial writer for *Harper's Weekly* from 1892 to 1898. **Margaretha Meyer Schurz** (1833-76), a student of the German educator Friedrich Fröbel, was influential in the establishment of kindergartens in the United States, and worked with her husband, assisting him in his social reform and political activities.

Schuyler, Philip John (1733-1804), American soldier and politician who served as major-general in the Continental Army during the Revolutionary War. He served three terms in the New York senate between 1780 and 1797, and was one of the first two U.S. senators from New York (1789-91 and 1797-98). *See also:* Revolutionary War in America.

Schuylkill River, river rising in east-central Pennsylvania and flowing southeast 130 mi (210 km) into the Delaware River near Philadelphia. The river is used for hydroelectric power, for Philadelphia's water supply, and as a route for coal barges.

Schwartz, Delmore (1913-66), U.S. poet admired for his rhapsodic yet philosophic style. His works include *In Dreams Begin Responsibilities* (1938), *Summer Knowledge* (1959), and *Last and Lost Poems of Delmore Schwartz* (1979). He also wrote short stories, a play, and a children's book.

Schwartz, Melvin (1932-   ), U.S. physicist. Schwartz, Leon Lederman, and Jack Steinberger won the 1988 Nobel Prize in physics for their work in using streams of subatomic neutrinos and their discovery of the muon neutrino. The work was conceived at Columbia Univ. in 1960 and executed at Brookhaven National Laboratory in 1962. *See also:* Neutrino.

Schwarzkopf, Elisabeth (1915-   ), German soprano noted for performances in Mozart and Strauss operas in Europe, and later for her expressive *Lieder* recitals there and in the United States. *See also:* Opera.

Schwarzkopf, H. Norman (1935-   ), commander in chief, U.S. Central Command (CENTCOM), responsible for the planning and direction of all U.S. and coalition armed forces in the Persian Gulf War (1991). He was Deputy Chief of Staff for Operation and Plans (1986-87) and Deputy Commander, Joint Task Force, in Grenada (Oct. 1983). He served two consecutive tours in Vietnam. Schwarzkopf graduated from the U.S. Military Academy at West Point (1956). He has received numerous awards and decorations, including 2 Distinguished Service Medals, 3 Silver Stars, and 3 Bronze Stars with a "V" for valor. *See also:* Persian Gulf War.

Schweitzer, Albert (1875-1965), German physician, theologian, missionary, musician, and philosopher. He was an authority on Bach and a noted performer of Bach's organ music. He abandoned an academic career in theology to study medicine and became (1913) a missionary doctor in French Equatorial Africa (now Gabon). He devoted his life to the hospital he founded there. His many writings include *The Quest of the Historical Jesus* (1906), and *The Decay and Restoration of Civilization* and *Civilization and Ethics* (1923), the first two volumes of his *Philosophy of Civilization*. Schweitzer won the 1952 Nobel Peace Prize for his inspiring humanitarian work.

Schwinger, Julian Seymour (1918-   ), U.S. physicist who shared with Richard P. Feynman and Japan's Shinichiro Tomonaga the 1965 Nobel Prize in physics for independent work in formulating the theory of quantum electrodynamics.
See also: Quantum electrodynamics.

Sciatica, pain in the distribution of the sciatic nerve in the leg caused by compression or irritation of the nerve. The pain may resemble an electric shock and be associated with numbness and tingling in the skin area served by the nerve. One of the most common causes is a slipped disk in the lower lumbar spine.
See also: Nervous system.

Science, systematic study of nature and of individual and social human behavior. Science is distinguished from other intellectual disciplines, like the arts and humanities, by several key characteristics. It is based upon observation, either by the unaided senses or with the help of instruments that increase the power of the senses, like microscopes or telescopes. Science requires the careful collection and organization of data. Above all, science employs a rigorous method of reasoning about what it observes. The scientific method relies upon logic to draw conclusions from evidence and tests its reasoning with experiments. As study progresses, a larger pattern or underlying law begins to emerge that helps explain phenomena like the formation of gases, the motion of planets, or the division of cells. Scientists attempt to state those laws or patterns in the form of theories or hypotheses, and those statements are also subjected to experiments. Some hypotheses prove useful and enduring, others are refuted or superseded by new experiments or new findings. Finally, science expresses itself mathematically, in formulas that state numerically the dynamics or relations underlying what we see. Neither the arts nor the humanities are rigorous in the way that science is; the questions they ask, the methods they use, and their findings and results are different.
The scope of science is vast. It is broken up into a great many fields and specialties. But a few major divisions are still useful for an overview. The physical sciences are, historically, probably the oldest and include astronomy, meteorology, chemistry, physics, and geology. These fields cover inanimate nature. Life and living beings are studied by the life sciences, including biology, zoology, botany, physiology, and paleontology. The social sciences study human beings as they reveal themselves in individual behavior and in society and its institutions. Such studies include political science, economics, psychology, anthropology, and sociology. To the extent that these disciplines are less successful than the natural sciences in expressing their findings mathematically, they have been criticized for lacking the rigor of pure science. Finally, although they are not themselves sciences in

the strict sense, mathematics and logic are essential to science. Though in many ways the two overlap, mathematics provides science with symbols and procedures for measuring and for calculating relations. Logic discovers the ratio and procedures of accurate reasoning.

The development of science has led to an explosion of knowledge unprecedented in human history. Allied with mechanical ingenuity, it led to technology, the application of scientific knowledge to practical problems. The results have completely transformed the world. In partnership with modern industry, finance, and the state, science has produced a mixed legacy, creating tools that heal and destroy, that enhance life and threaten it with annihilation.

History. Science's earliest manifestation was among the Greeks who were the first people to reason logically about the natural world. Instead of accepting occult explanations for what they observed, the Greeks tried to discover intelligible laws underlying things. They developed logic and mathematics and made impressive contributions to human knowledge. In the 4th century B.C., Hippocrates laid down elementary principles for the practice of medicine. One hundred years later, Aristotle attempted an exhaustive classification of phenomena based upon logical categories and direct observation. Euclid and Archimedes were great mathematicians and Ptolemy's description of the motion of the planets would not be improved upon for nearly 1,500 years.

With the fall of the Roman Empire and the onset of the Middle Ages in the West, it was left to Islam to pursue some of the promise of the Greeks. To mention only a few great Muslim thinkers, Alhazan in optics, Aricanna in medicine, and Al-Khwarizmi in algebra made important contributions that had their greatest impact on Christian Europe in the late Middle Ages. Schooled in logical rigor by the Scholastics and with access to Islamic work and the Hindu-Arabic numerical notation, Europe was ripe for intellectual change. It came first in Italy between the 14th and 16th centuries in the Renaissance. The use of perspective in painting and architecture that explored principles laid down by the Greeks and Romans fostered a spirit of inquiry that led to detailed studies of human anatomy and innovations in mechanics and virtually every branch of human knowledge. Men like Galileo and da Vinci pointed the way for the rest of Europe. Nicolaus Copernicus, the Polish astronomer, put an end to the medieval view of the world with his theory, based upon careful telescopic observation, that the earth was not the center of the universe but only one of several planets that revolves around the sun. The Copernican revolution sent profound shock waves throughout Europe, and combined with the impact of the discovery of the Americas, inspired the best minds of Europe to turn to science.

In the 17th century, Descartes in France laid the philosophical foundations of the scientific method. In the same century, the Englishman Newton and the German Leibniz simultaneously discovered calculus, and Newton wrote the *Principia Mathematica* in which he proposed his law of universal gravitation. His countryman, William Harvey, described the circulation of blood and Robert Boyle advanced the science of chemistry.

Building upon the work of the previous century, the 18th century saw rapid advances. In chemistry came the discoveries of gases, among them chlorine, hydrogen, and carbon dioxide. Carolus Linnaeus developed a system for the classification of animals and Luigi Galvani, Alessandro Volta, and Benjamin Franklin made advances in the study of electricity. In addition, the sciences had an impact outside of the laboratory in the rationalisms and skepticism of Voltaire, Hume, Diderot, and the work of Adam Smith, whose *Wealth of Nations* marked the advent of the modern study of economics. In the 19th century, Darwin did his pioneering work on natural selection and evolution, presenting theories that would have almost as profound an effect upon social and political thought as they did in science. Michael Faraday and Joseph Henry pioneered work in electromagnetism. James Clark Maxwell studied the laws of electricity and magnetism, and great advances were made in modern medicine, typified by the work and career of Louis Pasteur. Progress in medicine and in the care and treatment of the sick led to a dramatic increase in life expectancy.

Much of the early optimism felt about science began to be lost in the era of World War I, a grim demonstration of what the new knowledge and technology could do when applied to war. But the decades between World War I and World War II saw perhaps the most fertile and creative years of 20th-century science with the work of Einstein, who proposed his theory of relativity, as well as Max Planck and Nils Bohr, who deepened our understanding of the structure and mechanics of the atom. It was their work that made possible the creation of the atomic bomb, a weapon which revolutionized both war and peace.

In the latter half of the 20th century, science has become a highly complex and competitive intellectual pursuit, engaging the talents of many of the best minds throughout the world and tackling problems as diverse as the origin's of the universe to the perfecting of high-definition TV or the next generation of high-speed computers. Modern science is pursued almost entirely in the laboratories of universities, governments, or private industries, and research and development commands billions of dollars every year. But no matter how large or complex the facilities and supporting institutions, the basic work of science requires a combination of intellectual rigor, intuitive power, ambition, and a desire to know that are the characteristics of the individuals who pursue science.

Science fiction, literary genre based on speculation about scientific or social development. With the works of Jules Verne and H.G. Wells, science fiction broke from supernatural fantasy. In the United States in the 1920s "pulp" magazines popularized but all too often debased the form. John W. Campbell's magazine *Astounding* (founded 1937, now called *Analog*) revitalized the genre through its consistently high literary standards; it nurtured writers who today lead the field, among them Isaac Asimov, Robert Heinlein, Poul Anderson, Hal Clement, and Eric Frank Russell. Many science fiction writers, such as Asimov, Arthur C. Clarke, Ray Bradbury, Kurt Vonnegut, and John Wyndham, are well known outside the field. The critical acclaim they and writers no less accomplished but less well known receive indicates that the best science fiction may be considered to rank with the best contemporary general fiction.

Science project, independent project in which the student studies, explores, and demonstrates principles of science. Such projects include building models of anatomical structures or machines, collecting plant or animal specimens, demonstrating chemical reactions, or conducting controlled experiments on heredity in insects. The subject of these studies is not only the area of science involved but also the scientific method itself.

Scientific creationism, belief that current forms of life did not evolve from simpler forms over millions of years but were created more or less as they exist now. According to scientific creationists, neither logic nor physical evidence (fossils) supports the ideas of differentiation and transitions between life forms that are central to the theory of evolution. The scientific creationist movement developed in the mid-20th century, particularly with the activities of Henry M. Morris, cofounder of the Creation Research Society (1963) and founder of the Institute for Creation Research (1970s).

Scientology, religio-scientific movement stressing self-redemption, which originated in the United States in the 1950s and was incorporated as a church in 1965. It was founded by L. Ron Hubbard. Based on Hubbard's theory of dianetics, a "modern science of mental health," scientology holds that all aspects of individual human behavior are linked and must be harmonized; it also posits a life energy in the universe at large that affects human behavior.

Scipio, Publius Cornelius (Scipio Africanus Major, Scipio the Elder; 234?-183? B.C.), Roman general. Scipio defeated the Carthaginian forces under Hannibal in the Second Punic War (218-201 B.C.), fighting in Spain and winning decisively at Zama, in North Africa (202 B.C.). In 199 B.C. he was elected to public office, serving until 184 B.C.
See also: Punic Wars.

Scissors, cutting tool made of 2 metal blades joined at a pivot point. Cutting occurs between the blades as they are brought together when the handles at one end are squeezed together. Scissors may have been invented as early as the Bronze Age. They were in use in ancient Rome, China, Japan, and Korea, and came into regular domestic use in Europe in the 16th century. Among specialized scissors are *shears* (large scissors) and *pinking shears* (sawtooth scissors that cut fabric leaving zigzag edges).

Scoliosis, curvature of the spine to one side, with twisting. It occurs as a congenital defect or may be secondary to spinal diseases. Severe scoliosis causes hunchback deformity and loss of height, and may restrict cardiac or lung function. Scoliosis becomes apparent in adolescence or earlier, and it occurs more often in girls than in boys. Severe cases may require surgery, after which a body cast is worn for several months.
See also: Spine.

Scone, Stone of, ceremonial stone in Westminster Abbey, London, on which British monarchs are crowned. The stone originated in the village of Scone, Scotland, where it was used to crown Scottish kings. It was brought to London by Edward I of England in 1296.
See also: Westminster Abbey.

Scopes trial, 1925 prosecution of a biology teacher, John T. Scopes, for breaking a Tennessee law forbidding the teaching of evolution in state-supported schools. For the defense Clarence Darrow unsuccessfully pitted himself against the orthodoxy of William Jennings Bryan; the Tennessee supreme court reversed the conviction on a technicality, but the law was not repealed until 1967.
See also: Evolution.

Scopolamine, or hyoscine, alkaloid drug derived from plants of the Solenaceae (nightshade) family (especially genus *Scopolia*) and used as a depressant. Toxic unless given in very small quantities, it is administered to control tremors of Parkinson's disease and other disorders, to combat motion sickness, and in combination with morphine, as an analgesic and amnesic drug (reducing pain and inducing forgetfulness) before childbirth or surgery.

Scorpion, any cf an order (Scorpionida) of terrestrial arachnids having two claws held in front of the head and a stinging tail curled forward over the back. All scorpions have a poisonous sting but few are dangerous to humans. The sting is usually used in defense or, with the palps, in catching prey. Scorpions are restricted to dry, warm regions of the world and feed on grasshoppers, crickets, spiders, and other arthropods.

Scorpionfly, harmless insect (family Panorpidae) with transparent or colored wings and long, dangling legs. Some species are wingless. The long legs are used to trap smaller insects, which are then bitten and eaten. The caterpillar-like larvae are also flesh eaters.

Scorsese, Martin (1942-   ), U.S. film director. His first and somewhat experimental feature-length film, *Who's That Knocking at My Door?* (1968), was followed by the semi-autobiographical *Mean Streets* (1973), which he co-wrote. Other films include *Taxi Driver* (1976), *Raging Bull* (1980), the controversial *The Last Temptation of Christ* (1988), based on a novel by Nikos Kazantzakis, *GoodFellas* (1990), *Cape Fear* (1992), *Casino* (1995), and *Kundun* (1998). Scorsese received the Lifetime Achievement Award (1996).

Scotland, former kingdom now part of the United Kingdom. It is bounded by England in the south, the Atlantic Ocean in the north and west, and the North Sea in the east.
Land. Covering northern Britain and the Hebrides, Orkney, and Shetland islands, Scotland is 30,414 sq mi (78,772 sq km) in area. It is divided into 3 main land regions: the Highlands, the Central Lowlands, and the Southern Uplands. Great Britain's highest peak, Ben Nevis (4,406 ft/1,343 m) is located in the Highlands. Scotland's most important river is the River Clyde.
People. Over 50% of the population is urban; major cities include Edinburgh, the capital and cultural center; Glasgow, the industrial center; Aberdeen; and Dundee. English is spoken everywhere, but some 77,000 Scots in the northwest also speak Gaelic.
Economy. Scotland was one of the first industrialized countries; its economy rests on iron and steel, aluminum, shipbuilding, chemicals, North Sea oil, and the whiskey industry. Agriculture, mainly grain, sheep and cattle, and fishing are also important.
History. Scotland's original inhabitants were the Picts, displaced by the Scots, Britons, and Angles. United under Kenneth I MacAlpin (9th century A.D.) the country maintained an embattled independence from England, ensured by Robert the Bruce (Robert I; r. 1306-29). A brief Renaissance under James IV (r. 1488-1513) ended in disaster at Flodden Field. In the turmoil of the Reformation, James VI (James I of England) united the crowns of Scotland and England, but union of government came only in 1707. It was widely resented, and England fueled this by attacking Scottish autonomy and

prosperity; this helped incite the two Jacobite rebellions (1715 and 1745). A great cultural rebirth followed, but also the hardships of the Industrial Revolution and Highland depopulation for sheep farming. Devolution (i.e., greater autonomy) was defeated by referendum vote in 1979, although there continued to be a movement for greater autonomy. As a result of a referendum in 1997 Scotland received greater autonomy, such as a parliament and a greater say regarding the levy of taxes. Parliamentary elections will most likely be held in 1999.
See also: United Kingdom.

Scotland Yard, headquarters of the Criminal Investigation Department (CID) of the London Metropolitan Police since 1829. Its jurisdiction covers 786 sq mi (2,036 sq km) containing more than 8 million people. It also coordinates police work throughout Britain and provides national and international criminal records.

Scott, Barbara Ann (1928-   ), Canadian figure skater. In 1947 she became the first non-European to win a world title in figure skating, and in 1948 she won the Olympic gold medal. She then became a professional skater, featured in *Hollywood Ice Revues*, and subsequently, a competitor in equestrian events.

Scott, Robert Falcon (1868-1912), English explorer remembered for his fatal attempt, on his second antarctic expedition, to be the first to reach the South Pole. In 1911 he led 4 men with sleds 950 mi (1,529 km) from the Ross Ice Shelf to the South Pole. They arrived on Jan. 18, 1912, only to discover that Roald Amundsen had reached the Pole a month before. Scurvy, frostbite, starvation, and bitter weather hampered the grueling 2-month return journey, and the last 3 survivors died in a blizzard, only 11 mi (18 km) from the next supply point.
See also: South Pole.

Scott, Sir Walter (1771-1832), Scottish poet and the foremost romantic novelist in the English language. Scott was the inventor of the historical novel, and his vivid recreations of Scotland's past were widely read throughout Europe. He started by writing popular narrative poems, including *The Lay of the Last Minstrel* (1805). After these successes he turned to fiction and completed 28 novels and many nonfiction works. His novels included *Waverly* (1814), *The Heart of Midlothian* (1818), and *Ivanhoe* (1819).

Scott, Winfield (1786-1866), U.S. political and military leader, known as "Old Fuss and Feathers" for his obsession with procedure and detail and for his elaborate uniforms. Scott became a hero in the War of 1812. He was active in the Indian wars and in 1846 was appointed a commander in the Mexican War. He captured Mexico City. In 1852 he was the unsuccessful Whig presidential candidate. He commanded the Union Army until 1861.
See also: Mexican War; War of 1812.

Scottish deerhound, dog bred by the Scottish nobility since the 16th century to hunt deer. It stands 30 in (76 cm) or more and weighs 76-110 lb (34-50 kg), with a frame much like the greyhound but more heavily built. Its wiry coat is light gray to yellow brown. In the United States the breed is used to hunt wolves.

Scottish terrier, or Scottie, breed of dog with short legs, stocky body, large head, and a gray, tan, or black wiry coat. Scotties originated in the Scottish highlands in the 19th century, where they were used to hunt small game. They average 10 in (25 cm) at the shoulder and 18-22 lb (8-10 kg).

Scottsboro Cases, U.S. legal cases involving nine black youths accused in 1931 of raping two white women on a freight train in Alabama. Indicted and tried in Scottsboro, all the youths were found guilty, and eight were sentenced to death. They had no defense counsel until two lawyers volunteered to aid them on the day of the trial. The first Scottsboro case, *Powell* v. *Alabama*, reached the U.S. Supreme Court in 1932. The court reversed the convictions on the ground that failure to provide adequate counsel for the boys violated the due process clause of the 14th Amendment. Three years later the second case, *Norris* v. *Alabama*, reached the U.S. Supreme Court; it reversed the convictions because blacks had been excluded from the grand jury that indicted the youths. By 1976 all of the youths but one (who had escaped in 1948) were released from prison.

Scottsdale (pop. 88,622), city in south-central Arizona and now a suburb of Phoenix. First settled in 1888 by Major Winfield Scott, a Union chaplain during the Civil War, it became a stagecoach stop and agricultural community. It grew rapidly after World War II with the local development of the electronics industry. Scottsdale is a center for artists and craftspeople, and Frank Lloyd Wright's architecture school, Taliesin West, is located nearby. In the winter its desert climate attracts many tourists.

Scotus *See:* Duns Scotus, John.

Scouring rush *See:* Horsetail.

Scout *See:* Boy Scouts; Girl Scouts and Girl Guides.

Scranton (pop. 88,117), city in northeastern Pennsylvania, situated on the Lackawanna River near the Pocono Mountains. Permanent settlements date to the 1780s. It is located near large coal deposits, which helped make it a center for the iron industry; George W. Scranton, for whom it was named, established an iron works there in 1840. As coal mining declined in the 1950s, the city went into an economic decline, and has worked to attract textile and other industries. Scranton's educational institutions include Marywood College and the Univ. of Scranton, and it shares with the neighboring city of Wilkes-Barre the Northeastern Pennsylvania Philharmonic orchestra.
See also: Pennsylvania.

Scranton, William Warren (1917-   ), entrepreneur and politician, governor of Pennsylvania, 1963-67. He studied law before serving as a pilot in World War II. A member of the family for which the city of Scranton was named, Scranton became a businessman in that city. Before his governorship he served in the U.S. House of Representatives (1961-63). He lost a bid for the Republican presidential nomination in 1964. He was named by Richard Nixon as head of the Presidential Commission on Campus Unrest in 1970, and served as ambassador to the UN (1976-77).

Screw, simple machine consisting of a cylindrical or conical body around which is wrapped a spiral plane or thread, and used as a fastener, propeller, and part of many more complex machines. Screws were developed by the ancient Greeks and used in presses (to extract oil or juice) and weight-lifting devices. They came into wide use as fasteners in the 1500s, with major refinements in the 1800s including the development of the sharp-tipped wood screw. Screws that modify force and motion, such as are used in vises and drilling tools, are called power screws.

Scriabin, Alexander (1872-1915), Russian composer and pianist. He wanted performances of his tone poem *Prometheus* (1911) to be accompanied by a play of colored lights corresponding to the musical tones.

Scribe (Latin *scrivere*, "to write"), person hired to write out letters, books, and documents by hand. Scribes were particularly important in ancient times, as most people were illiterate. They were involved in legal, political, and business transactions as well as personal communication. In Europe, before the widespread use of the movable-type printing press, many books were copied out by monks, one of the most literate segments of the population. Highly trained scribes are still used to copy out Jewish sacred texts according to precise ritual standards.

Scribe, Augustin Eugène (1791-1861), French playwright and opera librettist. His "well-made plays," realistic dramas constructed according to a formula including a climactic revelation that dictates consequences of the characters' actions, influenced such modern playwrights as George Bernard Shaw and Arthur Miller. Among his works are the plays *Adrienne Lecouvreur* (1849) and *The Ladies' Battle* (1851) and the opera librettos for Auber's *Fra Diavolo* and Meyerbeer's *The Huguenots*.

Scribner, family name of U.S. book publishers. **Charles Scribner** (1821-71) co-founded the publishing company in New York City in 1846. His 3 sons served in turn as president of Charles Scribner's Sons, as the firm became known, but **Charles** (1854-1930) held the position the longest, from 1879 to 1928, during which time it published such major U.S. and British authors as Henry James, Ernest Hemingway, Ring Lardner, and Rudyard Kipling. The founder's grandson **Charles** (1890-1952) and great-grandson **Charles** (1921-) also served as company presidents.

Scripps, Edward Wyllis (1854-1926), U.S. newspaper publisher, founder of the first newspaper chain and of the wire service that eventually became United Press International (UPI). Beginning in the Midwest and West, his chain spread into 15 states by 1922, when Roy Howard, manager of UPI, became a partner. The Scripps-Howard organization subsequently acquired newspapers in nearly every state in the Union.

Scripps Institution of Oceanography, center for advanced study and research in oceanography, in La Jolla, Calif. Founded in 1903, it became part of the Univ. of California in 1912.
See also: Ocean.

Scrofula, tuberculosis of the lymph nodes of the neck, usually acquired by drinking infected milk. The eradication of tuberculosis in cattle and the pasteurization of milk have substantially reduced the incidence of scrofula. Treatment includes antituberculous chemotherapy.
See also: Lymphatic system; Tuberculosis.

Scruple, in the system of apothecaries' weights, unit equal to 20 grains (1.296 g). Three scruples equal 1 dram. These measures are used by pharmacists to measure drugs.

Scuba diving *See:* Diving, deep-sea; Skin diving.

Sculpin, bullhead, or sea scorpion, family of bottom-dwelling fishes (Cottidae) distinguished by a long body, large, wide head, and spiny gills and dorsal fin. Sculpins are found most often in the shallows of seas in northern regions. Bony and sometimes covered with spines, they have little food value, and sometimes steal bait and eat shrimp and young food fish. They are sometimes used as bait. The miller's thumb (*Cottus goblo*) is a common freshwater sculpin of Europe that grows to about 4 in (10 cm). The bullrout *(Myoxocephalus scorpius)* is a larger marine sculpin of Europe, North America, and the Arctic. The largest species grow to a length of 2 ft (60 cm).

Sculpture, artistic creation of three-dimensional forms in materials such as stone, metal, wood, or even foam rubber.
High cost and durability tended to make ancient sculpture an official and conservative art form. This is evident in the monumental sculpture of Egypt, which changed little in 2,000 years. Greek sculptors aimed to portray beauty of soul as well as body, and idealized the human form. In the archaic period (about 630-480 B.C.) Egyptian influence is evident in the frontal, stylized figures, showing little movement or emotion. Greater realism led to the classical perfection of Phidias, and in the 4th century to Praxiteles, with his more sensuous forms and wider range of expression. The Hellenistic Age favored an exaggerated style, of which the *Laocoön* sculpture and the *Winged Victory of Samothrace* are fine examples. Roman sculpture was deeply indebted to Greek art but was also under Etruscan influence and excelled at realistic portraiture.
The Western tradition revived about A.D. 1000 with the elongated, stylized figures of Romanesque art leading to the more graceful and expressive sculptures of Gothic art. Renaissance sculpture, starting about 1350, was dominated by the Italians. Lorenzo Ghiberti and Donatello treated classical models in a new spirit, and Michelangelo gave to works, such as his *David*, an inner tension quite foreign to classicism. The elegant mannerism of Benvenuto Cellini and the elaborate baroque style of Gian Bernini gave way about 1800 to the neoclassical reaction of Jean-Antoine Houdon, Antonio Canova, and Bertel Thorvaldsen. The great 19th-century sculptor Auguste Rodin created a style of partially unworked figures, such as his *Balzac*, influencing Jacob Epstein. This century has seen the abstract art of Constan-

tin Brancusi and Jean Arp, while Henry Moore and Alberto Giacometti showed interest in the human form. Outstanding U.S. sculptors are David Smith and Alexander Calder, who utilized mobiles to create movable sculpture.

Scurvy, disease caused by the gross deficiency of vitamin C. It is characterized by extreme weakness, spongy gums, and a tendency for hemorrhages to occur under the skin, membranes, and periosteum (the membrane covering the bones).

Scylla and Charybdis, in Greek mythology, perils faced by Odysseus in the Straits of Messina. Scylla was a six-headed monster who ate all within reach and Charybdis was a whirlpool. The phrase "between Scylla and Charybdis" means a straight, narrow course between two dangers.
See also: Mythology.

Sea anemone, cylindrical marine polyp with a ring of tentacles, belonging to the division of the animal kingdom known as Cnideria, or Coelenterata. Anemones are related to the jellyfish. The body of the anemone consists of a hollow sac with a mouth at one end. The base of the sac is fastened to a rock and the mouth is surrounded by a ring of tentacles armed with stinging cells, or *nematocysts*. Sea anemones feed on fish and other small animals, which they catch with their tentacles and force into their mouths. While most anemones are fixed to rocks, some burrow in the sand, some can float free, and many can creep over the rocks. Certain sea anemones live on the shells of hermit crabs. Sea anemones reproduce by laying eggs that develop into minute, floating larvae. They can also split in two.

Seabees (from CB, Construction Battalion), members of the U.S. Navy battalions that build, maintain, and defend overseas bases for the Navy and Marines. The Seabee battalions first came into existence in 1942, and were particularly active in the Pacific theater during World War II.
See also: Navy, United States.

Seaborg, Glenn Theodore (1912-), U.S. physicist who shared the 1951 Nobel Prize for physics with E.M. McMillan for his work in discovering several actinides: americum and curium (1944), berkelium and californium (1949). Later discoveries were einsteinium (1952), fermium (1953), mendelevium (1955), and nobelium (1957).
See also: Element; Physics.

Sea cow, any of an order (Sirenia) of tropical, herbivorous, aquatic mammals. Probably evolved from a marsh-dwelling ancestor related to the elephant, all serenians are completely seal-like with forelimbs modified into flippers and hindlimbs fused into the horizontal flukes of a whalelike tail. Genera include *Trichechus* (the manatee) and *Dugong* (the dugong).

Sea cucumber, any of a class (Holothuroidea) of sea animal of the echinoderm group, which also contains sea urchins and starfish. The leathery, flexible, cucumber-shaped animals grow up to 3 ft (1 m) in the tropics but are smaller in cooler waters. Tentacles around the mouth of the sea cucumber are used to catch food, and suction disks on the tube feet along the body provide locomotion. The animal can eject internal organs to distract attackers, regenerating these organs later.

Sea elephant *See:* Seal.

Sea fan, colony of coral animals called polyps (genus *Gorgonia*) common to shallow, warm waters of the Atlantic and Pacific oceans. The tiny, cylindrical polyps grow together in a flat, treelike form 2-24 in (5-60 cm) across. Coloration commonly ranges from yellows to reds to purples.

Sea gull *See:* Gull.

Seahorse, small marine fish of the Syngnathidae family (genus *Hippocampus*) found mostly in tropical waters, the head and forepart of which strongly resemble the head and neck of a horse. The seahorse is generally under 6 in (15 cm) long, with a body covered with bony plates and a long prehensile tail used to anchor the fish to plants. The female lays eggs in a pouch on the underside of the male, where they are fertilized and mature until they are released as live young.

Sea Islands, chain of more than 100 islands off the coasts of South Carolina, Georgia, and Florida. Settled by the Spanish in the 16th century, the islands were the first important North American cotton-growing region in the early 19th century. Many are now resorts or wildlife sanctuaries.